Over the last decade there has been a growing interest in interpersonal relationships in the scientific community as well as in the general public. Until now, no volume has comprehensively covered the many different types of interpersonal relationships, such as the relationships between friends, lovers, colleagues, neighbors, siblings, and parents and children. Ann Elisabeth Auhagen and Maria von Salisch have responded to this gap in the literature with *The Diversity of Human Relationships*, first published in German and later revised for English-speaking readers especially for Cambridge University Press.

The Diversity of Human Relationships draws together findings from social, developmental, and organizational psychology, sociology, biology, and the research on personal relationships. It reviews the multiplicity of research approaches and results on interpersonal relationships and how they change over the life span. It also elaborates the characteristics of the different types of relationships.

The Diversity
of Human
Relationships

The Diversity of Human Relationships

Edited by

Ann Elisabeth Auhagen
Free University Berlin

Maria von Salisch
Free University Berlin

CAMBRIDGE
UNIVERSITY PRESS

Published by the Press Syndicate of the University of Cambridge
The Pitt Building, Trumpington Street, Cambridge CB2 1RP
40 West 20th Street, New York, NY 10011-4211, USA
10 Stamford Road, Oakleigh, Melbourne 3166, Australia

Originally published as *Zwischenmenschliche Beziehungen*, © 1993 Hogrefe.

First published in English, 1996

Printed in the United States of America

Library of Congress Cataloging-in-Publication Data
Zwischenmenschliche Beziehungen. English
The diversity of human relationships / edited by Ann Elisabeth
Auhagen, Maria von Salisch; translated by Ann Robertson.
p. cm.
Includes bibliographical references and indexes.
ISBN 0-521-47463-9. – ISBN (invalid) 0-521-47983-5 (pbk.)
1. Interpersonal relations. I. Auhagen, Ann Elisabeth.
II. Salisch, Maria von, 1956– . III. Title.
HM132.Z9213   1996
302 – dc20   96-3885
                                                      CIP

A catalog record for this book is available from the British Library

ISBN   0-521-47463-9 hardback
ISBN   0-521-47983-5 paperback

Chapters 2–5, 7–8, and 10–14 were translated by Ann Robertson.

Contents

Contributors

Ann Elisabeth Auhagen
Institut für
  Entwicklungspsychologie,
  Sozialpsychologie und Methoden
  der Psychologie
Freie Universität Berlin
Habelschwerdter Allee 45
D-14195 Berlin
Germany

Victoria Hilkevitch Bedford
University of Indianapolis
University Heights
1400 East Hanna Ave.
Indianapolis, IN 46227-3697
U.S.A.

Hans Werner Bierhoff
Fakultät für Psychologie
Ruhr Universität Bochum
D-44780 Bochum
Germany

Dieter Frey
Universität München
Leopoldstr. 13
D-80802 München
Germany

Anne Gaska
Institut für Psychologie an der
  Christian-Albrechts-Universität
  Kiel
Olshausenstr. 40
D-24118 Kiel
Germany

Robert A. Hinde
St. John's College
Cambridge, CB2 1TP
United Kingdom

Peter Kaiser
Interdisziplinäre
  Familienwissenschaftliche
Forschungsstelle der
  Universität Oldenburg
Postfach 2503
D-26015 Oldenburg
Germany

Lothar Krappmann
Max-Planck-Institute for Human
  Development and Education
Lentzeallee 94
D-14195 Berlin
Germany

Kurt Kreppner
Max-Planck-Institute for Human
  Development and Education
Lentzeallee 94
D-14195 Berlin
Germany

Christian Melbeck
Universität Mannheim
Mannheimer Zentrum für
  Sozialwissenschaften
Postfach 103642
D-68137 Mannheim
Germany

Gerold Mikula
Institut für Psychologie
Karl-Franzens-Universität Graz
Universitätsplatz 2/II
A-8010 Graz
Austria

Oswald Neuberger
Institut für Sozioökonomie
Wirtschafts- und
  Sozialwissenschaftliche Fakultät
Universität Augsburg
Memmingerstr. 14
D-86159 Augsburg
Germany

Virginia Rutter
Department of Sociology DK-40
University of Washington
Seattle, WA 98115
U.S.A.

Maria von Salisch
FB Erziehungswissenschaften,
  Psychologie und
  Sportwissenschaft
Freie Universität Berlin
Königin-Luise-Str. 24-26
D-14195 Berlin
Germany

Yvonne Schütze
Humboldt Universität zu Berlin
FB Erziehungswissenschaften
Unter den Linden 9
D-10117 Berlin
Germany

Pepper Schwartz
Department of Sociology DK-40
University of Washington
Seattle, WA 98115
U.S.A.

Acknowledgments

Above all we would like to thank our authors, who spent much time in writing their thoughtful chapters and made cooperation so pleasant for us. In addition, we are very happy that we found Ann Robertson, who translated most of the chapters. We appreciate her competent and creative work. Last but not least, we are deeply indebted to Hans Oswald, who in his own way made this book possible.

Ann Elisabeth Auhagen   *Maria von Salisch*

Introduction

Ann Elisabeth Auhagen and Maria von Salisch

People interweave in a multitude of relationships. Adults are addressed daily as a romantic partner, as a child or a parent, as a colleague or a friend, as a neighbor or a housewife, or in their occupational role. This list could easily be extended. It indicates that people's everyday lives are not only shaped by "major" relationships, such as romantic or parent–child relationships, but that they are often filled with a variety of actions and expectations from other relationships. Changes in the traditional "normal biography," increasing employment among women, high divorce rates, and the many different forms of communal living arrangements (phenomena described as "pluralization in the forms of living") have led to the development of relationships other than "classic" relationships with partners, children, and parents, and these have gained significance in the lives of a great many people. Consequently, one major aim of this book is to broaden vision beyond the types of relationship generally favored by research so far, and to encompass the whole range of relationships experienced in everyday life. In so doing, this book complements in-depth examinations of particular relationship types or studies that classify human relationships according to perspectives, dimensions, or particular variables.

This volume is also designed to give insights into current theories, empirical findings, and new ideas on the diverse interpersonal relationships in everyday life. Each contribution focuses on a particular type of relationship and presents its essential characteristics. Of course, opinions may be divided on the specific characteristics of certain types of relationship. We have invited a number of experts to write about the various relationship types. The authors united to form an interdisciplinary and international team offering a wide range of theories and results. At the same time the individual chapters have numerous topics and points of interest in common so that wherever possible we have provided readers with brief cross-references.

The third aim of this book is to consider changes in interpersonal relationships during the life span. It is plausible that social relationships change depending on the stage of development of the participants, and that relationships become more differentiated during childhood and adolescence. It should also be considered that during adulthood shifts take place in the significance of certain relationships depending on varying needs and obligations. No matter whether the tasks that confront people at different stages of their lives are sought intentionally or whether they occur independent of the will or wishes of those involved, they certainly contribute toward the framework of their interpersonal relationships. Changing developmental impulses and demands may well be reflected in the structures and topics of interpersonal relationships. As experiences accumulate in life, it can be assumed that the quality of interpersonal relationships also changes. Or do people repeatedly engage in the "same" way in relationships? These thoughts on the interconnection of individual biography, developmental tasks, and interpersonal relationships have so far led a Cinderella existence in empirical research. In this respect our book also has its limitations but it attempts to point out these gaps and encourages their examination.

Our book tries to throw more light on the characteristics of relationship types. With this in mind, Part I covers the foundations of interpersonal relationships while Parts II–V are each dedicated to a different relationship category. Within these parts the individual chapters focus on particular types of relationship. What is a relationship type? Can relationship types be differentiated further or regrouped? There is no simple answer to these questions and, as Gerold Mikula points out in his concluding summary, there is no general scientific taxonomy of interpersonal relationships. While choosing the different types of relationship discussed in this book, we were guided by a variety of considerations: our everyday understanding of social relationships, the categorization of relationships in everyday language, and of course the scientific discussions and studies on the topics. Despite these many sources of information and inspiration, this volume still defied rigorous structuring, and it was not always possible to solve the connected problems to our satisfaction. Take, for example, private relationships: there is no general term that covers friendships and relationships between neighbors and acquaintances. "Private nonkin relationships" may cover the content in question, but it is not particularly elegant. In the case of partnerships it is difficult to make fine differentiations among partnership, courtship, romantic (love) relationship, marital relationship, companionship, and similar terms. Unfortunately, these are often confounded in international research, although, for example, a partnership does not necessarily imply love. Other relationships such as extramarital love relationships, which are often officially denied by society but unofficially practiced by millions, are almost completely ignored by current research into love relationships. Yet these relationships exist and are often experienced as "very loving" by those involved. In cases such as this, relationship research should reflect to what extent insights into reality are being obscured by the unquestioned acceptance of widespread thought. As this book cannot offer solutions to these complex problems, nor present the great variety of relationship forms, we have decided to restrict our differentiation to cross-sex and same-sex romantic partnerships. *conclu*

[In view of the many different kinds of interpersonal relationships present in everyday life in our culture alone, it would be presumptuous to imagine they could all be portrayed between the two covers of a single book. We gave the book the title *The Diversity of Human Relationships* because its central concern is the great variety of interpersonal relationships, not because it tells us everything about such relationships. On the contrary, because of the particular focus we chose, many important aspects of human relationships are only touched on marginally or briefly discussed. This means that the contributions can at most claim validity in Western cultures. Unfortunately, it was not possible to include cultural comparisons of interpersonal relationships and, despite their undoubted significance, too little space was available for the investigation of societal and historical backgrounds or connections and processes underlying the development and maintenance of relationships. Similarly, very little is mentioned about interdependencies and influences of individual relationships and relationship types on other relationships and relationship types. Although not completely excluded, aspects of interpersonal relationships associated with such keywords as networks, groups, and (family) systems also receive relatively little attention. Finally, the reader will not find any contributions representing purely clinical-psychological or methodological perspectives.

Briefly, the considerations underlying the structure of the book can be summarized as follows: the main focus centers on the dyad, the relationship between two people. Relationship types are ordered more or less in keeping with the life course progressing from childhood through adulthood. In addition, various types of relationship are collected in thematically related groups. We decided not to sketch the contents of each chapter in this short introduction as this would hardly have done justice to their contents. Each chapter is an independent unit presented within one of the following thematic groups: foundations, relationships within the family, partnerships, private nonkin relationships, and relationships at work. An epilogue on relationship research concludes the book.

With this work we wish to present an overview of current research into particular types of relationship and the foundations of relationships. Its level of success is of course relative because science is by nature a function of processes. The same applies to the topic of this book: relationships are by no means static but are involved in a permanent process of change. In this sense, we hope that our readers will consume its contents with critical interest and feel inspired to contribute their own new ideas and insights to the area of interpersonal relationships – both in theory and in practice.

PART I

Foundations

1

Describing relationships
Robert A. Hinde

Introduction

Can there be a science of relationships?

For nearly all of us, relationships are the most important part of our lives. Early development depends on an adequate relationship with a caregiver. Subsequently, relationships with other family members, with peers, with teachers, shape the developing personality. In preadolescence, close relationships with peers, and especially with opposite-sex peers, become important, and remain so throughout life. An adequate network of personal relationships forms an important protection against psychological and physical ill health.

Not surprisingly, perhaps, we all think we know about relationships. Indeed, we have been learning about relationships since we were born, and there are reasons for thinking that we are adapted to learning about relationships quickly and to using our knowledge with skill. Furthermore, every culture has its own folk psychology about which relationships are desirable and how relationships should be managed. Such folk psychology is all very well, but its beliefs can be based on wishful thinking by those who want to rationalize their own behavior or manipulate others to their own advantage. Or it can provide contradictory conclusions – for instance that similarity and difference each provides a basis for interpersonal attraction.

What we must work toward, therefore, is a science – used here in the sense of an ordered body of knowledge – of interpersonal relationships. We need to formulate each piece of knowledge about interpersonal relationships in a manner that will enable it to be incorporated alongside others, and thus to contribute to the edifice of knowledge. During the last 15 years remarkable progress has been made in the study of relationships, and much new knowledge about their nature and dynamics has been gained. Yet the very vigor of its growth inevitably produces obstacles to the development of a scientific discipline, or at least of a disciplined science. The creativity of those working in this exciting field demands that they should be allowed to fashion concepts to suit their problems, yet the diverse ways in which concepts like intimacy, commitment, love, and satisfaction have been defined makes comparison between studies difficult, if not impossible. Furthermore, many studies seem to be aimed for a purely parochial audience – would a Chinese psychologist know what a "dating relationship" is, for instance? And even within one society, can one really generalize about love from what teenagers do?

It is going to be extremely difficult to find the right balance between the flexibility and creativity necessary in a rapidly developing field of endeavor, and the discipline that will enable it to become a science. This is even more the case since the problems just mentioned, all in principle solvable, must be seen against the background of the great complexity of human relationships. A relationship between X and Y is not the sum of X and Y but has new properties of its own; it is not just a matter of what X and Y do together, but of what X thinks of Y and what X thinks Y thinks of X and so on; it is not even just a matter of X and Y, because the relationship affects and is affected by their friends and relations, their culture, their physical situation. This chapter does not set out to solve these problems, but focuses solely on a basic requirement for the building of a science: description.

A science involves systematic and formulated knowledge and requires a descriptive base. Biology became a science when the theory of evolution by natural selection provided a basis for the work of taxonomists and systematists. Chemistry became a science when Mendeleyev's periodic table provided a means for systematizing knowledge. Human relationships are infinitely more diverse than the chemical elements, and the generalizations we reach are likely to be applicable to some but not to others. Only with an adequate descriptive base can we specify the limits of the generalizations we reach. But relationships are not relatively static entities, like chemical elements or the taxonomist's species, but dynamic, involving ongoing processes. We must therefore remember that any description we make refers to processes over a slice of time.

Furthermore, in seeking to establish a science of human relationships, we must move toward a very special sort of science. Most sciences aim to produce simplifying generalizations that integrate diverse phenomena – the law of gravity or $e = mc^2$, for instance. We need generalizations, but we need them partly in order to understand individual relationships. We need a science not only to build a society in which creative relationships flourish, but one that will help us to manage our own relationships and to help and advise others. This means we must seek not, or not only, for ubiquitously applicable generalizations, but for generalizations whose limitations are precisely specified so that we know which do and which do not apply to any particular relationship. We must approach the complexity of human relationships with humility.

In this contribution, intended as background to subsequent chapters on relationships of specific types, the emphasis is on the nature of relationships and how we can describe them. Research on attraction, short-term interactions, the study of communication processes (a growing point in research), family systems, and many other issues are therefore underrepresented (see, e.g., Cook & Wilson, 1979; P. Minuchin, 1985; S. Minuchin & Fishman, 1981).

The nature of relationships

In the terminology used here, an *interaction* between two individuals involves at a minimum individual A showing behavior X to individual B. B may respond with behavior Y. There may be a number of repetitions of this sequence, involving behavior that is consistent or different, but an interaction is essentially limited in time. A *relationship* involves a series of such interactions between individuals who know each other, such that each interaction is affected by preceding ones and usually by the expectation of future interactions (see also Bateson, 1979; Rogers & Millar, 1988). That the distinction between a long interaction and a relationship is a shady one is an issue that need not detain us.

Neither interactions nor relationships can occur without behavior, but of course behavior is not all: both are accompanied by emotions, hopes, regrets, wishes, and so on. These emotional and cognitive concomitants may persist between the interactions of a relationship, and play an important role in its persistence. More importantly, relationships involve communication. Communication is indeed the essence of relationships and, as Duck and Pond (1989) have so clearly emphasized, the day-to-day background of small talk may be just as important as dramatic episodes in the course of a relationship.

Interaction and relationship, it will be apparent, refer to distinguishable levels of social complexity: relationships have properties that would be simply irrelevant to individual interactions. For instance a relationship may consist of one, a few, or many types of interaction, but this dimension of

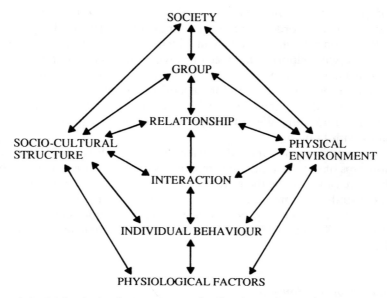

Figure 1.1. Dialectical relations among levels of social complexity.

uniplex versus multiplex would be irrelevant for interactions. Furthermore we tend to use different explanatory concepts in attempting to understand interactions and relations: thus the occurrence of an interaction might be explained in terms of the immediately eliciting factors or short-term moods, while relationships might be referred to in terms of family factors (e.g., sibling rivalry) or longer-term traits of the participants.

Although the distinction between interaction and relationship is heuristically useful, there are dialectical relations between them. Relationships are dynamic, and every interaction within a relationship may affect the future course of that relationship: conversely, the nature of every interaction is affected by that of the relationship in which it is embedded – for instance by memories of past interactions or expectations of future ones (Hinde, 1979, 1990; Park & Waters, 1988).

These two levels of social complexity can be regarded as part of the series *intraindividual systems, individual behavior, interactions, relationships, groups,* and *society* (see Figure 1.1). Each level has properties not relevant to the preceding level: for instance, the relationships within a group may be arranged hierarchically, centripetally, and so on, but these properties are irrelevant to a relationship. And each level has dialectical relations with those on either side. Thus the nature of a group both influences and is influenced by the relationships within it, and influences and is influenced by the society of which it forms part.

We must also consider two further levels, though here "level" is being used in a somewhat different sense. One is the *physical environment*, which both influences and is influenced by each of the levels of social complexity so far mentioned. For instance, the interaction between a car driver and her companion may be affected by obstacles on the road, and the skill with which she manipulates the controls may be affected by her anxieties or hopes about their relationship. The other is the *sociocultural structure*, or system of beliefs, values, myths, conventions, institutions with their constituent roles, and so on. Some of these will be shared by all members of the society, some by particular groups within it, some by particular dyads – indeed these beliefs, values, and so on, merge with those idiosyncratic to individuals. It is because the various elements of such a system may influence each other that we refer to the sociocultural *structure*. The sociocultural structure is to be seen as residing in the heads of the individuals concerned. It may both affect and be affected by each interaction, each relationship, and indeed all the levels of social complexity. For instance, the behavior of a couple to each other will be influenced in part by local cultural conventions and values concerning how couples ought to behave; and how couples actually behave affects cultural conventions about how they should behave (see Figure 1.1).

Finally, all the levels are to be thought of not as entities but as involving processes continually influenced by the dialectical relations between levels. The distinctions between the levels of complexity shown in Figure 1.1 are heuristically useful, but it is essential to remember the dynamic nature of the phenomena and the two-way relations between them (Hinde, 1987, 1990).

The task of description

A complete description of any one relationship would be impossible and relationships are almost infinitely diverse. This, however, is a problem present to some degree in every scientific endeavor, and it is always necessary to be selective. An initial decision concerns the level of complexity at which description should be attempted. One approach, that of Kelly et al. (1983), focuses on the interaction level, or rather on the component actions and subjective phenomena within interactions. They picture a relationship as the interconnections between the temporal chains of two individuals' affect, thought, and action, and suggest description in terms of (a) the nature of the events in each chain that are interconnected; (b) the pattern, (c) strength, (d) frequency, and (e) diversity of interconnection; (f) the extent to which the interconnections facilitate or interfere with the chain of actions, (g) the symmetry or asymmetry of the interconnections, and (h) the duration of the interaction or relationship. This provides a valuable conceptual

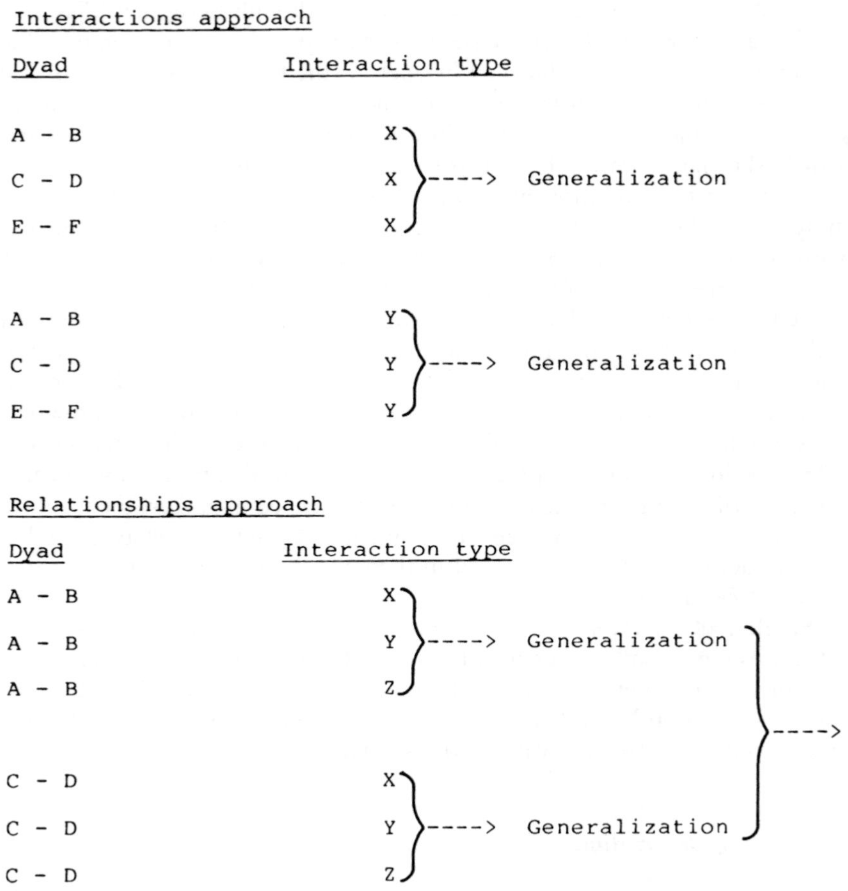

Interactions approach

Dyad   Interaction type

A - B   X ⎤
C - D   X ⎬----> Generalization
E - F   X ⎦

A - B   Y ⎤
C - D   Y ⎬----> Generalization
E - F   Y ⎦

Relationships approach

Dyad   Interaction type

A - B   X ⎤
A - B   Y ⎬----> Generalization ⎤
A - B   Z ⎦   ⎥
                                                    ⎬----->
C - D   X ⎤   ⎥
C - D   Y ⎬----> Generalization ⎦
C - D   Z ⎦

Figure 1.2. The difference between an interaction-oriented and a relationship-oriented approach to the study of social behavior. In the first case studies of the same type of behavior in different dyads form the basis for generalization. In studying relationships, it is necessary to study a number of types of behavior in each dyad, make a generalization about each relationship, and only then make a generalization across dyads about the type of relationship in question.

framework for analyzing the course of interactions, and the authors emphasize that each interaction may influence the "causal conditions" for subsequent ones. The emphasis, however, is on the analysis of interactions, rather than relationships.

It is in fact the case that most research in psychological science involves interactions rather than relationships. For instance, a developmental psychologist may study interactions in which one child is aggressive to another, or helps another, and from many such instances may propose generalizations about aggressive behavior or helping behavior. But the different interactions within a relationship affect each other, and one cannot derive a generalization about peer relationships from generalizations about helping behavior or aggressive behavior. Rather one must describe each dyadic relationship and then make generalizations about relationships (see Figure 1.2).

An alternative approach, and the one adopted here, is to select, at any rate initially, the level of analysis at which we habitually talk about relationships and aspects of relationships that appear to us to be important in everyday life. This approach can be justified by the view that we have been shaped, culturally and/or biologically, to be reasonably good prognosticians about relationships (e.g., Humphrey, 1976; Osgood, 1969). It also seems more likely to be useful clinically. As a way of ordering the almost limitless data about relationships, it was earlier suggested that the more important dimensions fall into eight categories (Hinde, 1979). The present scheme, involving some amendments to the earlier one, involves ten categories. They move from categories concerned primarily with the nature of interactions to categories concerned more with the nature of the relationship as a whole, and from more objective to more subjective aspects. They will be discussed in the following sections.

Before proceeding, however, it must again be emphasized that each of the levels in Figure 1.1 is to be thought of in terms of processes. In describing, we are not describing a static entity, but a set of interacting processes. And, related to this, description inevitably refers to a span of time – a span of time that is seldom explicitly specified.

Categories of dimensions

The content of interactions

The initial basis for discriminating types of relationship concerns what the individuals do together. This may be applied either to major categories of relationships (e.g., the difference between child–mother and child–teacher relationships) or to individual differences within major categories (e.g., mothers who play with their children vs. mothers who do not). We know, for instance, that the content of the child–mother relationship may differ from that of the child–father relationship (Lamb, 1976; Lytton, 1980), and friends do different things together from nonfriends. Usually, of course, such labels imply a range of types of interaction not all of which are essential for inclusion in the category: a mother does not have to cuddle her child for us to label their relationship as a mother–child relationship.

It is important to recognize that categories of relationships based on the content of interactions can be used in two ways. On the one hand, they may be used to refer to particular examples in the real world: for instance, we might study a sample of married couples in Berlin. On the other hand, such labels may be used to refer to an aspect of the sociocultural structure – to what the participants in a particular type of relationship are supposed to do in the society in which they live. Teachers are supposed to behave in certain ways with their pupils, and not to behave in others. Married couples are expected to do certain things together, and couples who do not may be referred to as "married only in name." It is possible, therefore, to consider each type of relationship as governed by rules that help to ensure that the participants in the relationship achieve their goals, and whose abrogation is likely to lead to a deterioration of the relationship. Most of these rules refer to aspects of the relationship discussed later in this chapter. Rules in this sense intergrade with conventions and norms that are less crucial to the continuation of the relationship. Argyle and Henderson (1985) have reviewed the rules relevant to a number of types of relationship, as revealed by questionnaire methods. Of course it may be that relationships as specified in the value system of the society are never realized in practice, but they may nevertheless serve as a goal: thus married couples may strive to achieve an ideal of married bliss. Furthermore, the label, with its implications concerning rules and conventions, may affect how outsiders treat the participants.

What individuals do in a relationship reflects their motivations, so that a classification of relationships in terms of what the individuals do together is also in some degree a classification in terms of the needs that that relationship satisfies or attempts to satisfy. We must remember, of course, that a given relationship may satisfy different needs in the two partners, yet analysis of individuals' need structures may be a guide to the sorts of relationships they will form (McAdams, 1988).

Not all relationships are defined in terms of what the participants do or should do together. For many kin relationships, for instance, there are no clear specifications. Of greater interest is the case of friendship, where the emphasis is on the qualities rather than the content of the interactions. Auhagen (1991, Chapter 10 of this volume) has taken an objective approach, defining friendship as a dyadic, personal, informal social relationship, involving reciprocity and mutual attraction, that is voluntary, long-lasting, positive in nature, and does not involve explicit sexuality. Others have attempted to define friendship in terms of its consequences or functions. For example, Wright (1984) has suggested that friendship has a self-referent character, facilitating the fulfillment or expression of an individual's desire to reaffirm his or her uniqueness or importance, to grow, or to avoid threats (see also Lea, 1989). Taking a different approach, Wiseman (1986) has argued that friendship involves an unwritten contract about the provision of aid and the repayment of kindness. Argyle and Henderson (1985) list the "rules" held to be important in friendship.

The lack of societal conventions about the content of the interactions means that behavior between friends is freely selected, and also that the relationship may lack societal support. The requirement of intimacy, on the other hand, demands that behavior between friends should fulfill certain expectations (see also Hays, 1985, 1989). Although the content of friendship appears to be free from societal constraints, a literature analysis by Contarello and Volpato (1991) indicates considerable consistency in friendship quality across the centuries.

One final point about the content of interactions must be made: there is no such thing as an interaction in which the two participants do nothing. Sitting quietly together, choosing to sit at a distance, quiet chit-chat, all contribute to the course of the relationship.

The diversity of interactions

A related characteristic concerns the diversity of types of interaction in the relationship. Some individuals do many different things together (multiplex relationship), whereas others do only one or a few (uniplex), for instance beer-drinking companions or golfing partners. How this is assessed depends, of course, in part on the level of analysis: a mother–child relationship could be regarded as uniplex, involving only maternal–filial responses, or multiplex, involving feeding, bathing, playing, and so on. Nevertheless the issue is important because the more things two individuals do together, the more opportunity there is for interactions to affect interactions, the more facets of the personalities of the participants are exposed, and the more shared experience is possible (cf. Hays, 1985).

The qualities of the interactions

This is one of the most important properties of a relationship, and yet one of the most difficult to assess. As yet we have few instruments for assessing the quality of interactions, and little information about the number of qualities that are important. Indeed, what is regarded as high-quality may be relationship-specific or even idiosyncratic (Montgomery, 1988). Furthermore, a given assessment may refer to all or only some of the interactions in the relationship, and to the behavior of one or both partners.

However, a variety of sources of information are available, such as the content of verbal utterances, the prosodic (e.g., intonation, stress) and paralinguistic (supporting gestures, etc.) (e.g., Crystal, 1975; Lyons, 1972; Noller, 1985; Pike & Sillars, 1985) aspects of conversation, and nonvocal signals (e.g., Ekman & Friesen, 1969, 1975). Such data have been used to assess marital relationships (e.g., Gottman, Markman & Notarius, 1977; Noller & Vernardos, 1986; Rutter & Brown, 1966) and mother–child relationships (e.g., Ainsworth, Blehar, Waters & Wall, 1978; Bugenthal & Love, 1975; Fraser, 1978), and for predicting relapse from psychiatric illness (Brown, Birley & Wing, 1972; Vaughn & Leff, 1976).

Nonverbal behavior may be even more indicative of the nature of an interaction than what is said: Gottman (1979) found that distressed couples did not differ from nondistressed couples in the overall extent of verbal disagreement, but were much more likely to express disagreement by nonverbal behavior. And the metacommunicational aspects of a verbal utterance may be conveyed by paralinguistic or prosodic aspects, or by accompanying nonverbal communication.

Another source of evidence concerns the extent to which the behavior of each partner meshes with that of the other: this has been shown to be a crucial aspect of the mother–child relationship (Ainsworth et al., 1978; Sander, 1977). Much of the work in this general area has been concerned with the minutiae of interactions: Capella (1984) has indicated the need to integrate such studies with those of longer-term relationships.

Relative frequency and patterning of interactions

Here we are concerned not with the individual interaction, but with how certain properties occur in relation to each other. Several issues are involved:

(1) Covariance of properties. Assessments of a relationship, for example as loving, sensitive, or competitive, usually depend not on just one type of interaction, but many. Thus assessments of, for instance, a marital relationship in terms of one or two measures, such as how often the couple kissed or quarreled, might be misleading, and a description of the relationship as warm or loving should depend on assessments of diverse interactions. Such assessments of "global" properties often have a special importance because the future course of the interaction may depend on how the participants assess its current nature in such terms.

(2) Ratio and derived measures. Often, the frequencies of interactions in a relationship are of less significance than their frequency relative to the

frequency with which one or both partners initiate them or want to initiate them. Thus what matters in a sexual relationship may be not how often a couple make love, but how often relative to how often one or the other partner wishes to.

(3) Relations between heterologous interactions. Some properties of relationships depend on the absolute and relative frequencies of different types of interaction. Consider, for instance, mother–child relationships in which the mothers vary in the frequency with which they initiate contact and reject the child's attempts to make contact. If the mother frequently initiates contact and seldom rejects the child's advances, we might call her warm (or possessive). If the opposite is the case, we would label her as a rejecting mother. If she often rejects and often initiates, or seldom does either, we might call her controlling or permissive, respectively. Although these labels are applied to the mother, they are actually properties of the relationship: the same mother might behave differently with a different infant.

More properly, however, we should consider the propensities of both partners. Imagine two individuals A and B who vary in the frequency with which they are prone to initiate interactions and to reject their partner's interactions (see Figure 1.3). The relationship A1–B1 might be described as mutual passivity; A2–B2 as mutual control (or animosity); A3–B3 as (mutual) cooperation; A4–B4 as mutual rejection; and A1–B2 as, perhaps, cowed submission by A or domination by B. Clearly other combinations are possible.

Another example, which has proven predictive value, concerns the relations between the parental dimensions of Warmth versus Hostility and Restrictiveness versus Permissiveness (Becker, 1964), or Accepting, Responsive versus Cold and Controlling versus Undemanding (Maccoby & Martin, 1983). Such dimensions have predictive value for child behavior in another context. For instance Baumrind (1971) identified three groups of parents, Authoritarian, Authoritative, and Permissive/Indulgent. Authoritarian parents were those attempting to control their children with an absolute sense of values and no allowance for the child's point of view. Authoritative parents expected mature behavior from their child, enforcing rules and standards firmly, but recognizing the rights of both children and parents and encouraging verbal give-and-take. Permissive parents take a tolerant, accepting attitude and make few demands. Baumrind found that the children of Authoritative parents had the most favorable outcomes on a number of dimensions. More recently Hinde, Tamplin, and Barrett (1994) have found that the 4-year-olds who were least aggressive in preschool were those whose mothers provided a balance between warmth and control.

(4) Patterning of interactions. Sometimes the sequencing of interactions is

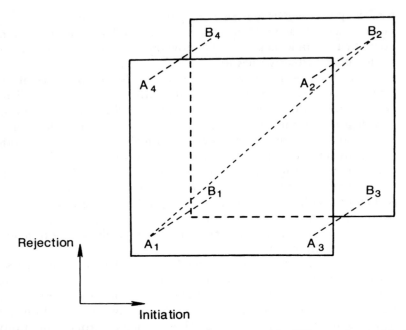

Figure 1.3. Possible relations between persons with different thresholds for initiating and terminating interaction.

important – for instance whether positive interactions are likely to be followed by negative ones, or vice versa (e.g., Gergen, 1969).

Reciprocity versus complementarity of the interactions

Reciprocal (or symmetrical, Bateson, 1979) interactions are those in which the partners do the same thing, either simultaneously or alternately, while in a complementary interaction they do different but complementary things. Thus an exchange of views between two equal friends would be a reciprocal interaction and a mother feeding a baby a complementary one. In both cases it is assumed that the actions of the two partners are functionally related (e.g., Ross, Cheyne & Lollis, 1988). As in some of the categories of dimensions mentioned already, the distinction depends to some extent on the level of analysis: thus a conversation might be reciprocal insofar as the partners spoke in turns, but complementary in that one was teaching and the other responding (see Ross et al., 1988, for further discussion).

Reciprocity depends on similarity in attributes between the partners, and there is considerable evidence that similarity is important in mate selection (e.g., Barry, 1970; Nias, 1979; Thelen, Fishbein & Tatten, 1985). However, relationships in which all interactions are reciprocal are probably rare, though some relationships between peers, colleagues, sports partners, and drinking companions approach that condition.

In part because of the hierarchical nature of most societies, and in part because many relationships involve partners who differ in sex or age or some other characteristic, relationships that are uniformly complementary are more common. Complementarity may involve dominance/subordinance, nurturance/succorance, pedagogy/learning, and many other dimensions. In practice, most relationships, and especially most intimate relationships, involve a complex and idiosyncratic patterning of reciprocal and complementary interactions.

An important dimension of complementarity, first studied in the context of the mother–child relationship (Ainsworth et al., 1978), but important also in adult relationships, and perhaps in all close relationships (Parkes & Stevenson-Hinde, 1982), concerns the extent to which one partner provides security for the other. Ainsworth and her colleagues demonstrated links between maternal sensitivity and warmth in infancy and a subsequent secure relationship for the child at 1 year of age. Other studies have documented relations between secure mother–child relationships at 1 year of age and subsequent adjustment of the child (Bretherton & Waters, 1985).

Much earlier work was concerned with the role of similarity in interpersonal attraction (Byrne, 1971). While powerful effects were demonstrated, it must be noted that (a) long-term relationships depend on more than initial attraction, and that the characteristics in which similarity matters may differ with the nature and stage of the relationship (Duck, 1977); (b) individuals have needs (e.g., for nurturance, succorance, dominance) that can be satisfied only by someone with complementary characteristics to themselves; and (c) individuals are involved in multiple relationships, and may find satisfaction of some needs in some relationships, others in others.

Conflict and power

Some degree of conflict is almost inevitable in every relationship. Conflicting needs for autonomy versus connectedness, for self-disclosure versus privacy, and for consistency versus novelty are inevitably present (Baxter & Wilmot, 1985). And in exchange theory terms, since social exchange entails obligations and expectations for the future, each participant may attempt not only to ensure that he or she is fairly treated, but also to create obligations in the partner in the expectation of future rewards (Blau, 1964). And there may be lack of agreement as to what is fair – equality, equity, or social justice may be taken as the criterion (Lerner & Lerner, 1981).

A number of techniques have been used to assess the amount of conflict in a relationship. These include questionnaire and interview methods (e.g., Engfer, Gavranidou & Heinig, 1988; Gottman, 1993), variants of the prisoners' dilemma game (Epstein & Santa-Barbara, 1975) and other experimental games (Deutsch & Krauss, 1965).

There has been an increasing tendency to see conflict as involving dysfunction in the relationship itself rather than, or as well as, a consequence of individual power assertion or psychopathology. Thus Patterson (1982), studying parent–child relationships, has demonstrated that particular patterns of interaction augment the conflict: ineffective parental discipline may reinforce negative child behavior, which in turn produces negative parent behavior. Similar principles have been applied to sibling conflict. Conflict within one dyad in a family may have repercussions throughout the whole family (Christensen & Margolin, 1988).

Related to conflict and how it is resolved is the issue of power in the relationship. Individuals differ in their need to have power over others, and this has diverse influences on marriage, success in public life, other aspects of the personality, and so on. Thus men with the trait of strong power motivation tend to have less successful heterosexual relationships (McAdams, 1988). The effects of the use of power in the parent–child relationship may have profound effects on personality development (Baumrind, 1971; Adler & Furman, 1988; Mills & Grusec, 1988).

Power can be defined in terms of the extent to which one individual can affect the quality of the other's outcomes. Power is, however, seldom absolute, and in many relationships one partner has power in some contexts and the other in others, the distribution being the result of negotiation between them (e.g., Collins, Kreitman, Nelson & Troop, 1971). In exchange theory terms, the nature of power varies with the resource exchanged (Foa & Foa, 1974). Thus if A influences B by giving B goods or money, A's own stocks will thereby be depleted. If A imparts information to B, A may become less able to influence B in the future, but A's own understanding may be enhanced by the process of teaching. And if A gives love to B, he may thereby augment his own resources.

Types of power have also been distinguished by French and Raven (1959) according to the means by which power is maintained. They distinguish reward power (maintained by A's potential to reward B); coercive power (capacity to punish B); expert power (A's special knowledge or skill); legitimate power (A's status) and referent power (maintained by B's identification with A). Kelvin (1977) has pointed out that reward and coercive power lead to compliance, and expert and referent power depend on acceptance.

However, except in extreme cases, there are many difficulties in assessing the power balance in a relationship: these result from the changing nature of individuals' goals and needs (McAdams, 1988), the diversity of dependent variables used (Sprey, 1972), and especially from the difficulty of deciding the level of analysis to be used. To exemplify the latter point, Collins et al. (1971), studying the power distribution in marriages of men who were alcoholic outpatients, found it necessary to distinguish three levels of activity: executive (e.g., who buys the tickets for the family holiday), executive decision making (who decides where to go), and how responsibility for executive decision making is decided (i.e., who decides who shall decide).

Conflict in marriage seems to become less frequent with time, though this may be because more harmonious marriages survive for longer. It is also less frequent in second marriages than in first. Among the factors leading to conflict in marriage are lack of social support, aspects of the personalities of the participants (especially neuroticism, social extroversion, and low impulse control), jealousy, unrealistic expectations, and, in some cases, the presence of small children and adverse economic circumstances (e.g., McGonagle, Kessle & Schilling, 1992). Rusbult, Verette, Whitney, Slovik and Lipkins (1991) showed that accommodation in conflict situations was related to the partners' commitment to the relationship, satisfaction and feelings about its centrality, investment in the relationship, perception of social support, perspective taking, femininity, and other factors (see also Holmes & Miller, 1976).

Mild conflict can be constructive: if the incompatible goals are trivial, conflict may provide a focus around which the relationship is built. Indeed, some would argue that conflict is essential if real intimacy is to be achieved (Gottman, 1993).

Self-disclosure

The concept of intimacy, sometimes equated with self-disclosure, is also often used in a rather broad sense. For instance, Reis and Shaver (1988) note that discussions of intimacy may include reference to such issues as self-validation and feelings of being understood and cared for. They link these "components of the intimacy process" in a model of the causes and consequences of disclosure. Similarly Tesch (1985) used a "Psychosocial Intimacy scale" which contained items relating to romantic love, supportiveness, and communication. Here, the current goal being description, and believing that description and explanation are usually best kept separate, we refer solely to the extent to which the participants in a relationship reveal themselves to each other experientially, emotionally, and/or physically. Although disclosure in a relationship may be one-sided and some individuals may be more prone to disclosure than others, disclosure is primarily a *relationship* characteristic, as what is disclosed may depend on the partner: attempts to characterize *individuals* as "disclosers" or "nondisclosers" (e.g., Jourard, 1971) have had only limited success.

An instrument for assessing self-disclosure within a relationship has been devised by Altman and Taylor (1973) and subsequently modified by others (e.g., Tschann, 1988), though such instruments inevitably have considerable cultural specificity.

Although disclosure is a relationship characteristic, it may be affected by personal characteristics, such as gender and marital status (Tschann, 1988). Furthermore, although what an individual discloses is specific to a particular other, this does not mean that the contributions of the partners are equal: for instance, Rubin, Hill, Peplau, and Dunkel-Schetter (1980) found that, in dating relationships, the women tended to disclose more than the men.

The degree of self-disclosure in a relationship is subject to social norms (see Gaska & Frey, Chapter 13 of this volume). In many role relationships intimacy is restricted, presumably because a revealed disagreement about basic issues could disrupt the relationship. In close personal relationships intimacy increases vulnerability and thus involves costs (e.g., Welch-Cline, 1989): conversely, intimacy with a stranger may be easier because vulnerability does not matter.

A need to share experiences, ideas, and feelings with others appears to be virtually ubiquitous, and inadequate opportunities to meet this need result in feelings of loneliness (Peplau & Perlman, 1982; Rook, 1988). However, at the same time some restraint on intimacy is present in nearly every relationship. Baxter and Wilmot (1985) have documented taboo topics in close relationships: an important issue here may be fear that discussion of the relationship may be deleterious to it, on the principle that when you plant a bulb you don't keep digging it up to see if it is growing. Kelvin (1977) has suggested that areas of privacy are areas in which the individual is not exposed to the power of others, and may therefore be defended. As an extreme case, denial of privacy appears to augment adherence to local group norms, as in the military. Burgoon et al. (1989) have shown that the importance of privacy, and the areas to which it refers, varies according to the type of relationship involved. Metts (1989) found that concealment or deception, and the reasons given for them, varied with the type of relationship: relationship satisfaction was associated with partner-focused reasons for deception (see also Montgomery, 1988, for a review of these and related issues).

Interpersonal perception

This category involves a number of dimensions that differ in their requirements for cognitive complexity.

(1) Does A see B as B "really" is?
(2) Does A see B as B sees B – in other words, does A "understand" B?
(3) Does B feel that A sees B as B sees A – in other words, does B feel "understood"?

Such issues obviously affect the processes of the relationship. Unless the partners are reasonably perceptive about each other, adequate meshing of their interactions is impossible. Their feelings about each other (and about themselves) may be affected by how they perceive each other, how they feel themselves to be perceived, and also by how far they believe their partner sees the world in the same way they do.

Several methods are available for assessing interpersonal perception. Each partner in the relationship may answer a questionnaire, and the answers are then compared (e.g., Cromwell, Olsen & Fournier, 1976). Of special interest are data obtained by asking an individual to fill in a questionnaire from more than one stance – for example what A thinks (or feels) about X and what A thinks B thinks about X (e.g., Drewery & Rae, 1969): comparisons between the replies of A and B permit answers to such questions as those in the list above. The questions may include reference not only to what A thinks B thinks about X, but also about what A thinks an ideal partner would think or believe (e.g., Murstein, 1972). This enables the investigator also to assess satisfaction with the relationship.

The validity of such self-report measures is reviewed by Harvey, Hendrick, and Tucker (1988). As recent examples of this approach, Saidla (1990) adapted Laing's Interpersonal Perception method (Laing et al., 1966) and used it in conjunction with other instruments to assess the quality of roommates' relationships, and White (1985) showed that, on high salience items, wives' understanding of husbands tended to be more accurate than husbands' understanding of wives.

Observational methods have also been employed (e.g., Ickes & Tooke, 1988): although revealing in many respects, they are costly in terms of time and equipment.

Commitment

This is used to refer to the extent to which the partners accept their relationship as continuing indefinitely, or strive to ensure its continuance or optimize its properties. It is useful to distinguish cases in which the emphasis is primarily on continuity, irrespective of content – as in Ruth's promise to Naomi, "Where thou goest, I will go" – from those in which the partners attempt to maintain or optimize the properties of the relationship but are not concerned if it is terminated, as with many next-door neighbor relationships. It is also useful to distinguish exogenous commitment, imposed from outside, as in arranged marriages, from endogenous commitment, arising as a relationship develops. The concept of commitment is linked to those of cooperation and trust (Hinde & Groebel, 1991) and intimacy (Rogers & Millar, 1988).

Commitment can, of course, be one-sided. While personal commitment reflects, and if acknowledged determines, many aspects of an individual's behavior, of equal importance is faith in the partner's commitment. For example, if each partner is to provide rewards now in the hope that they will be reciprocated in the future, some expectation of continuity is essential. Faith in the partner's commitment is essential for the growth of intimacy, for self-revelation increases vulnerability, and one must be sure that the partner would not exploit opportunities for harm. And belief in the partner's commitment to continuity may be essential for personal growth, because personal growth may require some change in the nature of a relationship.

Endogenous commitment usually progresses gradually. Initially, growing familiarity permits a gradual working out of the definition of the relationship. This may be followed by a private pledge involving a growing mutual awareness of commitment, which may then lead to public commitment. Public commitment may itself act as a cohesive force in the relationship.

A number of studies have assessed the determinants of commitment. Johnson (1982) suggested that personal commitment is based on satisfaction with the relationship, which in turn is based on outcomes, outcomes relative to expected outcomes, and equity. "Structural" commitment, by contrast, is associated with the costs consequent upon terminating the relationship. A variety of studies, not wholly consistent, bearing on this hypothesis, is reviewed by Michaels, Acock, and Edwards (1986). Lund (1985) found that what individuals feel that they have put into a relationship, and their perceived commitment to it, are better predictors of the continuity of the relationship than their outcomes or how much they love each other. In her view, effort and resources expended in a relationship are not to be viewed as costs, but as part of a process that strengthens the relationship (see also Lund, 1991; Rusbult, 1983).

Satisfaction with the relationship

This involves two elements: the participants' perceptions of the relationship and their satisfaction with it.

Just as an individual's interpersonal perception is often inaccurate, so may be their perceptions of the relationship. But perceptions may be crucial, for future action is inevitably affected by current perceptions, whether or not those perceptions are accurate. Of course, the partners may or may not agree in their perceptions of the relationship: in relationships with primarily reciprocal interactions, continuity of the relationship may (but need not) depend on agreement, but some relationships involving complementary interactions may depend on misperception by one or both participants.

Satisfaction with the relationship will depend on the correspondence between each partner's perception of the relationship and what each feels to be appropriate to the type of relationship in question; and on the availability of alternatives. For instance, Utne, Hatfield, Traupmann, and Greenberger (1984) showed that newlyweds who felt themselves to be equitably treated by their spouse would perceive their marriage to be more stable than those who felt the situation to be inequitable. The impact of noncorrespondence will depend on the alternative outcomes open to each partner in other situations or relationships (e.g., Thibaut & Kelley, 1959; Kelley, 1979). Again, of course, satisfaction may not be mutual.

What each partner feels to be appropriate may depend on gender, on personal attributes (e.g., Frazier & Esterly, 1990), and on norms or values about what is appropriate to the type of relationship in question. These norms may be held in common by all members of a society or group, may be specific to the dyad, or may even be idiosyncratic. A useful distinction here is that among rules, scripts, and prototypes (Davis & Todd, 1985; Ginsburg, 1988). Rules prescribe, proscribe, or permit particular types of behavior. They may be created by the dyad (Shotter, 1984) or shared more generally. They differ among types of relationships and among cultures (e.g., Argyle & Henderson, 1985; Peplau, 1983). Scripts are cognitive structures that organize comprehension and guide performance in particular situations – for instance at a wedding or in a restaurant. Prototypes are abstracted "best examples" from a range of patterns (Bartlett, 1932). The dimensions along which relationships are assessed differ between relationship types (Adler & Furman, 1988), and the concept of prototypes is useful in referring to ideological types of relationship, such as friendship (Hays, 1988) or romantic love (Lee, 1973; Shaver & Hazan, 1988; Hendrick & Hendrick, 1986) or parent–child relationships (Maccoby & Martin, 1983).

Another distinction useful here is that between communal and exchange relationships. In the former, participants feel an obligation and/or desire to be concerned with the other's welfare, as in relationships between family members or friends. In such relationships requests for favors with no offer of repayment are normal, and would not be accompanied by a decrease in satisfaction. Indeed, an offer of reciprocation might harm the relationship. In exchange relationships, by contrast, benefits are given as repayments for benefits received in the past or with expectations of future rewards, and what is considered "fair" is crucial (Clark & Waddell, 1985; see also Wright, 1984). This distinction is related to, but not coincident with, the distinction made by Foa and Foa (1974) between the different types of resource exchanged.

Categorizing relationships

Generalizations about the dynamics of relationships are unlikely to be ubiquitously applicable, and we need to be able to specify for which relationships they are useful and for which they are not. As we have seen, an initial classification of most relationships can be based primarily on the content of the interactions: most of the chapters in this book concern relationships defined ultimately in that way. Within those categories, further subdivisions may be necessary. For instance, we distinguish acquaintances, friends, close friends, and best friends: they have different characteristics, and what applies to one may not apply to others.

A number of schemes for categorizing relationships of particular types are to be found in the literature: two rather different ones will be mentioned as illustrations.

Bowlby's (1969, 1973) concept of "attachment" between child and caregiver, which has become of central importance in studies of child development, initially lacked a quantitative basis. However, the "Strange Situation" procedure, devised by Ainsworth (Ainsworth et al., 1978), permitted the classification of an infant's relationship with its caregiver into three (later four) categories: securely attached, insecurely/ambivalently attached, and insecurely/avoidantly attached (and later disorganized). The categorization is based on the infant's behavior during a series of structured episodes carried out in the laboratory and involving caregiver and infant being joined by a stranger, the caregiver departing, and so on. The attachment classification has considerable longitudinal stability in the absence of major changes in life circumstances, and is predictive of behavior in other childhood relationships (e.g., Bretherton & Waters, 1985; see also Kreppner, Chapter 4 of this volume).

More recently Hazan and Shaver (1987) devised a simple questionnaire for assessing "Attachment style" in adulthood, yielding three categories that were given the same names as Ainsworth's original ones. This simple instrument has shown a surprising number of relations with other aspects of the respondent's relationships and personality, though it must be noted that many of the data involve correlations between two sets of self-reports, with inherent possibilities of bias. Bartholomew (1990) has integrated the Ainsworth and the Hazan and Shaver schemes into a four-category one that is showing great promise (see also Bierhoff, Chapter 8 of this volume).

Fitzpatrick's typology of marital types is based on an instrument assessing three dimensions of the marriage as seen by the respondent: Ideology (beliefs about and standards for the relationship); Interdependence; and Conflict (tendency to avoid or engage in conflict). This enabled Fitzpatrick to characterize individuals as Traditionals – those holding a conventional ideology about marriage, seeing harmony and stability as important, seeking interdependence, and not avoiding conflict; Independents – those believing that relationships should not constrain individual freedom, maintaining a degree of physical separateness but a high degree of interdependence, and engaging in conflict; Separates – those ambivalent about ideology, with conventional ideas about marriage but nonconventional ideas about individual freedom, seeking less companionship and freedom than the other types.

Couples could then be divided into three "pure" types, where both partners were characterized in the same way, and a number of mixed types. Use of this typology has enabled Fitzpatrick and colleagues to demonstrate differences in marital dynamics, communication, satisfaction, the impact of childbirth, and so on (e.g., Fitzpatrick, Vangelisti & Firman, 1994).

Conclusion

It is worth emphasizing that the dimensions of relationships represent no more than convenient pigeonholes into which we may classify the issues that seem important about interpersonal relationships. As a scheme, it has already undergone considerable modification and it will certainly need more. The important point here, however, is that relationships are dynamic, with different processes important in different relationships. A major issue is that of how one cuts the cake: some properties of relationships, often referred to as unitary, in fact span several of the categories mentioned above. For example, relationships high on intimacy, interpersonal perception, and commitment might be referred to as trusting; and relationships involving interactions that are complementary and of an appropriate content and quality, and with high interpersonal perception, might be referred to as caring or nurturant.

Although this approach is less molecular than that advocated by Kelley et al. (1983), discussed earlier in this chapter, it is more molecular than that of Hendrick and Hendrick (1986). These authors used a questionnaire technique to differentiate varieties of love: each of their varieties would be expected to occur in relationships with several characteristics on the present scheme. Thus loving relationships involving primarily physical interactions of low diversity, intense but uncaring quality, in which intimacy, interpersonal perception, and commitment were low, might be high in *Eros* (i.e., physical desire and instense longing), while those with diverse intense interactions might be high in *Mania* (a possessive, dependent style of loving). It must be emphasized that these speculations are presented in order to demonstrate that the ten categories of dimensions listed do embrace properties of a more diffuse nature, but may also need much further revision: the test is whether they serve as convenient pigeonholes for what is important across a wide range of relationships.

However, some means for describing relationships and for specifying the limitations of generalizations is certainly essential. A number of examples of this have been given already. To stress the point, here are four more.

The first concerns the way lay persons perceive relationships: Kayser, Schwinger, and Cohen (1984) showed that individuals *perceived* different issues to be important in relationships of different types. Loving relationships, friendships, and work relationships were distinguished from each other on the basis of unique configurations of three features: affective climate, the goals of each participant, and the relative importance of the resources exchanged.

The second example emphasizes that normal and dysfunctional relationships do indeed differ in specific characteristics: Adler and Furman (1988), studying 11–12-year-olds, found differences in dimensions of warmth, conflict, relative status/power, and satisfaction.

The third concerns the subtlety of the distinctions that may be important. O'Conner and Brown (1984), noting that some studies had shown that a confiding relationship reduced the risk of depressive disorder (Brown, Birley & Wing, 1972) but that one major study did not (Henderson, Byrne & Duncan-Jones, 1981), produced strong evidence that the difference depended on whether the instrument used measured active support or merely felt attachment.

Finally, what is important may depend not only on the relationship itself, but on the network of relationships in which it is embedded. Radke-Yarrow, Richters, and Wilson (1988) studied parent–child relationships in "stable" and "chaotic" families. Higher rates of child compliance were related to more positive mother–child relationships only in stable families, and maternal use of harsh enforcement was associated with more negative mother–child relationships only in chaotic families (see also Hinde & Stevenson-Hinde, 1988).

Description is, of course, only the first stage in building a science of relationships. It must be followed by the development of understanding of the processes involved. In this field, as elsewhere in the social sciences, it would be a mistake to look for one universally applicable overarching theory. Progress seems more likely to come from theories of specified scope, whose limitations can be seen against a solid background of description (see Hinde, in press). Some theoretical tools are already available – personality theory, attribution theory, balance and dissonance theories, and exchange, equity, and interdependence theories. Others will certainly be developed.

A further need is to relate these several approaches – for instance, what sort of attribution is made by someone with this sort of personality in the context of that sort of exchange. Exciting developments here are likely to come from extensions of Foa and Foa's resource theory. As noted above, these authors pointed out that exchanges of resources of different types have different properties. Dividing resources into six categories, they showed that these vary along two dimensions: Particularity, implying that it matters with whom the exchange takes place, and Concreteness. Thus love is high and money is low on Particularity, food high and information low on Concreteness. The six categories can be arranged in a circular way, with adjacent resources most likely to be exchanged. Further developments of this approach, and its integration with others, are given in Foa, Converse, Tornblom, and Foa (1993).

References

Adler, T. F., & Furman, W. (1988). A model for children's relationships and relationship dysfunctions. In S. Duck (Ed.), *Handbook of personal relationships* (pp. 211–231). Chichester, England: Wiley.

Ainsworth, M. D. S., Blehar, R. C., Waters, E. & Wall, S. (1978) *Patterns of attachment: A psychological study of the strange situation.* Hillsdale, NJ: Erlbaum.

Altman, I., & Taylor, D. A. (1973). *Social penetration.* New York: Holt, Rinehart & Winston.

Argyle, M., & Henderson, M. (1985) *Anatomy of relationships.* London: Methuen.

Auhagen, A. E. (1991). *Freundschaft im Alltag.* Bern: Hans Huber.

Barry, W. (1970). Marriage research and conflict: An interpretive review. *Psychological Bulletin, 73,* 41–54.

Bartholomew, K. (1990). Avoidance of intimacy: An attachment perspective. *Journal of Social and Personal Relationships, 7,* 147–178.

Bartlett, F. C. (1932) *Remembering.* Cambridge University Press.

Bateson, G. (1979). *Mind and nature: A necessary unity.* New York: Dutton.

Baumrind, D. (1971). Current patterns of parental authority. *Developmental Psychology Monographs, 4* (1, part 2).

Baxter, L. A., & Wilmot, W. W. (1985). Taboo topics in close relationships. *Journal of Social and Personal Relationships, 2,* 253–270.

Becker, W. C. (1964). Consequences of different kinds of parental discipline. In M. L. Hoffman & L. Hoffman (Eds.), *Review of Child Development Research* (Vol. 1). New York: Russell Sage.

Blau, P. M. (1964). *Exchange and power in social life.* New York: Wiley.

Bowlby, J. (1969). *Attachment and loss.* Vol. 1: *Attachment.* London: Hogarth. (1973). *Attachment and loss.* Vol. 2: *Separation.* London: Hogarth.

Bretherton, I., & Waters, E. (Eds.) (1985). Growing points in attachment theory and research. *Monographs of the Society for Research in Child Development, 50* (Serial No. 209).

Brown, G. W., Birley, J. L. T., & Wing, J. K. (1972). Influence of family life on the course of schizophrenic disorders: A replication. *British Journal of Psychiatry, 121,* 241–258.

Bugenthal, D. E., & Love, L. R. (1975). Non-assertive expression of parental approval and disapproval and its relationship to child disturbance. *Child Development, 46,* 747–752.

Burgoon, J. K., Parrot, R., Le Poire, B. A., Kelly, D. L., Walther, J. B., & Perry, D. (1989). Maintaining and restoring privacy through communication in different types of relationships. *Journal of Social and Personal Relationships, 6,* 131–158.

Byrne, D. (1971). *The attraction paradigm.* New York: Academic Press.

Capella, J. N. (1984). The relevance of the microstructure of interaction to relationship change. *Journal of Social and Personal Relationships, 1,* 239–264.

Christensen, A., & Margolin, G. (1988). Conflict and alliance in distressed and non-distressed families. In R. A. Hinde & J. Stevenson-Hinde (Eds.), *Relationships within families* (pp. 263–282). Oxford: Clarendon.

Clark, M. S., & Waddell, B. (1985). Perceptions of exploitation in communal and exchange relationships. *Journal of Social and Personal Relationships, 2,* 403–418.

Collins, J., Kreitman, N., Nelson, B., & Troop, J. (1971). Neurosis and marital interaction. 3: Family roles and functions. *British Journal of Psychiatry, 119,* 233–242.

Contarello, A., & Volpato, C. (1991). Images of friendship: Literary depictions through the ages. *Journal of Social and Personal Relationships, 8,* 49–76.

Cook, M., & Wilson, G. (Eds.) (1979). *Love and attraction.* Oxford: Pergamon.

Cromwell, R. E., Olson, D. H. L., & Fournier, D. G. (1976). Tools and techniques for diagnosis and evaluation in marital and family therapy. *Family Process, 15,* 1–49.

Crystal, D. (1975). Paralinguistics. In J. Benthall & T. Polhemus (Eds.), *The body as a medium of expression* (pp. 162–174). London: Allen Lane.

Davis, K. E., & Todd, M. J. (1985). Assessing friendship: Prototypes, paradigm cases and relationship description. In S. Duck & D. Perlman (Eds.), *Understanding personal relationships* (pp. 17–38). London: Sage.

Deutsch, M., & Krauss, R. M. (1965). Studies of interpersonal bargaining. *Journal of Conflict Resolution, 6,* 52–76.

Drewery, J., & Rae, J. B. (1969). A group comparison of alcoholic and non-alcoholic marriages using the interpersonal perception technique. *British Journal of Psychiatry, 11,* 287–300.

Duck, S. (1977). Inquiry, hypothesis and the quest for validation: Personal construct systems in the development of acquaintance. In S. Duck (Ed.), *Theory and practice in interpersonal attraction* (pp. 379–404). London: Academic Press.

Duck, S., & Pond, K. (1989). Friends, Romans, countrymen, lend me your retrospections. In C. Hendrick (Ed.), *Close Relationships* (pp. 17–38). Newbury Park, CA: Sage.

Ekman, P., & Friesen, W. V. (1969). The repertoire of non-verbal behavior. *Semiotica, 1,* 49–98.

(1975). *Unmasking the face.* Engelwood Cliffs, NJ: Prentice-Hall.

Engfer, A., Gavranidou, M., & Heinig, L. (1988). Veränderungen in Ehe und Partnerschaft nach der Geburt von Kindern. *Verhaltensmedizin, 9,* 297–312.

Epstein, N. B., & Santa-Barbara, J. (1975). Conflict behaviour in clinical couples. *Family Process, 14,* 51–66.

Fitzpatrick, M. A. (1984). A typological approach to marital interaction: Recent theory and research. In L. Berkowitz (Ed.), *Advances in Experimental Social Psychology, 18,* 1–47. Orlando, FL: Academic Press.

Fitzpatrick, M. A., Vangelisti, A. L., & Firman, S. M. (1994). Perceptions of marital interaction and change during pregnancy: A typological approach. *Personal Relationships, 1,* 102–122.

Foa, U. G., Converse, J., Tornblom, K. Y., & Foa, E. B. (Eds.) (1993). *Resource Theory: Explanations and applications.* San Diego: Academic Press.

Foa, U. G., & Foa, E. B. (1974). *Societal structures of the mind.* Springfield, IL: Thomas.

Fraser, C. (1978). Communication in interaction. In H. Tajfel & C. Fraser (Eds.), *Introducing social psychology* (pp. 126–150). Harmondsworth, England: Penguin.

Frazier, P. A., & Esterly, E. (1990). Correlates of relationship beliefs: Gender, relationship experience and relationship satisfaction. *Journal of Social and Personal Relationships, 7,* 331–352.

French, J. R. P., & Raven, B. H. (1959). The basis of social power. In D. Cartwright (Ed.), *Studies in social power* (pp. 150–167). Ann Arbor: University of Michigan Press.

Gergen, K. J. (1969). *The psychology of behavior exchange.* Reading, MA: Addison-Wesley.

Ginsburg, G. P. (1988). Rules, scripts and prototypes in personal relationships.

In S. Duck (Ed.), *Handbook of personal relationships* (pp. 23–40). Chichester, England: Wiley.

Gottman, J. M. (1979). *Marital interaction: Experimental investigations.* New York: Academic Press.

(1993). *What predicts divorce.* Hillsdale, NJ: Erlbaum.

Gottman, J. M., Markman, H., & Notarius, C. (1977). The topography of marital conflict: A study of verbal and non-verbal behavior. *Journal of Marriage and the Family, 39,* 461–477.

Harvey, J. H., Hendrick, S. S., & Tucker, K. (1988). Self-report methods in studying personal relationships. In S. Duck (Ed.), *Handbook of personal relationships* (pp. 99–116). Chichester, England: Wiley.

Hays, R. B. (1985). A longitudinal study of friendship development. *Journal of Personality and Social Psychology, 48,* 909–924.

(1988). Friendship. In S. Duck (Ed.), *Handbook of personal relationships* (pp. 391–408). Chichester, England: Wiley.

(1989). The day-to-day functioning of close versus casual friendships. *Journal of Social and Personal Relationships, 6,* 21–38.

Hazan, C., & Shaver, P. R. (1987). Romantic love conceptualised as an attachment process. *Journal of Personality and Social Psychology, 52,* 511–524.

Henderson, S., Byrne, D. G., & Duncan-Jones, P. (1981). *Neurosis and the social environment.* London: Academic Press.

Hendrick, C., & Hendrick, S. S. (1986). *Liking, loving and relating.* Monterey, CA: Brooks Cole.

Hinde, R. A. (1979). *Towards understanding relationships.* London: Academic Press.

(1987). *Individuals, relationships and culture.* Cambridge University Press.

(1990). The interdependence of the behavioural sciences. *Philosophical Transactions of the Royal Society, 329,* 217–227.

(in press). *Understanding close relationships.* Hillsdale, NJ: Erlbaum.

Hinde, R. A., & Groebel, J. (Eds.) (1991). *Cooperation and prosocial behaviour.* Cambridge University Press.

Hinde, R. A., & Stevenson-Hinde, J. (Eds.) (1988). *Relationships within families.* Oxford: Clarendon.

Hinde, R. A., Tamplin, A., & Barrett, J. (1994). Home correlates of aggression in pre-school. *Aggressive Behaviour, 19,* 85–105.

Holmes, J. G., & Miller, D. T. (1976). Interpersonal conflict. In J. W. Thibaut, J. T. Spence & R. C. Carson (Eds.), *Contemporary topics in social psychology.* Mavistown, NJ: General Learning Press.

Humphrey, N. K. (1976). The social function of intellect. In P. G. Bateson & R. A. Hinde (Eds.), *Growing points in ethology* (pp. 303–318). Cambridge University Press.

Ickes, W., & Tooke, W. (1988). The observational method: Studying the interaction of minds and bodies. In S. Duck (Ed.), *Handbook of personal relationships* (pp. 79–98), Chichester, England: Wiley.

Johnson, M. P. (1982). Social and cognitive features of the dissolution of commitment to relationships. In S. W. Duck (Ed.), *Personal relationships, 4: Dissolving personal relationships* (pp. 51–74). London: Academic Press.

Jourard, S. M. (1971). *Self-Disclosure*. New York: Wiley.

Kayser, E., Schwinger, T., & Cohen, R. L. (1984). Layperson's conceptions of social relationships: A test of contract theory. *Journal of Social and Personal Relationships*, 1, 433–458.

Kelley, H. H. (1979). *Personal relationships*. Hillsdale, NJ: Erlbaum.

Kelley, H. H., Berscheid, E., Christensen, A., Harvey, J. H., Huston, T. L., Levinger G., McClintock, E., Peplau, L. A., & Peterson, D. R. (Eds.) (1983). *Close relationships*. New York: Freeman.

Kelvin, P. (1977). Predictability, power and vulnerability in interpersonal attraction. In S. Duck (Ed.), *Theory and practice in interpersonal attraction* (pp. 355–378). London: Academic Press.

Laing, R. D., Phillipson, H., & Lee, A. R. (1966). *Interpersonal perception*. London: Tavistock.

Lamb, M. E. (Ed.) (1976). *The role of the father in child development*. New York: Wiley.

Lea, M. (1989). Factors underlying friendship. *Journal of Social and Personal Relationships*, 6, 275–292.

Lee, J. A. (1973). *The colors of love*. Englewood Cliffs, NJ: Prentice-Hall.

Lerner, M. J., & Lerner, S. C. (1981). *The justice motive in social behavior*. New York: Plenum.

Lund, M. (1985). The development of investment and commitment scales for predicting continuity of personal relationships. *Journal of Social and Personal Relationships*, 2, 3–24.

   (1991). Commitment old and new. In R. A. Hinde & J. Groebel (Eds.), *Cooperation and prosocial behaviour* (pp. 212–222). Cambridge University Press.

Lyons, J. (1972). Human language. In R. A. Hinde (Ed.), *Non-verbal communication* (pp. 49–85). Cambridge University Press.

Lytton, H. (1980). *Parent–child interaction: The socialization process observed in twin and singleton families*. New York: Plenum.

Maccoby, E. E., & Martin, J. A. (1983). Socialization in the context of the family. In E. M., Hetherington (Ed.), *Handbook of child psychology* (Vol. 4, pp. 1–102). New York: Wiley.

McAdams, D. P. (1988). Personal needs and personal relationships. In S. Duck (Ed.), *Handbook of personal relationships* (pp. 7–22). Chichester, England: Wiley.

McGonagle, K. A., Kessle, R. C., & Schilling, E. A. (1992). The frequency and determinants of marital disagreements in a community sample. *Journal of Social and Personal Relationships*, 9, 507–524.

Metts, S. (1989). An exploratory investigation of deception in close relationships. *Journal of Social and Personal Relationships*, 6, 159–180.

Michaels, J. W., Acock, A. C., & Edwards, J. N. (1986). Social exchange and equity determinants of relationship commitment. *Journal of Social and Personal Relationships*, 3, 161–176.

Mills, R. S. L., & Grusec, J. E. (1988). Socialization from the perspective of the parent–child relationship. In S. Duck (Ed.), *Handbook of personal relationships* (pp. 177–192). Chichester, England: Wiley.

Minuchin, P. (1985). Families and individual development. *Child Development*, 56, 289–302.

Minuchin, S., & Fishman, H. C. (1981). *Family therapy techniques*. Cambridge, MA: Harvard University Press.

Montgomery, B. M. (1988). Quality communication in personal relationships. In S. Duck (Ed.), *Handbook of personal relationships* (pp. 343–361). Chichester, England: Wiley.

Murstein, B. I. (1972). Person perception and courtship progress among premarital couples. *Journal of Marriage and the Family*, 34, 621–626.

Nias, D. K. B. (1979). Marital choice: matching or complementation? In M. Cook & G. Wilson (Eds.), *Love and attraction* (pp. 151–156). Oxford: Pergamon.

Noller, P. (1985). Negative communications in marriage. *Journal of Social and Personal Relationships*, 2, 289–302.

Noller, P., & Vernardos, C. (1986). Communication awareness in married couples. *Journal of Social and Personal Relationships*, 3, 31–42.

O'Connor, P., & Brown, G. W. (1984). Supportive relationships: Fact or fancy? *Journal of Social and Personal Relationships*, 1, 159–176.

Osgood, C. E. (1969). On the whys and wherefores of E. P. & A. *Personality and Social Psychology*, 12, 194–199.

Park, K. A., & Waters, E. (1988). Traits and relationships in developmental perspective. In S. Duck (Ed.), *Handbook of personal relationships* (pp. 161–176). Chichester, England: Wiley.

Parkes, C., & Stevenson-Hinde, J. (Eds.) (1982). *The place of attachment in human behaviour*. New York: Basic Books.

Patterson, G. R. (1982). *A social learning approach. 3. Coercive family process*. Eugene, OR: Castalia.

Peplau, L. A. (1983). Roles and gender. In H. H. Kelley et al. (Eds.), *Close relationships* (pp. 220–264). New York: Freeman.

Peplau, L. A., & Perlman, D. (1982). Perspectives on loneliness. In L. A. Peplau & D. Perlman (Eds.), *Loneliness*. New York: Wiley.

Pike, G. R., & Sillars, A. L. (1985). Reciprocity of marital communication. *Journal of Social and Personal Relationships*, 2, 303–324.

Radke-Yarrow, M., Richters, J., & Wilson, W. E. (1988). Child development in a network of relationships. In R. A. Hinde & J. Stevenson-Hinde (Eds.), *Relationships within families* (pp. 48–67). Oxford: Clarendon.

Reis, H. T., & Shaver, P. (1988). Intimacy as an interpersonal process. In S. Duck (Ed.), *Handbook of personal relationships* (pp. 367–390). Chichester, England: Wiley.

Rogers, L. E., & Millar, F. E. (1988). Persuasion in personal relationships. In S. Duck (Ed.), *Handbook of personal relationships* (pp. 289–306). Chichester, England: Wiley.

Rook, K. S. (1988). Towards a more differential view of loneliness. In S. Duck (Ed.), *Handbook of personal relationships* (pp. 571–589). Chichester, England: Wiley.

Ross, H. S., Cheyne, J. A., & Lollis, S. P. (1988). Defining and studying reciprocity in young children. In S. Duck (Ed.), *Handbook of personal relationships* (pp. 143–160). Chichester, England: Wiley.

Rubin, Z., Hill, G. T., Peplau, L. A., & Dunkel-Schetter, C. (1990). Self-disclosure in dating couples. *Journal of Marriage and the Family*, 42, 305–317.

Rusbult, C. E. (1983). A longitudinal test of the investment model. *Journal of Personality and Social Psychology*, 45, 101–117.

Rusbult, C. E., Verette, J., Whitney, G. A., Slovik, L. F., & Lipkins, I. (1991). Accommodation processes in close relationships: Theory and empirical evidence. *Journal of Personality and Social Psychology*, 60, 53–68.

Rutter, M., & Brown, G. W. (1966). The reliability and validity of measures of family life and relationships in families containing a psychiatric patient. *Social Psychiatry*, 1, 38–53.

Saidla, D. D. (1990). The construct validity of individual and interpersonal correlates of roommate relationship quality. *Journal of Social and Personal Relationships*, 7, 311–330.

Sander, L. W. (1977). The regulation of exchange in the infant–caretaker system and some aspects of the context–content relationship. In M. Lewis & L. A. Rosenblum (Eds.), *Interaction, conversation and the development of language*. New York: Wiley.

Shaver, P. R., & Hazan, C. (1988). A biased overview of the study of love. *Journal of Social and Personal Relationships*, 5, 473–502.

Shotter, J. (1984). *Social accountability and selfhood*. Oxford: Blackwell.

Sprey, J. (1972). Family power structure: A critical comment. *Journal of Marriage and the Family*, 34, 235–238.

Tesch, S. A. (1985). The Psychosocial Intimacy questionnaire. *Journal of Social and Personal Relationships*, 2, 471–488.

Thelen, M. H., Fishbein, M. D., & Tatten, H. A. (1985). Interpersonal similarity: A new approach to an old question. *Journal of Social and Personal Relationships*, 2, 437–446.

Thibaut, J. W., & Kelley, H. H. (1959). *The social psychology of groups*. New York: Wiley.

Tschann, J. M. (1988). Self-disclosure in adult friendship. *Journal of Social and Personal Relationships*, 5, 65–82.

Utne, M. K., Hatfield, E., Traupmann, J., & Greenberger, D. (1984). Equity, marital satisfaction and stability. *Journal of Social and Personal Relationships*, 1, 323–332.

Vaughn, C. E., & Leff, J. P. (1976). The influence of family and social life on the course of psychiatric illness. *British Journal of Psychiatry*, 129, 125–137.

Welch-Cline, R. J. (1989). The politics of intimacy. *Journal of Social and Personal Relationships*, 6, 5–20.

White, J. M. (1985). Perceived similarity and understanding in married couples. *Journal of Social and Personal Relationships*, 2, 45–58.

Wiseman, J. P. (1986). Friendship: Bonds and binds in a voluntary relationship. *Journal of Social and Personal Relationships*, 3, 191–212.

Wright, P. H. (1984). Self-referent motivation and the intrinsic quality of friendship. *Journal of Social and Personal Relationships*, 1, 115–130.

2

The development of diverse social relationships in the social world of childhood

Lothar Krappmann

Adults live in a variety of relationships that differ in the individual form created by the people involved – for example, the relationship might be intense, superficial, full of conflicts, or boring – as well as in the basic type. These types include relationships with parents and children, love relationships, marital relationships, friendships and acquaintances, relationships with colleagues at work and with neighbors, relationships with people who share similar interests or convictions (members of a film club or a church community), and relationships with patients, clients, and superiors. All these relationships can be fulfilled to varying degrees of satisfactions: people can be bad or good fathers, lovers, or colleagues; they can also violate general conceptions of the relationship to such an extent that those affected, or observers, are of the opinion that someone who behaves in this way is not a father, a friend, or a colleague. Often people are very definite in this kind of judgment, although there is usually no written code of conduct for a particular type of relationship.

Although people often learn about a particular type of relationship only when they enter one in the course of life, the idea is widespread that fundamental skills in initiating and maintaining a relationship are already developed during childhood. According to attachment theory, these skills are rooted in the secure attachment built up in the first year of life between the child and the person caring for it (Ainsworth, Bell & Stayton, 1974; Bowlby, 1969). In all relationships where a person cares for someone else, it seems plausible that behavior is influenced by the caregiver–child relationship once experienced. However, in relationships characterized by egalitarian cooperation, this is more difficult to imagine. As it is, longitudinal studies in attachment theory show that early experience of secure attachment has a lasting influence on relationships that children develop with their peers (Grossmann & Grossmann, 1991; Sroufe, Carlson & Shulman, 1993; Suess, Grossmann & Sroufe, 1992).

Although important foundations for later relationships may be laid during early parent–child relationships, other experiences have to be undergone so that adults can act competently in the great variety of relationships that occur during their lifetime. These additional and novel experiences take place during childhood and youth, especially with others of the same age, as Piaget (1971) and Sullivan (1953) have shown. Children work out their plans together as partners of relatively equal standing. This experience of equality and reciprocity produces relationships that are structurally different from parent–child relationships (Youniss, 1980). This chapter poses the thesis that many of the relationships typical of adult life have their foundations in these earlier interactions with other children of the same age.

When studying research literature on the social relationships of children it is striking that there is no suggestion of looking for the beginnings of the great variety of relationships in adult life in the social world of children of the same age. The studies in question view children's peer relationships and friendships as a pattern of socializing in childhood and do not trace their connection to the relationships of later adults. This may be because studies on social relationships among children are based on a one-track model of development. This implicit developmental model assumes a change in children from relatively unstable relationships determined by external circumstances to stable relationships based on inner psychological interconnectedness that results from personal disclosure and mutual understanding and concern. According to this image of development, the social life of younger children is characterized by highly variable playmateships; middle childhood is dominated by close friendships; and from the beginning of adolescence romantic relationships play the central role (according to the concept of subsequent key relationships outlined by Buhrmester and Furman, 1986; see Figure 2.2). This developmental model represents a series of stairsteps along which the growing person abandons relationship forms that become unsatisfactory and enter into relationships that offer more reciprocity and intimacy.

Earlier ways of maintaining relationships seem like incomplete precursors in comparison to current key relationships. Consequently, according to Youniss and Volpe (1978), children progress from peer relationships to friendships to replace unfruitful symmetrical reciprocity with cooperation. Selman (1981) describes the development of the friendship concept in a way that suggests that relationships only reach fulfillment in personal relationships where the desire for reciprocal recognition of the self and intimate exchange with another is satisfied. This description sounds something like a love relationship. In this conceptualization of development each consecutive type of relationship represents a further step on the way toward the one aim: the realization of the ideal form of personal interdependence.

I do not mean to contradict this concept of children increasing their social competencies and, in so doing, gaining access to new ways of relating themselves to another person. But when investigating the gain in competencies and the new type of relationship that is discovered as a result of the gain in competencies, research should not lose sight of earlier types of relationship. Are these earlier types really abandoned in the course of development? In the following, I will present a developmental model of social relationships based on the assumption that earlier types of relationship do not disappear but instead continue to develop under the influence of increased competencies and still play an important role in their further developed form during adult life. These different types of adult relationships have a value of their own and are not simply "weak" forms or precursors of supposedly perfect relationships. It is not very meaningful, for example, to criticize a professional relationship for not being a friendship, nor a friendship for not being a love relationship. Each of these relationships harbors its own ideal, which is based on experiences within such relationships and extends back to precursors during childhood.

Various hints of the salience of this multitrack model of development have been collected from a number of empirical studies. Nevertheless, actual research work on this topic has yet to be carried out. Many studies do not differentiate relationships according to their qualities because they use sociometric methods rather than investigating the essential features characterizing distinct types of relationships. Mostly, relationships were not investigated directly, but inferred from reciprocal nominations (Asher & Hymel, 1981), although the sociometric method measures only social acceptance. It has only recently been proposed that methods should be sensitive to the quality of friendships (Berndt, 1984; Bukowski & Hoza, 1989; Bukowski, Hoza & Boivin, 1994; Parker & Asher, 1993). But even these studies have not led to a typology of different relationships between children that could be considered as the beginnings of the later variety of relationships. When examining different social experiences of children, research still almost exclusively refers to their peer status and categorizes the children in groups such as popular, rejected, neglected, controversial, and average children, but not according to the different quality of relationships.

How to conceive of social relationships?

It seems strange that the concept of social relationships has received little explicit attention in developmental psychology. The fact that children frequently meet or play together does not necessarily indicate that a relationship exists. According to Hinde and Stevenson-Hinde (1987), a relationship exists only when earlier interactions of the partners influence later ones. This view coincides with the ethological approach used to observe living beings that are personally unable to give information about their relationship. Mueller (1988) emphasizes that shared meanings are a central characteristic of relationships. These shared meanings develop from mutual experiences and influence future interactions. In this way relationships make it easier to create new meanings together (Fogel, 1993). A further element in a relationship is that the partners not only use mutual experiences and meanings when they interact, but they also develop a concept of their relationship which they try to confirm and secure by means of appropriate actions. It is not until adolescence that children are able to explain that they are not just acting in a certain way because of the partner, but because of the demands of the relationship (Keller, 1986; Youniss & Smollar, 1985).

Thus the influence exercised by the relationship on the interactions taking place between the partners depends on the fact that relationships create a social reality accessible to the participants comprising mutual experiences and shared meanings, expectations, and assessments. These interpretation patterns and ordering rules for relationships are negotiated between the partners on the one hand, but they also develop from sociocultural traditions that offer concepts of relationships (Cohen, 1966; Lopata, 1990). Consequently, although relationships are not dependent solely on the respective partners, but also on social norms, relationships nevertheless influence interactions and interactions influence relationships, either by changing their quality or by simply confirming the status quo (see Hinde, Chapter 1 of this volume). It is these feedback effects that particularly characterize relationships as dynamic systems in which the competencies of members are challenged.

To discover the special developmental incentives that specific relationships offer to interacting children, it is necessary to describe the different types of relationship in an appropriate way. Hinde (1976; see also Hinde, Chapter 1 of this volume) has suggested a number of dimensions for characterizing the peculiarities of individual relationships. These dimensions can also be used to describe types of relationship, as in the example of friendship. Referring to Hinde's dimensions, people in friendships characteristically emphasize the importance of mutual well-being and the willingness to support each other during the adversities and vicissitudes of life. Their behavior toward one another is varied and not restricted to one kind of interaction. The relationship is based on long-term satisfaction of each partner's wishes. Friends make an effort to keep in touch. Interactions often serve many purposes simultaneously: assistance, companionship, pleasure. Friends consider the perspective of the other person, disclose intimate feelings to one another and express their vulnerability in the knowledge that they can rely on support and protection (see also Auhagen, Chapter 10 of this volume).

It is certainly significant that people name friendship as the foremost example of a relationship outside the kin or primary caregiving context. Nevertheless, it should not be overlooked that although friendship is an important relationship during childhood and adult life, it is not the only one. It is characteristic of friendship that those involved choose each other voluntarily, that they defend their relationship in adverse conditions, and that friendship is based on interest in the other person as an individual (this is particularly evident in the European tradition as shown in the comparison of friendships in different cultures by Krappmann, 1995). Other relationships do not develop through freedom of choice, nor is the dominant interest of the partners in the individual person; here partners are brought together primarily by some task or activity. However, who the partner is is still not a matter of indifference, as it is often important that he or she has useful qualities for pursuing the particular task – as in the case of leisure companionship or colleagues at work. The colleague relationship differs from a friendship mainly because of the priority given to work-related collaboration over personal exchange. Sometimes a colleague relationship develops into a friendship, but the decisive criterion is reliable cooperation (see also Neuberger, Chapter 12 of this volume).

The wish to realize something one personally likes or to pursue a goal shared by a group can also form the starting point of a relationship, such as the decision to perform some kind of sport that would be impossible alone, or the intention to engage in a political campaign together with others. In such cases all people are welcome who have a minimum of qualifications, such as the willingness to abide by rules, to stick to agreements, and to share the effort. This also creates a basis for the development of relationships with those on whose participation one can rely, even though nothing much may be known about them as individuals. Nevertheless, even in this case relationships with others do not develop arbitrarily but rather with those who qualify for the relationship by offering certain prerequisites. Relationships of this type occur frequently in leisure, neighborhood, and political groups. Such relationships lack nothing, even if they do not develop into friendships (see also Melbeck, Chapter 11 of this volume).

Until now developmental research into social relationships has concentrated on the stages of childhood and adolescence throughout which friendships develop. But are not the precursors of these colleague and interest relationships also to be found in childhood? Their developmental beginnings may even reach back further than those of friendship because the personal nature of friendship, as a relationship type, makes relatively high demands on those involved, and consequently friendship does not emerge until young people are able to reflect on their perception of themselves in relation to others. In contrast, younger children may well be able to cope with tasks posed within less demanding relationships based on interests and preferred activities.

The beginnings of relationships in early childhood

It is not easy to distinguish when a child first perceives another child as a relationship partner independent of the situational context. During the last months of the first year of life children begin to show reactions to the presence or the behavior of other children that can be interpreted as social behavior (Vandell & Mueller, 1980; Howes, 1988). Toward the end of the first year differences become apparent in the behavior of the child toward the mother and children of the same age (Vandell, 1980). Hartup (1983) interprets these differences as signs of the development of a "specific peer repertoire." Although many of the interactions started by one child are not yet reciprocated, rudimentary forms of turn taking emerge and gradually develop into longer sequences that, however, are easily interrupted (Rauh, 1984; Vandell, Wilson & Buchanan, 1980). Whereas unsuccessful interactions among young children were once primarily ascribed to aggressive behavior and conflicts over possessions, they now tend to be attributed to lack of interactive skills.

Young children prefer partners who are socially more skilled and thus often choose somewhat older children (Rauh, 1987). Lewis, Young, Brooks, and Michalson (1975) also established that several children in a small group of 1-year-olds that they studied maintained "friendships" with children who were a few months older. At this age a seemingly small difference in age usually signifies a great difference in development. The greater social competence of the older peers facilitates the interaction because the older partners can partially balance out the lesser competence of the younger ones. In addition, the unequal-age peers fulfill other functions than same-age children. According to the study by Lewis et al. (1975), there was less body contact with the somewhat older children, they were imitated more frequently by the younger ones, the older ones offered toys more frequently to the younger ones, and the unequal-age children expressed more affection toward each other than "friends" of the same age.

It seems understandable that children seek social exchange with those children with whom they have less unpleasant experiences and more security than with socially less competent children. Nevertheless, the question still remains open whether these preferred contacts with some children can already be viewed as relationships. Although the literature on early interactions of children generally speaks of peer relationships and even of early friendships, usually no attempts are made to clarify what this concept might mean to children at this young age. There is in fact no concept that captures the quality of this developing mutuality. Nor is it possible to rely on the language of the children, who call all longer-term contacts "friendship" as soon as they know this word and use it in the context in which they have learned it (from about 3 years of age according to Hartup, 1975). They probably mean the fact of being together frequently rather than a relationship.

Chapman, Smith, Foot, and Pritchard have observed that, on a quantitative basis, children of preschool age do not play significantly more frequently with partners whom they previously described as their best friends than with others. This fact also warns against possible misinterpretation of children's statements (Chapman, Smith, Foot & Pritchard, 1979). Similarly, children's statements on the affective quality of their relationships offer little clarity, as, according to Bigelow (1977), younger children, like adolescents, emphasize that friends "like" each other. Children like others who do not disturb their own game; they like others who do not start arguments, and they like others because they sing nicely or have curly hair, as children's statements prove. Consequently, "liking" is not a definite sign of a relationship, even if the participants refer to a relationship as a friendship.

Evidence in favor of the development of relationships between children as early as near the end of the first year can be seen in the fact that from this age onward, as familiarity increases, children interact more and in more complex ways than children who are unfamiliar with each other (Lewis et al., 1975). Similar effects on behavior can also be observed among preschool children (Doyle, Connolly & Rivest, 1980). Here, earlier interactions influence subsequent ones, which, according to Hinde and Stevenson-Hinde (1987), documents the existence of a relationship. However, starting with the first encounter, new playmates also benefit from skills acquired during a relatively long process with another child (Becker, 1977). Consequently, it appears that a child does not develop a particular behavioral repertoire with a specific "friend" that differentiates that friend from others of the same age; rather, it acquires general competencies. This is facilitated by the presence of a counterpart with whom contacts last for some time and whose reactions gradually become predictable. It is difficult to decide whether these interactions are stimulated more by favorable circumstances or by some kind of attachment to one another.

Hartup concludes from existing studies that "peer relationships exist in babyhood only in the loosest sense" (1983, p. 114). In contrast to this, Lewis et al. (1975) already recognize friendships among 1-year-olds. Howes (1988) maintains that children in their first year do not yet have friendships, but that they certainly have preferred partners. She is of the opinion that friendships between children develop during their second and third years and that these friendships are based on reciprocal affective attachment. With the help of pictures, McCandless and Marshall (1957) succeeded in gaining details from 3-year-old children about the importance of others to them. The explanations children gave coincided well with the assessments of nursery teachers on friendships among these children. Hartup (1983) points out that, despite the increasing importance of same-age interaction partners, up until school entry a great deal of parallel play occurs among children without mutual orientation toward each other. Thus, the beginnings of relationships that influence the behaviors of the partners in a more consistent and effective way are seen in the older preschool years only.

Peer relationships

As the discussion about the beginnings of relationships between children shows, this question is confused by the unclear use of the concepts "friendship" and "peer relationship." To prevent the concept of friendship from becoming completely hollow, an attempt will be made to define this relationship as a special relationship type and to differentiate it in particular from the peer relationship. This would make possible the specific study of friendship development as one type of relationship and counteract the tendency to rashly equate the development of friendship with the development of relationships in general.

The concept "peer" is predominantly used synonymously with the expression "same-age child." Yet the word "peer" has a connotation that differentiates if from the expression "same-age child." The equality of "peers" does not depend primarily on age but on equality according to developed competencies and social rank (Hartup, 1978). This is reflected in the original meaning of the word, which denoted one of equal social standing or rank. Thus, not all children with whom a child interacts are necessarily peers but only children who interact at comparable levels of behavioral complexity (Lewis et al., 1975). Lewis and his colleagues point out that a child's recognition of another as a "peer" is initially related to the other child's function: "That is, a peer would be on one occasion all the children who could climb a tree, while on another occasion it would be those able to sing songs" (p. 58).

When certain age differences are compatible with two children's mutual acceptance as peers, the term "unequal-age peer" might be appropriate. If, however, the interaction with older children is being sought because the younger child is dependent on their more developed competencies, it would be helpful, for the purpose of clearly differentiating various types of relationship, not to call this a peer relationship. In this case the children are not equal in development and social rank. The above-mentioned evidence of specific behaviors among children who are unequal in age and level of development favors the assumption that these relationships constitute a particular domain of socialization: the mixed-age children's group. Biologists and ethologists have attributed to this group a specific phylogenetic function, namely that of practicing skills that are important for the survival of the group insofar as parents are unable to do this themselves. Konner (1975) points out that groups of same-age children developed relatively late in human evolution in comparison to the mixed-age group. On reaching school age children clearly ascribe different significance to same-age and unequal-age children. Older children help, teach, and give directions, but friends are found among children of the same age (French, 1984).

On the basis of these considerations every child of approximately the same age could qualify as a peer. But in order to graduate from being "simply" children of the same age to being peers, the prerequisite must be fulfilled that these children respect each other as equals. This does not mean that they have to accept each other in every respect. At first it is sufficient for them to consider themselves equally capable of carrying out an activity enjoyed at this time. Lewis et al. (1975) speak of "functions" that children can serve for one another. In some cases the ability to climb or the knowledge of songs may be of decisive importance. With regard to mutual play the demands on the peer consist of giving priority to coordinating plans and mutual activities, and avoiding conflicts.

Are children who are peers – that is, who regard themselves as of equal standing and prefer each other – in a relationship? Does this constitute the formation of a durable relationship between them? As the cited studies of the social world of younger children up to elementary school show, relationships that develop between children of the same age are certainly not based on the acceptance of others in their personal uniqueness but mainly on their reliable and predictable participation in common enterprises. At first even the influence of gender is small, as this only clearly separates girls' and boys' worlds from about 8 years of age (Feiring & Lewis, 1987; Thorne, 1994). Although all children can potentially become peers, each child has only a few peers in the narrower sense. These are the children of whom he or she expects that they will enter into shared activities time and again and also that they have the skills to do this. As this mutuality is experienced positively, a child "likes" its peers. If a peer moves away he or she may be difficult to replace and even children of preschool age express sadness at this loss – which, according to Hartup (1975), indicates the existence of a relationship. Thus the above-named criteria for a relationship are fulfilled. The relationships should be categorized as peer relationships in the narrow sense and should be differentiated from a friendship.

As soon as children are able to give information in interviews they express expectations toward their "friends" that coincide with this concept of peers. Four-year-olds say that someone is their friend because they do something together, especially play, and refer to various circumstances that create closeness. A quarter of the children also name attractive possessions as a reason. The answers of 6–7-year-olds are similar (Bigelow, 1977; Hayes, 1978). According to Selman (1981), younger children describe their friendships as situation-determined playmateships that often fail because they find it difficult to settle arguments. The arguments do not develop between children as individuals but about play and toys. Even in elementary school, friendship is still largely seen in a one-sided way because, to children, someone who does something they themselves like becomes a friend. The children also emphasize that they know friends better. By this they mean that they know what their friends like doing and consequently whether they can expect their own wishes to be fulfilled by them.

In general, these statements made by children are interpreted as fairly elementary descriptions of developing friendships. Admittedly, Selman also remarks that in the case of younger children "friendship is more accurately playmateship" (1981, p. 250). Nevertheless he sees this kind of togetherness as a primary stage of friendship understanding and investigates the transition from this stage to the following stages of closer friendship. However, the preparation of personal friendship is not the only function that peers perform in the developmental process. According to the thesis proposed in this chapter, these peer experiences form the basis of an independent type of relationship that continues to exist into adulthood, where it plays a specific, important role in the world of work and leisure.

There are indications that during middle childhood children do not transform all peer relationships into personal friendships and from then on solely maintain relationships of the friendship type. Rather, they appear to discover additionally for themselves relationships of the friendship type. In fact they often form friendships with children who were previously their peers in the above-mentioned sense. However, they continue peer relationships parallel to the new friendships. Indications of this can be found in the study carried out by Furman and Bierman (1984) in which children differentiate between friendships and acquaintances as early as the second grade, and more pronouncedly in the fourth and sixth grades. Affection and trust are mainly sought in friendships, while participation in mutual activities is offered by acquaintances that may well be continued, or newly formed, relationships of the peer type (Furman & Robbins, 1985).

This idea is corroborated in particular by a study carried out by LaGaipa (1979). The 6- to 13-year-olds he questioned made a contrast between "close" friends and "good" friends. He sees the so-called good friends as members of the peer group. According to his results they fulfill other functions than "close friends." Children seek trust and intimacy from close friends and acceptance and participation from good friends. Apart from this there are ordinary acquaintances. Differentiating who belongs to which category presents some difficulty and is a topic of conversation and gossip among adolescents: "Each individual is to some a social acquaintance, to another a good friend, and to a third a close or best friend" (1979, p. 210). It is often more complicated because close friends sometimes behave like children who simply have a peer relationship. LaGaipa emphasizes that it is still important to maintain peer-type relationships during middle childhood and adolescence, as they satisfy basic needs not met by close friendships. He sees the main significance of peer relationships, which are maintained parallel to friendships, mainly in their contribution toward the development of more realistic perceptions and assessments of the social world; toward learning to deal with conflicts; and toward acquiring a noncynical attitude in relationships. A study by Bukowski, Hoza, and Boivin (1993) also underlines different effects of peer relationships compared to those of friendships. Popularity, which indicates a good status among peers, is related to early adolescents' perception that they are part of the group, whereas friendship contributes toward avoiding feelings of loneliness.

Observational and interview studies carried out in a German elementary school offer evidence that 10-year-old girls and boys have close friendships, but at the same time maintain other relationships that can be seen as continued peer relationships (Krappmann & Oswald, 1995). Two other types of relationship exist alongside "intimate friendships": on the one hand there are still "playmateships," which are very similar to the peer relationships of 5- to 7-year-olds but which require a higher level of sociability at 10 years of age. Play is gradually replaced by other forms of pastime. On the other hand "partnerships" develop through specific mutual interests that children intensely pursue (a sport or hobby). Again, the partner is perceived less as an individual person and is primarily judged on account of what he or she can contribute to the favored occupation. It also proved difficult in this study to differentiate unequivocally between the different relationship types.

These studies hint at the existence of several forms of relationship between children of the same age. Parallel to friendships, relationships with peers appear to have their own function in the social development of young people. It would be incorrect to compare the qualities of these continuing peer relationships with those of friendships, as they enrich the social world of children in their own way. This contribution would be lost if all peers were to become friends. These peer relationships can undoubtedly be satisfying or unsatisfying. They should, however, be measured according to the purposes they serve and not according to features that characterize a friendship.

Friendships

In contrast to the peer relationship, friendship is characterized as a relationship type by mutual concern for the whole personality of the friend. Friends also expect the kind of mutual attention and assistance offered in peer relationships. The new aspect lies in the willingness to make personal disclosures, including areas of vulnerability, because friends trust that the other will not let them down but will support them in difficult situations. Friends accept each other as the people they are. This does not necessarily exclude arguments or attempts to influence each other's development or even the breakdown of friendship because of revealed differences. Children who are friends "like" each other. This also applies to other relationships, as Bigelow (1977) has shown. But "liking" in friendships is based on a new kind of understanding between people. Although some peer relationships turn into friendships, friendship does not generally replace the peer relationship.

Research on young people's expectations from friendship ("friendship concept") does not differentiate between friends and peers. It is not until the third developmental stage of expectations from friendship, recognized by Bigelow in his data, that a clear reference is made to the special quality of friendship. The 12- to 14-year-olds, who are at this third stage, demand empathy and mutual understanding (Bigelow, 1977). Further studies stress that personal loyalty, trust, and support of the other as a person do not manifest themselves until preadolescence (Berndt, 1982; Youniss & Volpe, 1978). Not all adolescents maintain friendships of this quality; boys maintain them less often than girls (LaGaipa, 1979; Youniss & Smollar, 1985).

According to Selman's (1981) model of the development of friendship concepts, friends do not acknowledge their differences until they are in stage two, the "fairweather friendships" among children who are usually of elementary school age. Their friendship is, however, still greatly threatened by the lack of ability to coordinate these different perspectives. It is not until preadolescence that friendship develops into a mutual, trusting relationship and young people start entering into intimate friendships. Several studies show that even 12-year-olds have difficulty in understanding their friendships, even under "fairweather" conditions, as a form of reciprocal exchange, and that in adolescence the majority of young people still do not consider mutual trust to be essential to friendship (Selman, 1980; Hoppe-Graff & Keller, 1988).

Studies on how experiences in friendships contribute to social and sociocognitive development show not only that friendships include pleasurable companionship and effective support, but also that friends refuse one another help, compete with each other, and argue intensely (compare overview in Hartup, 1989; Krappmann, 1991). These results help in understanding how friendships promote children's development. It appears that they stimulate development less by practicing particular behavioral patterns than by encouraging reciprocal support in exploring situations, examining problems, and experimenting with solutions. Even friends are often unable to agree on solutions (Hartup, Laursen, Stewart & Eastenson, 1988). Discussions between friends are less routine and consider far more aspects, so that their outcome is not predictable from the beginning, as is the case in discussions between nonfriends (Krappmann & Oswald, 1995). Unlike peer relationships, friendship is not defined by pleasurable activities but draws its attraction from the fact that one can rely on a friend, particularly in less pleasurable and trying conditions.

After the discovery of friendship as a relationship type, adolescents develop an increasingly complex concept of what good friendship is. They begin to concern themselves with a problem that, according to Selman (1981), encumbers the concept of friendship at stage three, that of "intimate relationships": close friends of both sexes tend to take possession of their counterpart. Selman concludes from his data that at a further stage of development adolescents are able to give their friendships a quality that combines reciprocal attachment and autonomy.

Friendships remain an important element of everybody's social life throughout life, also when love relationships are added to a person's relationship ensemble. Just as peer relationships have their own function and development and are not only a preparatory stage for friendships, it is by no means the main task of friendships to prepare the way for love relationships, although love relationships certainly benefit when people have learned to be good friends. Friendships are in fact maintained parallel to love and marriage relationships, which again represent different types of relationship, and make their own particular contribution toward mastering life's main tasks (Schütze & Lang, 1993).

Research faces the task of developing instruments for measuring the intensity and quality of friendships. As everyday use of the term "friend" is very imprecise, it is not sufficient simply to ask children and adolescents about their friendships. The more complex measuring devices developed in recent years will help to further differentiate friendship as a relationship type, and increase insights into the development of ways of being friends (Bukowski et al., 1994; Krappmann et al., 1991; Parker & Asher, 1993; overview in Furman, 1995).

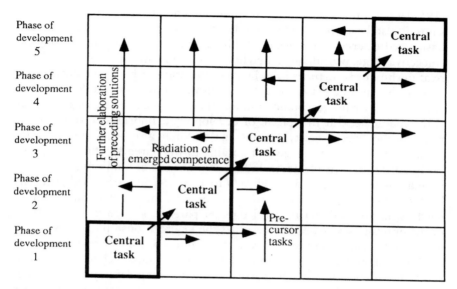

Figure 2.1. Basic principles of E. H. Erikson's developmental model. Source: Erikson (1956).

A genetic developmental model of relationship types

Descriptions young people give of their relationship show that the new way of relating to another person is seen more or less as a "discovery." Preparatory experiences are necessary for such discoveries. Once a type of relationship has been discovered it is further elaborated. Children talk about friendship not only when researchers ask them; they discuss among themselves what can be expected from friends and what one owes to them. These developmental processes cannot be represented by the above-mentioned ladder image of development. Another model is needed. One could refer to the Erikson diagram in which the developmental stages are ordered diagonally. Above and below each field, which depicts the task to be solved in each particular development phase and the competence to be acquired, there is room for preparation of the development task and for further development based on the solution found (Erikson, 1956; see Figure 2.1). A diagram of this kind also facilitates the design of a model of relationship types that illustrates both the consecutive "discoveries" and the progressing differentiation of relationship types.

The model of Buhrmester and Furman (1986), who take up Sullivan's

(1953) conception of embedding development in interpersonal relationships, is also based on the idea that during each stage of development a new basic need emerges. This need is fulfilled by a key relationship during the respective stage, possibly by a newly discovered relationship, by an existing relationship, or sometimes even by a combination of both (see Figure 2.2). During the juvenile era (according to Sullivan between 6 and 9 years), the child has to care for acceptance among others of the same age, as acceptance is the major need at this phase of development; Buhrmester and Furman refer to the "peer society." Same-age children also meet the need for companionship, at this stage still parallel to the parents, who were previously solely responsible for fulfilling this need. The additional need for intimacy emerges in preadolescence (9 to 12 years) and is fulfilled primarily by the same-sex peer who also contributes to the satisfaction of earlier needs, which are still partly satisfied by the parents. The search for a partner of the opposite sex, who then becomes the key relationship figure, starts in early adolescence, between 12 and 16. Same-sex friends and mixed-sex groups fulfill previous needs, although their importance declines in comparison to the friendship with the partner of the opposite sex. Relationships of the peer relationship type either disappear during preadolescence or are satisfied by cliques. Parents are no longer regarded as important relationship partners in the preadolescent stage, although Sullivan (1953), to whom the authors refer, drew particular attention to the relationship with the parents to show that relationships have to change continually.

Buhrmester and Furman's model is based on the idea that different relationships share in the satisfaction of needs. However, this appears to be a transitional phenomenon. From adolescence onward, the friend of the opposite sex certainly has priority in all areas. The model does not pay sufficient attention to the facts that relationships also change within the framework of a certain type and that needs also take on different forms. A developmental approach, which is based on Erikson's model, can be extended to overcome this limitation. The "genealogy" of emerging relationship types, as presented in Figure 2.3, is intended as a heuristic aid in understanding and further investigating the path from the undifferentiated mother–child interaction unit to the multiplex relationships of adult life. The examples of relationships entered in the boxes of the figure are designed to illustrate how the original relationship is continually differentiated; empty boxes indicate that other forms of relationship can be included. The order of the boxes and the arrows indicate how the relationships of the growing person transform and differentiate in relation to the line of development that represents the succession of newly discovered relationship types (heavily outlined boxes). Additional arrows could be added. There is, for instance, a lack of arrows indicating reciprocal influences within particular phases. It should be noted that in real development, transformation and

EMERGENT NEEDS AND KEY RELATIONSHIPS	INFANCY (0 to 2 yrs.)	CHILDHOOD (2 to 6 yrs.)	JUVENILE ERA (6 to 9 yrs.)	PREADOLESCENCE (9 to 12 yrs.)	EARLY ADOLESCENCE (12 to 16 yrs.)
SEXUALITY					**Opposite-sex partner**
INTIMACY				**Same-sex friend**	**Opposite-sex friend/romance** Same-sex friend
ACCEPTANCE			**Peer society**	**Friendship** Gang	**Heterosexual crowd** Friendship, Gang
COMPANIONSHIP		**Parents**	**Compeers** Parents	**Same-sex friend** Parents	**Opposite-sex friend/romance** Same-sex friend
TENDERNESS	**Parents**	**Parents**	**Parents**	**Same-sex friend** Parents	**Opposite-sex friend/romance** same-sex friend

Figure 2.2. Neo-Sullivanian model of emerging social needs and key relationships. During each developmental period (columns) a new need emerges (stairsteps) and is fulfilled by the key relationships (rows). Source: Buhrmester and Furman (1986, p. 43).

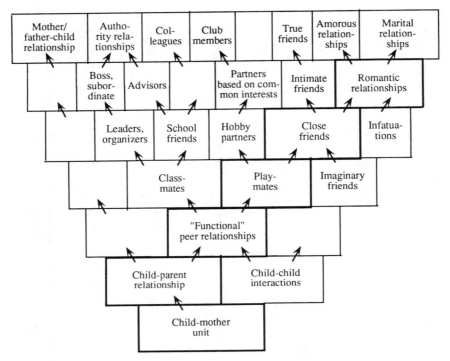

Figure 2.3. Developmental model of relationship types (following Erikson's model of development; see Figure 2.1).

differentiation do not progress in neatly outlined steps as suggested by this simplified figure.

The first stage in the development of relationships that a human being is capable of maintaining is the structuring of the parent–child relationship (compare Kreppner, Chapter 4 of this volume). Admittedly, the relationship with the parents generates fundamental interaction competencies, and the experienced attachment gives basic confidence in the self and in relationships to others (Sroufe et al., 1993). Also, social relationships between children are eased by various forms of parental support right into adolescence (Parke & Ladd, 1992). Nevertheless, as Piaget and Youniss have shown, relationships with others of the same age have characteristic structures that confront children with novel tasks and demand new competencies. Consequently, a new chapter begins on entering the same-age world.

This is where the line of development sets in that, as shown, leads from "functional" peer relationships to friendships, close friendships, and on to romantic relationships. At each stage, the newly entered relationship benefits from the patterns of relating to others that a person has already acquired. But the new relationship also opens up new perspectives: the child or adolescent develops a new type of relationship from which specific further developments emerge. At the same time, the new way of relating to others radiates onto existing types of relationship and influences their further development too.

The first peer relationships are still closely associated with relatively inconsistent "functions" (Lewis et al., 1975). A game or a practical joke may bring children together who share this preference. Pleasure and cumulative experiences help to continually improve action coordination. The next qualitative stage of development generates relationships with other children that center on longer-lasting tasks and occupations. Success and satisfaction increase when interacting with others with whom it is easy to agree, who are not looking for an argument, and who are reliable. In this way more constant "playmateships" develop. Another variation of this type can be seen in relationships with selected classmates who share problems of everyday school life and give mutual support. In both cases children often refer to playmates and schoolmates as friends, but this should not distract from the real nature of the relationships: attention is directed more toward mutual themes than toward persons.

These relationships with playmates and schoolmates not only provide the basis for qualitatively new friendships; they also change into more demanding forms of their own relationship type where the theme, rather than the person, is the focus of attention: these are important relationships maintained in schools, in higher education institutions, and at work (schoolmates, fellow students, colleagues), relationships held together by interests best pursued with others (hobby partners, group or club members), and relationships where people devote themselves to similar causes, share the same opinions, or are in a similar situation (neighbors, party members, members of grass-roots lobby groups). Sometimes friendships develop from these relationships. Despite this, they are not preliminary stages of friendship. Often a thematically oriented relationship can actually be complicated by friendship because its "irrelevant," "person-oriented" aspects can jeopardize giving priority to cooperation in solving the task.

As derivatives of the peer relationship, these relationships are based on equality of the participants. It is tempting to follow up the idea that on this basis a type of relationship develops in which influence and competencies are unevenly distributed. It can in fact be seen that even in relationships and groups that emphasize the equality of their members, there are always members who are more skilled, more imaginative, or better at problem solving. They gain influence, become spokespersons or advisors, and finally are elected to committees or become recognized leaders or bosses. The special position of *primus inter pares* is already accepted by children when leadership is both to their benefit and linked with specific tasks. Damon (1979) examined the stages in which adolescents develop an understanding of authority based not on prescribed differences in social rank but on the recognition of superior competence, which imposes special responsibility. Sullivan (1953) also presented the viewpoint that experiences with peers modify the parental authority of early childhood, thus creating the prerequisite for a lifelong parent–child relationship. It is also conceivable that this modifying experience represents a path toward entering into democratic structures of authority in which differences in responsibility do not prevent mutual respect.

The path from playmateships leads not only to further, theme-oriented relationships but also to close friendships in which the other is sought as the person he or she is. In directing attention toward the person, the close relationship adds a further dimension to the ways of forming relationships with others. Friends disclose their innermost thoughts to each other and trust one another, especially in psychic emergencies, not because the others are able to "do everything" like the parents, nor to found an interest group, but because friends are concerned about the life of the other without primarily expecting external rewards. Friends, especially younger ones, also play with each other. They also initially benefit from the fact that games and other favorite pastimes scaffold otherwise easily destabilized "fairweather friendships." The close childhood friendship further develops as a type throughout life. The more mature friendships of adolescents and adults are characterized by the challenges and problems of the particular phase in life. They are not abandoned when romantic relationships start occupying life. Often, different types of relationship maintained by a person provide a framework in which the specific advantages of relationship types are accumulated and disadvantages are compensated.

The emphasis given here to the development of children's or adolescents' relationships with persons of the same age does not imply that relationships with other generations – that is, with adults such as teachers or caregivers – are of minor significance to personal development. Experiences with siblings, if children have any, are doubtless also of importance, as von Salisch (in Chapter 3 of this volume) has shown. Nevertheless, relationships with peers are fundamentally different from relationships within the family and outside one's own generation. In a peer or friendship relationship a child succeeds in winning over another person who is not obliged to the child by family ties or an institutionalized role. This is an amazing achievement on the part of the child, the first major social achievement in the process of growing up. At the same time the child succeeds in taking a fundamental step toward the manifold social forms within which adults' lives interlink.

References

Ainsworth, M. D. S., Bell, S. M., & Stayton, D. J. (1974). Infant–mother attachment and social development. In M. P. Richards (Ed.), *The integration of a child into a social world* (pp. 99–135). Cambridge University Press.

Asher, S. R., & Hymel, S. (1981). Children's social competence in peer relations: Sociometric and behavioral assessment. In J. D. Wine & M. D. Smye (Eds.), *Social competence* (pp. 125–157). New York: Guilford.

Becker, J. M. (1977). A learning analysis of the development of peer-oriented behavior in nine-month-old infants. *Developmental Psychology, 13,* 481–491.

Berndt, T. J. (1982). The features and effects of friendship in early adolescence. *Child Development, 53,* 1447–1460.

   (1984). Sociometric, social-cognitive, and behavioral measures for the study of friendship and popularity. In T. Field, J. L. Roopnarine & M. Segal (Eds.), *Friendships in normal and handicapped children* (pp. 31–52). Norwood, NJ: Ablex.

Bigelow, B. J. (1977). Children's friendship expectations: A cognitive developmental study. *Child Development, 48,* 246–253.

Bowlby, J. (1969). *Attachment and loss,* Vol. 1: *Attachment.* New York: Basic Books.

Buhrmester, D., & Furman, W. (1986). The changing functions of friends in childhood: A Neo-Sullivanian perspective. In V. J. Derlega & B. A. Winstead (Eds.), *Friendship and social interaction* (pp. 41–62). New York: Springer.

Bukowski, W. M., & Hoza, B. (1989). Popularity and friendship: Issues in theory, measurement, and outcome. In T. J. Berndt & G. W. Ladd (Eds.), *Peer relationships in child development* (pp. 15–45). New York: Wiley.

Bukowski, W. M., Hoza, B., & Boivin, M. (1993). Popularity, friendship, and emotional adjustment during early adolescence. In B. Laursen (Ed.), *New Directions for Child Development,* Vol. 60: *Close friendships in adolescence* (pp. 23–37). San Francisco: Jossey-Bass.

   (1994). Measuring friendship quality during pre- and early adolescence: The development and psychometric properties of the Friendship Qualities Scale. *Journal of Social and Personal Relationships, 11,* 471–484.

Chapman, A. J., Smith, J. R., Foot, H. C., & Pritchard, E. (1979). Behavioural and sociometric indices of friendship in children. In M. Cook & G. D. Wilson (Eds.), *Love and attraction* (pp. 127–130). Oxford: Pergamon.

Cohen, Y. A. (1966). Patterns of friendship. In Y. A. Cohen (Ed.), *Social structure and personality* (pp. 351–386). New York: Holt, Rinehart & Winston.

Damon, W. (1979). *The social world of the child.* San Francisco: Jossey-Bass.

Doyle, A., Connolly, J., & Rivest, L. (1980). The effects of playmate familiarity on the social interactions of young children. *Child Development, 51,* 217–223.

Erikson, E. H. (1956). The problem of ego identity. *Journal of the American Psychiatric Association, 4,* 56–121.

Feiring, C., & Lewis, M. (1987). The child's social network: Sex differences from three to six years. *Sex Roles, 17,* 621–636.

Fogel, A. (1993). *Developing through relationships.* New York: Harvester & Wheatsheaf.

French, D. C. (1984). Children's knowledge of the social function of younger, older, and same-age peers. *Child Development, 55,* 1429–1433.

Furman, W. (1995). The measurement of children's and adolescents' perceptions of friendships: Conceptual and methodological issues. In W. M. Bukowski, A. F. Newcomb & W. W. Hartup (Eds.), *The company they keep: Friendships in childhood and adolescence.* Cambridge University Press.

Furman, W., & Bierman, K. L. (1984). Children's conceptions of friendship: A multimethod study of developmental changes. *Developmental Psychology, 20,* 925–931.

Furman, W., & Robbins, P. (1985). What's the point? Issues in the selection of treatment objectives. In B. H. Schneider, K. H. Rubin & J. E. Ledingham (Eds.), *Children's peer relations: Issues in assessment and intervention* (pp. 41–54). New York: Springer.

Grossmann, K. E. & Grossmann, K. (1991). Attachment quality as an organizer of emotional and behavioral responses in a longitudinal perspective. In C. M. Parkes, J. Stevenson-Hinde & P. Marris (Eds.), *Attachment across the life cycle* (pp. 93–114). London: Routledge & Kegan Paul.

Hartup, W. W. (1975). The origins of friendship. In M. Lewis & L. A. Rosenblum (Eds.), *Friendship and peer relations* (pp. 11–26). New York: Wiley.

(1978). Children and their friends. In H. McGurk (Ed.), *Issues in childhood social development* (pp. 130–170). London: Methuen.

(1983). Peer relations. In P. H. Mussen (Ed.), *Handbook of child psychology,* Vol. 4: *Socialization, personality, and social development* (ed. by E. M. Hetherington) (pp. 103–196). New York: Wiley.

(1989). Behavioral manifestations of children's friendships. In T. J. Berndt & G. W. Ladd (Eds.), *Peer relationships in child development* (pp. 46–70). New York: Wiley.

Hartup, W. W., Laursen, B. S., Stewart, M. I., & Eastenson, A. (1988). Conflict and the friendship relations of young children. *Child Development, 59,* 1590–1600.

Hayes, D. S. (1978). Cognitive bases for liking and disliking among preschool children. *Child Development, 49,* 906–909.

Hinde, R. A. (1976). On describing relationships. *Journal of Child Psychology and Psychiatry and Allied Disciplines, 17,* 1–19.

Hinde, R. A., & Stevenson-Hinde, J. (1987). Interpersonal relationships and child development. *Developmental Review, 7,* 1–21.

Hoppe-Graff, S., & Keller, M. (1988). Einheitlichkeit und Vielfalt in der Entwicklung des Freundschaftskonzeptes. *Zeitschrift für Entwicklungspsychologie und Pädagogische Psychologie, 20,* 195–213.

Howes, C. (1988). Peer interaction of young children. *Monographs of the Society for Research in Child Development* (Serial No. 217). Chicago: Society for Research in Child Development.

Keller, M. (1986). Freundschaft und Moral: Zur Entwicklung der moralischen Sensibilität in Beziehungen. In H. Bertram (Ed.), *Gesellschaftlicher Zwang und moralische Autonomie* (pp. 195–223). Frankfurt a.M.: Suhrkamp.

Konner, M. (1975). Relations among infants and juveniles in comparative perspective. In M. Lewis & L. A. Rosenblum (Eds.), *Friendships and peer relationships* (pp. 99–129). New York: Wiley.

Krappmann, L. (1991). Sozialisation in der Gruppe der Gleichaltrigen. In K. Hurrelmann & D. Ulich (Eds.), *Neues Handbuch der Sozialisationsforschung* (pp. 355–375). Weinheim and Basel: Beltz.

(1995). Amicitia, drujba, shin-yu, philia, freund, friendship – On the cultural diversity of a human relationship. In W. M. Bukowski, A. F. Newcomb & W. W. Hartup (Eds.), *The company they keep: Friendship in childhood and adolescence.* Cambridge University Press.

Krappmann, L., & Oswald, H. (1995). *Alltag der Schulkinder.* Weinheim: Juventa.

Krappmann, L., Oswald, H., Salisch, M. von, Schuster, B., Uhlendorff, H., & Weiss, K. (1991). *Das Freundesinterview. Ein Instrument zur Erhebung der Sozialbeziehungen von Kindern im Alter von sechs bis zwölf Jahren.* Unpublished manuscript, Max-Planck-Institut für Bildungsforschung Berlin.

LaGaipa, J. J. (1979). A developmental study of the meaning of friendship in adolescence. *Journal of Adolescence, 2,* 201–213.

Lewis, M., Young, G., Brooks, J., & Michalson, L. (1975). The beginnings of friendships. In M. Lewis & L. A. Rosenblum (Eds.), *Friendships and peer relationships* (pp. 27–66). New York: Wiley.

Lopata, H. Z. (1990). Friendship: Historical and theoretical introduction. In H. Z. Lopata & D. R. Maines (Eds.), *Friendship in context* (pp. 1–19). Greenwich, CT: JAI Press.

McCandless, B. R., & Marshall, H. R. (1957). A picture sociometric technique for preschool children and its relation to teacher judgments of friendship. *Child Development, 28,* 139–148.

Mueller, E. (1988). Toddlers' peer relations: Shared meaning and semantics. In W. Damon (Ed.), *Child Development – Today and tomorrow* (pp. 312–331). San Francisco: Jossey-Bass.

Parke, R. D., & Ladd, G. W. (Eds.) (1992). *Family–peer relationships.* Hillsdale, NJ: Erlbaum.

Parker, J. G., & Asher, S. R. (1993). Friendship and friendship quality in middle childhood: Links with peer group acceptance and feelings of loneliness and social dissatisfaction. *Developmental Psychology, 29,* 611–621.

Piaget, J. (1971 [1926]). *The language and the thought of the child.* New York: Hartcourt & Brace.

Rauh, H. (1984). Soziale Interaktion und Gruppenstruktur bei Krabbelkindern. In C. Eggers (Ed.), *Bindungen und Besitzdenken beim Kleinkind* (pp. 204–232). München: Urban & Schwarzenberg.

(1987). Social development in infant peers. In H. Rauh & H. C. Steinhausen (Eds.), *Psychobiology and early development* (pp. 257–274). Amsterdam: North-Holland.

Schütze, Y., & Lang, F. R. (1993). Freundschaft, Alter und Geschlecht, *Zeitschrift für Soziologie*, 22, 209–220.

Selman, R. L. (1980). *The growth of interpersonal understanding: Developmental and clinical analyses.* New York: Academic Press.

(1981). The child as a friendship philosopher. In S. R. Asher & J. M. Gottman (Eds.), *The development of children's friendships* (pp. 242–272). Cambridge University Press.

Sroufe, L. A., Carlson, E., & Shulman, S. (1993). Individuals in relationships: Development from infancy through adolescence. In D. C. Funder, R. D. Parke, C. Tomlinson-Keasey & K. Widaman (Eds.), *Studying lives through time. Personality and development)* (pp. 315–342). Washington, DC: American Psychological Association.

Suess, G. J., Grossmann, K. E., & Sroufe, L. A. (1992). Effects of infant attachment to mother and father on quality of adaptation in preschool: From dyadic to individual organization of self. *International Journal of Behavioral Development*, 15, 43–65.

Sullivan, H. S. (1953). *The interpersonal theory of psychiatry* (ed. by H. S. Perry & M. L. Gawel). New York: Norton.

Thorne, B. (1994). *Gender play: Girls and boys in school.* New Brunswick, NJ: Rutgers University Press.

Vandell, D. L. (1980). Sociability with peer and mother during the first year. *Developmental Psychology*, 16, 355–361.

Vandell, D. L., & Mueller, E. C. (1980). Peer play and friendships during the first two years. In H. C. Foot, A. J. Chapman & J. R. Smith (Eds.), *Friendship and social relations in children* (pp. 181–208). New York: Wiley.

Vandell, D. L., Wilson, K. S., & Buchanan, N. R. (1980). Peer interaction in the first year of life. *Child Development*, 51, 481–488.

Youniss, J. (1980). *Parents and peers in social development: A Sullivan-Piaget perspective.* Chicago: University of Chicago Press.

Youniss, J., & Smollar, J. (1985). *Adolescent relationships with mothers, fathers, and friends.* Chicago: University of Chicago Press.

Youniss, J., & Volpe, J. (1978). A relational analysis of children's friendships. In W. Damon (Ed.), *New directions for child development*, Vol. 1: *Social cognition* (pp. 1–22). San Francisco: Jossey-Bass.

3

Relationships between children: Symmetry and asymmetry among peers, friends, and siblings

Maria von Salisch

Introduction

Children are involved in a great variety of relationships, with members of previous generations, such as parents (see Kreppner, Chapter 4 of this volume), grandparents, or other relatives (see Kaiser, Chapter 7 of this volume), and with members of their own generation. Among these "other children" the most important are the child's own siblings, with whom about two-thirds of the children in Western countries still grow up. Apart from these, there are the children whom the child meets outside the family, for example on the street and the playground, in kindergarten and at school, in scouts' groups and leisure activity circles. In the following, these nonrelated, similar-aged children will be called peers. Children learn counting rhymes and games, rules and principles, and expectations and norms valid in the childhood world from their peers and siblings (e.g., Opie & Opie, 1970).

This chapter makes comparisons between children's relationships with peers and with siblings. As inequality in age, and thus in power too, is a prominent characteristic in sibling relationships during childhood, the comparison is restricted to clarifying the aspect of symmetry and asymmetry in these two social relationships between children. Comparisons will be made on two levels: first, on the level of face-to-face interactions; secondly, on the level of relationships. Relationships and interactions are not viewed as on the same level because, even in symmetrically structured relationships, children sometimes behave asymmetrically or complementarily with each other.[1] The type of relationship creates the opportunities or conditions for the interactions of the participants to proceed predominantly symmetrically or asymmetrically (on the question of interaction and relationship see Hinde, Chapter 1 of this volume).

The question of symmetry and asymmetry in relationships and interactions between children is of interest because developmental theoreticians, such as Piaget (1986), Sullivan (1953), and Youniss (1980), argue that special impulses for cognitive and social development are connected with symmetrical relationships. According to Youniss's (1980) definition of symmetrical-reciprocal interaction, where both partners in an interaction have the same possibilities of influencing the actions and views of the other, the partners will have a better chance of working out a solution to a problem *together* than when one person is permanently superior in strength or knowledge. Youniss points out that children who are friends can benefit from one another in their social development because friendships give children the chance to experience that others who are similar to themselves understand or even share characteristics that they may not appreciate in themselves. These experiences prevent an over- or underestimation of oneself and help the child to develop sensitivity toward differences in others (Youniss, 1980).

In the opinion of the constructivist theoreticians, Piaget and Youniss, different impulses in development are provided by complementary relationships, the foremost example of which is the parent–child relationship. In these relationships children tend to adopt the concepts of the wiser or more powerful; here, the child's own constructive contribution is relatively small. With respect to social development, Youniss (1980) surmises that the desire to be accepted by superior or valued persons misleads children into presenting the nicest possible image of themselves while hiding nonappreciated aspects of themselves from these valued persons.

Relationships between siblings and between peers

In the following, various aspects that render relationships symmetrical or asymmetrical will be listed; on the basis of this the respective sibling and peer relationships will be compared. Asymmetry occurs in both social relationships because of the participants' difference in age; in the case of the peer relationship it is also due to the different social (sociometric) status among same-age children. Symmetrical relationship structures result from different factors: first, from the relation to adults, whom children define as a group separate from themselves and in principle equal; second, from the mutual familiarity of the children; third, from the nonterminability of the sibling relationship; and fourth, from the sustainable power balance in freely agreed-upon friendships. These points will be explained below.

Asymmetrical aspects of the relationships

Relationships among siblings contain a conspicuous element of inequality, namely the different ages of the children. Apart from the rare case of twins, one child is always ahead of the other in years and, usually, in development. As development progresses at a rapid rate during early and middle childhood, the stages where siblings spend most time together, the resulting power difference molds the sibling relationship in this period. From school-age onward children increasingly choose peers of the same age as playmates or friends (Oswald, Krappmann, Chowdhuri & von Salisch, 1987), but when 6- to 10-year-olds are observed outside school, it is noticeable that they spend up to 40% of their time in mixed-age peer groups, though the frequency decreases as they get older (Ellis, Rogoff & Cromer, 1981). School-age children have a clear idea of what can be expected from older and younger children: they can turn to older children when they want to learn something, and younger children can be taught things. Friends are best found among agemates (French, 1984).

Inequalities in power and influence also exist among children of the same age. Among other reasons, they develop because some children invest more effort, are quicker, are more imaginative, have greater social skills, or are in some other way more active and attractive than others and eventually take on leading positions. Sociometric choices reflect these differences: when children in a school class are asked which of their classmates they like and dislike, four different groups emerge: (1) children who receive many positive votes and few negative votes and are thus generally popular, (2) children who receive few positive votes and many negative ones and are thus rejected by their classmates, (3) children who attract neither positive nor negative votes and are thus neglected by the other children, and finally (4) children who attract both positive and negative votes and are thus viewed controversially by the class (e.g., Dodge, Coie & Brakke, 1982). These differences in the sociometric status of a child often persist for years (Coie & Dodge, 1983); they display very little change over time, especially for children who were actively rejected by others (Parker & Asher, 1987). It is quite obvious that the sociometric status of a child influences the relationships he or she enters into with his or her classmates.

Symmetrical aspects of the relationships

Symmetry with reference to adults. A symmetrical relationship among children develops in the first place with reference to adults. Schoolchildren form a unit of basically equal persons (Parsons, 1955), as opposed to teachers, janitors, and other adults in the institution of the school; in a family the children belong to one generation and consequently, as siblings, are in principle entitled to the same rights (and duties). Similar to the peer community of the school class, the subsystem of siblings in a family also develops special behavioral conventions and rules; the norm not to tell tales – that is, to settle arguments without adult intervention – is upheld both in the school class and in the family. Children who do not stick to this principle face sanctions (Oswald, 1991).

Symmetry through mutual familiarity. A second form of symmetry is promoted within the family by interdependence among siblings. During early childhood, siblings spend a great deal of time together, sometimes more than twice as much as with their parents (Dunn, 1983). Sharing everyday life over a long period creates a high level of familiarity between siblings. This familiarity is mutual and contributes to symmetry in the relationship in that it sets limits on the power exercised by one over the other; it gives both partners a means to "repay" any eventual injuries. Younger siblings know the strengths and weaknesses, likes and dislikes, fears and worries, the "sore points," of their older brothers and sisters, almost as well as vice versa. Consequently siblings are particularly well equipped to make fun of, annoy, manipulate, or hurt each other (Dunn, 1983). Dunn and Munn (1985) observed that they develop this ability very early, from about 14 to 18 months and onward. On the one hand, this "balance of forces" can lead to symmetrical escalation in arguments (Watzlawick, Beavin & Jackson, 1967). On the other hand, siblings who depend on one another within the framework of everyday family life are under a great deal of pressure to make peace again and again.

Mutual familiarity has another aspect that also promotes symmetry in the relationship: as siblings share their lives together they can often develop greater mutual empathy than with their parents or other adults. "Since what distresses, pains or excites a sibling is very close to what distresses, pains or excites the child, the child is likely to be far better placed to understand and find remedies for a sibling's distress than for the distress of an adult" (Dunn, 1983, p. 793). Sibling relationships grow over a long period of time, during which children get to know each other in their innermost selves (Bank & Kahn, 1982). Attempts to bluff the other are quickly discovered and usually dismissed. Thus there are two sides to the familiarity between siblings: on the one hand it offers siblings the opportunity to recognize themselves in the other and, in so doing, to develop; on the other hand it harbors the danger of great mutual vulnerability. In a similar way to the friendships described by Youniss (1980), sibling relationships also offer the possibility of developing together within the relationship without denying or distorting parts of oneself. A difference between the two relationship types results from the fact that, on account of their family context, siblings are more often tempted to exploit their own developmental advantages or the idiosyncrasies of the other in order to hurt the brother or sister. Children often find it hard to resist this temptation, as toys, living space, and parental attention have to be shared in the family and their availability is often limited. In addition, one child sometimes succeeds in fulfilling its wishes or aims to the disadvantage of its siblings; or occasionally all the children in a family have similar needs at the same time.

In comparison, relationships among peers are less conflictual, as each child lives in its family and can withdraw there if dealings with friends, classmates, or playmates prove unsatisfactory. But even in the world of peers children face the temptations of competition and social comparison, outdoing others or treating them arrogantly (Sullivan, 1953). If a child tries to stand out against others without understandable cause, its peers will call it a "show-off" and turn away. Peers insist on the principle of equality in their relationships (Selman, 1980).

Symmetry through nonterminability of the relationship. Siblings relate to one another in the long term as well, in fact in a way that they can hardly influence themselves. People become siblings because of their parents, by the "chance" of their birth in the same family, and they remain siblings for the rest of their lives. This third aspect of symmetry makes a sibling relationship a stable and relatively secure relationship that exists independent of the intentions or actions of the participants, and that can be relied on in cases of emergency (Bank & Kahn, 1982; see Bedford, Chapter 6 of this volume).

Symmetry in behavior. Friendships are essentially at greater risk than sibling relationships because people can only be, and remain, friends when the choice is mutual and all participants contribute to the maintenance of the friendship. The fact that interest in one another has to be reciprocal promotes long-term symmetry in behavior. Friendships in which a child permanently exercises power at the expense of another will be terminated (Selman, 1980). External factors contribute toward ensuring that the structural differences between friends do not become too pronounced: during middle childhood and preadolescence, children mainly choose friends of the same age and the same gender, from a similar social stratum, with similar views (Kandel, 1978), and with similar grades at school (Krappmann, 1985). Symmetry in the sense of reciprocity in behavior gains prominence around 9 years (stage two) in the concept children have of friendship (Selman, 1980). From about this age, too, children expect that help given by one friend to another should be returned, not immediately, but at some time in the future (Youniss, 1980).

Interactions among siblings and among peers

As in the case of relationships, symmetrical and asymmetrical elements are also identifiable in interactions between peers and between siblings. Asymmetry in interactions fundamentally manifests itself in that the action of one participant is controlled by the contribution of the other (Youniss, 1980). If nothing is known about the reaction of the counterpart or the broader context, categorization of a particular type of behavior becomes difficult. As some types of behavior (e.g., imitation) occur in different contexts, they can appear in both categories. Short-term, symmetrical forms of interaction emerge when both interaction partners do the same thing and get involved directly with each other. Long-term symmetrical forms of interaction can emerge in relation to third parties, for instance in the mutual support children give each other vis-à-vis adults.

Asymmetrical aspects of interactions between siblings

The behavior of older and younger siblings is overtly complementary in many areas. This is perfectly clear when, for instance, older siblings try to cheer up or help look after their baby sisters or brothers. Parents welcome such efforts (Schütze, 1986), which further a positive relationship between siblings (Dunn & Kendrick, 1982). According to Schütze (1986), the relationship between brothers and sisters develops in three phases during the first 18 months of the second child's life: in the first phase, the parents support the relationship, which is almost complementary in nature; the second phase begins when the younger child starts to crawl at about 9 months; and the third phase begins when the younger child starts to talk at about 16 months. During the second phase antagonistic forms of behavior on the part of the older child gain prominence; at the same time, the development of an independent sibling relationship can be observed. During the third phase the independent relationship consolidates itself between the two children. Symmetrical elements in the interactions of the siblings increase as the baby develops from a helpless infant into a playmate with basic competencies such as talking and walking.

In most areas, interactions between siblings at this age are nevertheless highly complementary. For example: older brothers and sisters generally turn down the younger ones' offers to play. Younger siblings imitate their older sisters and brothers and in this way try to stimulate them into mutual play (Schütze, 1986). When the younger child is about 18 months old, its siblings of preschool age tend to take the initiative more often, both in prosocial as well as antagonistic behavior. The younger ones imitate the older ones far more frequently than vice versa. Asymmetrical elements in the interaction decline somewhat by the time the younger child reaches 3 years of age (Abramovitch, Corter, Pepler & Stanhope, 1986). When the younger sibling is of preschool age and the older child is of school age, initiating games and setting up rules usually depends on the older child. Older brothers and sisters tend more to manipulate or bribe younger ones, to help them, to show tenderness and comfort them, to ask them to do something, and to involve them in disputes about objects, rather than vice versa (Abramovitch et al., 1986). Seven- to 8-year-olds praise their younger sisters and brothers, teach them more, and generally behave more dominantly than a comparison group of 8-years-olds who were observed with their older siblings. As might be expected, the differences in behavior of older and younger siblings are greater with increasing differences in age (Minnett, Vandell & Santrock, 1983). Again, this indicates that the different levels of development in children are a basic determining factor of their complementary behavior.

Older siblings of 10 to 11 years tend to help their younger sisters or brothers with an air of disparagement and discouragement (Bryant & Crockenberg, 1980). In contrast to this, the younger siblings tend to react with annoyance and anger on the one hand (Bryant & Crockenberg, 1980), and a greater tendency to self-deprecation on the other (Minnett et al., 1983). A questionnaire study among 11- to 13-year-olds (Furman & Buhrmester, 1985b) confirmed that older siblings have more power than younger ones and that this difference declines as development progresses. The loadings on the "power" factor reflect the double nature of complementary social behavior because, alongside items that describe dominance in behavior, this factor also contains items that indicate admiration or nurturance.

The results referred to above can be summarized in a table (see Table 3.1). It contains examples of those types of behavior that define the relationships between the participants as implicitly asymmetrical (Watzlawick et al., 1967), or react to these relationship definitions. This table does not refer to the fit between the siblings' behavior. The behavior of both children in their mutual relation is defined as a dyadic concept, as a complementary form of the interaction (see Hinde, Chapter 1 of this volume).

Two aspects in this schema are of particular importance. First, in view of the double nature of power (Furman & Buhrmester, 1985b), complementary behavior is depicted on the horizontal axis, which extends from "nurturing and encouraging" to "fighting and invalidating." Most types of sibling behavior probably do not lie at these extremes but along the continuum between. Others contain elements from both areas. Thus praise may contain elements of criticism and assistance may occasionally be associated with invalidation (Bryant & Crockenberg, 1980; Krappmann & Oswald,

Table 3.1. *Complementary forms of interaction between older and younger siblings*

	Asymmetrical behavior	
	Nurturing and encouraging the other $\Leftrightarrow$	Fighting and invalidating the other
Older sibling	E.g., praise, encourage, teach, watch over, protect, nurture $\Updownarrow$	E.g., hit, boss, control, disapprove, criticize, invalidate $\Updownarrow$
Younger sibling	E.g., admire, imitate, learn, send ahead in difficult situations, express need	E.g., obey, submit, self-deprecate, ingratiate oneself, annoy the other, provoke, ridicule

1991). In contrast to the custom of some authors, the two poles are not labeled "positive" and "negative" or "prosocial" and "antagonistic," because this would imply an individualistic perspective that removes the behavior from the context of the interaction. For example: when younger siblings defend themselves against the infringements of their older brothers and sisters, should this be considered "prosocial" because everyone in a community has the right to their own development? Or should this behavior be seen as "antagonistic" because it sometimes includes insults and physical attacks?

This difficulty leads to the second point. If the interaction between two people is viewed as a system in which both partners relate reciprocally in their behavior (Watzlawick et al., 1967), then evaluation of the behavior retreats into the background, as it can only be carried out from a superior standpoint. The system view emphasizes the *interdependence* of the behavior. That the nurturing and the fighting behavior of older and younger siblings fundamentally depend on one another is indicated by the vertical arrows between the blocks. These arrows simultaneously show that each contribution to a face-to-face interaction contains a definition of the (momentary) relationships to which the interaction partner may react differently. If an older child bosses a younger child, the younger – assuming the simplest case – may accept the implied relationship definition by, for instance, acquiescing. Alternatively, it can refuse the definition by, for instance, provoking the older brother or sister in return. In other words: asymmetrical relationship definitions also require confirmation by the partner. Which form the interaction takes is continually negotiated in the reciprocal exchange of relationship definitions, even if this process is often implicit and the participants are not conscious of it (von Salisch, 1991b).

The fact that siblings influence each other over longer periods of time can be illustrated by two studies on infants and toddlers. Negative behavior displayed by older siblings toward their younger brothers or sisters between 8 and 16 months is seldom repaid by the younger ones in the same way during this phase. Negative reactions on the part of the younger ones do not occur until the next phase. Younger children learn ways of defending themselves against their older siblings (Schütze, 1986). Prosocial actions of older children toward their 18-month-old siblings correlate with conciliatory, cooperative, and cognitively progressive behavior on the part of the younger ones six months later (Dunn & Munn, 1986). According to Dunn and Munn, the actions of the older children stimulate the relatively advanced behavior of the younger ones. Over a period of time interactions between the siblings produce impulses that stimulate the cognitive development of the individual children (Dunn, 1988) and change the relationship between them both. How influential the quality of the sibling relationship can also be in emotional development is illustrated by the fact that those children of about 3 years of age who were observed using arguments when quarreling with their older siblings were better able to understand a doll's feelings in various everyday situations seven months later than their agemates who quarreled with their siblings without the use of arguments (Slomkowski & Dunn, 1992). Dunn, Brown, Slomkowski, Tesla, and Youngblade (1991) corroborate that a friendly and cooperative sibling relationship contributes to the acquisition of emotional and cognitive perspective taking.

Asymmetrical aspects of interaction between peers

Interactions between older and younger children display many of the elements of complementary behavior described above in sibling relationships. Nine- and 10-year-olds are more prepared to keep group members to the point, obtain their opinions, and assume responsibility for the result when making a communal decision in a group of younger children than when they have to come to an agreement with their agemates (French, Waas, Stright & Baker, 1986). Nine- and 11-year-old girls who are asked to explain the rules of a boardgame adapt to the development level of a younger child by repeating things more often; they also tend to give advice and praise more often than when giving instructions to agemates (Ludeke & Hartup, 1983). Similar to older siblings, the older children are less prepared to observe younger children (Brody, Stoneman, MacKinnon & MacKinnon, 1985), to imitate them, or to take up their suggestions than vice versa (Brody & Stoneman, 1981).

Asymmetrical forms of interaction also occur between agemates. They are often created by the sociometric status of the child in the class. Behavioral offers made by children who are rejected by their classmates are turned down more often than those of other children (Dodge et al., 1982; Dodge, 1983). Behavioral interdependence manifests itself in that many rejected children are more inclined than their agemates to threaten others verbally or physically (Coie & Kupersmidt, 1983; Dodge, 1983). This results in mutual rejection and refusal. When trying to discover how these undesirable cycles in the exchange of asymmetrical relationship definitions originated, it is advisable to study the behavior of rejected children in newly constituted peer groups where their reputation as a "rejected child" has not yet influenced the behavior of the other children. Coie and Kupersmidt (1983) and Dodge (1983) did exactly this. They showed that within a brief period of time the rejected children (in this case boys) again followed the above described behavioral pattern of pressurization and refusal. Consequently, it was hardly surprising that in these newly constituted children's groups they were also stigmatized as rejected outsiders within a short space of time. Prosocial offers from children who are neglected by their classmates are also ignored more frequently; they are simply left out (Dodge et al., 1982; Dodge, 1983). This form of asymmetrical interaction is particularly invalidating because it does not even acknowledge the other as an interaction partner (Laing, 1969).

Relationships between children of the same age can take on a temporary asymmetrical form, which is often classified as "prosocial," in situations where one child helps another. If a child requires or needs to know something that another child has or knows, then "power" is unequally distributed between them. Many children use this opportunity to define the momentary relationship with the interaction partner asymmetrically: 41% of all requests for help among 10-year-old classmates are refused or combined with different types of disparagement (Krappmann & Oswald, 1991). The concrete form of these problematical attitudes toward helping is reminiscent of the cycles of invalidation on the part of the older children and resentment or self-deprecation on the part of the younger ones that Bryant and Crockenberg (1980) observed when sisters solved a problem together.

Symmetrical aspects of interactions between siblings

An early form of symmetry is mutual imitation. A child does something, the other imitates the action and changes it, the first child takes over the changed form, and so on. When a pair of siblings of preschool age bounce together on the couch, move a toy train together, or sing a "duet" of rhymes or songs, both of their faces are full of joy and excitement. Action procedures of this kind strengthen the positive feelings the siblings feel for one another (Dunn, 1983). Abramovitch et al. (1986) report that pairs of siblings of preschool age establish symmetry in giving and taking, in the expression of physical attraction and in physical forms of dispute. It has already been mentioned that siblings are in a particularly favorable position when the question of recognizing and alleviating distress in a brother or sister arises. Social perspective taking, which develops during the second year of life, is a prerequisite of symmetrical action (Dunn, 1983) in thinking out practical jokes together as well as provoking each other (Brown & Dunn, 1992). Siblings of 2 to 3 years of age can comfort one another and give assurance when coping with difficult situations (Dunn, 1983).

Although siblings are of unequal age, which results in different functions toward the parents, with the older ones acting as pioneers or translators and the younger ones giving loyal support, the interactions of the siblings may well be symmetrical and balanced at a different level. With reference to the parents, siblings often give each other mutual support. In this case neither helps one "more" than the other. On the basis of case studies, the psychotherapists Bank and Kahn (1982) report that intense loyalty between siblings can develop when parents die or are no longer emotionally accessible to the children for other reasons. According to Bank and Kahn (1982), the prerequisites of the development of such an unusually close sibling bond are that (1) at least one parent was warm and accessible during early childhood, providing an example of such behavior; (2) the parents did not play the children off against each other, so that interactions between the siblings were predominantly harmonious and balanced; (3) the siblings grew up together; and (4) they were close in age and shared interests and developmental tasks together. Further preconditions are that the siblings felt sympathy toward one another and were really dependent on each other because no (or almost no) other supporting adults were available after the loss of their parents.

Symmetrical aspects of interactions between peers

Children who are close in age but not siblings also develop many forms of symmetrical interaction. From the age of 2 months infants establish eye contact with other children; they later crawl toward them and follow them. One-year-olds offer each other toys, laugh at, and imitate each other (Rauh, 1984). The main difficulty in interactions between these young children is coordinating actions. Awakening the partner's interest often proves difficult for children of around 2 years of age.[2] Many of their offers are simply lost. The majority of interactions between 2-year-old peers are accompanied by smiles and laughter (Ross & Goldman, 1976). Similar to siblings, the nonrelated children repeat their actions, imitate each other and enjoy their play. Reciprocal imitation and positive affect are forms of interaction found among preschool and schoolchildren, who call this "fun." This includes such diverse activities as splashing with water, whistling on pen caps, or initiating playful chases (Oswald et al., 1987). Children who are popular with their classmates often succeed in striking this jovial tone, which creates mutuality and is rewarding for all participants (Dodge, 1983). How important unrestrained exuberance is for children in middle childhood is also reflected in children's own reports that 90% of them have "fun" or can be silly with their friends (Krappmann, von Salisch & Oswald, 1990). The "fun factor," the possibility of having fun together, seems to be a central category in assessing friends among 8- to 10-year-olds (see also von Salisch, 1996).

Classmates support each other in the face of teachers. Whispering prompts, copying, or lending things can be interpreted as acts of mutual assistance. This occurs approximately two or three times during a lesson, particularly between children who are friends (Krappmann & Oswald, 1985). Here, the balance between giving and taking is most likely squared in time. The temporary asymmetry that occurs in the act of helping was already mentioned above.

Interactions between siblings and friends: A comparison

When comparing how friends and siblings interrelate, the immediate idea is to observe the behavior of a child with children of both groups. Brody, Stoneman, and MacKinnon (1982) have compared the ways in which same-sex sibling pairs aged between 5 and 10 years play together, with the ways in which the older siblings play with their best friend of the same sex. Although the age difference between the siblings is only two to three years, the interactions between pairs of friends tend to be more symmetrical than between pairs of siblings. When siblings are at play, the older ones tend to explain things to the younger ones, to show them how to do things, but also to give orders and to assert their own position. In the case of best friends, the older one also tends to take on the role of teacher more often than vice versa (home advantage!), but overall, symmetrical forms of behavior predominate. Younger brothers or sisters often agree to the asymmetrical relationship definitions of their older siblings. They tend to allow themselves to be "managed," while older siblings slip into the "manager" role more often. When choosing a game, the older ones adapt to the abilities of their younger sibling: boys tend to avoid games with their younger brothers that involve the same amount of physical strength; girls are more likely to play ritualized children's games that are better suited to the level of development of their younger sisters. At the same time, a study by Stoneman, Brody, and MacKinnon (1984) points out a gender difference. In contrast to sisters, behavior among brothers is characterized less by egalitarian playmate roles and more by demonstrations of strength such as arguing, hitting, or pushing.

In the studies reported above, the behavior of *all* the older siblings toward their friends was compared with their behavior toward their younger siblings at home. Whether and to what extent *individual* children behave similarly toward these different partners was the topic of three additional investigations: Berndt and Bulleit (1985) found that the behavior of children toward their playmates in kindergarten hardly coincides with the behavior they display toward their younger siblings. As expected, correlations are higher when the brother or sister is close in age – less than two years' difference. No consistent pattern could be established in the correlations between the behavior of kindergarten children (Abramovitch et al., 1986) and schoolchidren (Stocker & Dunn, 1990) toward their siblings and friends. Consequently, what children learn in their sibling relationships is not directly transferred to other child–child relationships (or vice versa) (Dunn, 1994, ch. 6).

Conflicts between friends and between siblings

Studies of conflicts show particularly clearly that children and adolescents sometimes behave differently toward their friends and siblings. More detailed surveys of this topic are offered by Shantz and Hobart (1989) and Vandell and Bailey (1992).

Eleven- to 13-year-olds consider the relationship with their siblings to be more conflict-laden than those with their friends (Furman & Buhrmester, 1985a). This is probably due not only to the difference in age, as twins between 10 and 14 years of age also report more conflicts in their sibling relationship than with their respective friends (Furman & White, 1991). In contrast to this, conflict seems to be almost taboo in some friendships: 23% of all the preadolescent subjects maintained that they *never* argue with their best friend (Rafaelli, 1989). The cause of conflicts also appears to be different. While siblings argue predominantly about possessions, family tasks, and violations of the private sphere by verbal insults, female friends argue more often about relationship topics such as neglect or untrustworthiness. Male friends come into conflict more often because of physical abuse. Whether one controls or bosses the other, or shares sufficiently, are questions that give rise to disagreement at an almost equal level in sibling relationships and friendships among 11- to 14-year-olds (Rafaelli, 1989). Siblings state that they quarrel "out of habit," whereas friends need a particular cause for this (Rafaelli, 1991).

In a study by Furman and Buhrmester (1985b), conflict between siblings is associated with the fact that parents are perceived as biased. If parents are considered to have a "blind spot," the frequency of disputes between siblings increases. This result indicates how much the behavior of parents influences that of siblings toward each other. In 17% of conflicts between siblings parents intervene directly. (In comparison, only 2% of conflicts among friends are ended by adult intervention.) Whereas siblings often let the conflict escalate because they can be certain that the parents will step in, friends have to come to terms on their own. Girls who disagree with their girlfriends tend to part without immediate settlement; they let the relationship lapse and apologize later. Boys tend to settle a dispute with their same-sex friends immediately and show no open signs of repairing their relationship later (Rafaelli, 1989).

On the basis of these questionnaire results, Rafaelli reaches the conclusion that conflicts between siblings primarily serve the purpose of self-assertion. A child who does not defend itself against the insults of a brother or the demands of a sister comes off worse because children cannot withdraw from the indissoluble sibling relationships. The necessity to create demarcations against a brother or sister challenges children to continually make sure what their own needs, abilities, preferences, and characteristics are and thus define themselves as individuals (Shantz & Hobart, 1989). Children also get to know themselves better in conflicts with friends when they confront the opinion of the other with their own. However, it is more difficult to settle disputes in freely agreed-upon friendships because (1) the conflict has to be solved without the intervention of parents, and (2) the conflict may place the friendship at risk. Thus, friendship pairs face the dilemma of needing to air their criticism and negative feelings on the one hand, yet at the same time having to consider the feelings of the friend and to protect the relationship (von Salisch, 1991a). If the friendship is to continue (or even be intensified), preadolescent friends have to develop some skill when negotiating on relevant relationship topics such as promise and trust, neglect and jealousy, or power and subordination; that the children often first part without reaching a settlement is hardly surprising considering the difficulty of this task. The developmental theoreticians Sullivan (1953) and Youniss (1980) emphasize that such negotiations stimulate friends to think about themselves, their partner, and their relationship, and thus grow in themselves and in their relationship.

From childhood to youth

During youth the relationship between siblings and other members of the family relaxes (Larson & Richards, 1991). Between 9 and 18 years of age the warmth and closeness that young persons experience with their siblings decline, and conflicts between them occur less often and become less intense (Buhrmester & Furman, 1990). As siblings grow older and converge in their level of development their relationship is perceived as more balanced and egalitarian.

The increasingly symmetrical relationship between the siblings challenges them to renegotiate the relationship. As adolescent siblings become less dependent on one another, their relationship can develop in two directions. If the sibling relationship is based on sympathy and goodwill it can become as supportive as freely agreed-upon friendships usually are. If the relationship is conflict-laden or characterized by injuries, then the siblings have the chance of relaxing it and continuing it on a level satisactory to both. To what extent sibling relationships are cultivated in adulthood depends on the agreements reached by the participants, as in the case of friendships. As cohesion through the family of origin loses its importance in adulthood, the relationship between siblings depends on mutual sympathy and affection similar to friendships (see Auhagen, Chapter 10 of this volume). Formally, the relationship between siblings continues throughout their lifetime, but inspiring these relationships with life calls for efforts on the part of both participants (see Bedford, Chapter 6 of this volume).

Notes

1. Complementary interactions can depend on many factors: on differences in the interaction partners with respect to power, gender, emotional support, etc. (Hinde, 1979). This chapter is concerned with the complementary distribution of power in relationships. The concepts "complementary" and "asymmetrical" are thus interchangeable in this text.
2. Whether older siblings reject play offers made by the younger ones more often than they reject the offers of equally familiar, but nonrelated, older peers is an interesting research question. It could give insights into the role played by developmental differences versus the sibling relationship during such interactions.

References

Abramovitch, R., Corter, C., Pepler D., & Stanhope, L. (1986). Sibling and peer interaction: A final follow-up and a comparison. *Child Development, 57,* 217–229.

Bank, S., & Kahn, M. (1982). *The sibling bond*. New York: Basic.

Berndt, T., & Bulleit, T. (1985). Effects of sibling relationship on preschoolers' behavior at home and at school. *Developmental Psychology, 21*, 761–767.

Brody, G. H., & Stoneman, Z. (1981). Selective imitation of same-age, older and younger peers. *Child Development, 52*, 717–720.

Brody, G. H., Stoneman, Z., & MacKinnon, C. (1982). Role asymmetrics among school-aged children, their younger siblings and their friends. *Child Development, 53*, 1364–1370.

Brody, G. H., Stoneman, Z., MacKinnon, C., & MacKinnon, R. (1985). Role relationships and behavior between preschool-aged and school-aged sibling pairs. *Development Psychology, 21*, 124–129.

Brown, J., & Dunn, J. (1992). Talk with your mother or your sibling? Developmental changes in early family conversations about feelings. *Child Development, 63*, 336–349.

Bryant, B., & Crockenberg, S. (1980). Correlates and dimensions of prosocial behavior: A study of female siblings with their mothers. *Child Development, 51*, 529–544.

Buhrmester, D., & Furman, W. (1990). Perceptions of sibling relationships during middle childhood and adolescence. *Child Development, 61*, 1387–1398.

Coie, J., & Dodge, K. (1983). Continuities and change in children's social status: A five-year longitudinal study. *Merrill Palmer Quarterly, 29*, 261–282.

Coie, J., & Kupersmidt, J. B. (1983). A behavioral analysis of emerging social status in boys' groups. *Child Development, 54*, 1400–1416.

Dodge, K. A. (1983). Behavioral antecedents of peer social status. *Child Development, 54*, 1386–1399.

Dodge, K. A., Coie, J., & Brakke, N. (1982). Behavior patterns of socially rejected and neglected preadolescents: The roles of social approach and aggression. *Journal of Abnormal Child Psychology, 10*, 389–410.

Dunn, J. (1983). Sibling relationships in early childhood. *Child Development, 54*, 787–811.

(1988). *The beginnings of social understanding*. Oxford: Blackwell.

(1994). *Young children's close relationships*. Newbury Park, CA: Sage.

Dunn, J., Brown, J., Slomkowski, C., Tesla, C., & Youngblade, L. (1991). Young children's understanding of other people's feelings and beliefs: Individual differences and their antecedents. *Child Development, 62*, 1352–1366.

Dunn, J., & Kendrick, C. (1982). *Siblings: Love, envy and understanding*. London: McIntyre.

Dunn, J., & Munn, P. (1985). Becoming a family member: Family conflict and the development of social understanding in the second year. *Child Development, 56*, 480–492.

(1986). Siblings and the development of prosocial behavior. *International Journal of Behavioral Development, 9*, 265–284.

Ellis, S., Rogoff, B., & Cromer, C. (1981). Age segregation in children's social interactions. *Developmental Psychology, 17*, 399–407.

French, D. (1984). Children's knowledge of the social functions of younger, older and same-age peers. *Child Development, 55,* 1429–1433.

French, D., Waas, G., Stright, A., & Baker, J. (1986). Leadership asymmetries in mixed-age children's groups. *Child Development, 57,* 1277–1283.

Furman, W., & Buhrmester, D. (1985a). Children's perceptions of the personal relationships in their social networks. *Developmental Psychology, 21,* 1016–1024.

(1985b). Children's perceptions of the qualities of the sibling relationships. *Child Development, 56,* 448–461.

Furman, W., & White, A. (1991, April). *The link between twins' relationship with each other and their friends.* Paper presented at the Meeting of the Society for Research in Child Development, Seattle.

Hinde, R. (1979). *Towards understanding relationships.* London: Academic Press.

Kandel, D. (1978). Similarity in real-life adolescent friendship pairs. *Journal of Personality and Social Psychology, 36,* 306–312.

Krappmann, L. (1985). The structure of peer relationships and possible effects on school achievement. In R. Hinde, A. N. Perret-Clermont & J. Stevenson-Hinde (Eds.), *Social relationships and cognitive development* (pp. 149–166). Oxford: Clarendon Press.

Krappmann, L., & Oswald, H. (1985). Schulisches Lernen in Interaktion mit Gleichaltrigen. *Zeitschrift für Pädagogik, 31,* 321–337.

(1991). Problems of helping among ten-year-old children – Results from a qualitative study in natural settings. In H. W. Bierhoff & L. Montada (Eds.), *Altruism in social systems.* Toronto: Hogrefe.

Krappmann, L., Salisch, M. von, & Oswald, H. (1990). Spielkameraden, Freunde und beste Freunde. In D. Frey (Ed.), *Bericht über den 37. Kongreß der Deutschen Gesellschaft für Psychologie in Kiel 1990.* Göttingen: Hogrefe.

Laing, R. D. (1969). *Self and others.* Harmondsworth, England: Penguin.

Larson, R., & Richards, M. (1991). Daily companionship in late childhood and early adolescence: Changing developmental contexts. *Child Development, 62,* 287–300.

Ludeke, R., & Hartup, W. W. (1983). Teaching behaviors of nine- and eleven-year-old girls in mixed-age and same-age dyads. *Journal of Educational Psychology, 75,* 908–914.

Minnett, A., Vandell, D. L., & Santrock, J. W. (1983). The effects of sibling status on sibling interaction: Influence of birth order, age spacing, sex of child and sex of sibling. *Child Development, 54,* 1064–1072.

Opie, I., & Opie, P. (1970). *Children's games in street and playground.* Oxford: Clarendon Press.

Oswald, H. (1991). Negotiation of norms and sanctions among children. In P. & P. Adler (Eds.), *Sociological studies of child development* (Vol. 5). Greenwich, CT: JAI Press.

Oswald, H., Krappmann, L., Chowdhuri, I. & Salisch, M. von (1987). Gaps and bridges – Interactions between girls and boys in elementary school. In

P. & P. Adler (Eds.), *Sociological studies of child development* (Vol. 2, pp. 205–223). Greenwich, CT: JAI Press.

Parker, J., & Asher, S. (1987). Peer relations and later personal adjustment. Are low-accepted children at risk? *Psychological Bulletin, 102,* 357–389.

Parsons, T. (1955). Family structure and the socialization of the child. In T. Parsons & R. F. Bales (Eds.), *Family socialization and interaction* (pp. 35–131). Glencoe, IL: Free Press.

Piaget, J. (1986 [1932]). *Das moralische Urteil beim Kinde.* München: dtv.

Rafaelli, M. (1989, April). *Conflict with siblings and friends in late childhood and early adolescence.* Paper presented at the Meeting of the Society for Research in Child Development, Kansas City, MO.

(1991, April). *Interpersonal conflict with siblings and friends. Implications for early adolescent development.* Paper presented at the Meeting of the Society for Research in Child Development, Seattle.

Rauh, H. (1984). Soziale Interaktion und Gruppenstruktur bei Krabbelkindern. In C. Eggers (Ed.), *Bindungen und Besitzdenken beim Kleinkind* (pp. 204–232). München: Urban & Schwarzenberg.

Ross, H. S., & Goldman, B. D. (1976). Establishing new social relations in infancy. In T. Alloway, P. Pliner & L. Krames (Eds.), *Advances in the study of communication and affect: Attachment behavior* (Vol. 3, 61–79). New York: Plenum.

Salisch, M. von (1991a). *Kinderfreundschaften. Emotionale Kommunikation im Konflikt.* Göttingen: Hogrefe.

(1991b, September). *Emotionale Regulierung in face-to-face Interaktionen.* Paper presented at the 10. Tagung Entwicklungspsychologie der Deutschen Gesellschaft für Psychologie, Köln.

(1996). Emotional processes in children's relationships with siblings and friends. In S. Duck (Ed.), *Handbook of personal relationships,* 2d ed. Chichester, England: Wiley.

Schütze, Y. (1986). Der Verlauf der Geschwisterbeziehung während der ersten beiden Jahre. *Praxis der Kinderpsychologie und Kinderpsychiatrie, 35,* 130–137.

Selman, R. (1980). *The growth of interpersonal understanding. Developmental and clinical analyses.* New York: Academic Press.

Shantz, C., & Hobart, C. (1989). Social conflict and development: Peers and siblings. In T. Berndt & G. Ladd (Eds.), *Peer relationships in child development* (pp. 71–94). New York: Wiley.

Slomkowski, C. L., & Dunn, J. (1992). Arguments and relationships within the family: Differences in young children's disputes with mother and sibling. *Developmental Psychology, 28,* 919–924.

Stocker, C., & Dunn, J. (1990). Sibling relationships in childhood: Links with friendship and peer relationships. *British Journal of Developmental Psychology, 8,* 227–244.

Stoneman, Z., Brody, G. H., & MacKinnon, C. (1984). Naturalistic observation of children's activities and roles while playing with their siblings and friends. *Child Development, 55,* 617–627.

Sullivan, H. S. (1953). *The interpersonal theory of psychiatry.* New York: Norton.

Vandell, D. L., & Bailey, M. (1992). Conflicts between siblings. In C. U. Shantz & W. W. Hartup (Eds.), *Conflict in child and adolescent development* (pp. 242–269). Cambridge University Press.

Watzlawick, P., Beavin, J., & Jackson, D. (1967). *Pragmatics of human communication.* New York: Norton.

Weiss, R. (1974). The provisions of social relationships. In Z. Rubin (Ed.), *Doing unto others.* Englewood Cliffs, NJ: Prentice-Hall.

Youniss, J. (1980). *Parents and peers in social development.* Chicago: University of Chicago Press.

PART II

Relationships within the family

4

Parent–child relationships: Childhood and adolescence
Kurt Kreppner

Introduction

In relationships between parents and children all the components can be found that normally characterize interpersonal relationships. However, these components retreat into the background when a closer look is taken at the special features of this relationship. The parent–child relationship displays a number of characteristics that make it fundamentally different from other social relationships. The following contribution sketches out interaction and communication between parents and children during two different age phases that are generally regarded as crucial for the further development of the child: childhood and adolescence. These two age phases can also be taken as examples of how research into early childhood first concentrated solely on the isolated dyadic relationship between mother and child, or in the case of adolescence, how investigations, before interest grew in the parent–child relationship, focused on the individual child and the developmental process of its autonomy, its self, and its orientation toward peers. Finally, the question of how the parent–child relationship is embedded within the whole family is covered, that is, the overall framework that modifies the particular mother–child and father–child relationships.

Special features of the parent–child relationship

How do parent–child relationships differ in comparison to other relationships such as friendship, marriage, and teacher–student relationships? Relationships between children in particular are often highlighted as a counterpart to the parent–child relationship (Youniss, 1980) and are viewed as particularly important for development. The possibility of creating reality together with other children in a *symmetrical* relationship is seen as genuinely different from the parent–child relationship, which, in principle, is assumed to be unilaterally *complementary*, that is, one-sided and asymmetrical. According to Youniss, the main difference between child–child relationships and parent–child relationships is that children *build* a relationship of reciprocity and equality *by themselves*. Within the framework of the parent–child relationship, the child goes through a variety of experiences that are certainly fundamental for developing its competence for later social relationships outside the family, including the possibility of building symmetrical relationships. A generalization of the parent–child relationship as complementary, in the sense of hierarchical, thus seems rather problematic when viewing the period of childhood and adolescence as a whole. There is, however, a series of features that do actually differentiate parent–child relationships from other relationships and that belong to a category other than the differentiation between symmetrical and complementary.

Genetic components and the emotional history of dyadic relationships

The child is born into a family where it experiences forms of relationships. These and the accompanying experiences with its parents remain with the child throughout its lifetime. In addition, apart from a genetically determined similarity in external appearance and various abilities and preferences, there is also the experience of a shared framework of experience that acts as a filter and interpretation grid for events in the outside world. Emotionality is also characterized by the history of the dialectics between dependency and autonomy. In this respect in particular, communication between parents and the child always has its own emotional history, which none of the interacting partners can neglect in the later course of the relationship.

When parent–child relationships are compared with other relationships such as friendships or marital relationships, it is the presence of biological ties, high emotionality, and the interminability of the relationship throughout life that lends the parent–child relationship a different status. Consideration of the significance of the parent–child relationship leads to a broader view of the child in the whole family. Here, it is not only the direct experiences in the dyadic relationships with the mother or father that are of relevance, but also the process of growing up within a family, that is, in a group with other family members of different generations (siblings, parents, grandparents), where the child has the opportunity of observing other dyadic relationships from the outside. In this sense the family is an *arena of dyadic relationships* and the child can follow these interactions as if on a monitor. It should, however, be emphasized that "family" is not to be understood as a static concept and relationship structure but as a unit complex that itself develops along with changes in the relationships between the members over the life span (Aldous, 1978; Duvall, 1977; Olson & McCubbin, 1983).

The concept of a "dynamic context" in which the child grows up with its parents and within the family has a long tradition. Kurt Lewin (1931, 1946) was one of the first to emphasize the importance of the environment in understanding developmental processes of children. Prior to this, in his "Psychology of Early Childhood," William Stern (1927) concentrated his contribution to the heredity–environment debate on the role of the "personal proximal zone"in which the child grows up. He viewed the "personal proximal zone" as a central component of successful or unsuccessful development. Finally, during the 1930s, Lev Vygotsky (1978) launched the concept of the "zone of proximal development," which is of decisive importance in individual development (see Valsiner, 1984; Valsiner, 1988, pp. 140–150). These theories on the quality of contextual conditions surrounding the child are insufficient in that they hardly elaborate on the concrete relationships between children and their parents, the quality of their experiences in actual everyday life, and the differences in forms of communication.

Reciprocity and activity

Specific observations of the parent–child relationship often characterize this relationship type as unilateral or complementary, but it should be remembered that this relationship also contains the most essential characteristic of all human relationships, namely reciprocity. In the final instance, both partners influence each other from the beginning of the early parent–child relationship (Bell, 1968). Reciprocity in the regulation of a relationship is visible, for example when the emotional exchange between mother and infant is observed more closely (Tronick, 1989; Tronick & Cohn, 1989). In so-called still face experiments, where the mother is asked to keep a completely straight face in front of her children, it was observed that even 6-week-old children produced up to nine different forms of facial expression in order to draw their accustomed interaction partner back into communication.

The activity of the child in shaping its relationships is also an important component when considering early childhood (Lerner, 1982; Lerner & Busch-Rossnagel, 1981). When mother and child try to adjust to one another and in so doing permanently try to balance out their misunderstandings, certain misunderstandings can naturally occur that depending on the child's level of development, can later be overcome, for instance when the child can specify its activities by evolving new communicative skills in the course of its development (Stern, 1977). However, during early childhood the balancing process is basically carried out between two unequal partners, because the maintenance of the relationship between the child and its parents, with its mother and its father, is of existential importance and without alternatives, whereas the reverse does not apply (Hinde & Stevenson-Hinde, 1990).

Effects thus operate in *both directions*, although, as in the case of early childhood, they certainly occur in very different proportions at first. But reciprocity within the parent–child relationship becomes clearer when viewed over the life span. During adolescence the independent activity of the youngster acts as an initiator of change in the relationship between parents and child, and this often results in crises in the existing forms of interaction.

In the course of its development, the meanings of the different contexts change for the child. Whereas the quality of the relationship in the mother–child and father–child dyads within the family is fundamental to the young child's further development, on entering school and later during puberty it will use persons outside the family, such as friends and teachers, as orientations for its own development goals. Whereas during early childhood the parent–child relationship plays a decisive role in the *building* of social relationships, during adolescence it contributes toward the success or failure of the *separation process* parallel to the development of autonomy and identity.

Thus research favors the following phases in the development of the parent–child relationship: early childhood, when a pair have their first child (Cowan & Cowan, 1987; Osofsky & Osofsky, 1984; Palkovitz & Sussman, 1988); the period of family expansion when further children are born (Brüderl, 1989; Kreppner, 1988), and the separation process of the children when they mature from childhood to youth (Collins & Russell, 1991; Kidwell, Fischer, Dunham & Baranowski, 1983). Adolescence is also an interesting period for the whole of the family because two phases in the development of children and parents coincide and this in particular can give rise to conflicts between the generations (Cooper, Grotevant & Condon, 1983; Grotevant & Cooper, 1985; Steinberg, 1981; Youniss, 1983). The way in which the relationship and reciprocal behavior are formed during this period is of great importance for further development. This has been shown in longitudinal studies of both ethnically and socioeconomically heterogeneous samples. Young people ranging from 14 to 18 years of age were classified according to different parenting styles (authoritative, indulgent, neglectful, and authoritarian); a year later they were examined to establish the continuity of certain personality traits. It was seen that even after a year the adolescents still differed greatly in social competence, school performance, behavioral problems, and somatic symptoms, depending on their respective parenting styles (Steinberg, Lamborn, Darling, Mounts & Dornbusch, 1994).

Early childhood

Family context

The child not only grows up in the mother–child relationship; it is born into a family where there are other caregivers besides the mother, such as the father, siblings, grandparents (Belsky, 1981). The child is also affected in different ways by the various contexts that form the closer and broader environment of the family. In early childhood these contexts are not experienced directly but are substantially mediated by the family, which acts more or less as a filter to outside influences by letting them in or keeping them out. The neighborhood, kindergarten and school, and external economic and cultural living conditions also have to be considered as influencing factors when assessing the experiences of the child within the framework of the parent–child relationship (Bronfenbrenner, 1979; Bronfenbrenner & Crouter, 1983). For instance, the quality of the relationship between marriage partners during pregnancy and their living conditions during this time are also of great significance for the future formation of the family relationship during the first three years of the infant's life (Belsky & Rovine, 1990). The quality of the relationship between the parents during early childhood seems to have a greater influence on the behavior of children than clinical symptoms, such as depression in one of the parents (Miller, Cowan, Cowan, Hetherington & Clingempeel, 1993).

The significance of a constant and secure mother–child relationship during early childhood was emphasized in the 1960s and 1970s by Schaffer and Emerson (1964), Bowlby (1969, 1973), Sander (1969), Bell (1968), and Lamb (1976). The family as a proximal context was first seriously discussed when the mother–child and the father–child relationships were compared and similarities and differences between them were defined (Lamb, 1975, 1976, 1977; Parke, 1976, 1979; Pedersen, 1980). The contribution of the sibling relationship toward the child's socialization and the special nature of this child–child relationship in the family was a topic treated in particular by Judy Dunn in the early 1980s. She emphasized that the concept of the family constituted more than just the mother–child or the father–child relationship (Belsky, 1981; Dunn, 1983; Dunn & Kendrick, 1979, 1982a, 1982b). Apart from the extension of the mother–child relationship by that of the father, the role of the father was also discussed as a factor of indirect influence on the mother–child relationship (Clarke-Stewart, 1978; Hinde, 1989). In this case it is a question of the influence of a third party on a dyadic relationship. If, for example, a mother interacts with the child and the father or another third person, such as a sibling, is not actually present, these will still influence the formation of the dyadic relationship. This potential influence, even of someone who is not actually present, again stresses the necessity of considering the whole family context instead of just single dyads.

Many researchers who have carried out longitudinal studies on early childhood (Cowan & Cowan, 1989; Cowan, Cowan, Coie & Coie, 1978; Cox, Tresch-Owen, Lewis & Henderson, 1989; Sroufe & Fleeson, 1986, 1988) have repeatedly indicated the importance of the family and the parent–child and sibling relationships within it, describing it as the environment that influences the child most strongly. According to Sroufe and Fleeson (1986, 1988), experiences during early childhood appear to be decisive for the development of social competencies in later stages of life, for instance during the preschool phase.

The parent–child relationship has a considerable influence on the formation of emotional attachment (Ainsworth, Blehar, Waters & Wall, 1978; Bowlby, 1969, 1973): it is the main model for structuring the internal working model of social relationships (Main, Kaplan & Cassidy, 1985); it promotes or hinders cognitive development as well as the growth of self-assurance (Kagan, 1979, 1981) because it creates the framework of the child's "apprenticeship" (Kaye, 1982), and it forms the way in which the child creates its own self-image and its identity. The experience of contingency or incontingency in the mother–child relationship (Malatesta, Culver, Tesman & Shepard, 1989) and attachment can be seen as keystones of emotional security or insecurity in social interaction. The first signs of self-development can be established toward the end of the second year of life, as shown in experiments where children recognized their own reflection in a mirror (Lewis, 1981; Lewis & Brooks-Gunn, 1979). In the psychoanalytical considerations of Mahler, Pine, and Bergman (1975) and Abelin (1971, 1975, 1980), the process has been described as "triangulation," in which the child is stimulated by the growing attraction of the father and starts separating from the symbiotic relationship with the mother. Here, the child sees itself neither as mother nor father, but as a third element, something else; it starts perceiving itself as an independent self. This fundamental development of the self lays the foundations for the further development of the person long before the peer experiences of childhood and youth.

Attachment

The security offered by the mother–child relationship is of existential importance to the child. It forms the basis of all further development. At about 1 year of age there are quite different forms of attachment between children and their parents that are expressed in different types of behavior when the mother leaves the child and returns. A combination of ethological methodology and a comparative cultural approach in the observation of early mother–child interactions has led to an experimental paradigm that is one of the standard experimental procedures currently used to investigate the quality of relationships between young children and their parents. Mary Ainsworth's (1967) study on early childhood in Uganda and a comparative study in Baltimore (Ainsworth et al., 1978) laid the foundations for this paradigm; it has since become fairly standardized and is now used to examine the concept of attachment developed by Bowlby (1969, 1973).

The classification of differences established by Ainsworth in her Baltimore study form the keystone to the individual steps in the so-called strange situation. This laboratory paradigm consists of eight episodes, each of three minutes in length: (1) introduction of mother and child into the laboratory; (2) mutual play between mother and child; (3) a stranger enters the laboratory; (4) mother leaves the room and the child stays behind with the stranger; (5) first reunification with the mother, the stranger leaves the room; (6) second separation, the mother leaves the room and the child remains alone; (7) second entrance of the stranger; (8) second return of the mother. As a result of this experiment a distinction was made between three types of child behavior (with subclassifications) when the mother reentered after separation: children who ignore the mother on reentry, who appear not to perceive her and pretend to carry on playing (children with an insecure-avoidant [A] quality of attachment); children who greet their mother on her return, let her pick them up, and then carry on playing (children with a secure [B] quality of attachment); and finally, children who cannot be comforted, cling to their mother, and cannot be motivated to carry on playing or exploring (children with an insecure-ambivalent [C] quality of attachment). Longitudinal studies have shown that securely attached children (B1–B4 children) later demonstrate more social competence, less complicated behavior, and more success when assessed than children classified according to the other two qualities of attachment (A and C children) (Grossmann, 1988; La Freniere & Sroufe, 1985; Süß, 1987; Sroufe, 1983; Wartner, Grossmann, Fremmer-Bombik & Suess, 1994).

This experimental approach has also proved successful in conducting intercultural comparisons of qualities of attachment between the child and the caregiver (Grossmann & Grossmann, 1990; Main, 1990; Van IJzendoorn, 1990; Van IJzendoorn & Kroonenberg, 1988). As a result of this comparative research the quality of emotional attachment between the parents and child as well as the different reactions to separation are assumed to be universal. Current research into possible causes for the different quality of mother–child attachment is being carried out in a great variety of directions, for example into the further differentiation of subcategories (Cassidy & Berlin, 1994) and the comparison of different sleeping habits in earliest childhood (Sagi, Van IJzendoorn, Aviezer, Donnell & Mayseless, 1994). In the "strange situation" there is a pattern in the way of dealing with emotional stress on separation that definitely remains relevant in later stages of development (Main & Cassidy, 1988; Resnick, 1989; Sagi et al., 1994).

Internal working model

While investigating emotional attachment and the different reactions to separation from the caregiver, Bowlby (1969, 1973) developed a concept to describe the process of *internalization* of experiences with social relationships. It contains the idea of a working model of relationship experiences in the child. The model is based on the assumption that experiences collected in the parent–child relationship are aggregated to form a reservoir of expectations for forming future social relationships. In this reservoir, which Bowlby calls an "internal working model," the child then collects a kind of arsenal of social relationships and their emotional meanings. Main et al. (1985) elaborated this concept, focusing on the cognitive aspect. In so doing, they expanded the concept to include the idea that the child *actively* undertakes the aggregating process, that is, it more or less independently sorts its experiences and forms its own cognitive representations of things. Its attitudes of expectation are structured according to its working model. In their expanded concept, Main et al. (1985) specified the major aspects of internal working models of relationships as follows: (1) the working models include both emotional and cognitive components; (2) they are integral components of the behavioral repertoire of the child; (3) they are formed by general representations of events; and (4) they exist outside of consciousness and tend toward stability (Main et al., 1985, p. 76). In addition, the internal working models are "transported" into new relationships (Sroufe & Fleeson, 1986), thus contributing toward the generation of new, reinforcing experiences.

   However, the concept of the "internal working model" leaves open the question as to how the internalization of aggregated relationship experiences during early childhood actually functions and how expectations and the anticipation of certain definitions build up on entering new relationships. The notion of the internal working model, of a "script" or "blueprint" in a child's mind, is certainly a way of explaining recurring patterns. The construction process, which effectively takes place beyond the awareness of the subject, as it were, and which can only be changed later with great difficulty, calls for the definition of an experience level behind the level of concrete events and behavior. Gregory Bateson (1973) developed the idea of deutero learning, or second-order learning, which offers a theoretical explanation to the development of expectations and the tendency to repeat forms of social behavior. In second-order learning, the individual sets up a *framework*. All other first-order learning processes, that is, stimulus–response learning or instrumental learning, then take place within this framework, where, for instance, the success or failure of an action is "interpreted." This "learning to learn," or second-order learning, consolidates forms of behavior that an individual continually transfers to all new situations and that can thus develop into a kind of personality trait.

From childhood to adolescence

Coming to terms with family change

For a long time adolescence research focused on theoretical questions and empirical studies on ego development, autonomy, self-confidence, and risk-taking behavior among children. It was the general view that these aspects, together with the interaction of adolescents with their peers and the separation process from the family, essentially characterize the process of change from the child to the adolescent. However, more recent studies on adolescence have indicated that orientation toward peers, risk-taking behavior, and increased efforts toward autonomy are just one side of the coin. Sullivan and Sullivan (1980) and Youniss (1983) have demonstrated that gaining autonomy and continuing connectedness to the parents are by no means antagonistic variables, in fact they complement one another. Thus it is not a question of either autonomy or connectedness when assessing further development; it is a question of harmony or disharmony of these two characteristics. Research into the parent–child relationship concerning the development of autonomy during childhood and adolescence has tended to be neglected. This has hindered a differential view and insights into the reciprocal influences of autonomy and connectedness on ego development and the acquisition of social competencies in social interactions between adolescent peers (Krappmann, 1991), particularly where the analysis of the development of the self is concerned (Paikoff, 1991).

Because early adolescents develop new interests, abilities, and needs, an adaptation process becomes necessary that, depending on the family's previous experience of restructuring existing forms of interaction, can vary in the level of crisis. Hill (1982) described the transition to adolescence for the family as the fastest and most dramatic changes in the human organism since early childhood (p. 1410). The phases of transition can be compared with crises in which families tend to react to particular events with certain types of behavior (Reiss, 1981; Reiss & Klein, 1987; Steinglass, 1987). But *normally* the transition from childhood to adolescence is a restructuring process, not necessarily a crisis threatening to the existence of the family. However, it becomes necessary to adapt existing rules to the new conditions created by the dramatic changes in the child; previously existing norms that were valid in everyday family life have to be redefined (Hill & Holmbeck, 1986; Kidwell et al., 1983). During this phase the parents also go through a period of change as individuals that can have a decisive effect on the formation of the transitional phase, but that may not be directly attributable to the concrete behavior of the child. The parents are usually about 35 to 45 years old. In view of their confrontation with increasing criticism from their children about living styles and standards, and in view of the increasing orientation of the children toward the outside world, they start reviewing their life to date and develop new goals beyond the tasks of child rearing (Hamill, 1988; Silverberg & Steinberg, 1987, 1990; Steinberg, 1980, 1981). How little research has been focused on the family role of the father in connection with the child's transition in adolescence is illustrated by a number of recent studies. These studies, which concentrate on the emotional relationship between adolescents and their fathers and include comparisons to those with mothers, emphasize the great importance of the relationship both for the youngsters and their fathers (Larson, 1993; Montemayor, McKenry & Julian, 1993).

Autonomy and the acceptance of rules

Studies on the communication between parents and their adolescent children have shown that the relationship to the parents is of great importance for ego development during adolescence (Bell & Bell, 1983; Hauser et al., 1984; Powers, Hauser, Schwartz, Noam & Jacobson, 1983). In cases where communication within the family was assessed as supportive and not depreciative, the quality of ego development among adolescents was rated higher than in families where communication tended to be depreciative, avoidant, or conflict-laden. The ability to develop ideas and activities independently and the willingness to create and solve developmental tasks for oneself (Havighurst, 1953) are performed within the context of family communication and interaction forms. This creates the basis for excursions into areas of social interaction outside the family. In so doing, decisive new experiences are generated that are important for self-development in that they can further or inhibit it.

On the question of how differential trajectories of ego development come about, Smetana (1991) refers to the concept of accepted or nonaccepted parental "competence" for decisions in the parent–child relationship. From childhood onward there are accepted forms of "competence" for certain areas within the family concerning decisions as to whether a particular kind of behavior is in keeping with the family code or not. But there are also areas that, from early childhood onward, children consider do not belong to the area of parental concern. Studies with various age groups have shown that this assessment of various areas of everyday life changes during adolescence and that divergent assessments by parents and adolescents eventually create conflicts. Smetana proposes that children who do not recognize any regulations and competence of their parents generate more conflicts than adolescents who, while growing up, accept rules as general rules and leave the specific competence for particular decisions to their parents. Under the perspective of the development of self and autonomy, the following conclusions can be drawn: adolescents who generate conflicts by questioning parental jurisdiction and authority, that is, who strive, in a traditional sense, for independence and autonomy, construct their own "still-being-a-child" status by contributing to the fact that their parents remain in the role of "child-regulating parents" for longer than when adolescents accept parental jurisdiction in certain domains (Smetana, 1991). They do not recognize parental authority and consequently remain longer in a state of dependence (Smetana, 1988). During the late teens conflict frequency rapidly declines. On the whole, Smetana established quite different opinions between parents and adolescents in respect of decision regulation in various areas of daily life. Whereas on a majority of topics parents tended to consider norm-oriented and conventional decision patterns as correct, usually with parental jurisdiction, adolescents tended primarily toward a decision structure that gave the personal interests of the participants priority (Smetana & Asquith, 1994).

Consensus and divergence

A study by Carlson, Cooper, and Spradling (1991) investigated congruence and divergence within familial dyads; comparisons were made between adolescents' assessments of their own self-esteem and competence and the assessments made by the parents. Results show that congruence and divergence of evaluations within the family depend essentially on the quality of communication and the possibility to compare and negotiate differing views. In normal families the greatest divergences are found in the areas concerning autonomy and independence. Studies that compared the conflict frequency between mothers and adolescent children in two-parent and single-parent families found no difference in frequency but some in the perception of conflicts. While adolescents in two-parent families viewed their relationship as disharmonious, adolescents in single-parent families expressed greater satisfaction with the relationship and the level of agreement with their mother (Smetana, Yau, Restrepo & Braeges, 1991).

When these studies focusing on the development of autonomy during adolescence are related to studies focusing on the development of independence and separation during infancy and early childhood, one can draw the conclusion that there is a common element in early childhood as well as in adolescence that can be used as a kind of gauge for successful or unsuccessful affective attachment: the degree of mutuality in communication and the possibility to negotiate controversial issues within the family and to find a common solution. This, for example, has been demonstrated for the early childhood period by the concept of a medium level of "contingency" behavior of mother and child (Malatesta et al., 1989), as well as for the period of adolescence by the concept of harmony or disharmony between dependency and autonomy (Sullivan & Sullivan, 1980; Youniss, 1983).

Differences in parent–child relationships during adolescence: Boys and girls

Studies on differences in the behavior of mothers and fathers toward boys and girls, especially during the transition from childhood to adolescence, have shown that, for instance, the areas of communication between mothers and children are richer than those between fathers and children (Youniss & Smollar, 1985). Fathers are less directive in their interactions with children than mothers (Russell & Russell, 1987), whose communication during this phase generally appears more disturbed than that between fathers and children (Gjerde, 1988; Hill, 1988; Steinberg, 1987, 1988).

To a varying degree, the parent–child relationship also influences not only the well-being of the parents but also gender-specific behavior between the parents and their children. When the relationship between the parents was bad, mothers were less likely to make compromises with their daughters. Daughters from families where the marital relationship was less satisfying showed less obedience toward their fathers (Kerig, Cowan & Cowan, 1993).

There are a variety of functions that indicate the specific nature of the parent–child relationship through various age stages. Intensive studies on inner-familial communication in connection with identity development among adolescents (Grotevant & Cooper, 1985, 1986) produced greatly differing communication variables for the various dyads of father–son, father–daughter, and mother–son, mother–daughter. Data on identity were gathered by Grotevant and Cooper, who developed an identity interview that used the fields of friendship and acquaintance with the opposite sex in the discovery of self-identity in Erikson's sense: sons with a high level of identity, for instance when communicating with their father but not with their mother, made their suggestions more directly or openly showed that they did not agree with their father. In such cases fathers took up the suggestions more readily and showed their disagreement less often. By means of their communicative behavior, they thus gave their sons the opportunity to show autonomy and self-confidence, in contrast to sons with a low level of identity. On the other hand, paternal behavior toward daughters was different. In the father–daughter dyads there were few components indicating reciprocity; the fathers made more interrupting comments and signaled that they were of a different opinion. In contrast to sons, daughters with a high level of identity introduced their suggestions into discussions more indirectly. Daughters with a high level of identity also displayed less common interests with their mothers. In their interpretation, the authors emphasize the great significance of the differences in behavior with both parents. They come to the conclusion that identity development is furthered by the different parental models and that, as in the case of triangulation at the end of the second year of life, the experience of the parent–child relationship as being different from the others and yet still connected to them, represents one of the major characteristics of positive ego development.

This is also shown in analyses in which the above-described characteristics of inner-familial communication were related to the ability to form friendships (Cooper & Grotevant, 1987). Hauser et al. (1987) found similar peculiarities in father–son communications, compared with mother–son or father/mother–daughter communications. On the question of assessment of social support by the family and the feeling of solidarity, Carlson, Cooper, and Spradling (1991) discovered a marked difference between boys and girls. In the case of girls, a high level of concurrence in parental assessment and a high level of familial support was associated with a positive evaluation of the self and competence; in contrast, boys showed more positive self-esteem when their evaluations diverged from those of their parents and when the general level of familial support and the feeling of solidarity were rated low.

When compared with studies on earlier childhood, these studies showed that the transition from childhood to adolescence is linked to growing differentiation in the parent–child relationships according to the gender of the child. They also showed that, for instance, the growth of symmetry and influence is present in some parent–child constellations but not in others. The experience of *different* forms of relationships within the family, as indicated in the context of gender-specific interactions, is likely to be an important aspect in the development of autonomy in the child.

Reflections on the differential analysis of parent–child relationships

Differences in setting the parental framework

In so-called normal families a high degree of flexibility in possible interaction and communication forms can be assumed in the organization of everyday life and in the methods of treating and solving critical situations within the family. During the 1970s and 1980s a number of models were developed for this topic. They concentrate on different aspects in their description of family systems, such as dimensions of distance regulation over time, space, and energy distribution (Kantor & Lehr, 1975), crisis definition, crisis configuration, and crisis management (Reiss, 1981; Reiss & Klein, 1987), or adaptability and closeness (Olson & McCubbin, 1983).

Despite the many differences in these models they share a common denominator: even in cases of greatest flexibility a *framework* is set up within which the parent–child relationships take place. Going beyond this framework signifies a challenge to the existing equilibrium and a questioning of the normative system. When, for instance, the existing partner relationship is extended by the arrival of the first child and the family constitutes itself after the birth, the partnership also has to be adapted because it can no longer function under the old canon of rules. For example, a study by Cowan and Cowan (1987) on the transition to parenthood of young married couples observed the behavior of the mother in the decisive first months after the birth of the first child; the study found that many young mothers always intervened when the father wanted to participate in child care. Either the father was turned down immediately or his awkwardness or lack of routine with the child was cited so that, especially in the period right after birth, paternal participation was prevented by the mother. The resulting pattern of paternal nonparticipation then gave cause to continual reproaches from the mother about just this. Cowan and Cowan compared this paradoxical situation with a gavotte in which the dancing partners repeatedly move closer together and then separate again.

After the birth of the first child it is one of the young family's most important tasks to achieve a balance in the distribution of child care that satisfies the needs and desires of all the participants. The birth of a second child presents a new challenge to the equilibrium of the family and requires a new definition of relationships between parents and children because the relationship is no longer particularistic between the parents and their first child. The existence of the second child thus confronts the family with a new developmental task (Kreppner, 1988). For example, after the arrival of the second child, the parents have to come to terms with the new problem of sibling rivalry when the first child sees itself pushed out of its unique position as a single child by the intruder and starts to actively defend itself. The parents are now no longer mother and father of the single child "Peter" or "Susan" but the parents of "children"; as a rule it is not until after the birth of the second child that they recognize themselves as members of a generation within the family, in contrast to the children's generation.

The specificity of each child's experience within the family

The fact that different children develop completely differently within the same family has been intensely discussed over the past 10 years, particularly in the field of behavioral genetics, where research has focused on twins and adoptive children (Plomin & Rowe 1979; Plomin & Daniels, 1987; Rowe & Plomin, 1979, 1981; Scarr & McCartney, 1983). This research proposes that similarities in children in the family are not created by growing up in the same environment, as was previously assumed, but by the 50% common genetic endowment (in biological families). According to this proposition, the dissimilarity of the children is caused by the environment, which is different for each child within the same family. Thus, each child experiences a completely different scenario in its family, an environment shared by nobody else that forms the framework of all social experiences.

The concept of the nonshared environment is of great interest, particularly with reference to the development of identity within the family. According to this concept, the family exercises a *time-specific* and *unique* influence on the child, that is, every child has different experiences in the same family depending on the life phase of the parents and the sibling constellation into which the child is born. A second child, for example, is born into a very different family from a first child. The second child has always had a sibling and can always observe another parent–child relationship without being personally involved. These differences continue to exist and are intensified during school age. In addition, the effort of individuals to differentiate themselves from their siblings increases as time goes by

(Dunn & Plomin, 1990; Dunn, Plomin & Daniels, 1986; Plomin, 1986; Plomin, Loehlin & DeFries, 1985).

Although Dunn, Plomin, and Nettles (1985) discovered in a comparative longitudinal study that mothers treated their first and second children similarly during particular age phases (where the age difference was approximately three years), this by no means creates an identical experience of the family context for the children. When, for example, the second child is 12 months old, it will experience a mother who, despite her reproduction of similar behavior toward the child, also gives her attention to an older child. In so doing she displays different types of behavior more appropriate to the age of the older sibling. Thus the whole family scenario for the second child cannot be compared with the scenario into which the first child is born. When comparing the first and the second child it should also be taken into account that the parents are also at different stages in their own development during the transition from a childless couple to competent parents. The combination of genetic design and environment has given rise to various methodological considerations, as familial environments are by nature also shaped by the parents in a variety of ways that make it difficult to create a clear division between the two components in question (Plomin & Bergeman, 1991; Plomin, Reiss, Hetherington & Howe, 1994).

Assumptions on the development of general differential socialization patterns

Different patterns of socialization forms in the family are readily available in a great number of results from research on toddlers, children, and adolescents, but are generally viewed as unrelated or divergent. Belsky, Steinberg, and Draper (1991) discussed a theoretical proposition for interpreting these different patterns. The authors focus on differences in the willingness of the parents to invest in their children, children's attachment behavior, divorce behavior of the parents, and the onset of puberty in children. They conceive two general patterns that are designed to optimize the offspring in different environmental conditions (favorable or unfavorable). In accordance with this, socialization in families with favorable environmental conditions creates the opportunity to develop recurring patterns of careful partner selection, high parental investment, positive attachment of the children to the family, and a long period of residence in the family. Under unfavorable environmental conditions, energies are needed for the survival of the individual and are not available for the careful selection of a partner or excessive investment in the children, nor for closer attachment of the children to the parents.

Despite critical objections to the suggested evolutionary perspective (Hinde, 1991; Maccoby, 1991), the proposition that it is possible to trace back developmental trajectories to two principally different experiences of parent–child relationships can contribute to future research, inasmuch as more systematic differences in the fundamental quality of parent–child relationships could be analyzed under a mutual perspective. For instance, the above-mentioned cooperation or noncooperation of fathers in everyday socialization is an example of the different world of experience into which each child is born. Whereas families in which fathers do not participate in child care display a higher level of stress and the children are exposed to greater control by the mother (Kreppner, 1990), stress is reduced in families in which fathers participate in child care from the beginning; the controlling activity of the mother for the whole family is also lower in this case. Results in studies by Cox et al. (1989), Sroufe and Fleeson (1986, 1988), as well as Cowan and Cowan (1989), seem to confirm this trend. The atmosphere was generally more relaxed and the psychological condition of the married couple was better in cases where fathers actually took on some of the child-care activities.

The inclusion of the familial context as a whole and the observation of continuity and change in transitional periods from one phase of family development to another help us to recognize differential patterns of interaction at particular times during development. However, the question still remains open as to how children develop their concepts of the quality of their parent–child relationships in the various scenarios in which they grow up, and which criteria they use to determine their own social behavior in new situations. Here, more research into details is necessary in order to obtain information on the internal mechanisms of the parent–child relationship that further or inhibit *time-specific* development processes, or generate pathological forms that can no longer be compensated or overcome during later development (Lewis, Feiring, McGuffog & Jaskir, 1984). As Alison Clarke-Stewart (1988) wrote in a contribution summarizing the last 10 years of research into parental influence on the development of the child, future research will have to be devoted to more – and more extensive – longitudinal studies, larger samples, and higher methodological standards.

References

Abelin, E. L. (1971). The role of the father in the separation-individuation process. In J. McDevitt & C. F. Settlage (Eds.), *Separation-individuation: Essays in honor of Margaret S. Mahler* (pp. 229–253). New York: International Universities Press.

(1975). Some further comments and observations on the earliest role of the father. *International Journal of Psychoanalysis, 56,* 293–302.

(1980). Triangulation, the role of the father and the origins of core gender identity during rapprochement subphase. In R. Lax, A. J. Burland, & S. Bach (Eds.), *Rapprochement: The critical subphase of separation* (pp. 151–169). New York: Jason Aronson.

Ainsworth, M. D. S. (1967). *Infancy in Uganda: Infant care and the growth of love.* Baltimore: John Hopkins University Press.

Ainsworth, M. D. S., Blehar, M. C., Waters, E., & Wall, S. (1978). *Patterns of attachment.* Hillsdale, NJ: Erlbaum.

Aldous, J. (1978). *Family careers.* New York. Wiley.

Bateson, G. (1973). The logical categories of learning and communication. In G. Bateson (Ed.), *Steps to an ecology of mind* (pp. 250–279). Frogmore: Paladin.

Bell, D. C., & Bell, L. G. (1983). Parental validation and support in the development of adolescent daughters. In H. D. Grotevant & C. R. Cooper (Eds.), *Adolescent development in the family* (pp. 27–42). *New Directions for Child Development,* 22. San Francisco: Jossey-Bass.

Bell, R. Q. (1968). A reinterpretation of the direction of effects in studies of socialization. *Psychological Review, 75,* 81–95.

Belsky, J. (1981). Early human experience: A family perspective. *Developmental Psychology, 17,* 3–23.

Belsky, J., & Rovine, M. (1990). Patterns of marital change across the transition to parenthood: Pregnancy and three years postpartum. *Journal of Marriage and the Family, 52,* 5–19.

Belsky, J., Steinberg, L., & Draper, P. (1991). Childhood experience, interpersonal development, and reproductive strategy: An evolutionary theory of socialization. *Child Development, 62,* 647–670.

Bowlby, J. (1969). *Attachment and loss,* Vol. 1: *Attachment.* London: Hogarth. (1973). *Attachment and loss,* Vol. 2: *Separation.* London: Hogarth.

Bronfenbrenner, U. (1979). *The ecology of human development.* Cambridge, MA: Harvard University Press.

Bronfenbrenner, U., & Crouter, A. C. (1983). The evolution of environmental models in developmental research. In W. Kessen (Ed.), P. H. Mussen (Series Ed.), *Handbook of child psychology: History, theory, and methods* (Vol. 1, pp. 357–414). New York: Wiley.

Brüderl, L. (1989). *Entwicklungspsychologische Analyse des Übergangs zur Erst- und Zweitelternschaft.* Regensburg: S. Roderer Verlag.

Carlson, C. I., Cooper, C. R., & Spradling, V. Y. (1991). Developmental implications of shared versus distinct perceptions of the family in early adolescence. In R. L. Paikoff (Ed.), *Shared views on the family during adolescence* (pp. 13–32). *New Directions for Child Development,* 51. San Francisco: Jossey Bass.

Cassidy, J., & Berlin, L. J. (1994). The insecure/ambivalent pattern of attachment: Theory and research. *Child Development, 65,* 971–991.

Clarke-Stewart, K. A. (1978). And daddy makes three: The father's impact on mother and young child. *Child Development, 49,* 466–478. (1988). Parents' effects on children's development: A decade of progress? *Journal of Applied Developmental Psychology, 9,* 41–84.

Collins, W. A., & Russell, G. (1991). Mother–child and father–child relationships in middle childhood and adolescence: A developmental analysis. *Developmental Review, 11,* 99–136.

Cooper, C. R., & Grotevant, H. D. (1987). Gender issues in the interface of family experience and adolescents' friendship and dating identity. *Journal of Youth and Adolescence, 16,* 247–264.

Cooper, C. R., Grotevant, H. D., & Condon, S. M. (1983). Individuality and connectedness in the family as a context for adolescent identity formation and role-taking skill. In H. D. Grotevant & C. R. Cooper (Eds.), *Adolescent development in the family* (pp. 43–59). *New Directions for Child Development, 32.* San Francisco: Jossey-Bass.

Cowan, C. P., & Cowan, P. A. (1987). Men's involvement in parenthood: Identifying the antecedents and understanding the barriers. In P. W. Berman & F. A. Pedersen (Eds.), *Men's transition to parenthood* (pp. 145–174). Hillsdale, NJ: Erlbaum.

Cowan, C. P., Cowan, P. A., Coie, L., & Coie, J. D. (1978). Becoming a family. The impact of a first child's birth on the couple's relationship. In W. B. Miller & L. F. Neuman (Eds.), *The first child and family formation* (pp. 296–324). Chapel Hill NC: Carolina Population Center.

Cowan, P. A., & Cowan, C. P. (1989). *From parent adaptation in pregnancy to child adaptation in Kindergarten.* Paper presented at the Biennial Meeting of the Society for Research in Child Development, April 27–30, 1989, Kansas City, MO.

Cox, M. J., Tresch Owen, M., Lewis, J. M., & Henderson, V. K. (1989). Marriage, adult adjustment, and early parenting. *Child Development, 60,* 1015–1024.

Dunn, J. (1983). Sibling relationships in early childhood. *Child Development, 54,* 787–811.

Dunn, J., & Kendrick, C. (1979). Interaction between young siblings in the context of family relationships. In M. Lewis & L. D. Rosenblum (Eds.), *The child and its family* (pp. 143–168). New York: Plenum.

(1982a). *Siblings: Love, envy, and understanding.* Cambridge, MA: Harvard University Press.

(1982b). Siblings and their mothers: Developing relationships within the family. In M. E. Lamb & B. Sutton-Smith (Eds.), *Sibling relationships: Their nature and significance across lifespan* (pp. 39–60). Hillsdale, NJ: Erlbaum.

Dunn, J., & Plomin, R. (1990). *Separate lives. Why siblings are so different.* New York: Basic Books.

Dunn, J., Plomin, R., & Daniels, D. (1986). Consistency and changes in mothers' behavior toward young siblings. *Child Development, 57,* 348–356.

Dunn, J., Plomin, R., & Nettles, M. (1985). Consistency in mothers' behavior toward infant siblings. *Developmental Psychology, 21,* 1188–1195.

Duvall, E. (1977). *Marriage and family development.* New York: Lippincott.

Gjerde, P. F. (1988). Parental concordance on child rearing and the interactive emphases of parents: Sex-differentiated relationships during the preschool years. *Developmental Psychology, 24,* 700–706.

Grossmann, K. E. (1988). Longitudinal and systemic approaches in the study of biological high- and low-risk groups. In M. Rutter (Ed.), *The power of longitudinal data: Studies of risk and protective factors for psychosocial disorders* (pp. 138–157). Cambridge University Press.

Grossmann, K. E., & Grossmann, K. (1990). The wider concept of attachment in cross-cultural research. *Human Development, 33,* 31–47.

Grotevant, H. D., & Cooper, C. R. (1985). Patterns of interaction in family relationships and the development of identity exploration in adolescence. *Child Development, 56,* 415–428.

(1986). Individuation in family relationships. *Human Development, 29,* 82–100.

Hamill, S. B. (1988, March). *The family at adolescence: The coincidence of parental midlife crisis and children's adolescence.* Paper presented at the Biennial Meeting of the Society for Research on Adolescence, Alexandria, VA.

Hauser, S. T., Book, B. K., Houlihan, J., Powers, S., Weiss-Perry, B., Follansbee, D., Jacobson, A. M., & Noam, G. G. (1987). Sex differences within the family: Studies of adolescent and parent family interactions. *Journal of Youth and Adolescence, 16,* 199–220.

Hauser, S. T., Powers, S., Jacobson, A., Noam, G., Weiss, B., & Follansbee, D. (1984). Family contexts of adolescent ego development. *Child Development, 55,* 195–213.

Havighurst, R. J. (1953). *Human development and education.* New York: McKay.

Hill, J. P. (1982). Guest editorial (Special issue on early adolescence). *Child Development, 53,* 1409–1412.

(1988). Research on adolescents and their families: Past and prospect. In C. E. Irwin (Ed.), *Adolescent social behavior and health* (pp. 13–31). *New Directions for Child Development, 37.* San Francisco: Jossey Bass.

Hill, J. P., & Holmbeck, G. N. (1986). Attachment and autonomy during adolescence. In G. W. Winterhurst (Ed.), *Annals of child development* (Vol. 3, pp. 145–189). Greenwich, CT: JAI Press.

Hinde, R. A. (1989). Reconciling the family systems and the relationships approaches to child development. In K. Kreppner & R. M. Lerner (Eds.), *Family systems and life-span development* (pp. 149–163). Hillsdale, NJ: Erlbaum.

(1991). When is an evolutionary approach useful? *Child Development, 62,* 671–675.

Hinde, R. A., & Stevenson-Hinde, J. (1990). Attachment: Biological, cultural and individual desiderata. *Human Development, 33,* 62–72.

Kagan, J. (1979). Family experience and the child's development. *American Psychologist, 34,* 886–891.

(1981). *The second year.* Cambridge, MA: Harvard University Press.

Kantor, D., & Lehr, W. (1975). *Inside the family.* San Francisco: Jossey Bass.

Kaye, K. (1982). *The mental and social life of babies.* Brighton, England: Harvester.

Kerig, P., Cowan, P. A., & Cowan, C. P. (1993). Marital quality and gender differences in parent–child interaction. *Developmental Psychology, 29,* 931–939.

Kidwell, J., Fischer, J. L., Dunham, R. M., & Baranowski, M. (1983). Parents and adolescents: Push and pull of change. In H. I. McCubbin & C. R. Figley (Eds.), *Stress in the family: Coping with normative transitions* (pp. 74–89). New York: Bruner/Mazel.

Krappmann, L. (1991). Sozialisation in der Gruppe der Gleichaltrigen. In K. Hurrelmann & D. Ulich (Eds.), *Neues Handbuch der Sozialisationsforschung* (pp. 355–375). Weinheim: Beltz.

Kreppner, K. (1988). Changes in parent–child relationships with the birth of the second child. *Marriage and Family Review, 12,* 157–181.

(1990, October). *Differences in parents' cooperation patterns after the arrival of a second child.* Paper presented at the International Conference BABY XXI, Lisbon, Portugal.

La Freniere, P. J., & Sroufe, L. A. (1985). Profiles of peer competence in the preschool: Interrelations between measures, influence of social ecology, and relation to attachment history. *Developmental Psychology, 21,* 56–69.

Lamb, M. (1975). Fathers: Forgotten contributors to child development. *Human Development, 18,* 245–266.

(1976). *The role of the father in child development.* New York: Wiley.

(1977). The development of mother–infant and father–infant attachments in the second year of life. *Developmental Psychology, 13,* 637–648.

Larson, R. W. (1993). Finding time for fatherhood: The emotional ecology of adolescent–father interactions. In S. Shulman & W. A. Collins (Eds.), *Father–adolescent relationships* (pp. 7–25). *New Directions for Child Development, 62.* San Francisco: Jossey Bass.

Lerner, R. M. (1982). Children and adolescents as producers of their own development. *Developmental Reviews, 2,* 342–370.

Lerner, R. M., & Busch-Rossnagel, N. A. (1981). Individuals as producers of their own development: Conceptual and empirical bases. In R. M. Lerner & N. A. Busch-Rossnagel (Eds.), *Individuals as producers of their own development. A life span perspective.* New York: Academic Press.

Lewin, K. (1931). Environmental forces in child behavior and development. In C. Murchison (Ed.), *Handbook of child psychology* (pp. 94–127). Worcester, MA: Clark University Press.

(1946). Behavior and development as a function of the total situation. In L. Carmichael (Ed.), *Manual of child psychology* (pp. 791–844). New York: Wiley.

Lewis, M. (1981). Self-knowledge: A social cognitive perspective on gender identity and sex-role development. In M. E. Lamb & L. E. Sherrod (Eds.), *Infant social cognition: Empirical and theoretical considerations* (pp. 395–414). Hillsdale, NJ: Erlbaum.

Lewis, M., & Brooks-Gunn, J. (1979). *Social cognition and the acquisition of self.* New York: Plenum.

Lewis, M., Feiring, C., McGuffog, C., & Jaskir, J. (1984). Predicting psychopathology in six-year-olds from early social relations. *Child Development, 55,* 123–136.

Maccoby, E. E. (1991). Different reproductive strategies in males and females. *Child Development, 62,* 676–681.

Mahler, M. S., Pine, F., & Bergman, A. (1975). *The psychological birth of the human infant.* New York: Basic Books.

Main, M. (1990). Cross-cultural studies of attachment organization: Recent studies, changing methodologies, and the concept of conditional strategies. *Human Development, 33,* 48–61.

Main, M. B., & Cassidy, J. (1988). Categories of response to reunion with the parent at age six: Predicted from infant attachment classifications and stable over a one-month period. *Developmental Psychology, 24,* 415–426.

Main, M. B., Kaplan, N., & Cassidy, J. (1985). Security in infancy, childhood, and adulthood: A move to the level of representation. In I. Bretherton & E. Waters (Eds.), Growing points of attachment theory and research. *Monographs of the Society for Research in Child Development, 50* (1–2), 66–104.

Malatesta, C. Z., Culver, C., Tesman, J. R., & Shepard, B. (1989). The development of emotion expression during the first two years of life. *Monographs of the Society for Research in Child Development, 54* (1–2), 1–104.

Miller, N. B., Cowan, P. A., Cowan, C. P., Hetherington, E. M., & Clingempeel, W. G. (1993). Externalizing in preschoolers and early adolescents: A cross-study replication of a family model. *Developmental Psychology, 29,* 3–18.

Montemayor, R., McKenry, P. C., & Julian, T. (1993). Men in midlife and the quality of father–adolescent communication. In S. Shulman & W. A. Collins (Eds.), *Father–adolescent relationships* (pp. 59–72). *New Directions for Child Development, 62.* San Francisco: Jossey Bass.

Olson, D. H., & McCubbin, H. I. (1983). *Families.* London: Sage.

Osofsky, J. D., & Osofsky, H. J. (1984). Psychological and developmental perspectives on expectant and new parenthood. In R. D. Parke (Ed.), *Review of child research,* Vol. 7: *The family* (pp. 372–397). Chicago: University of Chicago Press.

Paikoff, R. L. (Ed.) (1991). *Shared views in the family during adolescence. New Directions for Child Development, 51.* San Francisco: Jossey Bass.

Palkovitz, R., & Sussman, M. B. (1988). *Transitions to parenthood.* New York: Haworth.

Parke, R. D. (1976). Parent–infant interaction: Progress, paradigms, and problems. In G. P. Sackett & H. C. Haywood (Eds.), *Application of observational-ethological methods to the study of mental retardation.* Baltimore: University Park Press.

⸻ (1979). Perspectives on father–infant interaction. In J. D. Osofsky (Ed.), *Handbook of infant development* (pp. 549–590). New York: Wiley.

Pedersen, F. A. (1980). *The father–infant relationship.* New York: Praeger.

Plomin, R. (1986). *Development, genetics, and psychology,* Hillsdale, NJ: Erlbaum.

Plomin, R., & Bergeman, C. S. (1991). The nature of nurture: Genetic influence on "environmental" measures. *Behavioral and Brain Sciences, 14,* 373–427.

Plomin, R., & Daniels, D. (1987). Why are children in the same family so different from one another? *Behavioral and Brain Sciences, 10,* 1–60.

Plomin, R., Loehlin, J. C., & DeFries, J. C. (1985). Genetic and environmental components of "environmental" influences. *Developmental Psychology, 21,* 391–402.

Plomin, R., Reiss, D., Hetherington, E. M., & Howe, G. W. (1994). Nature and nurture: Genetic contributions to measures of the family environment. *Developmental Psychology, 30,* 32–43.

Plomin, R., & Rowe, D. C. (1979). Genetic and environmental etiology of social behavior in infancy. *Developmental Psychology, 15,* 62–72.

Powers, S. I., Hauser, S. T., Schwartz, J. M., Noam, G., & Jacobson, A. M. (1983). Adolescent ego development and family interaction: A structural-developmental perspective. In H. D. Grotevant & C. R. Cooper (Eds.), *Adolescent development in the family* (pp. 5–25). *New Directions in Child Development, 22.* San Francisco: Jossey Bass.

Reiss, D. (1981). *The family's construction of reality.* Cambridge, MA: Harvard University Press.

Reiss, D., & Klein, D. (1987). Paradigm and pathogenesis. A family-centered approach to problems of etiology and treatment of psychiatric disorders. In T. Jacob (Ed.), *Family interaction and psychopathology* (pp. 203–255). New York: Plenum.

Resnick, G. (1989). *Individual differences in adolescent attachment and its relationship to family cohesion and adaptability: An exploratory study.* Unpublished doctoral dissertation, Tufts University.

Rowe, D. C., & Plomin, R. (1979). A multivariate twin analysis of within family environmental influences. *Behavioral Genetics, 9,* 519–525.

(1981). The importance of nonshared (E1) environmental influences in behavioral development. *Developmental Psychology, 17,* 517–531.

Russell, G., & Russell, A. (1987). Mother–child and father–child relationships in middle childhood. *Child Development, 58,* 1573–1585.

Sagi, A., Van IJzendoorn, M. H., Aviezer, O., Donnell, F., & Mayseless, O. (1994). Sleeping out of home in a kibbutz communal arrangement: It makes a difference for infant–mother attachment. *Child Development, 65,* 992–1004.

Sagi, A., Van IJzendoorn, M. H, Scharf, M., Koren-Karie, N., Joels, T., & Mayseless, O. (1994). Stability and discriminant validity of the adult attachment interview: A psychometric study in young Israeli adults. *Developmental Psychology, 30,* 771–777.

Sander, L. W. (1969). The longitudinal course of early mother–child interaction: Cross-case comparison in a sample of mother–child pairs. In B. M. Foss (Ed.), *Determinants of infant behaviour* (Vol. 4, pp. 189–227). London: Methuen.

Scarr, S., & McCartney, K. (1983). How people make their own environments: A theory of genotype–environment effects. *Child Development, 54,* 424–435.

Schaffer, H. R., & Emerson, P. E. (1964). Patterns of response to physical contact in early human development. *Journal of Child Psychology and Psychiatry, 5,* 1–13.

Silverberg, S. B., & Steinberg, L. (1987). Adolescent autonomy, parent–adolescent conflict, and parental well-being. *Journal of Youth and Adolescence, 16,* 293–312.

(1990). Psychological well-being of parents with early adolescent children. *Developmental Psychology, 26,* 658–666.

Smetana, J. G. (1988). Adolescents' and parents' conceptions of parental authority. *Child Development, 59,* 321–335.

(1991). Adolescents' and mothers' evaluations of justifications for conflicts. In R. L. Paikoff (Ed.), *Shared views on the family during adolescence* (pp. 71–86). *New Directions for Child Development, 51.* San Francisco: Jossey Bass.

Smetana, J. G., & Asquith, P. (1994). Adolescents' and parents' conceptions of parental authority and personal autonomy. *Child Development, 65,* 1147–1162.

Smetana, J. G., Yan, J., Restrepo, A., & Braeges, J. L. (1991). Adolescent–parent conflict in married and divorced families. *Developmental Psychology, 27,* 1000–1010.

Sroufe, L. A. (1983). Infant–caregiver attachment and patterns of adaptation in preschool: The roots of maladaptation and competence. In M. Perlmutter (Ed.), *Minnesota Symposium on Child Psychology* (Vol. 16, pp. 41–81). Hillsdale, NJ: Erlbaum.

Sroufe, L. A., & Fleeson, J. (1986). Attachment and the construction of relationships. In W. Hartup & Z. Rubin (Eds.), *Relationships and development* (pp. 51–71). Hillsdale, NJ: Erlbaum.

(1988). The coherence of family relationships. In R. A. Hinde & J. Stevenson-Hinde (Eds.), *Relationships within families: Mutual influences* (pp. 27–47). Oxford: Oxford University Press.

Steinberg, L. D. (1980). *Understanding families with young adolescents.* Carrboro, NC: Center for Early Adolescence, University of North Carolina at Chapel Hill.

(1981). Transformations in family relations at puberty. *Developmental Psychology, 17,* 833–840.

(1987). The impact of puberty on family relations: Effects of pubertal status and pubertal timing. *Developmental Psychology, 23,* 451–460.

(1988). Reciprocal relations between parent–child distance and pubertal maturation. *Developmental Psychology, 24,* 122–128.

Steinberg, L. D., Lamborn, S. D., Darling, N., Mounts, N. S., & Dornbusch, S. M. (1994). Over-time changes in adjustment and competence among adolescents from authoritative, authoritarian, indulgent, and neglectful families. *Child Development, 65,* 754–770.

Steinglass, P. (1987). A systems view of family interaction and psychopathology. In T. Jacob (Ed.), *Family interaction and psychopathology* (pp. 25–65). New York: Plenum.

Stern, D. (1977). *The first relationship. Infant and mother.* London: Open Books.

Stern, W. (1927). *Psychologie der frühen Kindheit.* Leipzig: Quelle und Meyer.

Sullivan, K., & Sullivan, A. (1980). Adolescent–parent separation. *Developmental Psychology, 16,* 93–99.

Süß, G. (1987). *Auswirkungen frühkindlicher Bindungserfahrungen auf Kompetenz im Kindergarten.* Dissertation, Universität Regensburg.

Tronick, E. Z. (1989). Emotions and emotional communication in infants. *American Psychologist, 44,* 112–119.

Tronick, E. Z., & Cohn, J. (1989). Infant–mother face-to-face interaction: Age and gender differences in coordination and the occurrence of miscoordination. *Child Development, 60,* 85–91.

Valsiner, J. (1984). Construction of the zone of proximal development in adult–child joint action: The socialization of meals. In B. Rogoff & J. V. Wertsch (Eds.), *Children's learning in the "zone of proximal development"* (pp. 65–76). *New Directions for Child Development, 23.* San Francisco: Jossey Bass.

(1988). *Developmental psychology in the Soviet Union.* Bloomington: Indiana University Press.

Van IJzendoorn, M. H. (1990). Developments in cross-cultural research on attachment: Some methodological notes. *Human Development, 33,* 3–9.

Van IJzendoorn, M. H., & Kroonenberg, P. M. (1988). Cross-cultural patterns of attachment: A meta-analysis of the Strange Situation. *Child Development, 59,* 147–156.

Vygotsky, L. (1978). *Mind in society: The development of higher psychological processes.* Cambridge, MA: Harvard University Press.

Wartner, U. G., Grossmann, K., Fremmer-Bombik, E., & Suess, G. (1994). Attachment patterns at age six in South Germany: Predictability from infancy and implications for preschool behavior. *Child Development, 65,* 1014–1027.

Youniss, J. (1980). *Parents and peers in social development.* Chicago: University of Chicago Press.

(1983). Social construction of adolescence by adolescents and parents. In H. D. Grotevant & C. R. Cooper (Eds.), *Adolescent development in the family* (pp. 93–110). *New Directions for Child Development, 22.* San Francisco: Jossey Bass.

Youniss, J., & Smollar, J. (1985). *Adolescent relations with mothers, fathers, and friends.* Chicago: University of Chicago Press.

5

Relationships between adult children and their parents
Yvonne Schütze

Intergenerational solidarity: myths and findings

Relationships between elderly parents and their adult children are not a traditional topic for those research disciplines that otherwise concern themselves with parent–child relationships during childhood and youth – that is, family sociology, developmental psychology, and socialization research. The subject started to interest researchers when a demographic change became more evident during the 1950s: a steady increase in the number of elderly and very old people. Interest began to focus on the sociostructural effects of this previously unknown type of age structure on intergenerational relationships between aging parents and their adult offspring.

Early studies showed that, contrary to general opinion, lively relationships existed between adult children and their parents, but that both parents and children preferred not to live under the same roof. At almost the same time new expressions were coined, such as "inner closeness through external distance" (Tartler, 1961) and "intimacy at a distance" (Rosenmayr & Köckeis, 1965), that still aptly characterize attitudes of parents and children today. Virtually the same results were found in the United States (Shanas et al., 1968; Sussman, 1965). Despite this, the opinion was, and is still being upheld, that traditional care for the elderly within the family is coming to an end as a result of modernization processes such as urbanization, bureaucratization, and individualization. Although this sweeping statement is unfounded, as historical family research shows (Mitterauer, 1976; Ehmer, 1982), the never-ending lamentations of cultural pessimists about vanishing family solidarity still beg confirmation. In 1979 the American sociologist,

Ethel Shanas, mockingly likened these incessant complaints to the mythical many-headed Hydra:

> each time evidence has been presented that old people are not alienated from their families, new adherents rise up, not only among the mass media and the writers for the popular press, but also among research investigators and even among old people themselves. (Shanas, 1979, p. 3)

Old people are often convinced, according to Shanas, that old parents are left in the lurch by their children and that things are completely different only in their own family. The elderly who have no children of their own are even more critical of relationships between adult children and their parents.

Shanas's perception of a repeatedly revived myth was to a certain extent overoptimistic, in that she assumed that *new* evidence was always adduced for the supposed decay of family solidarity. But 10 years later, Troll (1989) took the matter up again only to discover that the same old evidence was being recycled. It begins with the claim that aid is lacking in intergenerational relationships and ends with the claim that children push their parents into homes. However, numerous studies confirm that, next to the spouse, children provide the main source of support for older people (Senator für Gesundheit und Soziales, 1988), that only 4% of over-65-year-olds live in institutional homes, and that it is not even certain how many of these are without children (Bäcker, 1991).

At present – and this is not the first time – the family is suspected of being in a state of decay. It is maintained that, as a result of progressing individualization processes at both a societal level and the individual psychological level, deinstitutionalization of the family can no longer be stemmed (Beck, 1986; Kohli, 1985; Rossi, 1987). This view perceives an interlock of societal and personality structures to the extent that society is organized around market mechanisms and thus requires "individuals who are not 'handicapped' by marriage and family" (Beck, 1986, p. 191). As a result people develop into ego-centered individuals who are no longer in a position to make a permanent "commitment" (Rossi, 1987). In the following, intergenerational relationships will first be looked at from the perspective of societal demands. After this, our focus will shift to the psychological constellation between adult children and their aging parents.

The "isolated nuclear family" and the "householdless family"

In his famous and much-quoted 1943 essay "The Kinship System of the Contemporary United States," Talcott Parsons developed the concept of the "isolated nuclear family" that still forms the basis of thinking on intergenerational relationships. Parsons proposed that the structure of the North American kinship system – in contrast, for example, to Asian kinship systems – brings about the isolation of the nuclear family because, when a young couple marries, it forms a unit spatially and economically independent of the original families. Relationships within the nuclear family involve the father, mother, and their dependent children; they take priority over all other relatives, including both of the families of origin.

> Ego, by marriage, that is, is by comparison with other kinship systems drastically segregated from his family of orientation, both from his parents and their forebears – and from his siblings. His first kinship loyalty is unequivocally to his spouse and then to their children if and when they are born. Moreover, his family of procreation, by virtue of a common household, income, and community status, becomes a solidarity unit in the sense in which the segregation of the interests of individuals is relatively meaningless, whereas the segregation of these interests of ego from those of the family of orientation tends relatively to minimize solidarity with the latter. (Parsons, 1949, p. 239)

The separation of the family of origin and the family of procreation corresponds with the functional requirements of a modern meritocracy where positions in the status hierarchy are not acquired through lineage as in traditional societies, but by individual achievements. Only those who are exempt from duties toward their family of origin are able to meet the needs of the job market and the structures of the profession, which require geographical and social mobility. The concept of the isolated nuclear family has since been interpreted and criticized as it suggests that separation of the family of origin and the family of procreation paralyzes solidarity relationships between parents and their adult children (Litwak, 1965; Sussman, 1958, 1965).

As an alternative to the isolated nuclear family, Litwak (1965) developed the model of the modified extended family. Although parents and children no longer live in the same household, they still maintain lively relationships and provide mutual support. Admittedly, this alternative is not visible because, even in the modified extended family, the family of origin and the family of procreation are structurally independent units (see Tyrell, 1976). At best, the consequences for Parsons and for Litwak are different. Whereas from Parsons's viewpoint, intergenerational solidarity between segregated nuclear families is improbable but in principle not impossible, from Litwak's point of view solidarity is more probable, but not imperative. This means that in principle the model of the "isolated nuclear family" remains impregnable to empirical studies, which demonstrate numerous contacts and forms of solidarity between the generations.

What can be questioned in the case of both Parsons and Litwak is their concept of the family, which refers exclusively to the combined household of father, mother, and minor children. This definition, which is still in current use (e.g., Neidhardt, 1975), ignores all the functions that people carry out for each other *because* they are family members, even though these members do not live in the same household. Examples here include the divorced parent who takes on responsibility for the children although he or she does not have custody of them; the increasing number of parents who support their economically dependent children into their thirties although they have long left home (Vaskovics, 1990); and adult children who care for their aging parents although they do not live in the same household. As René König discovered during the 1940s, there is also the "householdless family" for which he forecasted "wide distribution" in the future (König, 1974, p. 67), a prediction that seems to be proving correct in view of the current "pluralization of family forms" (Kaufmann, 1990).

A further aspect of the separation of the family of origin and the family of procreation is worth considering: this separation is functional, as it gives young adults the right and the duty to embark on an independent career and earn their own living. Today this applies to both men and women. But even in Parsons's model, where the woman is not fully employed but might at most have some part-time job or volunteer activity, separation from the family of origin, applies equally to her because she gains her social status through her husband. But does this segregation prove itself functional at the end of the life course of a family? Certainly not from the point of view of society. Faced with increasing costs in care for needy elderly citizens, the state is pressuring family members to become more involved in care. Apart from this, economic independence of the various generations also has its limits. Depending on their own economic situation, family members are obliged to contribute toward the support of both old and young who are without income. The majority of middle-aged children with elderly parents have to remain mobile because of their professional obligations, which means they are unable to provide the necessary physical care. Geographical mobility, at least, has declined since the 1950s and 1960s. Forty percent of people born in German rural areas between 1929 and 1931, 1939 and 1941, or 1949 and 1951 still live in their place of birth in their thirties; in the case of those born in large conurbations the rate is 50% to 60% (Wagner, 1989). Only a third of those born during these periods, and who have left the parental home, live more than 30 kilometers from their parents (Mayer & Schwarz, 1989). Geographical distance is by far the best predictor for frequency of visits between adult children and aging parents (De Wit, Wister & Burch, 1988; Frankel & De Wit, 1989). It should, however, be noted that frequency of visits alone tells us nothing about the level of satisfaction with intergenerational relationships (Lee, 1985; Mancini & Blieszner, 1989).

This means that from a societal perspective, the segregation of adult children from their elderly parents tends to be dysfunctional; and from the individual perspective, segregation during this life phase is no longer functional.

Development-theoretical aspects of relationships between parents and children in the life course

Whereas Parsons's structural-functionalistic theory, from which he derives the concept of the "isolated nuclear family," focuses mainly on economic independence as well as social and geographical mobility, socialization theory and developmental psychology are more interested in processes of emotional independence in intergenerational relationships. The phase of total dependency and close emotional attachment during the early parent–child relationship is followed by adolescence and separation from the parents, which is the prerequisite of self-identity development – a process usually experienced as a series of crises by those involved. During early adulthood, the relationship balances out at a new level. A more realistic attitude toward the parents (Blos, 1973) replaces the distance that the youngster has to gain during adolescence in order to relinquish the dependence of early childhood. In older concepts of adolescence an emphasis is laid on inner and outer separation from the parents. In their book *The Adolescent Experience*, Douvan and Adelson begin the chapter on the family with the characteristic sentence "The guiding term for this chapter will be departure" (Douvan & Adelson, 1996, p. 119). In more recent literature, this view is criticized as being too one-sided. Here the family is seen not only as an institution from which a person separates; continuing relationships with the parents and individualization are not regarded as mutually exclusive (Youniss, 1983, p. 96f; see also Kreppner, Chapter 4 of this volume).

It is difficult to decide whether there has been a shift solely in theoretical perspectives or whether the reality of parent–child relationships has changed too. Whatever the case, empirical studies come to the unequivocal conclusion that relationships between parents and their adolescent children are not primarily characterized by conflicts but by mutual trust and affection (Fischer, Fuchs & Zinnecker, 1985; Allerbeck & Hoag, 1985; Oswald, 1989).

With the exception of therapeutical case studies based on recollections of relationships, no empirical research has been carried out to find out to what extent the quality of relationships between parents and children during early childhood and adolescence influences their relationships during adulthood. Some hints are provided in the study by Rossi and Rossi (1990), a simulated longitudinal study in which almost 3,000 family members from three generations were questioned. The members of the middle generation (G2) made statements on both their present relationships with their parents (G1) as well as on their recollections of these relationships when they were 10, 16, and 25 years old. The G2 parents were also asked about their relationships with their children (G3), who themselves represented a very heterogeneous age group. The range stretched from toddlers to adults over 40 years of age. The G2 retrospective showed that emotional closeness to their parents reached a low during adolescence, that it gradually rose again during early adulthood and sank again slightly during middle age. Results on relationships between the G2 parents with their children were similar but not so pronounced. This seems to indicate the presence of cohort effects. Adolescence of the majority of the G2 subjects took place during the era of student and youth protest in the 1960s and 1970s, whereas the majority of the G3 children experienced their adolescence during the relatively peaceful 1980s. However, it is quite possible that the G1 parents were less liberal, so that the adolescence of the G2 subjects was more conflictual than that of their own G3 children. This tends to coincide with the liberalization in child-rearing methods established by other studies in recent years (Fischer et al., 1985; Allerbeck & Hoag, 1985). When differentiating the parent–child relationships according to gender, it was clear in all three groups (G1, G2, and G3) that mothers and daughters had the closest emotional relationships. G2 mothers also had closer emotional ties with their G3 sons than G2 fathers with their G3 sons. However, G2 daughters felt closer to their fathers than G2 sons, who felt equally close to both mothers and fathers.

The emotional distance that members of the G2 generation recalled during their adolescence seemed to be of no significance in the further course of the relationship. According to Rossi and Rossi (1990), emotional closeness and willingness to help elderly parents are not influenced by recalled relationships during adolescence but certainly by the recalled relationships during childhood. Rossi and Rossi do not attempt to explain why lacking emotional closeness during childhood should have a negative influence on the later relationships of the adult child, whereas a similar lack during adolescence does not. We can surmise that different interpretation patterns are in operation depending on whether childhood or adolescence is being recalled. People who missed emotional closeness as a child can only find reasons for this in rejection by the parents. It is almost impossible to imagine someone assuming that he or she was the one who did not love his or her parents as a child. But, when remembering adolescence, it is not difficult to recall that one was also actively involved in creating emotional distance from the parents. Emotional distance during adolescence is after all a cultural norm. However, if someone felt rejected by their parents as a child it can often present a lifelong problem.

Apart from the emotional relationship, difficulties such as financial need and unemployment that the families of those questioned had to combat during their childhood also appear to have a positive influence on later relationships. This seems plausible, in that the model of earlier family cohesion has a kind of delayed effect on later approaches to difficult situations, for instance when elderly parents need practical or emotional assistance. These results coincide with the so-called *support bank thesis* (Antonucci, 1985). Based on a combination of attachment and exchange theories, this thesis assumes that adult children more or less "repay" the affection and support they received during their childhood.

The support bank thesis implies that only children who have reason to be grateful are prepared to take on responsibility for elderly parents. Yet it has been shown in other studies that investigated motives for undertaking the most taxing of all responsibilities – nursing an elderly mother or father – that this is not always the case. The actual motives for looking after an aging parent are by no means clear to the caregivers themselves and can only partially be interpreted as "repayment" for once-received affection. Willingness to care for the elderly may result from unresolved childlike dependency needs or from the desire to be finally accepted by the parent, at least at the end of the family life course, after having missed this acceptance throughout life (Bracker, Dallinger, Karden & Tegethoff, 1988; Bruder, 1988; Goldfarb, 1965; Klusmann, Bruder, Lauter & Lüders, 1981). Caring for an elderly parent is often seen as a duty that, despite an unhappy relationship during childhood, is unavoidable.

In a pilot study I carried out on intergenerational relationships, one woman who had already cared for her completely confused mother for four years was asked, "Have you always had a good relationship with your mother?" and gave the following reply:

> No, I didn't have a particularly bad relationship, but it wasn't particularly good either. I don't know, well unfortunately, the relationship with my mother was never good. But not so bad that you could say I couldn't stand her. I really took her in out of, well what would you call it, a sense of duty. (Schütze, 1989, p. 96)

Of the 14 study subjects whose mothers or fathers were not in need of care, 6 classified their relationship as absolutely positive, while 8 saw the relationship as strongly ambivalent. Nevertheless, all of them were prepared to help the parent should the need arise, even though they did not wish to nurse them in the event of total disability (Schütze, 1989).

Thus, it can be assumed that intergenerational solidarity between adult children and their parents is furthered by an emotionally satisfying relationship, but that a norm is also operative that prescribes that aid should be given to those in need, especially when the person is a family member.

As in the case of all general norms, this one also leaves some leeway to interpret to what extent it should be followed. Nobody is compelled to care for their elderly mother or father for 24 hours a day even if such care becomes necessary. Yet if people completely neglect their old and needy parents, they will have to contend with external sanctions (disapproval of others in their environment) and with inner sanctions (feelings of guilt), which are indicators of norm infringements. To my knowledge there are no studies yet on the extent of disapproval expressed by the environment. On the question of guilt feelings, the study by Klusmann et al. (1981) shows that, for example, anticipated feelings of guilt were also given as a reason for caring for an elderly parent. In addition, Tobin and Kulys (1981) report that the majority of questionnaire subjects who had found a place in a home for a parent suffered from feelings of guilt. A further indication for the existence of a norm prescribing intergenerational solidarity can be seen in the result that, among friends and relations, parents and children feel the most obligations toward one another (Rossi & Rossi, 1990).

Apart from emotional ties and the normative duty to help, I can suggest another potentially fruitful research area in the analysis of intergenerational relationships at the end of the family life course from the perspective of developmental psychology: To what extent do psychodynamic changes in midlife affect relationships with parents? As this question is not directly addressed by research on adults in midlife (Hunter & Sundel, 1989; Smelser & Erikson, 1980; Whitbourne & Weinstock, 1982), I shall have to restrict myself to a few available hints and speculations derived from them.

In Erikson's stage theory, adulthood is characterized by generativity and, in the most unfavorable instance, by self-absorption. Generativity refers in the narrow sense to parenthood and in the broader sense to guidance and advancement of the younger generation. However, nothing is mentioned about whether, or in which way, this phase also has implications for relationships with the parents or members of the previous generation in general.

Only the next phase of mature adulthood, which Erikson subsumes under the concept of integrity versus despair and disgust, makes some reference to the relationship with the parents and with members of previous generations in general. In this context integrity means:

> a new, a different love of one's parents, free of the wish that they should have been different, and an acceptance of the fact that one's life is one's own responsibility. It is a sense of comradeship with men and women of distant times and of different pursuits, who have created order and objects and sayings conveying human dignity and love. (Erikson, 1964, p. 224)

Margaret Blenkner (1965) follows a similar train of thought with her concept of filial maturity. Blenkner assumes that sons and daughters aged between 40 and 50 experience a filial crisis during which they have to recognize that the parents are no longer primarily a source of support to them but vice versa, the parents become increasingly dependent on aid from the children. Consequently, the parent–child relationship goes through yet another new phase in which a person no longer turns to the parent as a child but as a mature adult,

> with a new role and a different love, seeing him for the first time as an individual with his own rights, needs, limitations, and life history that, to a large extent, made him the person he is long before his child existed. (Blenkner, 1965, p. 58)

By finally overcoming the earlier dependency on the parents, the filial crisis opens up into filial maturity, which enables the person to take on responsibility for the parents without simultaneous role reversal.

When, in Erikson's sense, people no longer make their parents responsible for their own situation in life and when – as Blenkner postulates – they perceive the parents as persons with their own life history, this presumably also means that they can react in a more relaxed way toward the parents' behavioral patterns and attitudes that previously led to conflicts. I know of no empirical studies that investigate the question of changes in the relationship with parents during the children's transition from early to middle adulthood. According to Roberts and Bengtson (1990) and Rossi and Rossi (1990), discrepancies between one's own values and those of the parents do not impair willingness to support elderly parents.

If it were possible to show in longitudinal studies that the phase of middle adulthood is characterized by the fact that past pain and injustices caused by the parents may still be recalled, but that they tend to lose their sting, then this could provide a different explanation for willingness to take on responsibility, in contrast to the one postulated by the support bank thesis. This would mean that the actual experiences of early childhood do not directly determine the relationship with the parents toward the end of the family life course. Rather, as a result of the personal growth process and experiences of life, the relationships are reinterpreted to provide a measure for the degree of responsibility one is able to adopt for aging parents without being caught up in renewed dependency.

According to Blenkner, the phase of filial maturity is also characterized by personal involvement with one's own aging. To what extent reflections on one's own remaining life span, which Neugarten (1968) designates as the prominent characteristic of middle adulthood, influences relationships with parents, is an open empirical question. It can be surmised that, while recognizing that after the death of the parents one is no longer anybody's child but has graduated into the highest family generation, one also wonders how the relationships with one's own children will turn out in old age and what conclusions the children will draw from one's own example. It can also be surmised that the objective possibility and the subjective willingness to take on responsibility for elderly parents are facilitated if the person's own children are already grown and no longer need parental care.

Studies on middle adulthood report that men of about 50 years of age show less involvement in their career, which is usually complete, and develop more interest in the family (Fiske, 1980; Gutmann, 1977; Vaillant, 1977). On the other hand, women – especially those who had no career in employment – start looking for new occupations again (Fiske, 1980). But this new interest of men in the family hardly appears to include taking on responsibility for aging parents, as in the majority of cases it is still daughters who, for instance, nurse and care for aging parents (Lehr, 1987; Senator für Gesundheit und Soziales, 1988). However, it should be noted that empirical studies on care for the elderly primarily target daughters, while studies that include sons as caregivers are relatively rare (see Arber & Gilbert, 1989; Horowitz, 1985).

Summary

Theoretical concepts on relationships between children and parents and the end of the family life course concentrate mainly on the question: How is intergenerational solidarity possible between independent units when the families of origin and families of procreation are separated? The implicit assumption here is that constitutive solidarity in the family only extends to those members who are present in a communal household. This construction makes it impossible to systematically investigate intergenerational solidarity, although it has often been empirically proved, and degrades it to an exception. No attention is paid to the fact that relationships between adult children and their aging parents are regulated by a norm that prescribes mutual aid in cases of need, despite physical, economic, and spatial independence. While referring to the developmental psychological concepts of Erikson (1966) and Blenkner (1965), one can also surmise that relationships with parents go through a new phase characterized by the increasing needs of the parents on the one hand and the children's sense of responsibility on the other, and that this phase transcends past and present conflicts. However, filial maturity still remains solely a concept. Whether and how it presents itself in reality would be an inviting topic for future research.

References

Allerbeck, K., & Hoag, W. J. (1985). *Jugend ohne Zukunft?* München: Piper.
Antonucci, T. C. (1985). Personal characteristics, social support, and social

behavior. In R. H. Binstock & E. Shanas (Eds.), *Handbook of aging and the social sciences* (pp. 94–128). New York: Van Nostrand Reinhold.

Arber, S., & Gilbert, G. N. (1989). Transitions in caring: Gender, life course and the care of the elderly. In B. Bytheway, T. Keil, P. Allatt & A. Bryman (Eds.), *Becoming and being old: Sociological approaches to later life.* London: Sage.

Bäcker, G. (1991). Pflegebedürftigkeit und Pflegenotstand. *WSI Mitteilungen, 2,* 88–103.

Beck, U. (1986). *Risikogesellschaft. Auf dem Weg in eine andere Moderne.* Frankfurt am Main.

Blenkner, M. (1965). Social work and family relationships in later life with some thoughts on filial maturity. In E. Shanas & G. F. Streib (Eds.), *Social structure and the family* (pp. 46–59). Englewood Cliffs, NJ: Prentice-Hall.

Blos, P. (1973). *Adoleszenz – Eine psychoanalytische Interpretation.* Stuttgart: Klett.

Bracker, M., Dallinger, U., Karden, G., & Tegethoff, U. (1988). *Die Pflegebereitschaft der Töchter.* Wiesbaden: Die Bevollmächtigte der Hessischen Landesregierung für Frauenangelegenheiten.

Bruder, J. (1988). Filiale Reife – ein wichtiges Konzept für die familiäre Versorgung kranker, insbesondere dementer alter Menschen. *Zeitschrift für Gerontopsychologie und -psychiatrie, 1,* 95–101.

De Wit, D. J., Wister, A. V., & Burch, T. K. (1988). Physical distance and social contact between elders and their adult children. *Research on Aging 10(1),* 56–80.

Douvan, E., & Adelson, J. (1966). *The adolescent experience.* New York: Wiley.

Ehmer, J. (1982). Zur Stellung alter Menschen in Haushalt und Familie – Thesen auf der Grundlage von quantitativen Quellen aus europäischen Städten seit dem 17. Jahrhundert. In H. Konradt (Ed.), *Der alte Mensch in der Geschichte.* Wien: Verlag für Gesellschaftskritik.

Erikson, E. H. (1964). Growth and crisis of the healthy personality. In C. Kluckhohn & H. A. Murray (Eds.), *Personality in nature, society, and culture.* New York: Knopf.

(1966). *Identität und Lebenszyklus. Theorie 2.* Frankfurt am Main: Suhrkamp.

Fischer, A., Fuchs, W., & Zinnecker, J. (1985). *Jugendliche und Erwachsene 85* (Bd. 1–5). Opladen: Leske und Budrich.

Fiske, M. (1980). Changing hierarchies of commitment in adulthood. In N. J. Smelser & E. H. Erikson (Eds.), *Themes of work and love in adulthood* (pp. 238–264). Cambridge, MA: Harvard University Press.

Frankel, B., & DeWit, D. J. (1989). Geographic distance and intergenerational contact: An empirical examination of the relationship. *Journal of Aging Studies, 3(2),* 139–162.

Goldfarb, A. I. (1965). Psychodynamics and the three-generation family. In E. Shanas & G. F. Streib (Eds.), *Social structure and the family* (pp. 10–45). Englewood Cliffs, NJ: Prentice-Hall.

Gutmann, D. C. (1977). The cross-cultural perspective: Notes toward a comparative psychology of aging. In J. E. Birren & K. W. Schaie (Eds.), *Handbook of the psychology of aging* (pp. 302–326). New York: Van Nostrand Reinhold.

Horowitz, A. (1985). Sons and daughters as caregivers to older parents: Differences in role performance and consequences. *Gerontologist, 25,* 612–617.

Hunter, S., & Sundel, M. (Eds.) (1989). *Midlife myths.* Newbury Park, CA: Sage.

Kaufmann, F.-X. (1990). *Zukunft der Familie. Stabilität, Stabilitätsrisiken und Wandel der familialen Lebensformen sowie ihrer gesellschaftlichen Bedingungen.* München: Beck.

Klusmann, D., Bruder, J., Lauter, H., & Lüders, I. (1981). *Beziehungen zwischen Patienten und ihren Familienangehörigen bei chronischen Erkrankungen des höheren Lebensalters.* Teilprojekt A 16. Sonderforschungsbereich 115 der Deutschen Forschungsgemeinschaft. Hamburg.

Kohli, M. (1985). Die Institutionalisierung des Lebenslaufs. Historische Befunde und theoretische Argumente. *Kölner Zeitschrift für Soziologie, 37,* 1–29.

König, R. (1974 [1945]). Zwei Grundbegriffe der Familiensoziologie: Desintegration und Desorganisation der Familie. *Materialien zur Soziologie der Familie* (pp. 55–87). Köln: Kiepenhauer und Witsch.

Lee, G. R. (1985). Kinship and social support of the elderly: The case of the United States. *Aging and Society, 5,* 19–38.

Lehr, U. (1987). *Zur Situation der älter werdenden Frau. Bestandsaufnahme und Perspektiven bis zum Jahre 2000.* München: Beck.

Litwak, E. (1965). Extended kin relations in an industrial democratic society. In E. Shanas & G. F. Streib (Eds.), *Social structure and the family* (pp. 290–323). Englewood Cliffs, NJ: Prentice-Hall.

Mancini, J. A., & Blieszner, R. (1989). Aging parents and adult children: Research themes in intergenerational relations. *Journal of Marriage and the Family, 51,* 275–290.

Mayer, K. U., & Schwarz, K. (1989). The process of leaving the parental home: Some German data. In E. Grebenik, C. Höhn & R. Mackensen (Eds.), *Later phases of the family cycle. Demographic aspects* (pp. 145–163). Oxford: Clarendon Press.

Mitterauer, M. (1976). Auswirkungen von Urbanisierung und Frühindustrialisierung auf die Familienverfassung an den Beispielen des österreichischen Raums. In W. Conze (Ed.), *Sozialgeschichte der Familie in der Neuzeit Europas.* Stuttgart: Klett.

Neidhardt, F. (1975). *Die Familie in Deutschland. Gesellschaftliche Stellung, Struktur und Funktion.* Opladen: Leske und Budrich.

Neugarten, B. L. (1968). The awareness of middle-age. In B. L. Neugarten (Ed.), *Middle-age and aging* (pp. 93–98). Chicago: University of Chicago Press.

Oswald, H. (1989). Intergenerative Beziehungen (Konflikte in der Familie). In M. Markefka & R. Nave-Herz (Eds.), *Handbuch der Familien- und*

Jugendforschung, Band II: Jugendforschung (pp. 367–381). Neuwied & Frankfurt: Luchterhand.

Parsons, T. (1949). *Essays in sociological theory – pure and applied.* Glencoe, IL: Free Press.

Roberts, R. E. L., & Bengtson, V. L. (1990). Is intergenerational solidarity a unidimensional construct? A second test of a formal model. *Journal of Gerontology: Social Sciences, 45,* 12–20.

Rosenmayr, L., & Köckeis, E. (1965). *Umwelt und Familie alter Menschen.* Neuwied & Berlin: Luchterhand.

Rossi, A. S. (1987). Parenthood in transition: From lineage to child to self-orientation. In J. B. Lancaster, J. Altmann, A. S. Rossi & L. R. Sherrod (Eds.), *Parenting across the life span* (pp. 31–81). New York: de Gruyter.

Rossi, A., & Rossi, P. (1990). *Of human bonding: Parent–child relationships across the life course.* Hawthorne, NY: Aldine.

Schütze, Y. (1989). Pflicht und Neigung: Intergenerationelle Beziehungen zwischen Erwachsenen und ihren alten Eltern – Ergebnisse einer Pilotstudie. *Zeitschrift für Familienforschung, 1,* 72–102.

Senator für Gesundheit und Soziales (1988). *Strukturanalyse pflegebedürftiger Menschen. Eine statistische Analyse.* Berlin.

Shanas, E. (1979). Social myth as hypothesis: The case of the family relations of old people. *Gerontologist, 19,* 3–9.

Shanas, E., Townsend, P., Wedderburn, D., Friis, H., Milhoj, P., & Stehouwer, J. (Eds.) (1968). *Old people in three industrial societies.* London: Routledge and Kegan Paul.

Smelser, N. J., & Erikson, E. H. (1980). *Themes of work and love in adulthood.* Cambridge, MA: Harvard University Press.

Sussman, M. B. (1958). The isolated nuclear family: Fact or fiction. *Social Problems, 6,* 333–340.

(1965). Relationships of adult children with their parents in the United States. In E. Shanas & G. F. Streib (Eds.), *Social structure and the family* (pp. 62–92). Englewood Cliffs, NJ: Prentice-Hall.

Tartler, R. (1961). *Das Alter in der modernen Gesellschaft.* Stuttgart: Enke.

Tobin, S. S., & Kulys, R. (1981). The family in the institutionalization of the elderly. *Journal of Social Issues, 37,* 145–157.

Troll, L. E. (1989). Myths of midlife intergenerational relationships. In S. Hunter & M. Sundel (Eds.), *Midlife myths* (pp. 210–231). Newbury Park, CA: Sage.

Tyrell, H. (1976). Probleme einer Theorie der gesellschaftlichen Ausdifferenzierung der privatisierten modernen Kleinfamilie. *Zeitschrift für Soziologie, 5,* 393–417.

Vaillant, G. (1977). *Adaptation to life.* Boston: Little, Brown.

Vaskovics, L. A. (Ed.) (1990). *Familienabhängigkeit junger Erwachsener und ihre Folgen.* (Forschungsbericht der Sozialwissenschaftlichen Forschungstelle.) Bamberg: Universität Bamberg.

Wagner, M. (1989). *Räumliche Mobilität im Lebensverlauf.* Stuttgart: Enke.

Whitbourne, S. K., & Weinstock, C. S. (1982). *Die mittlere Lebensspanne.* München: Urban & Schwarzenberg.

Youniss, J. (1983). Social construction of adolescence by adolescents and parents. In H. D. Grotevant & C. R. Cooper (Eds.), *Adolescent development in the family* (pp. 93–110). *New Directions for Child Development, 22.* San Francisco: Jossey Bass.

6

Relationships between adult siblings[1]
Victoria Hilkevitch Bedford

Introduction

An invisible relationship

Despite the fact that nearly everyone has a literal sibling, and those without have probably "adopted" a surrogate (Cumming & Schneider, 1961), adult sibling relationships have been one of the more invisible categories of personal relationships in social science research. Even sibling relationships in childhood have received modest attention compared to the parent–child bond (Irish, 1964; Johnson, 1982). This vertico-centric bias was interrupted briefly in the adult literature with the discovery that solidarity with siblings was perceived by older adults (age 50–80) to be "stronger than that which they perceive between themselves and their parents" (Cumming & Schneider, 1961, p. 502). This unexpected finding was credited to the egalitarian character of sibling relationships, a characteristic that is more in tune with the values of American society than the hierarchical structure of parent–child ties. Preference for sibling ties was also credited to the nonobligatory structure of the sibling relationship, which provides a flexibility more suited to the mobility needed by modern nuclear families to follow economic opportunity (Rosenberg & Anspach, 1973).

Subsequent empirical studies, however, did not support these claims. Compared to those of parents and their adult children, geographical availability of siblings, contact frequency (Leigh, 1982), and help exchanges (Scott, 1983; Myers & Dickerson, 1990; Coward, Horn & Dwyer, 1991; Wellman, 1990) were less. Also, the sibling relationship's vitality seemed to depend upon parental kinkeeping (Rosenberg & Anspach, 1973), because, when parents died, sibling interaction was often attenuated (Allan, 1977; Berardo, 1967; Townsend, 1957; Young & Willmott, 1957; Johnson, 1982).

Limitations of the literature

Knowledge about the sibling bond has been tentative and incomplete. A preoccupation with the vertical bond (e.g., Mancini, 1989; Mangen, Bengtson & Landry, 1989) continues to define the parameters by which original family relationships are conceptualized. Consequently, researchers' questions and perceptions about sibling ties have been restricted. For instance, anthropologists failed to notice that some societies are actually structured successfully by siblingship rather than by descent, as recently discovered in Oceania (Marshall, 1983). Also, almost no longitudinal studies are reported and studies using more than one sibling informant are rare. Often the sibling set is analyzed as a unit, obscuring the personal bond between specific partners, or the sibling targeted for study is not representative. Rarely are there systematic in-depth studies of the subtleties and nuances of what appears to be a complex and elusive bond. Finally, the relationship is rarely considered within the larger systems that subsume it (Matthews & Sprey, 1989). Despite these limitations, an initial body of knowledge has been amassed, awaiting replication and further development. For instance, with the use of thematic analyses of sibling interview data, response categories relevant to sibling relationships are now unfolding (Ross & Milgram, 1982; Gold, 1989a; Mosatche, Brady & Noberini, 1983). A literary scholar alludes to the rewards these efforts should reap:

> Only gradually did I fully apprehend how much is changed if we free ourselves from the notion that the relation of mother to child is the paradigmatic human relation and set next to it as equally significant the relation of sibling to sibling. (Downing, 1988, p. 4)

A list of many of the studies referenced here and descriptions of their samples appear in Table 6.1. Readers are urged to use the table to keep themselves informed of the restrictions on the data from which conclusions are drawn throughout this chapter.

Purpose

This review surveys the literature regarding the nature of sibling relationships in adulthood and the influences that shape it. In the spirit of this

Table 6.1. *Summary of adult sibling studies and methods used*

Study by author(s) and date: Number of subjects; Age; Sampling; Urban/ Rural; Location; Method

Adams, 1967a, 1968: 697; age 25–45; random block; urban; North Carolina; survey.

Allan, 1979: 41 (23 households); three diverse city blocks; commuter village in Essex, England; multiple interviews.

Auhagen, 1990: 18 pairs of adult friends, 18 pairs of adult siblings (same sex); Berlin, Germany; 60 consecutive days of double diary data.

Bank & Kahn, 1982: 250, all ages; clinical interview.

Bedford, 1989a, 1989b: 60; age 30–69; random within middle-class neighborhood; middle-sized town; Indiana; personal interview.

Bedford, 1989c: 71; age 20–89; convenience sample; Indiana; personal and small-group-administered survey.

Bedford, 1990: 54; age 34–73; first follow-up of 1989a study.

Bedford, 1992, 1993a, 1993b: 39; age 39–78; second follow-up of 1989a study.

Berardo, 1967: 821 women, 272 men; average age 40; white middle-class, highly educated, mostly of Southern background; survey.

Cicirelli, 1977: 32; mean age 75.9; nursing home and community dwelling volunteers from medium-sized Midwestern city; personal interview.

Cicirelli, 1980: 100; undergraduate women; survey.

Cicirelli, 1981: 140; age 30–70; representative, small Midwestern town; individual interviews using structured interview-questionnaire.

Cicirelli, 1989: 83; age 61–91; independently living elders; medium-sized Midwestern city.

Connidis, 1989: 298; age 65–92; random sample; residing in community; London, Canada; personal interview.

Gold, 1987, 1989a; Gold et al. 1990: 60; age 65 and older; purposive sample, white, middle-class, well-functioning; Chicago; intensive personal interview.

Gold, 1989b: 54; age 67 and older; mail questionnaire; follow-up of 1987 study.

Johnson, 1982: 74 Italian-American and 98 intermarried families sampled from marriage license records and 56 matched Protestant (European background) families (using newspaper wedding announcements); mean age 44; Syracuse, New York; personal interviews.

Kendig, Coles, Pitteldow & Wilson, 1988; 620; age 60 and over; random sample; urban; Sidney, Australia; survey.

Leigh, 1982: secondary analysis of Adams's (1968) survey using 799 respondents plus 478 small-town Indiana residents (58% response rate).

Table 6.1. *(cont.)*

Study by author(s) and date: Number of subjects; Age; Sampling; Urban/
Rural; Location; Method

Matthews & Rosner, 1988: 50 sibling groups with parents aged 75 and
  older; age 33–78; geographically dispersed volunteers surveyed by mail;
  23 sister pairs in which one was employed were interviewed.

Matthews & Sprey, 1989: 49 brother pairs, all-male sibling groups drawn
  from Matthews & Rosner (1988) sample; written questionnaire and
  personal interview.

Mosatche, Brady & Noberini, 1983: 47; mean age 59.3 years; lower
  socioeconomic status; New York City; personal interview.

Myers & Dickerson, 1990: 309; age 60–91; low-income African-Americans,
  Mexican-Americans, and Anglos from seven states (mostly Texas)
  participating in a foster grandparent program.

Peterson, 1990: 121 households; age 16–92; two rural and one urban
  community; below poverty level; random selection of households within
  each of three settings; both male and female heads of households
  interviewed; Benguet Province, Philippines.

Pulakos, 1989: 115; age 17–25; survey of college undergraduate psychology
  class; mostly Caucasian.

Rosenberg & Anspach, 1973: 1,368 (1,000 couples included); age 45–79;
  random sample; blue-collar, Caucasian, urban; Philadelphia; survey.

Ross & Milgram, 1982: 75 volunteers; age 22–93; urban; grouped into 13
  discussion groups, in-depth individual discussion with 10.

Wiehe, 1990: 150, age 18–77, volunteers.

volume the focus here is on the interpersonal relationship within pairs of
siblings, not on the dynamics of the sibling group or larger family system.
The targeted sources of variability among sibling pairs are gender and the
life course. Some of the other important potential mediators of the relationship that cannot be addressed directly at this time are ethnicity, geographical proximity, and social class.

The nature of the sibling bond

Sibling variants

It is important to note the ethnocentric bias of most sibling research.
Siblings are assumed to be offspring of the same parents (Cicirelli, 1993;

Weisner, 1989). Other siblings are seen as deviations from this standard. Using both anthropological and lay terminology, siblings by adoption lack the biological link, "part-siblings" or half-siblings share one biological parent, stepsiblings have different biological parents who are married to each other, "quasi-siblings" have different biological parents who are not married to each other but live together (Weisner, 1989, p. 12), and socially designated "fictive" siblings and cousins are interchangeable with siblings in many societies (Marshall, 1983).

Sibships compared to friendships and other ties

In dominant Western societies, adult siblings do not appear to play a prescribed role in one another's lives. Some normative trends have been identified, however. Due to its egalitarianism (e.g., Scott, 1983), the sibling relationship bears some resemblance to friendship, but it is more like the parent–child bond in other ways. For instance, with siblings, obligation plays a far greater role in contact motivation than with friends, and social activities are less frequent (Adams, 1967b; Pulakos, 1989). In early adulthood at least, sibship differs from friendship in that the range of topics discussed is dramatically narrower (Pulakos, 1989), contact is more often symbolic (in thought) than direct, support is more instrumental and less emotional (Auhagen, 1990), and affectional closeness (Pulakos, 1989) and value consensus (Adams, 1967b) are considerably less.

Uniquenesses of sibling ties

The sibling relationship has features not shared by most friendship or intergenerational family ties. One feature is the remarkable persistence of the sibling tie (Allan, 1979); it is the longest enduring human bond, spanning most of the life of each member. Within the family of orientation, the sibling is the most egalitarian relationship (Scott, 1983), and, except for very old friends, it is the only peerlike relationship with a shared past (e.g., Goetting, 1986). A near-universal "dormant" characteristic is that siblings can be turned to in times of crisis. Another feature is that contact with siblings will almost always be maintained at least for its own sake, whether directly or through other family members (Allan, 1977).

Sex differences and sibling relationships

Sex differences are expected to influence the quality of interpersonal relationships. This expectation reflects cultural prescriptions for women to display more expressive and nurturant behavior (Cicirelli, 1989; Walker, 1992), personality differences describing women as more empathic than men (Chodorow, 1978), and the need for superior interpersonal skills such as role taking by those who are dependent on a more powerful other to gain access to vital resources (Barber, 1984).

Whether sex differences affect sibling relationships is frequently asked by researchers. Results differ on whether sex differences in sibling relationships are a function of the "femaleness" of the dyad (the more females included in the dyad, the more intimate, etc.) (Suggs, 1989; Gold, 1989a), the partners' gender likeness (like-sex dyads are closer than cross-sex dyads) (Gold, 1989a), or the developmental period of the partners (gender becomes less relevant with age) (Cicirelli, 1993).

Femaleness

Although the results of many studies indicate that respondents with a sister are emotionally closer than those with a brother (Cicirelli, 1989, p. 214; Gold, 1989a; Adams, 1968), this is not always the case. Connidis (1989) reported that gender composition of sibling dyads predicted neither whether respondents considered a sibling to be a close friend nor whether they confided in their siblings. Femaleness of the dyad (whether composed of none, one, or two women) affects whether it will be a "type" of relationship that is especially positive and/or intense. In a small sample of older men and women, Gold (1989a) found that the modal type of relationship across gender was loyal, but sisters were more than twice as likely to be in intimate types of relationships, more than four times as likely to be in congenial ones, and about one-eighth as likely to be in apathetic ones. Using a different methodology, Scott (1983) essentially replicated this pattern with respect to intimate and apathetic types.

Femaleness also has a differential effect on the well-being of its members. Using projective data, Cicirelli (1977) found that women who had sisters were more socially challenged, whereas men with sisters felt more secure, but having brothers made no difference. In another study, degree of closeness to a sister was related to fewer symptoms of depression in both men and women, but closeness to a brother was not (Cicirelli, 1989). Among recent widows, only contact with sisters predicted positive affect (O'Bryant, 1988).

Same-sex siblings

Brother pairs and sister pairs are noted throughout the sibling literature for the intensity of feeling they have for one another, whether positive or negative (e.g., Bank & Kahn, 1982; Gold, Woodbury & George, 1990). For some, the same-sex tie might be "the most stressful, volatile, ambivalent one we will ever know" (Downing, 1988, p. 12). Based on clinical and literary sources, whether same-sex sibling pairs are male or female appears to affect the partners' level of emotional interdependence, which is related to the intensity of their interidentification (Bank & Kahn, 1982). A common theme is that interidentification is problematic for sister pairs, but not for brother pairs (Downing, 1988). This putative interidentification problem of sisters is based on the psychoanalytic formulation that women's identity formation is incomplete (McGoldrick, 1989).

Cultural values are likely to account for some gender differences found between brother pairs and sister pairs. For instance, the greater level of conflict found between sisters than between brothers (Bedford, 1989a; Lowenthal, Thurnher & Chiriboga, 1975) might be influenced by the "culture's devaluation of female characteristics" (McGoldrick, 1989, p. 245). Brothers' relationships, on the other hand, seem to be more affected by achievement values than are sisters' (e.g., Form & Geschwender, 1962), which explains Adams's (1967a) finding that in brother pairs composed of a blue-collar and a white-collar member, each is unlikely to identify with or feel close to the other. For sisters who are socioeconomically disparate, the pattern is similar for the advantaged partner but not for the disadvantaged sister who idealizes her white-collar sister and feels close to her (Adams, 1967a).

Because of the many sources of similarity between same-sex sibling pairs, competition is likely to be magnified, particularly between those who occupy first and second birth positions. The amount of competitiveness is sometimes presumed from the degree to which they "deidentify" from one another – assign themselves an identity that is the opposite of the other (Schachter et al., 1976). Even in non-Western cultures, such as Oceania, where siblings are expected to share and cooperate because same-sex siblings are treated as equivalent, they are more likely to compete (Marshall, 1983).

Cross-sex versus same-sex dyads

Adult brothers and sisters often perform different tasks within the family, as seen in the Philippine Highlands (Peterson, 1990). In Oceania the brother–sister dyad is much desired and admired because of its complementary tasks assignment, where sisters have spiritual and brothers have secular predominance (Marshall, 1983). Regarding parent care, one of the few cases of an enterprise shared by adult siblings in Western societies (Matthews & Sprey, 1989), task differentiation is also greatest in mixed-gender siblingships compared to same-gender ones (Cicirelli, 1993). However, the differences in this traditionally female enterprise (caregiving) can be seen as quantitative as well as qualitative (e.g., Matthews & Rosner, 1988).

Age variation of sex differences

There is considerable evidence that men and women become more androgynous in later years, when earlier sources of differentiation, such as traditional parental and economic roles, are less prominent (e.g., Gutmann, 1987). Sex differences, therefore, should diminish with age. The sibling caregiving literature (concerned with caring for dependent parents or siblings) does not support a lessening of gender distinctions with advancing age. In his review of this literature Cicirelli (1993) concluded that men and women continue to follow sex-stereotyped roles. Women engage in the more personal and time-intensive aspects, whereas men provide financial help, transportation, and advice. Further, he concluded that sisters tend to share caregiving roles more equitably than do brothers.

Many studies find sisters continue to be more affectionally close than brothers in later life (Gold, 1989a; Ross & Milgram, 1982; Cumming & Henry, 1961), but others fail to support this finding (Scott, 1983; Bedford, 1989a; Connidis, 1989). For instance, in a four-year follow-up of 30- to 69-year-old adults, men caught up to the level at which women rated their affectional closeness toward their same-sex sibling (Bedford, 1990). Contact frequency studies also tend to support an absence of sex differences in old age (Scott, 1983). Finally, sex composition of the dyads was not a significant predictor of sibling association (activities and interaction) for either black or white old people in rural North Carolina (Suggs, 1989).

Critique of sex-differences findings

The lack of consensus on the contribution of sex differences to the nature of sibling relationships is not surprising in view of the variety of methods employed in the studies compared. The contradictions also point to a need for greater conceptual clarity on the goals of the research. Both the relational qualities of interest and the aspects of maleness and femaleness to be studied need to be carefully delineated. For instance, gender is used at times to index stereotypic personality or behavioral characteristics such as nurturance and instrumentality, and at other times it is used to index the enactment of particular roles such as that of kinkeeper. Rarely is the behavior, personality characteristic, or role itself measured in addition to gender. To do so would tease out the relative contributions of gender and whatever it is assumed to index. For instance, is there any difference between the sibling interaction of equally nurturant brothers and sisters?

Another flaw is that the relational qualities targeted for studies of sex differences are often gendered within the research enterprise. For instance, affectional closeness is typically "feminized" as emotional expressiveness, when the same inner experience might be expressed in other ways, such as by instrumental acts (Walker, 1991). Also, the sibling experience of men and women might seem to be different because of gender differences in the language they use to talk about feelings (Matthews & Sprey, 1989), the narrower range of responses men use when rating their sibling relationships compared to women (Bedford, 1989a), and possible differences in men's and women's awareness of their feelings toward their siblings (Bedford, 1989b).

Life-course variation of siblingships

Due to a dearth of longitudinal research on adult sibling relationships, much of the information about patterns of relational change comes from retrospective and cross-sectional data and from comparisons between age-specific studies. Problems inherent in these designs include confounding age with cohort influences, distortions in remote memory, and inferring intraindividual change from inter-age-group differences. Attempts to draw conclusions from these data are, therefore, only tentative approximations of change along a time continuum.

Stability and change

Although psychoanalytic concepts are often discredited by researchers for their resistance to empirical study, the idea that there are "levels of awareness" helps to understand disparate findings about whether sibling relationships change. The psychoanalytic paradigm provides a framework that allows for the possibility that this long-lived relationship follows different trajectories of stability and change at different levels of awareness.

Suppressed feelings toward siblings. It is generally accepted that experiences lodged in the deeper levels of awareness are resistant to change without radical intervention. Because the earliest experiences of the infant and young child reside there, early feelings toward siblings might have little opportunity to change during the life course. Clinical data and studies that use clinical techniques to access information offer some support. Laverty (1962) suggested that early sibling rivalry can be reactivated in residents of nursing homes because of a staff–resident configuration that simulates the early family environment. Berezin (1977) described how early hostilities that had been long forgotten often erupt when adult sibling interaction escalates during events surrounding the care and death of parents. Abarbanel (1983) demonstrated longitudinally that women's feelings about their own sibling were revived during their pregnancy with a second child, as they anticipated a sibling for the first child.

Conscious representations of siblingships. The sibling relationship adults describe is usually quite different from the one reactivated under special circumstances. Conscious descriptions appear to be more susceptible to social pressures, personal inhibitions, life experiences, and personality changes. Without longitudinal data the extent to which these representations change fundamentally is not known. However, recent statistics on sibling abuse in childhood provide a crude baseline for considering the life-course trajectory of sibling conflict.

Most children experience considerable conflict with a sibling. Conservative estimates of sibling physical abuse indicate that 80% of American children carry out at least one violent act toward a sibling during a typical year, and 20% "beat up" a brother or sister during the survey year (Straus, Gelles & Steinmetz, 1980). Sibling sexual abuse was remembered by 15% of women and 10% of men in a New England student sample. Of those sexually abused, 25% characterized it as exploitative (Finkelhor, 1980).

What happens to this conflict in the adult relationship? Studies of adult sibling conflict are rare. Using survey methods, Cicirelli (1981) found that in middle adulthood only 2% of men and women frequently felt competitive with a sibling and 3% had frequent arguments. Analyses by age indicated further declines. In contrast, using small, supportive discussion groups, Ross and Milgram (1982) found that of the 71% of their respondents who remembered experiencing rivalrous feelings, 45% said these feelings remain active. Greater proportions of adults also report negative feelings when circumstances require frequent interaction with siblings, as in the case of parent care (Brody, Hoffman, Kleban & Schoonover, 1989; Matthews & Rosner, 1988). This wide discrepancy in reporting sibling conflict juxtaposed with the data-eliciting methods used suggests that in the conscious relationship conflict disappears precipitously in adulthood, whereas when deeper levels of awareness are aroused, the underlying conflict often emerges intact.

Sibling abuse victims' reports provide insight into the denial of negative feelings toward siblings by adults. Among volunteers responding to widely distributed advertisements, over half the victims of emotional, psychological, and sexual abuse eventually recognized that they were very angry at the perpetrator today (Wiehe, 1990). A common pattern was to deny the experience altogether or to deny associated feelings, often by blaming oneself. Denial served to avoid reexperiencing painful feelings of shame, guilt, despair, and anger toward the perpetrator. The highly positive picture old respondents paint of their sibling relationships (e.g., Cicirelli, 1981; Gold, 1989a), therefore, might reflect fundamental change in some cases, and a coming to terms with the earlier conflicts. Yet the high incidence of sibling abuse and reasons for its denial suggest that the same picture could also reflect selective perceptions if not distortions of childhood experiences (Goetting, 1986).

Theoretical perspectives on life-course variation within siblingships

Does the sibling relationship change predictably over the course of life? If so, are these changes guided by an invariant sequence of developmental tasks, family career stages, or normative adult personality/cognitive changes? Some illustrations of theoretical frameworks follow.

The family career perspective predicts that changes in the sibling relationship are consequences of a time-energy budget (Leigh, 1982). Given a fixed quantity of time and emotional energy, young adults should be involved with their siblings until marriage, children, or other "social-clock" projects (Helson & Moane, 1987) monopolize these resources. Once these competing demands subside (children depart, careers peak and decline or level off, retirement begins, widowhood occurs), the sibling relationship resumes and sometimes intensifies.

Following the tradition of Havighurst (1972), developmental tasks of siblingships (Goetting, 1986) are a sequence of empirically derived subgoals that adults need to meet and master in order to lead a successful life. Goetting describes them as "prosocial and expected behaviors" emphasizing the social construction more than the personal construction of the task (p. 704). In early and middle adulthood, the tasks are the provision of companionship and emotional support of childhood at the level of "a passive concern for how the other is getting along" (p. 711); cooperating in caring for elderly parents and the events surrounding their death, which should initiate a sustained higher level of socioemotional involvement; and providing occasional aid and services such as help during illness, babysitting, sharing possessions, and lending money. Old-age tasks are validation of earlier perceptions by means of reminiscence, resolution of sibling rivalry, provision of aid and direct services when called upon, and intensification of the level of sibling support to compensate for social losses (Goetting, 1986).

Attachment is an affectional bond with a specific person, and it is a behavioral system designed to provide protection or solace. Protection is provided by means of proximity-seeking behaviors that serve the evolutionary function of protecting one's genes so that they will be transmitted to subsequent generations (see Bowlby, 1969; Bierhoff, Chapter 8 of this volume; Kreppner, Chapter 4 of this volume). Adults sustain attachments with one another through distal means such as the telephone and even in the absence of contact because of their ability to evoke symbolic representations of the attachment person. The idea that attachment has a protective function has implications for the life course of sibling relationships. Illness, dependency needs, and negative feelings toward siblings threaten the well-being of the attached person, requiring protective behavior. Because such events and feelings are more frequent and/or more threatening in old age, the need for protection is greater. Attachment feelings and their expression, therefore, should increase with advancing age (Cicirelli, 1989).

Empirical trends

These frameworks are consistent with the prediction that sibling involvement decreases in early adulthood, reaches a low point during the middle years, and rises in later years, accompanied by more positive feelings and fewer negative feelings. Findings of some empirical studies seem to support this trend, which has been referred to as "the hourglass effect" (Shanas, 1979).

A few studies scan the entire adult life course. Using cross-sectional data, the rate of overt interaction between siblings provided modest support for the hourglass effect (Leigh, 1982). Subjective reports on intensity of affectional closeness, again using cross-sectional data, followed the same trend (Ross & Milgram, 1982). Interestingly, neither study found this pattern with parents; both contact and closeness remained constant in adulthood. Another study, using thematic analyses of open-ended interview questions (Mosatche et al., 1983), found significant shifts in the emphasis of the relationship at two of the four adult periods sampled. Positive affect, reciprocity, compatibility, similarity, and shared activities marked both the beginning of marriage and the death of a parent, with a long latency period in between (birth of respondent's first child and when the respondent's children left home). Similarly, White and Riedmann (1992) found a nonlinear increase in viewing siblings as a potential source of support.

In a more recent study, sibling contact frequency does not follow this U-curve. Using a representative sample from the National Survey of Families and Households, White and Riedmann (1992) found a pattern of decline that varied in degree at different life periods. Corroboration of the hourglass effect by age-specific studies is considered next.

Decline in involvement during early adulthood. Studies of young adulthood are especially rare. In a study of college students, decline in sibling involvement was evident when compared with friendship. Respondents preferred to discuss most topics with their best friend than with their closest sibling. They engaged in more activities, felt more close and less different, and valued the relationship with the friend more (Pulakos, 1989).

Other studies found important exceptions to the pattern of decline. Although circumstances supporting rivalry should no longer be operative when siblings leave the parental home (Adams, 1968; Allan, 1979), there are potential new grounds for conflict, suggesting greater involvement, albeit negative. Adams (1968) noted that differences in occupational levels at this time, especially between brothers, accounts for competitiveness, ambivalence, and jealousy. For women, the involvement appears to be more positive (Adams, 1968). For instance, the emotionally closest sibling of college women compared favorably with parents (Cicirelli, 1980). These women felt more supported by this sibling than by their father and the same as by their mother.

The dormant years. Findings from other studies of white middle-class samples concur that sibling relationships undergo a hiatus during child-rearing, career-building years. The relationship has been described as "dormant" (Bank & Kahn, 1982), "attenuated" (Irish, 1964), or "transformed" (Brady & Noberini, 1987) as the partners' nonshared concerns take precedence. For instance, Adams (1968) found that younger to middle-aged respondents (aged 20 to 45) do not show a tendency toward sibling solidarity. Their sibling relationships are largely constrained by different values and interests.

Perhaps an unidentified task of this dormant period is separation from close siblings. Projective stories told by men and women who are raising children contain significantly more sibling separation themes than those whose children have departed (Bedford, 1989a). Adults who were busy raising children told stories indicating concern with the loss of their siblings, decrease in contact, the separate paths they took, and the many obstacles that keep them apart. Separation themes were usually accompanied by expressions of sadness, anger, or guilt.

Sibling separation in adulthood has eluded most researchers' notice, with the exception of a small clinical literature. Defining separation as "an intrapsychic process that includes affective differentiation of self from others" (Adelman & Siemon, 1986), these studies have focused on twins, for whom separation can be especially poignant (Siemon, 1980). In the one study of the interpersonal relationship between well-functioning adult twins (20 pairs), only cross-sex twins achieved psychological separation (Schave & Ciriello, 1983). Apparently the costs of intimacy and independence are "themes that resonate throughout the lives of many twins" (Adelman & Siemon, 1986, p. 99).

As parents age, overt involvement among siblings appears to increase. Although positive consequences of parent care to the quality of sibling relationships have been noted (Brody, 1990; Matthews & Rosner, 1988), a growing literature chronicles the tensions and resentments engendered by this event (e.g., Strawbridge & Wallhagen, 1991).

Increased involvement in later life. Rates of contact between siblings give conflicting results as to whether sibling involvement increases. Retrospectively, more than half of a middle-class sample of elders reported increased contact with their siblings (Gold, 1987), although in a follow-up two years later no further increase had occurred (Gold, 1989b). Targeting available siblings only (those living within the same metropolitan area), however, the proportion who had seen a sibling in the past week dropped from 68% for those aged 44 to 54 to 47% for those aged 65 and older (Rosenberg & Anspach, 1973). Findings by Young and Willmott (1957), Berardo (1967), and Shanas et al. (1968) support this downward turn. Whether contact increases or decreases in old age seems to depend on whether the interaction is only face-to-face or includes distal modes (mail, telephone). Face-to-face contact is more likely to decrease when mobility problems increase in old age, especially if residential propinquity decreases (Rosenberg & Anspach, 1973), but distal modes can compensate for this loss (Allan, 1979).

There is considerable agreement on the late-life rise in sibling involvement using indicators of positive affect toward the sibling. Cumming and Henry's (1961) confirmation of this trend has since been replicated on nearly 30 years of adjacent cohorts (e.g., Gold, 1989a; Cicirelli, 1981; Ross & Milgram, 1982). Bedford (1990) compared sibling affect ratings separated by four years for adults ranging from middle to old age. In general, positive affect was as likely to increase as decrease; but for men an increase was more frequent, probably because it began at a lower level, whereas the women's level had reached a ceiling earlier. When examining the direction of longitudinal change within each age group, however, the rate of increase in positive affect declined monotonically by age group (from 22% to 8%) until the oldest group, in which the increase was dramatic (47%), lending further support to the rise in positive affect later in life (Bedford, 1990).

Most studies report that old people show little variance in their extremely positive ratings of all family relationships (Bedford, 1992; Mangen et al.,

1989; Scott, 1983), raising questions about the validity of these findings. This exaggerated and uniform positive response has been attributed to a greater vulnerability to desirability effects in the old (Minkler, 1985) and to perceptual distortions and selection serving the developmental need for a sense of integrity (Goetting, 1986).

Several studies have looked for changes within the course of old age on specific positive aspects of the sibling relationship. Kendig, Coles, Pitteldow and Wilson (1988) found that in a 60- to 64-year-old group, the older members confided in their sibling more than the younger members, but in two older groups no age differences were seen. Gold (1989b) too found that with advanced old age, interaction rate, closeness, and emotional support leveled off after a rise in sibling involvement. Acceptance/approval and psychological involvement, however, continued to increase.

One developmental task of old age is the resolution of sibling rivalry (Goetting, 1986). The rise in sibling involvement in late life usually implies a decrease in negative feelings, indicating the successful completion of this task. This decline in sibling conflict has been illuminated by teasing apart changes in the intensity and frequency of negative affect. Bedford (1989c) found that the intensity of conflict increased with age in response to a few specific elicitors, but the likelihood of these elicitors occurring decreased precipitously with age. Perhaps old people take precautions to avoid known sources of sibling conflict to assure that their interactions will be satisfying.

Finally, historical changes can account for the reported drop in sibling conflict in late life as a cohort effect. Stearns (1988) found that the sibling relationships of cohorts born before 1920 experienced less conflict (jealousy and rivalry) than those born between 1920 and 1960. Demographic changes and family practices during this period contributed to a fertile environment for engendering intense rivalry between siblings. These changes include an increase in the intensity of maternal affection, less severe discipline, the use of hospitals for delivery of infants, and smaller families (Stearns, 1988).

Future directions

The sibling relationship sometimes remains important even after death. Studies of grief reactions to sibling death underline the variability of the sibling relationship (Moss & Moss, 1989), its intensity (Zisook & Lyons, 1988), and its symbolic nature (Troll & Smith, 1976), qualities that contribute to its elusiveness in Western society. To study this elusive, emotionally charged, memory-laden tie requires a search for creative methodologies that the infant science of interpersonal relations is hardly ready to tackle (Hinde,

1979). Several attempts appear to be promising, such as thematic analyses of qualitative data (Mosatche et al., 1983; Ross & Milgram, 1982; Gold, 1989a), diary entries (Auhagen, 1990), and adaptations of projective tests (Bedford, 1989a). Whether they can systematically and convincingly tap into those complex, covert phenomena especially important to sibling relationships (identification, psychological separation, and underlying feelings) remains to be seen.

Demographic changes will necessitate a renewed focus on the overt sibling relationship as well. As life expectancy continues to increase, siblings are more likely to be jointly engaged in parent care and for longer periods of their lives (see Cicirelli, Coward & Dwyer, 1992; Stoller, Forster & Duniho, 1992). As family size continues to shrink and divorce rates remain high, the old will be left more often with neither a spouse nor an adult child (the primary support resources of the old). Thus, the dormant support function of siblings might have to be activated (Avioli, 1989). Are those of the aged who are physically capable likely to respond to the chronic health care and psychological needs of a dependent sibling? Does the positive affect reported in late life translate into tangible and sustained aid?

In some cases, an important obstacle to the desire to provide sibling care and its successful enactment might be unresolved early conflicts. For instance, it is not clear whether the increased interaction involved in this task improves the relationship (Bedford, 1990) or reactivates earlier conflicts (Allan, 1979). Other life events are being identified as well that seem to initiate change in feelings (positive and negative) toward siblings (Ross & Milgram, 1982; Bedford, 1990). An understanding of the principles involved in changing the direction and intensity of feelings toward siblings should have important implications for the prevention and repair of problematic sibling outcomes in late life.

The study of sibling relationships highlights interpersonal issues, which should have relevance to other relationships as well. For instance, how does the symbolic relationship interface with actual interactions? How is the relationship differentially affected when motivations for contact are based upon obligation rather than volition? Does the need for separation require the loss of intimacy? A challenging research agenda lies ahead.

Note

1. I wish to express my appreciation to Drs. Paula Avioli, Deborah Gold, and Elizabeth Paul for their helpful comments on an earlier version of this manuscript.

References

Abarbanel, J. (1983). The revival of the sibling experience during the mother's second pregnancy. *Psychoanalytic Study of the Child, 38*, 353–357.

Adams, B. (1967a). Occupational position, mobility, and the kin of orientation. *American Sociological Review, 32*, 364–377.

(1967b). Interaction theory and the social network. *Sociometry, 30*, 64–78.

(1968). *Kinship in an urban setting.* Chicago: Markham.

Adelman, M. B., & Siemon, M. (1986). Communicating the relational shift: Separation among adult twins. *American Journal of Psychotherapy, 40*(1), 96–109.

Allan, G. (1977). Sibling solidarity. *Journal of Marriage and the Family, 39*, 177–184.

(1979). *A sociology of friendship and kinship.* London: Allen & Unwin.

Auhagen, A. E. (1990). Friendship and sibling dyads in everyday life: A study with the new method of double diary. Paper presented at the Fifth International Conference on Personal Relationships, Oxford, England.

Avioli, P. S. (1989). The social support functions of siblings in later life: A theoretical model. *American Behavioral Scientist, 33*(1), 45–57.

Bank, S. P., & Kahn, M. D. (1982). *The sibling bond.* New York: Basic.

Barber, C. E. (1984). The influence of power and dependency on role-taking accuracy in three-generational families. *Australian Journal of Sex, Marriage, and Family, 5*(3), 77–87.

Bedford, V. H. (1989a). A comparison of thematic apperceptions of sibling affiliation, conflict, and separation at two periods of adulthood. *International Journal of Aging and Human Development, 28*(1), 53–66.

(1989b). Ambivalence in adult sibling relationships. *Family Relations, 10*(2), 211–224.

(1989c). Understanding the value of siblings in old age: A proposed model. *American Behavioral Scientist, 33*(1), 33–44.

(1990). *Changing affect toward siblings and the transition to old age.* Unpublished manuscript.

(1992). Memories of parental favoritism and the quality of parent–child ties in adulthood. *Journal of Gerontology, 47*(4), S149–S155.

(1993a). Attachment, intimacy and other relational links to well-being: Which apply to sibling relationship? In V. H. Bedford (Chair), *Social support revisited: Costs and benefits of personal relationships.* Symposium conducted at the annual convention of the American Psychological Association, Toronto.

(1993b). Differential parental treatment in childhood and the quality of sibling relationships in adulthood. Paper presented at the Biennial Scientific Meeting of the Society for Research in Child Development, New Orleans.

Berardo (1967). Kinship interaction and communications among space-age migrants. *Journal of Marriage and the Family, 29*, 541–554.

Berezin, M. A. (1977). Partial grief for the aged and their families. In E. Pattison (Ed.), *The experience of dying.* Englewood Cliffs, NJ: Prentice-Hall.

Bowlby, J. (1969). *Attachment and loss*, Vol. 1: *Attachment*. New York: Basic Books.

Brady, E. M., & Noberini, M. R. (1987, August). Sibling support in the context of a model of sibling solidarity. Paper presented at the 95th Annual Meeting of the American Psychological Association, New York.

Brody, E. M. (1990). *Women-in-the-middle: Their parent care years.* New York: Springer.

Brody, E. M., Hoffman, C., Kleban, M. G., & Schoonover, C. B. (1989). Caregiving daughters and their local siblings: Perceptions, strains, and interactions. *Gerontologist, 29,* 529–539.

Chodorow, N. (1978). *The reproduction of mothering: Psychoanalysis and the sociology of gender.* Berkeley: University of California Press.

Cicirelli, V. G. (1977). Relationship of siblings to the elderly person's feelings and concerns. *Journal of Gerontology, 131,* 317–322.

(1980). A comparison of college women's feelings toward their siblings and parents. *Journal of Marriage and the Family, 42,* 111–118.

(1981). *Helping elderly parents: The role of adult children.* Boston: Auburn Books.

(1989). Feelings of attachment to siblings and well-being in later life. *Psychology and Aging, 4*(2), 211–216.

(1993). Sibling relationships in adulthood. *Marriage and Family Review, 16*(3/4), 291–310.

Cicirelli, V. G., Coward, R. T., & Dwyer, J. W. (1992). Siblings as caregivers for impaired elders. *Research on Aging, 14,* 331–350.

Connidis, I. A. (1989). Siblings as friends in later life. *American Behavioral Scientist, 33*(1), 81–93.

Coward, R. T., Horne, C., & Dwyer, J. W. (1992). Demographic perspectives on gender and family caregiving. In J. W. Dwyer & R. T. Coward (Eds.), *Gender, families, and elder care.* Newbury Park, CA: Sage.

Cumming, E., & Henry, W. E. (1961). Growing old. New York: Basic Books.

Cumming, E., & Schneider, D. M. (1961). Sibling solidarity: A property of American kinship. *American Anthropologist, 63,* 498–507.

Downing, C. (1988). *Psyche's sisters: Reimagining the meaning of sisterhood.* San Francisco: Harper and Row.

Finkelhor, D. (1980). Sex among siblings: A survey on prevalence, variety, and effects. *Archives of Sexual Behavior, 9*(3), 171–194.

Form, W. H., & Geschwender, J. A. (1962). Social reference basis of job satisfaction: The case of manual workers. *American Sociological Review, 27,* 232–233.

Goetting, A. (1986). The developmental tasks of siblingship over the life cycle. *Journal of Marriage and the Family, 48,* 703–714.

Gold, D. T. (1987). Siblings in old age: Something special. *Canadian Journal on Aging, 6*(3), 211–227.

(1989a). Sibling relationships in old age: A typology. *International Journal of Aging and Human Development, 28*(1), 37–51.

(1989b). Generational solidarity: Conceptual antecedents and consequences. *American Behavioral Scientist, 33*(1), 19–32.

Gold, D. T., Woodbury, M. A., & George, L. K. (1990). Relationship classification using grade of membership analysis: A typology of sibling relationships in later life. *Journal of Gerontology, 45*(2), S43–S51.

Gutmann, D. L. (1987). *Reclaimed powers.* New York: Basic Books.

Havighurst, R. J. (1972). *Developmental tasks and education.* New York: McKay.

Helson, R., & Moane, G. (1987). Personality changes in women from college to midlife. *Journal of Personality and Social Psychology, 53*(1), 178–187.

Hinde, R. A. (1979). *Toward understanding relationships.* New York: Academic Press.

Irish, D. P. (1964). Sibling interaction: A neglected aspect of family life research. *Social Forces, 42,* 279–288.

Johnson, C. L. (1982). Sibling solidarity: Its origin and functioning in Italian-American families. *Journal of Marriage and the Family, 44,* 155–165.

Kendig, H. L., Coles, R., Pitteldow, Y., & Wilson, S. (1988). Confidants and family structure in old age. *Journal of Gerontology: Social Sciences, 43*(2), S31–S40.

Laverty, R. (1962). Reactivation of sibling rivalry in older people. *Social Work, 7,* 23–30.

Leigh, G. K. (1982). Kinship interaction over the family life span. *Journal of Marriage and the Family, 44*(1), 197–208.

Lowenthal, M. F., Thurnher, M., & Chiriboga, D. (1975). *Four stages of life.* San Francisco: Jossey-Bass.

Mancini, J. (1989). *Aging parents and adult children.* Lexington, MA: Lexington Books.

Mangen, D. J., Bengtson, V. L., & Landry, Jr., P. H. (1989). *Measurement of intergenerational relations.* Newbury Park, CA: Sage.

Marshall, M. (1983). *Siblingship in Oceania.* Monograph No. 8. New York: University Press of America.

Matthews, S. H., & Rosner, T. T. (1988). Shared filial responsibility: The family as the primary caregiver. *Journal of Marriage and the Family, 50,* 185–195.

Matthews, S. H., & Sprey, J. (1989). Older family systems: Intra- and intergenerational relations. In J. A. Mancini (Ed.), *Aging parents and adult children* (pp. 63–77). Lexington, MA: Lexington Books.

McGoldrick, M. (1989). Sisters. In M. McGoldrick, C. M. Anderson, & F. Walsh (Eds.), *Women in families* (pp. 244–266). New York: Norton.

Minkler, M. (1985). Social support and health in the elderly. In S. Cohen & S. L. Syme (Eds.), *Social support and health* (pp. 199–217). New York: Academic Press.

Mosatche, H. S., Brady, E. M., & Noberini, M. R. (1983). A retrospective lifespan study of the closest sibling relationship. *Journal of Psychology, 113,* 237–243.

Moss, S. Z., & Moss, M. S. (1989). The impact of the death of an elderly sibling: Some considerations of a normative loss, antecedents and consequences. *American Behavioral Scientist, 33*(1), 94–106.

Myers, D. R., & Dickerson, B. E. (1990). Intragenerational interdependence among older, low-income African American, Mexican American, and Anglo siblings. *Family Perspective, 24,* 217–243.

O'Bryant, S. L. (1988). Sibling support and older widows' well-being. *Journal of Marriage and the Family, 50*(1), 173–184.

Peterson, J. T. (1990). Sibling exchanges and complementarity in the Philippine Highlands. *Journal of Marriage and the Family, 52,* 441–451.

Pulakos, J. (1989). Young adult relationships: Siblings and friends. *Journal of Psychology, 12*(3), 237–244.

Rosenberg, G. S., & Anspach, D. F. (1973). Sibling solidarity in the working class. *Journal of Marriage and the Family, 33,* 108–113.

Ross, H. G., & Milgram, J. I. (1982). Important variables in adult sibling relationships: A qualitative study. In M. E. Lamb & B. Sutton-Smith (Eds.), *Sibling relationships: Their nature and significance across the lifespan* (pp. 225–249). Hillsdale, NJ: Erlbaum.

Schachter, F. F., Shore, E., Feldman-Rotman, S., Marquis, R. E., & Campbell, S. (1976). Sibling deidentification. *Developmental Psychology, 12,* 418–427.

Schave, B., & Ciriello, J. (1983). *Identity and intimacy in twins.* New York: Praeger.

Scott, J. P. (1983). Siblings and other kin. In. T. Brubaker (Ed.), *Family relationships in later life* (pp. 47–62). Newbury Park, CA: Sage.

Shanas, E. (1979). Social myth as hypothesis: The case of the family relations of old people. *Gerontologist, 19*(1), 3–9.

Shanas, E., Townsend, P., Wedderburn, D., Friis, H., Milhoj, P., & Stehouver, J. (Eds.) (1968). *Old people in three industrial societies.* London: Routledge & Kegan Paul.

Siemon, M. (1980). The separation-individuation process in adult twins. *American Journal of Psychotherapy, 34*(3), 1–14.

Stearns, P. N. (1988). The rise of sibling jealousy in the twentieth century. In C. Z. Stearns & P. N. Stearns (Eds.), *Emotion and social change* (pp. 193–222). New York: Holmes & Meier.

Stoller, E. P., Forster, L. E., & Duniho, T. S. (1992). Systems of parent care within sibling networks. *Research on Aging, 14*(1), 28–49.

Straus, M. A., Gelles, R. J., & Steinmetz, S. K. (1980). *Behind closed doors: Violence in the American family.* New York: Anchor.

Strawbridge, W. J., & Wallhagen, M. I. (1991). Impact of family conflict on adult–child caregivers. *Gerontologist, 31*(6), 770–777.

Suggs, P. K. (1989). Predictors of association among siblings: A black/white comparison. *American Behavioral Scientist, 33*(1), 70–80.

Townsend, P. (1957). *The family life of old people: An inquiry in East London.* Glencoe, IL: Free Press.

Troll, L. E., & Smith, J. (1976). Attachment through the life span: Some questions about dyadic bonds among adults. *Human Development, 19,* 156–170.

Walker, A. J. (1991). Conceptual perspectives on gender and family caregiving. In J. W. Dwyer & R. T. Coward (Eds.), *Gender, families, and elder care.* Newbury Park, CA: Sage.

Weisner, T. S. (1989). Comparing sibling relationships across cultures. In P. G. Zukow (Ed.), *Sibling interaction across cultures: Theoretical and methodological issues* (pp. 11–25). New York: Springer-Verlag.

Wellman, B. (1990). The place of kinfolk in personal community networks. *Marriage and Family Review, 15,* 195–228.

White, L. K., & Riedmann, A. (1992). Ties among adult siblings. *Social Forces, 71,* 85–102.

Wiehe, V. R. (1990). *Sibling abuse: Hidden physical, emotional, and sexual trauma.* Lexington, MA: Lexington Books.

Young, M., & Willmott, P. (1957). *Family and kinship in East London.* Baltimore: Penguin.

Zisook, S., & Lyons, L. (1988). Grief and relationship to the deceased. *International Journal of Family Psychiatry, 9*(2), 135–146.

7

Relationships in the extended family and diverse family forms
Peter Kaiser

Introduction

The great variety of familial relationships and the significance of kinship contacts are often underestimated, because most disciplines, including psychology, tend to view the family simply as the *nuclear family*. Yet the family includes not only parents and children but also a more or less extensive number of relatives who belong to various generations and form a variety of relationships. These are augmented by the special family relationships in *stepfamilies*, which are gaining in significance as a result of increasing divorce rates, as well as the relationships in *foster families* and *adoptive families*.

In this chapter I shall concentrate on these somewhat neglected relationships between *not directly related* family members. This raises questions about living conditions, structures, and constellations that contribute toward the satisfactory functioning of the respective families. After first making some clarifying preliminary remarks on family psychology, I shall then consider the somewhat rudimentary theoretical and empirical studies of the most important kin relationships and discuss the perspectives of future research.

Family psychological foundations

The family should be understood as a group of persons with a communal past, present, and future, the members of which are formally linked to one another by blood relationships, marital or nonmarital companionship, fostering, or adoption – directly or via relatives. Informal family members may be nonrelated persons with whom close, stable connections exist (e.g., cohabitants). Depending on the degree of relationship or bonds, the members have more or less intensive social and emotional relationships, often combined with a high density of interaction (see Kramer, 1985; Mühlfeld, 1984; Nave-Herz & Markefka, 1989; Neidhardt, 1975; Schneewind, 1987). Life in the family takes place within a mutually shared private life of always the same members who demarcate themselves toward the outside. Membership in this communal living group aims toward permanence and continuity. Concurrent membership in several families is impossible (see Kaufmann, 1980; Schneewind, 1987; Tyrell, 1982).

While considering the many approaches and results on the psychology of the family, the family can be characterized in the following way:

- Families are autopoietic systems with pronounced interdependence and social networking among the members, who are prepared to learn and are flexible in shaping their structures (e.g., Hill, 1971; Kaiser, 1989; Nave-Herz, 1988; Neidhardt, 1975; Schneewind, 1987; Tyrell, 1982).
- Families found a communal world of living whereby the worlds of the members are not necessarily identical (Adamszek, 1994; Gilbert, Christensen & Margolin, 1984; Hess & Handel, 1975; Tyrell, 1982).
- Family life always has a processlike character, as the family itself constantly changes with the life cycles of its members as well as the family cycle, which stretches over generations; also, the family has to come to terms when environmental changes come about, or when it actively changes its environment itself, for example, as a result of unemployment (see Duvall, 1977; Carter & McGoldrick, 1980; Hill & Mattesich, 1979; L'Abate, 1990; Lewis, 1988; Schneewind, 1987; Sperling, 1988).

A family can be considered *well-functioning* when it is in a position to cope satisfactorily with the tasks and situations that occur in all the areas relevant to it. For these particular areas the family needs *competencies* tailored to the specific needs of the *system, area,* and *situation* (Kaiser, 1989; L'Abate, 1990). These also include the competencies and cooperation of the individual familial subsystems and their members who operate effectively together and who can support or temporarily replace each other in difficult situations, or when a subsystem or a member is unavailable. If, for instance, the parents are temporarily unavailable because of illness, relatives often replace them in many families and thus secure the functioning of the family. The availability of relatives is often of great importance when the nuclear family can no longer manage on its own. Contrary to certain (theoretical) opinions on the "functional irrelevance" of relatives (see

Lüschen, 1989; Parsons & Bales, 1955; Tyrell, 1979), recent studies increasingly show that familial relationships are by no means to be viewed solely within the nuclear family context (see Lüschen, 1989; Pfeil & Ganzert, 1973). For instance, in an intercultural study in four major cities in Germany, Finland, and Ireland, Lüschen, Haavio-Mannila, Stolte-Heiskamen, and Ward (1985) established the frequency and durability of contacts between relatives and how these are maintained with the help of rituals. Claessens and Menne (1973) assume "sympathy, dominance and objective structures" as the basis of kin relationships. The latter include rituals on special occasions such as religious or public holidays, anniversaries, births, marriages, and funerals, which usually unite large extended families. Here, an important role is played by falling birth rates, increasing divorce and remarriage rates, and increasing life expectancy. This also applies to changes in kin relationships. Thus there are, for example, a growing number of single children, whose (great-)grandparents are still alive (on intergenerational expansion of the family system, see Menken, 1985; Shanas et al., 1968). More and more grandparents have fewer grandchildren as a result of declining birth rates and higher marriage ages so that the overall size of the kinship network is declining (on intragenerational shrinkage, see Huinink, 1987; Nave-Herz, 1988). This indicates that in the course of time there is an increase in intergenerational and a decrease in intragenerational relationships (see Lüschen, 1989). As a result of their higher life expectancy, the lower average marriage age of women, and increasing divorce rates, which lead to more single-parent (mother) families, "feminization" of the family is growing (Lüschen, 1989).

Relatives are still the primary *support system* in most families. For example, aid is usually sought first among relatives, before nonrelated persons are approached, as this entails obligations. Among relatives, those persons are usually asked with whom closer relationships and thus greater loyalty exists, for example, parents-in-law, grandparents, or sisters- and brothers-in-law (see Nauck, 1987; Parish, Hao & Hogan, 1991; Veiel & Herrle, 1991). The kinship support system is still especially important during illness and crises (see Kaiser, 1989; Lüschen, 1989; Pfeil & Ganzert, 1973). According to Litwak's (1985) findings, old people only occasionally receive support from neighbors or friends during sickness or crises; when the situation is serious or they are ill for a longer period, they receive support from relatives. These results are also confirmed by intercultural findings (Lee, 1984; Rosenmayr, 1978; Segalen, 1985; Vaskovics, 1982; van Wetering, 1986). Having surveyed the relevant literature, Lüschen reaches the conclusion that contacts with friends and relatives are not interchangeable, rather they are *complementary*. In his study Lüschen (1989) found only a few families that centered exclusively on friends. In contrast, a relatively large number of families had close contacts with relatives only.

Let us now take a look at the different types of kin relationships.

Relationships between (great-)grandparents and their (great-)grandchildren

Relationships between great-grandparents or grandparents and their grandchildren will be considered together, as the literature pays little attention to great-grandparents, and there are many parallels between great-grandparents and grandparents. Where differences do exist, they will be discussed. Many people do not know very much about their great-grandparents, and although numbers are increasing because of the older gernerations' increasing life expectancy, only a few people know their great-grandparents personally. However, what they relate about them elucidates their importance in the family.

Grandparents who are still alive and available are often the closest, direct caregivers for grandchildren. Parents often maintain very close contacts with their own parents (Argyle & Henderson, 1986; Fünfter Familienbericht, 1994; Nauck, 1987; Schwob, 1988). Here, age and the particular phases in life and family cycles are of great significance. A representative American longitudinal study carried out by Parish et al. (1991) showed that more than two-thirds of young single mothers and about a third of young divorced mothers were taken in (with their children) and supported by the children's grandmothers. However, in most cases this arrangement was temporary and decreased with increasing age. Over 40% of the 19- to 26-year-old single mothers and about 20% of the married mothers were (still) able to rely on help in looking after the children. However, this was only the case where the grandmothers lived nearby and when no regular duties were involved over a longer period of time.

Many grandparents are just over 50 years old when their first grandchild is born. They are often very active in their occupations and are by no means "old" (Crawford, 1981). As far as their own duties and interests permit, such grandparents can be very active with their grandchildren, which is rarely possible for very old or frail (great-)grandparents. Often the whole family will meet, especially on festive occasions, at the home of (great-)grandparents who are still active and in good health. Grandparents often head the family hierarchy. It was noticeable that some (great-)grandparents in a study of over 300 multigeneration families (Kaiser, 1989) displayed special characteristics or were bearers of the family tradition, the family heritage, or the like. Some grandfathers influenced the lives of their grandchildren more by conveying traditional norms and models rather than by their behavior. This does not only apply to the strong and powerful but also to the weaker, more inconspicuous (great-)grandfathers. In this academic sample, a third of the subjects depicted their grandfathers as "patriarchs," but said that they tended to have a weak position within the family and that they "were not taken particularly seriously" (Kaiser, 1989). They often did not pay much attention to their grandchildren; according to the grandchildren, the "nice, kind grandad" was more the exception than the rule.

The relationship between grandparents and grandchildren is often uncomplicated when it is free of disciplinary responsibility (Argyle & Henderson, 1986). Grandparenthood is often just as important as parenthood to those involved: they relive their own youth but also identify themselves with their own grandparents. They enjoy spoiling their grandchildren. Grandmothers more often have a good relationship to granddaughters than grandfathers to grandsons. However, about a third of grandparents have difficulties with the role because of differing opinions on child rearing. A quarter of grandparents feel like "distant relatives" (Argyle & Henderson, 1986; Sperling, 1983). According to a study by Wood and Robertson (1976), grandchildren had little to do with life satisfaction in older people. Argyle and Henderson (1986) surmise that this is due to a lack of close relationships between grandchildren and grandparents. The relationship could only be of personal significance if there were close ties.

The relationships between grandparents and grandchildren are thus very much influenced by the quality and quantity of relationships between parents and grandparents and thus depend on family constellations, forms, and structures. The less the parents in the above-mentioned samples (Kaiser, 1989) were separated and independent of their families of origin, and the closer they lived together, the greater the claim – especially of grandmothers – that they influenced the raising of their grandchildren and family life in general. This was particularly the case

- when several generations lived in one house or on the same piece of property,
- when one parent was ill or absent for a long time (soldiers, sailors, long-distance truck drivers),
- when the parental relationship was dysfunctional or interrupted by separation,
- when parents were "single parents" and thus relying on the support of the grandparents,
- when the grandparents acted as foster parents to their grandchildren (see below).

The grandmother frequently has a special meaning within the family for her daughters and their families, whom she often supports materially with child care or in crises (Argyle & Henderson, 1986; Sperling, 1983).

According to other results (Kaiser, 1989; Jürgens & Norpoth, 1986), many grandmothers stepped in to help take care of their grandchildren when the mothers were employed or the parents were unable to do so. Some also looked after their grandchildren on weekends or during holidays. Reports of good relationships with their grandmothers are given in particular by grandchildren whose relationship with their mother was less satisfactory because of career or family reasons. In these cases the grandmother acted as a substitute mother; in some cases they represented a "refuge" from unsatisfactory conditions in the parental home.

When parents felt disadvantaged by too close a bond between grandparents and grandchildren, or when they felt the boundaries between generations or in the personal sphere were being violated, a frequent result was conflicts between parents and grandparents on the one hand and loyalty problems between grandparents and grandchildren on the other. When the grandmother takes over functions from the mother, the mother can easily drift into the position of an elder sibling in relation to the child, which questions the generation boundaries and the parental role. This has major effects on the overall functioning of the family and, as a result of the ensuing conflicts and climatic changes, there are repercussions in the relationship between grandparents and grandchildren. Grandmothers who have become substitute mothers experience not only an increase in power but also quite often find that the responsibilities they have taken on are not (or no longer) in keeping with their needs and psychophysical capabilities. If they feel "compelled" to make such sacrifices, they usually expect reciprocal payments of gratitude, such as subordination and care in old age. In such cases, grandchildren can be "the cause" of reciprocal obligations and conflicts between parents and grandparents. In this type of context parents often exercise a strong influence on the relationships between grandparents and grandchildren through unconscious expectation fantasies. These can extend as far as delegating the responsibility to act as substitutes in unsolved problems (Crawford, 1981; Fischer, 1983; Lieberman, 1979; Richter, 1969; Robertson, 1977; Schwob, 1988).

A direct and intensive relationship between grandparents and grandchildren is less likely to exist:

- the greater the age on both sides, especially after the grandchildren enter puberty,
- when the grandparents' health declines, thus reducing their capacity to give attention to their grandchildren,
- the greater the physical distance between them,
- the greater the social and socioeconomic distance between children, parents, and grandparents,
- the less favorable the structures in the family are (e.g. in stepfamilies);

- the less frequent contacts are with the family of the parent living outside after the remarriage of divorced parents, or when the child lives with foster or adoptive parents (see below).

Despite all this, *indirect* influence and relationships between grandparents and grandchildren should not be underrated, as the grandparents were initially the primary source of socialization to the parents of their grandchildren. In this respect grandparents influence family structures, value hierarchies, concepts of life, traditions, and so forth, which are transferred to the grandchildren. When grandparents functionalize their children up to and into adulthood as the substitute for a partner, a deceased relative, or the like, the children are unlikely to be able to cultivate independent and satisfying pair relationships because they cannot separate from their parents. Many families have traditions that continue through generations, for instance blood relationship ties and lines of descendency that are given higher priority than the pair relationship (Kaiser, 1989; Schwob, 1988; Sperling, 1988). Such traditions reflect (often unconscious) family model concepts of partnership and family that are handed down to the grandchildren. At the same time the influences of grandparents were and are shaped by the conditions of the historical-societal and economic context that indicate the meaning of the family for existential security.

Thalmann (1971) was able to establish connections between disturbances in the marital harmony of both pairs of grandparents and the symptoms of their grandchildren. The fathers and mothers reported:

- that they had been brought up more strictly when the marriage of their own parents was less good,
- that they agreed with their parents' style of upbringing when family life had been experienced as harmonious,
- that they were less depressive and nervous when they considered family life in their family of origin to be harmonious (mothers only),
- that their own marriage was harmonious when they described the marriage of their parents also as harmonious.

Parents in Thalmann's study population who disagreed with the "mild" style of upbringing of their own parents and those who disagreed with their own strict upbringing, had children displaying stronger symptoms (Mattejat, 1985). Robins (1966) established that children of parents who previously had psychosocial problems suffered psychological disturbances more often than a control group. According to Frommer and O'Shea (1973), mothers who had experienced parental loss during their childhood had more marital and child-rearing problems than a control group. The behavior of the mother and of the father is strongly determined by the experiences they had with their respective parents. Thus it was demonstrated, for example, that parents who abused their children had often been abused themselves during childhood (Jürgens & Norpoth, 1986; Oliver & Taylor, 1971). In a questionnaire study DeFrain (1979) found out from parents that the role model of their parents was the most important determinant of their own parental behavior. Gersick (1979) reached similar conclusions. Radin (1980) found that women who had had happy experiences with their own fathers during childhood also had husbands who were strongly involved in the upbringing of the children. According to Sagi (1982), highly involved fathers displayed "expressive" and "instrumental" activities, thus providing their sons with effective paternal models. In his criticism of these studies, Fthenakis (1985) maintained that they were retrospective and gave too little consideration to the historic situation of the individual generations. He reaches the conclusion that fathers who registered below a certain level of paternal involvement probably compensated for the deficient availability of their own father during childhood, whereas fathers who registered above this level probably tried to imitate or excel their own fathers.

Sometimes the significance of grandparents for parents and children does not become clear until they die: their death often comes as a hard blow to the family, depleting resources and imposing a burden on the children. According to a study by Walsh (1982), 41% of children whose grandparents died around the time of their birth later developed schizophrenia, whereas children in a control population displayed a far lower morbidity rate.

In the triangle of grandparents, parents, and grandchildren, grandchildren play an important role in the relationship between parents and grandparents. This is particularly evident when, for instance, "a new relationship" develops between parents and grandparents on the birth of a "son and heir." The arrival of the new family member transforms the whole system, which in turn affects the triadic and dyadic relationships (Kaiser, 1989). As grandchildren are often less affected by encumbered relationships between parents and grandparents, they can often mediate to the advantage of the whole family and are more likely to be able to draw the generations closer together (Schwob, 1988). Conversely, grandparents can buffer disturbances in the parent–child relationship and offer the children possibilities of support and identification that the parents are unable to provide. The interweaving of dyadic relationships within the system context of the whole family is most evident in the three-generation constellation.

Uncles and aunts, cousins, nieces, and nephews

For most authors the family ends with the grandparents: scientific analyses tend to focus on the broader family circle only sporadically or in an anecdotal way. As a result, this section is relatively brief, although, admittedly, more research in this area would be welcome. This research deficit makes the rather restricted view of the family in psychology apparent.

According to the available literature, the intensity and frequency of contacts with uncles and aunts, with great-uncles and great-aunts, and with cousins are lower than with primary relatives. Spacial proximity and other direct forms of contact are of particular significance (Argyle & Henderson, 1986). About a third of families consider contact with these relatives important (Lüschen et al., 1985). Generally, family rules do not consider contacts to be obligatory, as is the case with immediate relatives. Contact occurs at family reunions of parents or grandparents with their siblings. In this respect the relationships between uncles, aunts, nieces, nephews, and cousins are essentially influenced by the relationships of the parents or grandparents to their siblings and should thus be viewed in the triadic context. Tradition-conscious families with pronounced clan consciousness lay particular emphasis on the careful cultivation of family cohesion and regular contacts. Studies established this particularly in old, tradition-conscious farming families and occasionally in academic and entrepreneurial families. In all these cases economic or professional reasons played a major role: those involved were connected by kinship, a family enterprise, or business relationships (Kaiser, 1989).

The larger the family, the more intricate the kin relationships. This increases the scope for selecting certain members and developing special relationships with them that are attractive because of their voluntary nature. According to the results of Adams (1968) and Kaiser (1989, 1991), many family members have favorite aunts or uncles, favorite nieces or nephews, and favorite cousins with whom friendly relationships are cultivated, similar to those with parents or siblings. Relationships with aunts and their children are often closer because relationships between mothers and their sisters are usually closer than those between mothers and their brothers (Argyle & Henderson, 1986). According to the results of Parish et al. (1991), approximately 15% of single young mothers and 10% of married young mothers in the United States receive child-care help from aunts and especially nieces who live nearby.

In relationships between cousins, same-sex relationships are usually preferred. This is particularly the case when no same-sex siblings of approximately the same age are available, when the cousins are of similar social status, and when they share similar interests. In the case of mixed-sex cousins it is often unclear whether the incest taboo is recognized. Marriage is possible in principle and often occurs, although sometimes eugenic arguments and family tradition oppose such links. Marriage between cousins in quite common in some places where dynastic or economic considerations play a significant role (Lévi-Strauss, 1981). According to our observations, uncles and aunts with special gifts or characteristics often function as models and benefactors for nieces and nephews, especially when the parents have deficits in this area (Kaiser, 1989).

Relations by marriage

Relations through marriage include above all parents-in-law, their sons- and daughters-in-law, and brothers- and sisters-in-law and their respective relatives. These include the partners of cousins, uncles, and aunts as well as their relatives. Relationships between them are characterized by the fact that people foreign to the family become closely linked with family members. As a result their relatives also come into some kind of contact. Whether and how relationships between distant relatives through marriage develop depends (initially) on the relationships that lead to the contact.

When relatives grow closer because of marriage it increases the size of the familial support system, but it also entails competition over other privileged family relationships and possibly over possession rights (Fischer, 1983; Sabean, 1984). The instability of in-law relationships is thus structurally preprogramed and increases with contact frequency. For example, approximately two-thirds of those questioned by Nauck (1987) had contact with their parents-in-law once a week or more. The parents-in-law of 70% of the families studied by Buhr, Strack, and Strohmeier (1987) were within less than 15 minutes' reach; according to Fauser (1982) 26% of families lived under the same roof; in rural areas this was as high as 50%.

The double-sided nature of relationships with in-laws is created basically by their great significance as a support system. All recent studies on this topic show that in most families the parents-in-law and other relatives are the most important source of support after the parents and children. According to Nauck's (1987) results, about 20% of parents-in-law participated in financing and 12% in constructing the family home. About 15% of those interviewed were helped by their brothers-in-law and 5% by other in-laws in constructing their home. In contrast, financial assistance was given by friends in 0.7% of cases and practical assistance by 25%. The study conducted by Fauser (1982) showed that between 48% and 62% of families can rely on their parents-in-law to look after their children during brief periods of absence. In areas where there is a lack of day-care places or there are time limits on child-care facilities, young mothers can usually only take up gainful employment when the children are looked after by their grandparents – that is, in 50% of the cases, by the parents-in-law (see Buhr et al., 1987). Being accepted in this type of support system is often not easy.

The families of origin of young married couples usually represent a fairly rigid system and they are not always prepared to simply integrate a new member. This is especially the case when the young couples have not separated sufficiently from their respective families or when parents-in-law disagree with the choice of partner (Kaiser, 1989, 1991; Minuchin, 1977; Reich, 1987). It should be taken into consideration that, as a result of the choice of partners, two more or less strange families are brought together whose members do not choose each other but still have to get along with each other and occasionally may have to work together. This is of greater relevance when an extended family is involved in a family enterprise, or with property, than when small nuclear families live far away from each other. Thus the in-law relations have numerous indirect ways of influencing a couple's relationship that can cloud the relationship between the in-laws and the partner marrying into the family.

If the ties between the partners and their families of origin are not yet sufficiently relaxed, this can make the establishment and definition of the pair dyad difficult because of loyalty conflicts (Kaiser, 1989; Kemmler-Drews & Sewerin, 1989; Reich, 1987). If a young couple fails to agree on certain limits and rules of social intercourse with the respective families, or on the respective value systems, misunderstandings and conflicts can easily occur: what one partner considers to be welcome attention from his or her family may be considered as interference from the in-laws by the other partner. This is more likely to occur when the young couple is less self-sufficient and lives close to the parents-in-law. Grandmothers often want more contact with their grandchildren than the parents wish (see above). Acceptance of material goods, taking up residence in the home or on the land of the parents-in-law, or the acceptance of services (help in the home and with child care, etc.) often creates dependence and boundary violations that "entitle" parents-in-law to reciprocal demands, such as subordination, good behavior, or less distance (Argyle & Henderson, 1986; Fischer, 1983; Reich, 1987; Kaiser, 1989). As dependence increases the daughter- or son-in-law slips into the role of an additional (wanted or unwanted) child of the parents-in-law and sibling to the partner; such diffusion of roles can lead to or indicate grave structural crises in the family. The relationships between parents-in-law and daughter- or son-in-law can only develop constructively when both the partnerships and the generations have clearly demarcated contours that are mutually respected. If, however, the partnership of the parents-in-law is under pressure or even nonexistent (widowed, single, etc.), and the relationship with the adult child is so close that the child even acts as a substitute partner, then the parents-in-law and the daughter- or son-in-law can easily become dangerous rivals.

This also applies to relationships between brothers- and sisters-in-law, partners of cousins, partners of aunts or uncles, and other members of in-law families (Kaiser, 1992a). Each is moderated by the (triadic) influence of the more intimate relationships with the closer relatives such as (a) siblings, cousins, uncles, and aunts, and (*b*) the partners. If siblings do not get on well or if they are indifferent to one another, usually the partner and his or her relatives also "have to" keep at a distance, as partner loyalty takes precedence. When sibling relationships are very close with a high degree of loyalty, the relationship with the brother- or sister-in-law can easily turn into rivalry. This danger is greater when the respective partner has not separated enough from the family of origin or does not give the partnership enough visible priority, and when the pair dyad does not define itself sufficiently.

When a couple gets on well together they usually expect mutual acceptance between the families of origin and the siblings and adherence to certain rules governing social intercourse (Argyle & Henderson, 1986). Temporary partnership conflicts do not initially affect relationships with sisters- and brothers-in-law. In the case of continuing partnership problems or separation, the sibling relationship often regains priority over partner loyalty and the sibling takes sides against the (ex-)sister- or brother-in-law, who is increasingly excluded.

With the exception of the relationship to parents-in-law, a certain lightheartedness is ascertainable in relationships between in-laws: contacts are usually relaxed and can be extended or cultivated if desired, or they can be kept at a distance. Even so, certain rules of social intercourse still have to be observed (Argyle & Henderson, 1986).

Members of stepfamilies

Several million stepchildren live in the United States and Western Europe. They live in *primary* stepfamilies, in which one of the parents is not biologically related to the children. Most stepchildren have regular contact with the parent living outside; this other family is termed the *secondary* stepfamily (Hoffmann-Riem, 1989). When both partners introduce children from previous relationships into the family, or when they have common offspring alongside the stepchildren, this is termed a *combined* stepfamily (Furstenberg, 1987a; Hoffmann-Riem, 1989; Ihinger-Tallman & Pasley, 1987; Krähenbühl, Jellouschek, Kohaus-Jellouschek & Weber, 1979; Visher & Visher, 1979). A stepfamily is created in the psychological sense (the formal legal aspect is of less interest here) when: (a) widowed persons with children remarry; (b) divorcees with children from previous relationships remarry; or (c) a person establishes a nonmarital companionship with a single-parent family in which the parent is separated or widowed. In as much as sooner or later the majority of single parents enter a stable relationship, the *nonmarital* stepfamily is increasing in significance and may well represent the most widespread form of psychological stepfamily.

The stepparent enters the family *in addition* to the biological parent and does not replace him or her. Most stepchildren have a close relationship either with the parent living outside or with the stepparent. Mothers who live outside keep in closer contact with their children than fathers; contact often decreases over time (Coleman & Ganong, 1990).

As time progresses, single-parent families (single, widowed, or divorced) establish themselves as an *independent* system with its own structures and clear demarcations. If the mother or father enters a new relationship, this by no means implies that the old system is flexible enough to integrate the new partner. At first the new partner simply combines with the existing system. The new pair dyad can only consolidate itself under difficult circumstances. Here, the resources that each partner introduces into the relationship are of particular importance; so too is the level of satisfaction with their former single status (Crosbie-Burnett & Giles-Sims, 1991). If the partners chose each other out of love, this does not necessarily mean that the stepchildren and stepparents get along well and are emotionally open with each other (Heekerens, 1990). According to Furstenberg's results (1987a), a third of the children questioned did not regard their stepparents as family members on genealogical grounds. According to some studies, the relationships between stepparents and stepchildren, particularly in combined families, are generally weaker and become more conflict-laden over the years (Brand & Clingempeel, 1987; Coleman & Ganong, 1990). Other results indicate that parent–child relationships in stepfamilies need not be any worse than in other families (Coleman & Ganong, 1987; Ganong & Coleman, 1987), especially when the pair relationship of the parents is good.

There are a number of significant differences between stepfamilies and core familes (Furstenberg, 1987a, 1987b; Coleman & Ganong, 1990; Hoffmann-Riem, 1989; Jürgens & Norpoth, 1986; Kaiser, Rieforth, Winkler & Ebbers, 1990; Krähenbühl et al., 1986; Visher & Visher, 1979):

- Stepfamilies are typically handicapped by the prehistory of their members. They are often established as a result of previous critical situations: families break up as a result of death, divorce, or separation and the remaining members often enter into new relationships without having come to terms with the accompanying experiences or the characteristics that led to the separation, for example dysfunctional problem-solving strategies (Bernstein, 1990; Heekerens, 1990; Hoffmann-Riem, 1989; Kemmler-Drews & Sewerin, 1989; Reich, 1987; Visher & Visher, 1979).

- A stepfamily can include different types of children – the mother's children and the father's children from their previous relationship(s) or from previous divorced stepfamilies, and common offsprings. In combined stepfamilies there is no uniform sibling subsystem, but two or more different subsystems each with its specific internal structure and relationships to the biological parents and half-siblings.

- Stepfamilies contain different, competing family structures and cultures, to which members usually cling out of (un)conscious loyalty to their original family systems.
- Because of contacts with the external parent, there are often no clear family and pair boundaries and thus no protected private spheres, especially for the children, but also for the parents in relation to their former partners.
- Stepparents have actual parental duties toward and relationships with the stepchildren, but they have no parental rights, which usually remain with the external parent. This can lead to conflicts in role and loyalty and to ambivalence.
- The need to regulate and reach understandings is increased by the complicated structures and the prehistories and often does not correspond with the communicative skills and problem-solving competencies of those involved. Second and third marriages are often additionally handicapped by a tradition of problems and separations in the partners' families of origin (Heekerens, 1990; Kaiser, 1989; Reich, 1987). In view of the handicaps from family prehistory, the parental role often absorbs a great deal of time and energy at the expense of consolidating the pair relationship (Bernstein, 1990; Coleman & Ganong, 1990). Stepparents are also under pressure to counteract prejudices against the "nasty stepmother or stepfather" and this can make children wary at first (Ihinger-Tallman & Pasley, 1987). Especially stepmothers with small children feel easily stressed, and this can have a negative effect on the pair relationship (Kurdek, 1990). As a result many families find themselves caught up in continual endurance tests, which lead to renewed separation more often than in "normal" families (Furstenberg, 1987a, 1987b; Visher & Visher, 1979, 1989). Children from problematic stepfamilies suffer more from psychological and psychosomatic disturbances (e.g., Mattejat, 1985) and this affects all the members. In contrast to this, children from well-functioning stepfamilies show no signs of increased morbidity (Baydar, 1988; Clingempeel & Segal, 1986; Ganong & Coleman, 1987; Hetherington, Cox & Cox, 1985). According to Steinberg (1987), stepchildren are similar to those from single-parent families in that they are more strongly oriented toward their peers; they are more susceptible to antisocial behavior; they engage earlier in sexual relationships; and they marry earlier and have a more positive attitude toward divorce (Coleman & Ganong, 1987; Kinnaird & Gerrard, 1986).

Because of their structural problems, stepfamilies probably have a higher risk of illness, separation, and divorce. Many need family therapeutical help in order to transform the existing single-parent and sibling subsystems into a new, common, comprehensive system, and to develop and realize models and ideas of enjoyable cooperative living in such a complex group. Demarcating and cultivating the parental pair dyad seem to be of particular importance but also present the most difficulties.

Foster children and foster families

If a family does not wish, or is unable, to care for its child either permanently or temporarily, the child can live with relatives or in a foster family. Care by relatives (usually grandparents) is less restricted by legalities and can usually be organized in a more flexible way, as relationships between parents and grandparents are generally closer. A differentiation is made between two types of fosterage: (1) parental care is *complemented*; (2) parental care is *replaced* (Müller, 1991). Complementary fosterage in the form of hourly, daily, or interval child care (e.g., by a childminder) is organized by the parents or by a social institution when a child cannot be otherwise looked after. However, the child's life is still centered in the family of origin. In contrast, permanent fosterage replaces the family of origin and gives the child a new home when the parents are unable to care for their child (in an appropriate way), or when the child may even need to be protected from them.

Permanently fostered children have often suffered very trying experiences and privations early in life before they have been removed from their families and placed in foster families. But even foster families have their problems: usually, they not only take in children with difficulties but also have to come to terms with a complicated network of system interactions, including, for instance, the families of origin, previous foster families, institutions, legal representatives, and courts. In most countries fosterage is regulated by law.

Foster children and their family of origin

The family of origin of children who are being cared for by relatives is generally different from that of children in unrelated foster families: care by relatives is only possible when the family system is still in working order and able to balance out disturbances in some areas. When children are taken in by relatives they remain within the (extended) family of origin (see above), but change from one subsystem to another (e.g., grandparents, aunt). In this case, role competencies change within the family. There is a long tradition of children being cared for by relatives if possible, when parents are in a difficult situation. Single parents or couples who need help with child care during illness or in periods of work transition often resort to their own parents for this (see above). This can sometimes result in parents and their children shifting into a kind of sibling relationship as a result of the parental role taken on by the grandparents. Sometimes this can have a permanent effect on the family structure, relationships, and hierarchy (Kaiser, 1989, 1995a).

Permanently fostered children in unrelated families usually originate from families that often display dysfunctions over generations. Numerous structural problems in the family and difficult external conditions, such as single parents working away from home, often lead to disturbances and crises in the parent–child relationship and in child development (Jürgens & Norpoth, 1986; Kaiser, 1992b, 1993a, 1995a; Niederberger & Zeindl, 1989). Before the child is placed in a foster home it has almost always suffered from difficult circumstances for a long period. This often has a lasting effect on the triadic relations between the removed child, its foster family, and the family of origin (see below). The situation is often made more difficult by loyalty conflicts that the child experiences toward its foster parents and its biological parents if a competitive relationship develops between the two (DJI, 1987; Nienstedt & Westermann, 1989). These inter-action problems between two family systems often result in the end of the foster relationship: according to various studies, between 20% and 50% of foster children are "removed" one or more times. Heun (1984) reported up to 10, Olson (1982) up to 21 "replacements." It is not surprising that many of the affected children later have great difficulty in forming relationships (e.g., Blandow, 1972; Goldbeck, 1984; Janus, 1989; Niederberger & Zeindl, 1989; Schepank, 1987; Sonnewend, 1982). Let us now take a look at families who foster children.

Specific structures in foster families

Foster families are families that take children for a limited (usually longer) period of time into their homes. Foster families can be described as systems with specific structures. While only the internal family structure is changed when relatives care for the children, nonrelated foster families also come into contact with numerous other ecosocial systems. Both types of foster family are subject to specific biographically determined changes (e.g., Budde & Rau, 1981; Carter & McGoldrick, 1980; Kaiser, Rieforth, Winkler & Ebbers, 1988; Kaiser, 1993b, 1995a; Masur, 1982; Minuchin, 1977).

Families that foster nonrelated children do this with particular motives that are of consequence in the course of caring for the child: apart from social motivation, a role is also played by transgenerational patterns, the desire for new tasks in life, and improving the functioning of the family (Goldbeck, 1984; Kaiser et al., 1990; Maywald & Weißmann, 1994). Only in a few cases are the foster parents sufficiently informed about the child's family of origin, its history, and its problems.

When a foster child enters the family (Felgenhauer, 1983; Kaiser, 1993b, 1995a; Krähenbühl et al., 1986), changes such as the following are unavoidable:

- The (sub)system receives a new member with special status.
- The sibling subsystem and the family structures change.
- Two family subsystems (in the case of relatives who foster) or two different family systems (the family of origin and the foster family) confront each other, which causes definition, regulating, and loyalty problems.
- The foster family enters into complex interactions with institutions (child-care authorities, special schools, etc.) in which it has a very weak legal position, as it is not entitled to take any major independent decisions on behalf of the child.

Fosterage is designed to take into account the views of all participants, to satisfy wishes, and to solve problems. Conflicts are unavoidable, as the intentions of the participants are often highly divergent or incompatible: children who have suffered from their previous background are hardly in a position to help solve the problems facing their foster parents. Conversely, only a few foster parents are able and willing to take on therapeutic responsibilities toward the child or even its family. As a rule, neither the family of origin nor the foster family is usually in a position to predict the long-term effects and side effects of fosterage: when the foster family takes in and integrates a new member, this alters the sibling constellation and forces it into often undesired contact with authorities and the family of origin. Gradually the family of origin becomes alienated from its child, which in turn can lead to the legal prevention of reunion. In foster cases legal guardianship usually remains with the child's parents, which means that the foster parents are compelled to cooperate with them at all times. This often proves to be difficult and sometimes even impossible. After all, the child was usually officially removed from the parents because they were unable to care for their child in an appropriate way. The various forms of conflict between the family of origin and the foster family, the loyalty conflicts experienced by the child, and the uncertainty about the duration of the foster relationship often expose the relationship between the foster child and the foster family to tough endurance tests. Both sides desire interpersonal relationships that, according to the contract, should not be formed: double-bind and other problems are preprogrammed. Foster families are thus often delicate, easily destabilized systems that nonetheless can provide a harmonious home when foster parents succeed in securing a well-functioning family (Felgenhauer, 1983; Kaiser et al., 1990; Kaiser, 1993b, 1995a, 1995b; Müller, 1991).

Today, many experts (Kaiser, 1992b, 1995a, 1995b; Müller, 1991; Nienstedt & Westermann, 1989) plead in favor of providing families experiencing problems with speedy and comprehesive preventive counseling and support to improve their functioning, thus making placements in foster families an exception. Should such placements be necessary, then foster parents should be carefully selected, informed, trained, and offered refresher courses as well as the possibility of permanent supervision. Self-help groups and organizations of foster parents also play an important role here. After a relatively short period of time the decision should be taken – in the interest of the child's well-being – as to where it should stay permanently, so that it can form a continuous attachment. Replacements should be avoided on principle.

Adoptive children, their parents, and adoptive families

The problems in adoptive families are similar to those in foster families to the extent that in both cases the families have biologically nonrelated children. This section concentrates on the differences between adoptive families and foster families.

In Western industrialized countries, about 25% of marriages remain involuntarily childless (Parent, van Balen, Bierkens & van Tongeren, 1992). The comparatively small number of children available for adoption can be explained by the fact that many parents who are unable or do not wish to rear their child themselves are not prepared to have their child adopted. They prefer to place their child in a foster family or a home so that they can retain guardianship rights as well as the possibility of reclaiming the child (Hoksbergen, 1993; Müller, 1991; Swientek, 1986; Textor, 1993). For this reason, a sizable number of prospective adoptive parents make efforts to adopt children from countries outside their own, for example from developing countries.

Official institutions face a particular problem when forecasting the development of relationships between the adoptive child and members of the adoptive family, which often includes not only the parents but also their natural children and other relatives. Follow-up studies are not available as yet. According to Swientek (1986), the relationship can present problems when, as in 10% to 30% of cases, the parents unexpectedly produce a child, which might result in the adoptive child being forced into the background.

The original parents

Many studies on adoptive families tend to ignore the original (often unmarried) parents, although they are an indelible part of the history of the adoptive family with whom a kind of "nonrelationship" exists. The fact still remains that, for most mothers and many fathers, consenting to the adoption of their child represents a critical situation in their lives and as such affects both their personality and their future (Hoffmann-Riem, 1989; Kaiser, 1992b; Swientek, 1986). This is particularly the case when the parent or parents were pressured into adoption by authorities, social workers, or relatives (see Leuthold, 1959; Swientek, 1986). In the majority of cases, mothers consent to adoption primarily or exclusively for economic reasons (Kaiser, 1992b; Napp-Peters, 1978).

Many biological parents reported feelings of painful loss and sadness years after consenting to adoption. Many wish that their children know that they still think about them and would like to have some form of contact with them (Lifton, 1982; Sorosky, Baran & Pannor, 1979). Apart from the sadness, they also suffer from discrimination as "cruel parents" and the pressure of having to hide the problem (Swientek, 1986). The suffering of parents who have consented to adoption also has to be seen against the background of a difficult transgenerational prehistory: 28 of the 75 mothers who had consented to adoption and were interviewed by Swientek reported a nonexistent or difficult relationship with their own mothers. In their families of origin they had missed the experience of being wanted, loved, and accepted. More than a third of these mothers came from extremely desolate families with low functional capacity and pathogenic structures that provided no constructive parental role models (see also Kaiser, 1992b, 1995a).

As a rule, the children's natural fathers have a steady, usually long-term relationship with the mothers. In less than a quarter of the cases the father is only briefly encountered or unknown. A few cases record incestuous relationships. Just over a half of the fathers are foreign nationals (Swientek, 1986). In her overview of the relevant literature, Swientek concludes that there was more or less a balance between long-term relationships between the mother and the father who lived in difficult socioeconomic and psychosocial circumstances (including delinquency, poverty, psychological illness, family problems) and brief relationships. She also complains of a lack of research on the natural fathers of adoptive children. There are extremely few studies on family structures and conditions (for preliminary statistics in Germany, see Kaiser, 1992b), legal and institutional structures, and the behavior of authorities that investigate the system context in which consent to adoption comes about.

Adoptive children

Adoptive children are generally transferred to the adoptive family a few weeks after birth. As adoptive children are usually unwanted children of very young mothers or of mothers in conflict situations, it can be assumed that pregnancy and birth took place under difficult conditions that could have had a detrimental effect on the health and development of the child (Janus, 1989; see above). Because of legal regulations, adoptive children do not know their natural parents and at first do not know anything about their true origin. According to experts, young children sense very early on that something is amiss with their origin and are disconcerted in their relationship to their adoptive parents (Ebertz, 1987; Hawellek, 1990; Hoffmann-Riem, 1989; Hoksbergen, Juffer & Textor, 1994; Lifton, 1982; Keller-Thoma, 1987; Kowal & Schilling, 1985; Müller, 1991; Sorosky et al., 1979; Stein & Hoopes, 1985). The stronger the doubts and the later they are told about their origins, the more negative the effects are likely to be on the child's self-esteem and its relationship to the adoptive parents. The child is stuck between the adoptive parents and the fantasy of its natural parents, and this can lead to a lifelong ambivalence toward both. The continuity of the self in the past, present, and future is jeopardized in the case of adoptive children because their history is partially in the dark (Aselmeier-Ihrig, 1984; Ebertz, 1987; Mackie, 1982; Swientek, 1993). About half of the children are interested in getting to know their natural parents (Keller-Thoma, 1987; Knoll & Rehn, 1985). Usually the search is started during adulthood, in most cases by children with a less satisfactory relationship with their adoptive parents (Swientek, 1993; Textor, 1993). Adoptive children easily experience feelings of inferiority in peer groups, which can result in difficulty with contacts. When looking for a romantic partner later on, they are sometimes disconcerted by the thought that they may meet up with a true sibling without knowing that they are blood relations (Hawellek, 1990; Hoffmann-Riem, 1989; Hoksbergen et al., 1994).

Adoptive parents

The relationship with the child can develop differently depending on the status of the adoptive parents. Those eligible for adoption include:

- a relative, particularly when the parents die. In this case existing family relationships are intensified. Here, it is of significance whether the relatives' primary interest is family loyalty or interest in the child.

- a stepparent, when the natural mother or father declares agreement. In this case the above-mentioned discussion on stepparents applies.
- a nonrelated third person from the original, or a different, cultural background. Because of the large number of adoptive parents seeking children, many children come from developing countries. Racial, cultural, language, and other differences may give rise to numerous problems within and outside the family.

Many adoptive parents are still influenced by the often unresolved question of not being able to produce any (more) children. For many, this symbolizes a deficit in their sexual or pair identity as well as in their life plan. In such cases the adoption is often kept secret in order to create the appearance of a "normal" family (Hawellek, 1990; Hoffmann-Riem, 1989). Here, the adoptive child has the "task" of helping its adoptive parents to overcome this crisis in life. The arrival of the adoptive child often appears abrupt, as the usual preparatory process of pregnancy and birth, which gradually attunes the parents and their environment to the child, are missing in the case of adoption. Getting to know each other and overcoming the strangeness has to take place in the legally prescribed phase of "adoption care," which is about 12 months in the case of infants and somewhat longer in the case of older children.

In contrast to natural parents, adoptive parents also have the right to express preferences on gender, age, origin, and other characteristics before they receive a child. This means that from the start, criteria are fixed that the child later has to satisfy. If the child does not satisfy these criteria it is more or less "in breach of contract" (Hawellek, 1990; Müller, 1991). On the other hand and in contrast to natural parents or foster parents, prospective adoptive parents have to subject themselves to scrutiny by the appropriate authorities. Thus adoption is generally carried out by members of the middle class who are aware of their competencies as parents.

The natural parents, the adoptive child, and the adoptive family are thus linked for life. The natural parents can easily stand between the adoptive parents and the adoptive children in their imaginations. They can act as a fantasy target for associations such as longings, fears, or competitive feelings. This effect is increased by information deficits about the pre- and perinatal development of the child as well as about the nature and conditions of the actual birth. Such information is usually an essential part of family history and family structures in "normal" families. In addition, lay psychological attitudes interpret characteristics and behavior as forms of virtually unalterable hereditary or family predispositions, and this can encourage the idea of the pure-blooded family pedigree. The different and unknown prehistory further documents the palpable difference between adoptive parenthood and natural parenthood (Hoffmann-Riem, 1989;

Hoksbergen et al., 1994; Swientek, 1986, 1993). The unknown genealogy could be picked up later and used as an "argument" by the adoptive parents when difficulties arise, thus aggravating the situation.

According to present research results the development of adoptive children is more positive when:

- adoption takes place as early as possible,
- the child is informed as early as possible,
- the adoptive family has a positive attitude toward the child's prehistory and family of origin,
- the adoptive parent–child relationship is good,
- adoptive families are taken seriously as a special type of family,
- the social environment accepts adoption and talks about it openly.

Conclusion

The following conclusion can be drawn from the presented approaches and results: relationships in the extended family and different family forms can be formally described and explored in their (sub)cultural context. They can be differentiated according to intragenerational (e.g., cousins) and intergenerational (grandparents and grandchildren) relationships that are expressed, for instance, in age and status gradients. Further differences exist in the presence or absence of blood relations of second or more grades.

No matter how heterogeneous relationships in the extended family and different family forms may be, they still display certain similarities:

- They are mediated at first by close relatives or institutions and then formed within a framework of family rules and dynamics; without exception, they are all influenced by other close family relationships, structures, and constellations; they are changed, qualitatively and quantitatively, and sometimes even ended when more important family relationships call for this.
- They are subject to changes in life cycles and family cycles.
- Family relationships are subject to certain legal regulations that sometimes include permanent specifications (e.g., inheritance laws).
- They form the basis of mutual loyalty, dependence, and support relationships of a more or less obligatory nature, which extends the pool of resources of those involved but also creates conflict potential.

How the participants subjectively experience and shape these relationships depends not only on their formal and interactional characteristics but also on the family and social context, the situation, and other influencing variables. Family relationships thus take place and are embedded within a more complex context. This complexity presents a huge challenge to social scientific research methods. Thus, it is hardly surprising that a great number of wishes still remain unfulfilled in the development of theory and applied research on different family forms and relationships in the extended family.

References

Adamaszek, M. (1994). *Leibliches Befinden in Familienkontexten. Genographische Mehrebenenanalysen in der Gesundheitsbildung.* Unpublished dissertation, Universität Oldenburg.

Adams, B. N. (1968). *Kinship in an urban setting.* Chicago: Markham.

Argyle, M., & Henderson, M. (1986). *Die Anatomie menschlicher Beziehungen. Spielregeln des Zusammenlebens.* Paderborn: Junfermann.

Aselmeier-Ihrig, M. (1984). Das Selbstverständnis der Adoptivfamilie: Eine Familie wie jede andere – oder ganz anders? *Unsere Jugend, 36,* 238–241.

Baydar, N. (1988). Effects of parental seperation and reentry into union on the emotional well-being of children. *Journal of Marriage and the Family, 50,* 967–981.

Bernstein, A. C. (1990). *Die Patchworkfamilie. Wenn Väter oder Mütter in neuen Ehen weitere Kinder bekommen.* Zürich: Kreuz Verlag.

Blandow, J. (1972). *Rollendiskrepanzen in der Pflegefamilie.* München: Juventa.

Brand, E., & Clingempeel, G. (1987). The interdependence of marital and stepparent–stepchild relationships and children's psychological adjustment: Research findings and clinical implications. *Family Relations, 36,* 140–145.

Budde, H., & Rau, H. (1981). Unterbringung von verhaltensauffälligen Kindern in Pflegefamilien – Erfahrungen bei der Auswahl und Differenzierung im Rahmen eines Pflegeelternprojektes. *Praxis der Kinderpsychologie und Kinderpsychiatrie, 30*(5), 165–173.

Buhr, P., Strack, P., & Strohmeier, K. P. (1987). *Lebenslage und Alltagsorganisation junger Familien in Nordrhein-Westfalen – regionale Differenzierungen und Veränderungen im Zeitablauf.* Bielefeld: IBS-Materialien, 26.

Bundesverband der Pflege- und Adoptiveltern (1993). *Handbuch für Pflege- und Adoptiveltern.* Münster: Bundesverband der Pflege- und Adoptiveltern e.V.

Carter, E. A., & McGoldrick, M. (1980). *The family life cycle: A framework for family therapy.* New York: Gardner.

Claessens, D., & Menne, F. W. (1973). Zur Dynamik der bürgerlichen Familie und ihrer möglichen Alternative. In D. Claessens & P. Milhoffer (Eds.), *Familiensoziologie.* Frankfurt: Fischer.

Clingempeel, G., & Segal, S. (1986). Stepparent–stepchild relationships and the psychological adjustment of children in stepmother and stepfather families. *Child Development, 57,* 474–484.

Coleman, M., & Ganong, L. (1987). Marital conflict in stepfamilies: Effects on children. *Youth and Society, 19,* 151–172.

(1990). Remarriage and stepfamily research in the 1980's: Increased interest in an old family form. *Journal of Marriage and the Family, 52,* 925–940.

Crawford, M. (1981). Not disengaged: Grandparents in literature and reality. *Sociological Review, 29,* 499–519.

Crosbie-Burnett, M., & Giles-Sims, J. (1991). Marital power in stepfather families: A test of normative resource theory. *Journal of Marriage and the Family, 4,* 484–496.

DeFrain, J. (1979). Androgynous parents tell who they are and what they need. *Family Coordinator, 28,* 237–243.

DJI (Deutsches Jugendinstitut) (Ed.) (1987). *Handbuch Beratung im Pflegekinderbereich.* München: DJI.

Duvall, E. M. (1977). *Marriage and family development* (5th Ed.). New York: Lippincott.

Ebertz, B. (1987). *Adoption als Identitätsproblem. Zur Bewältigung der Trennung von biologischer Herkunft und sozialer Zugehörigkeit.* Freiburg: Lambertus.

Fauser, R. (1982). *Zur Isolationsproblematik von Familien.* München: DJI.

Felgenhauer, U. (1983). Perspektiven für Pflegekinder. *Jugendhilfe, 58,* 31–36.

Fischer, L. (1983). Mothers and mothers-in-law. *Journal of Marriage and the Family, 45,* 187–192.

Frommer, E. A., & O'Shea, G. (1973). The importance of childhood experience in relation to problems of marriage and family building. *British Journal of Psychiatry, 123,* 157–160.

Fthenakis, W. E. (1985). *Väter, Bd. 1: Zur Psychologie der Vater-Kind-Beziehung. Bd. 2: Zur Vater-Kind-Beziehung in verschiedenen Familienstrukturen.* München: Urban & Schwarzenberg.

Fünfter Familienbericht (1994). *Familien und Familienpolitik im geeinten Deutschland – Zukunft des Humanvermögens.* Bonn: Bundesministerium für Familie und Senioren.

Furstenberg, F. F. (1987a). Fortsetzungsehen. Ein neues Lebensmuster und seine Folgen. *Soziale Welt, 38,* 29–39.

(1987b). The new extended family: The experience of parents and children after remarriage. In M. Ihinger-Tallman & K. Pasley (Eds.), *Remarriage and stepparenting* (pp. 42–61). Newbury Park, CA: Sage.

Furstenberg, F., Jr., & Nord, C. (1985). Parenting apart: Patterns of child-rearing after marital disruption. *Journal of Marriage and the Family, 47,* 893–904.

Ganong, L., & Coleman, M. (1987). Stepchildren's perception of their parents. *Journal of Genetic Psychology, 148,* 5–17.

Gersick, K. E. (1979). Fathers by choice: Divorced men who receive custody of their children. In G. Levinger & O. C. Moles (Eds.), *Divorce and separation: Context, cause and consequences.* New York: Basic Books.

Gilbert, R., Christensen, A., Margolin, G. (1984). Patterns of alliances in nondistressed and multiproblem families. *Family Process, 23,* 75–87.

Goldbeck, L. (1984). Pflegeeltern im Rollenkonflikt – Aufgaben einer psychologischen Betreuung von Pflegefamilien. *Praxis der Kinderpsychologie und Kinderpsychiatrie, 33,* 308–317.

Hawellek, C. (1990). Die therapeutische Basis. *Familiendynamik, 2,* 113–124.

Heekerens, H. P. (1988/1990). *Die zweite Ehe. Wiederheirat nach Scheidung und Verwitwung.* Weinheim: Deutscher Studienverlag.

Hess, R. D., & Handel, G. (1975). *Familienwelten. Kommunikation und Verhaltensstile in Familien.* Düsseldorf: Econ.

Hetherington, E. M., Cox, M., & Cox, R. (1985). Long term effects of divorce and remarriage on the adjustment of children. *Journal of the American Academy of Child Psychiatry, 24,* 518–530.

Heun, H. D. (1984). *Pflegekinder im Heim. DJI-Forschungsbericht.* München: DJI.

Hill, R. (1971). Modern systems theory and the family: A confrontation. *Social Science Informations, 10,* 7–26.

Hill, R., & Mattesich, P. (1979). Family development theory and life-span development. In P. B. Baltes & O. G. Brim (Eds.), *Life-span development and behavior* (Vol. 2, pp. 161–204). New York: Academic Press.

Hoffmann-Riem, C. (1989). Elternschaft ohne Verwandschaft: Adoption, Stiefbeziehung und heterologe Insemination. In R. Nave-Herz & M. Markefka (Eds.), *Handbuch der Familien- und Jugendforschung* (Bd. 1). Neuwied: Luchterhand.

Hoksbergen, R. A. C. (1993). Auslandsadoptionen: Deutsche, niederländische und andere Forschungsergebnisse. In R. A. C. Hoksbergen & M. R. Textor (Eds.), *Adoption: Grundlagen, Vermittlung, Nachbetreuung, Beratung* (pp. 63–90). Freiburg: Lambertus.

Hoksbergen, R. A. C., Juffer, F., & Textor, M. R. (1994). Attachment und Identität von Adoptivkindern. *Praxis der Kinderpsychologie und Kinderpsychiatrie, 43,* 339–344.

Huinink, J. (1987). Soziale Herkunft, Bildung und Alter bei der Geburt des ersten Kindes. *Zeitschrift für Soziologie, 16,* 367–384.

Ihinger-Tallman, M., & Pasley, K. (1987). *Remarriage.* Newbury Park, CA: Sage.

Janus, L. (1989). *Psychoanalyse der vorgeburtlichen Lebenszeit und des Geburtserlebens.* Freiburg: Centaurus.

Jürgens, M., & Norpoth, A. (1986). *Familienstrukturen und Fremdplazierung. Eine Untersuchung über Herkunftsfamilien von Heim- und Pflegekindern.* Unpublished. Diplomarbeit. Oldenburg: Universität Oldenburg.

Kaiser, P. (1989). *Familienerinnerungen. Zur Psychologie der Mehrgenerationenfamilie.* Heidelberg: Asanger.

(1991). *Partnerwahl im Kontext der Mehrgenerationenfamilie. Schriftenreihe der Arbeitsgruppe Familientherapie 2.* Oldenburg: Universität Oldenburg.

(1992a). *Beziehungen unter angeheirateten Verwandten.* Oldenburg: Unveröffentlichtes Manuskript.

(1992b). Das Pflege-/Adoptivkind und seine Ursprungsfamilie. In Landesverband der Pflege- und Adoptiveltern in Bayern (Ed.), *Das Pflege-*

/Adoptivkind und seine Ursprungsfamilie. Dokumentation der Fachtagung des Landesverbandes der Pflege- und Adoptiveltern in Bayern e.V. vom 26.9. 1992 in Kitzingen (pp. 8–21). Aichach-Klingen: Landesverband der Pflege- und Adoptiveltern in Bayern.

(1993a). Pflegefamilien und ihre Systemkontexte. In P. Kaiser (Ed.), *Psycho-Logik helfender Institutionen. Beiträge zu einer verbesserten Nutzerfreundlichkeit der Einrichtungen des Sozial- und Gesundheitswesens* (pp. 79–104). Heidelberg: Asanger.

(1993b). Pflegefamilien im Netzwerk der Systeme. *Zeitschrift für Familienforschung, 5,* 5–41.

(1995a). Strukturelle Besonderheiten von Pflegefamilien. In M. R. Textor & P. K. Warndorf (Eds.), *Familienpflege: Forschung – Vermittlung – Beratung.* Freiburg: Lambertus.

(1995b). Beratung von Pflegefamilien nach dem Systemischen Mehrebenenmodell. In M. R. Textor & P. K. Warndorf (Eds.), *Familienpflege: Forschung – Vermittlung – Beratung.* Freiburg: Lambertus.

Kaiser, P., Rieforth, J., Winkler, H., & Ebbers, F. (1988). Selbsthilfe-Supervision und Familienberatung bei Pflegefamilien. *Praxis der Kinderpsychologie und Kinderpsychiatrie, 8,* 290–297.

(1990). Strukturprobleme von Pflegefamilien. *Familiendynamik, 2,* 125–140.

Kaufmann, F. X. (1980). *Sozialpolitik und familiale Sozialisation. Zur Wirkungsweise öffentlicher Sozialleistungen.* Stuttgart: Schriftenreihe des Bundesministers für Jugend, Familie und Gesundheit.

Keller-Thoma, P. (1987). *Adoption aus der Sicht des Adoptiv "kindes."* Zürich: Schweizerischer Gemeinnütziger Frauenverein/Adoptivkindervermittlung.

Kemmler-Drews, R., & Sewerin, C. (1989). *Familiale Hintergründe von Ehescheidungen – eine empirische Untersuchung.* Unpublished. Diplomarbeit. Oldenburg: Universität Oldenburg.

Kinnaird, K., & Gerrard, M. (1986). Premarital sexual behavior and attitudes toward marriage and divorce among young women as a function of their mother's marital status. *Journal of Marriage and the Family, 48,* 757–765.

Knoll, K. D., & Rehn, M.-L. (1985). *Adoption. Studie über den Adoptionserfolg und die psychosoziale Integration von Adoptierten.* Nürnberg: Diakonisches Werk Bayern.

Kohaus-Jellouschek, M. (1984). Nachwort. In U. Köhler, *Du bist gar nicht meine Mutter: Stiefmütter erzählen* (pp. 273–286). München: Droemer Knaur.

Kowal, K. A., & Schilling, K. M. (1985). Adoption through the eyes of adult adoptees. *American Journal of Orthopsychiatry, 55,* 354–362.

Kramer, J. R. (1985). *Family interfaces: Transgenerational patterns.* New York: Brunner & Mazel.

Krähenbühl, V., Jellouschek, H., Kohaus-Jellouschek, M., & Weber, R. (1986). *Stieffamilien: Struktur, Entwicklung, Therapie.* Freiburg: Lambertus.

Kurdek, L. A. (1990). Effects of child age on the marital quality and psychological distress of newly married mothers and stepfathers. *Journal of Marriage and the Family, 52,* 81–86.

L'Abate, L. (1990). *Building family competence. Primary and secondary prevention strategies.* Newbury Park, CA: Sage.

Lee, G. R. (1984). Status of the elderly: Economic and familial antecedents. *Journal of Marriage and the Family, 46,* 267–275.

Leuthold, E. (1959). *Ein Beitrag zur Problematik der Kindesadoption und deren psychische Rückwirkungen auf die leibliche Mutter.* Dissertation, Zürich.

Lévi-Strauss, C. (1981). *Die elementaren Strukturen der Verwandschaft.* Frankfurt a.M.: Suhrkamp.

Lewis, J. M. (1988). The transition to parenthood: II. Stability and change in marital structure. *Family Process, 27*(3), 273–284.

Lieberman, S. (1979). *Transgenerational family therapy.* London: Sage.

Lifton, B. J. (1982). *Adoption.* Stuttgart: Klett Cotla.

Litwak, E. (1985). *Helping the elderly.* New York: Guilford.

Lüschen, G. (1989). Verwandtschaft, Freundschaft, Nachbarschaft. In R. Nave-Herz & M. Markefka (Eds.), *Handbuch der Familien und Jugendforschung* (pp. 435–452). Neuwied: Luchterhand.

Lüschen, G., Haavio-Mannila, E., Stolte-Heiskamen, V., & Ward, C. (1985). Familie, Verwandtschaft und Ritual im Wandel. In H. W. Franz (Ed.), *Deutscher Soziologentag* (pp. 25–29). Opladen: Westdeutscher Verlag.

Mackie, A. J. (1982). Families of adopted adolescents. *Journal of Adolescence, 5,* 167–178.

Masur, R. (1982). *Eingliederung behinderter Kinder in Pflegefamilien.* München: Reinhardt.

Mattejat, F. (1985). *Familie und psychische Störungen.* Stuttgart: Enke.

Maywald, J., & Weißmann, R. (1994). Psychosoziale Aspekte der Verwandtenpflege. Leben in vertrauter Fremde. *Jugendhilfe, 32*(3), 138–144.

Menken, J. (1985). Age and fertility: How long can you wait? *Demography,* 469–483.

Minuchin, S. (1977). *Familie und Familientherapie.* Freiburg: Lambertus.

Mühlfeld, C. (1984). *Ehe und Familie.* Opladen: Westdeutscher Verlag.

Müller, B. (1991). *Handbuch für Pflege- und Adoptiveltern.* Münster: Bundesverband der Pflege- und Adoptiveltern.

Napp-Peters, A. (1978). *Adoption. Das alleinstehende Kind und seine Familien.* Neuwied: Luchterhand.

Nauck, B. (1987). *Erwerbstätigkeit und Familienstruktur. Eine empirische Analyse des Einflusses außerfamilialer Ressourcen auf die Familien.* Weinheim/München: Verlag Deutsches Jugendinstitut.

Nave-Herz, R. (Ed.) (1988). *Wandel und Kontinuität der Familie in der Bundesrepublik Deutschland.* Stuttgart: Enke.

Nave-Herz, R., & Markefka, M. (Eds.) (1989). *Handbuch der Familien- und Jugendforschung* (Bd. 1 u. 2). Neuwied: Luchterhand.

Neidhardt, F. (1975). Systemtheoretische Analyse zur Sozialisationsfähigkeit der Familie. In F. Neidhardt (Ed.), *Frühkindliche Sozialisation* (pp. 161–187). Stuttgart: Enke.

Niederberger, J. M., & Zeindl, T. (1989). Forschungs- und Erfahrungsberichte.

Karrieren fremdplazierter Kinder. Erste Daten aus einer schweizerischen Studie. *VHN, 58*(1), 46–62. Zürich: Universität Zürich.

Nienstedt, M., & Westermann, A. (1989). *Pflegekinder. Psychologische Beiträge zur Sozialisation von Kindern in Ersatzfamilien.* Münster: Votum Verlag.

Oliver, J. E., & Taylor, A. (1971). Five generations of ill-treated children in one family pedigree. *British Journal of Psychiatry, 119,* 473–480.

Olson, D. H. (1982). *Family inventories.* S. Paul: University of Minnesota Press.

Parent, A., Balen, F. van, Bierkens, P., & Tongeren, P. van (1992). *De zin van ouderschap.* Baarn: AMBO.

Parish, W. L., Hao, L., & Hogan, D. P. (1991). Family support networks, welfare, and work among young mothers. *Journal of Marriage and the Family, 53,* 203–215.

Parsons, T., & Bales, R. (1955). *Family, socialization and interaction process.* Glencoe, IL: Free Press.

Pfeil, E., & Ganzert, J. (1973). Die Bedeutung der Verwandten für die großstädtische Familie. *Zeitschrift für Sozialpsychologie, 2,* 47–58.

Porst, R. (1984). Haushalte und Familien. *Zeitschrift für Soziologie, 13,* 165–175.

Radin, N. (1980). Childrearing fathers in intact families: An exploration of some antecedents and consequences. Paper presented to the Study Group on "The Role of the Father in Child Development: Theory, Social Policy, and the Law," University of Haifa, Haifa, Isvael.

Reich, G. (1987). *Partnerwahl und Ehekrisen.* Heidelberg: Asanger.

Richter, H. E. (1969). *Eltern, Kind und Neurose.* Reinbek: Rowohlt.

Robertson, J. F. (1977). Grandmotherhood: A study of role conceptions. *Journal of Marriage and the Family, 39,* 165–174.

Robins, L. N. (1966). *Deviant children grown up.* Baltimore: Williams & Wilkens.

Rosenmayr, L. (Ed.) (1978). *Die menschlichen Lebensalter.* München: Piper.

Sabean, D. (1984). "Junge Immen im leeren Korb": Beziehungen zwischen Schwägern in einem schwäbischen Dorf. In H. Medick & D. Sabean (Eds.), *Emotionen und materielle Interessen.* Göttingen: Vandenhoeck & Ruprecht.

Sagi, A. (1982). Antecedents and consequences of various degrees of parental involvement in childrearing: The Israeli project. In M. E. Lamb (Ed.), *Nontraditional families: Parenting and child development* (pp. 205–232). Hillsdale, NJ: Erlbaum.

Schepank, H. (1987). *Psychogene Erkrankungen der Stadtbevölkerung.* Berlin: Springer.

Schneewind, K. A. (1987). Familienentwicklung. In R. Oerter & L. Montada (Eds.), *Entwicklungspsychologie.* Weinheim: Psychologie Verlags Union.

Schubert, H., (1990). Mitglieder der erweiterten Familie in persönlichen Hilfenetzen. Ergebnisse einer egozentrierten Netzwerkanalyse. *Zeitschrift für Familienforschung, 2,* 176–210.

Schwarz, K. (1984). Eltern und Kinder in unvollständigen Familien. *Zeitschrift für Bevölkerungswissenschaft, 10,* 3–36.

Schwob, P. (1988). *Großeltern und Enkelkinder. Zur Familiendynamik der Generationenbeziehungen.* Heidelberg: Asanger.

Segalen, M. (1985). Family change and social uses of kinship networks in France. *Historische Sozialforschung,* 22–29.

Shanas, E., Townsend, P., Wedderburn, D., Friis, H., Milhoj, P., & Stewhower, J. (Eds.) (1968). *Old people in three industrial societies.* New York: Atherton.

Simon, F. B. (1988). *Unterschiede, die Unterschiede machen.* Heidelberg: Springer.

Sonnewend, S. (1982). Auswirkungen prä-, peri- und postnataler Belastungsfaktoren auf die Einstellung der Mutter und die Entwicklung des Kindes. In S. Schindler (Ed.), *Geburt. Eintritt in eine neue Welt* (pp. 103–111). Göttingen: Hogrefe.

Sorosky, A. D., Baran, A., & Pannor, R. (1979). *The adoption triangle.* Garden City, NY: Anchor Books.

Sperling, E. (1983). Die Mehrgenerationen – Familientherapie. In K. Schneider (Ed.), *Familientherapie in der Sicht psychotherapeutischer Schulen* (pp. 301–313). Paderborn: Junfermann.

(1988). Familienselbstbilder. *Praxis der Kinderpsychologie und Kinderpsychiatrie,* 37, 226–331.

Stein, M. L., & Hoopes, J. L. (1985). Identity formation in the adopted adolescent: The Delaware Family Study. New York: Child Welfare League of America.

Steinberg, L. (1987). The impact of puberty on family relations: Effects of pubertal status and pubertal timing. *Developmental Psychology,* 23, 833–840.

Stierlin, H. (1976). "Rolle" und "Auftrag" in der Familientheorie und -therapie. *Familiendynamik,* 1, 36–52.

Swientek, C. (1986). *Die "abgebende" Mutter im Adoptionsverfahren.* Bielefeld: Kleine.

(1993). *Wer sagt mir, wessen Kind ich bin? Von der Adoption Betroffene auf der Suche.* Freiburg: Herder.

Textor, M. R. (1993). Inlandsadoptionen: Herkunft, Familienverhältnisse und Entwicklung der Adoptivkinder. In R. A. C. Hoksbergen & M. R. Textor (Eds.), *Adoption: Grundlagen, Vermittlung, Nachbetreuung, Beratung* (pp. 41–63). Freiburg: Lambertus.

Thalmann, H. (1971). *Verhaltensstörungen im Grundschulalter.* Stuttgart: Klett.

Tyrell, H. (1979). Familie und gesellschaftliche Differenzierung. In H. Pross (Ed.), *Familie – wohin?* (pp. 13–67). Reinbek: Rowohlt.

(1982). Familienalltag und Familienumwelt: Überlegungen aus systemtheoretischer Perspektive. *Zeitschrift für Sozialisationsforschung und Erziehungssoziologie,* 2, 167–188.

Vaskovics, L. A. (1982). Räumliche und soziale Distanz bei alten Menschen. In L. A. Vaskovics (Ed.), *Umweltbedingungen familialer Sozialisation.* Stuttgart: Enke.

Veiel, H. O. F., & Herrle, J. (1991). Geschlechtsspezifische Strukturen sozialer Unterstützungsnetzwerke. *Zeitschrift für Soziologie,* 20, 237–245.

Visher, E. B., & Visher, J. S. (1979). *Stepfamilies: A guide to working with stepparents and stepchildren.* New York: Brunner & Mazel.

(1989). *Old loyalities, new ties: Therapeutic strategies with stepfamilies.* New York: Brunner & Mazel.

Walsh, F. (1982). *Normal family process.* New York: Guilford.

Wetering, W. van (1986). Een sociaal vaugnet: quasi-verwantshap, religie en sociale order bij de creoolse surinamers in de Bijlmermeer. *Soziologische Gids*, 233–252.

Wood, V., & Roberston, J. F. (1976). The significant grandparenthood. In J. F. Gubrium (Ed.), *Time, roles and self in old age.* New York: Human Science Press.

PART III

Partnerships

8

Heterosexual partnerships: Initiation, maintenance, and disengagement

Hans Werner Bierhoff

Eibl-Eibesfeldt (1984) regards the development of love relationships as a milestone in evolution. Shaver, Hazan, and Bradshaw (1988) describe love as a concept that encompasses three biologically meaningful behavioral systems: attachment, caregiving, and sexuality. The psychological correlates of these three behavioral systems are trust, altruism, and passion. In a lecture on psychoanalysis as art and science, Bowlby traced fear of attachment in the child and later adult back to the expectation of rejection coupled with torturous anxiety. In this context he writes: "As a result there is a massive block against his expressing or even feeling his natural desire for a close trusting relationship, for care, comfort, and love – which I regard as the subjective manifestations of a major system of instinctive behavior" (Bowlby, 1988, p. 55). Bowlby, who presents attachment and love from an ethnological point of view, emphasizes the biological function of this behavior class and its preprograming by inborn behavioral tendencies that, together with the interplay of ecological influences (especially the behavior of the parents), determine the formation of attachment. Later (p. 65) he stresses that, when forming attachments to people later in life, a person acts on expectations that resemble the model of the parents. In agreement with these assumptions, longitudinal studies confirm a certain stability in styles of attachment (Grossmann & Grossmann, 1991). The style of attachment in the young child influences the type of friendship relationships that are built up 10 years later. Attachment styles developed during childhood can be seen as a relationship system into which later relationships are integrated (see Reis & Shaver, 1988, p. 375).

As heterosexual partnerships contain attachment, a taxonomy of attachment styles that Ainsworth, Blehar, Waters, and Wall (1978) developed from observations of young children will first be presented; this taxonomy was later extended by Bartholomew (1990) on the basis of theoretical considerations. Following this, different love styles will be described and an attempt will be made to compare attachment styles with love styles. Finally, investment theory (Rusbult, 1983) is discussed from an exchange-theoretical viewpoint of close relationships. The second section of this chapter addresses the progress of love relationships; the initiation of and disengagement from the relationship receive special attention.

Variety instead of unity: The many faces of love

The variety of human feelings that develop within a relationship preclude a view of romantic love as a unitary construct from the very start. It is much more appropriate to adopt a multidimensional approach when measuring love. It may at first sound surprising that the variable "love" can be measured just as well as other psychological variables. Yet there is no reason to view love as something irrational or intangible. Certain dimensions of love are measurable, although the claim cannot necessarily be justified that love scales are able to cover feelings of love in their total complexity, or that they are able to reflect the dynamics of the development of love. In order to limit the aims and possibilities of measuring attachment and love styles, it is advisable to consider the characteristics of love as a psychological character-istic (see Amelang, 1991).

Childhood attachment as a model for later love relationships

One of the most important ideas in John Bowlby's attachment theory (1969) is the assumption that infant attachment is condensed into internal working models of the relationship with the caregiver, and that these models integrate the child's attachment experiences with its personality development (Bretherton, 1985). These cognitive working models contain individual differences that can be traced throughout childhood (Grossmann & Grossmann, 1991; Main, Kaplan & Cassidy, 1985). The working models serve the child in its assessment of other people and its self, as well as in its assessment of relationships between its self and others. Ainsworth devel-oped a test situation designed to monitor the attachment behavior of children (Ainsworth et al., 1978). It consists of a brief separation and subsequent reunion of mother and child. On the basis of resulting observa-tions the attachment styles of the children were divided into three groups, described as *secure*, *insecure-ambivalent*, and *insecure-avoidant*. A secure attachment style appears to coincide with reliable positive reactions of the caregiver to the closeness needs of the child, an insecure-ambivalent style coincides with unpredictably positive or negative reactions on behalf of the caregiver to the child's approaches, and an insecure-avoidant style with regular rejection (see also Kreppner, Chapter 4 of this volume).

On the basis of this classification Hazan and Shaver (1987) differentiated between three adult attachment styles and gave the people they questioned three selection alternatives:

Secure: "I find it relatively easy to get close to others and am comfortable depending on them and having them depend on me. I don't often worry about being abandoned or about someone getting too close to me."

Anxious-ambivalent: "I find that others are reluctant to get as close as I would like. I often worry that my partner doesn't really love me or won't want to stay with me. I want to merge completely with another person, and this desire sometimes scares people away."

Avoidant: "I am somewhat uncomfortable being close to others; I find it difficult to trust them completely, difficult to allow myself to depend on them. I am nervous when anyone gets too close, and often, love partners want me to be more intimate than I feel comfortable being."

The respondents classified themselves according to one of the attachment styles. In a random sample of 620 persons, 56% classified themselves as secure in their attachment style, 19% as anxious-ambivalent, and 25% as avoidant (Hazan & Shaver, 1987). An initial differentiation based on the three attachment styles refers to secure and insecure attachment, respectively. The hypothesis seems plausible that a secure style of attachment coincides with a longer duration of relationships. This assumption is confirmed by Hazan and Shaver (1987), who report that persons who chose the secure alternative were together longer (10 years on average) and were divorced less often (6%) than persons who chose one of the other two alternatives (anxious-ambivalent: 6 years and 12% divorce rate; avoidant: 4.9 years and 10% divorce rate).

In their assessment of partnership experiences, the secure group differed from the other two groups on a variety of characteristics (e.g., persons in this group attributed to themselves more happiness and trust and less fear of closeness). The anxious-ambivalent group also displayed a number of characteristic features (e.g., persons in this group described themselves as more jealous, craving unity with their partner, more oriented toward reciprocity, and more lonely). The avoidant group differed from the others in their lower perception of acceptance and a tendency to expect that romantic feelings were not very stable.

The connection between the attachment styles measured by the trichotomized item of Hazan and Shaver and love attitudes and self-esteem, respectively, was made clear in a study by Feeney and Noller (1990). They covered the following variables:

- love attitudes (after Lee, 1973/1976);
- love addiction, that is, defining oneself in terms of the partner, or harboring dreams of fulfilling unfulfilled hopes (see Peele, 1988);
- limerence (Tennov, 1979), which includes obsessive preoccupation with individual topics, self-conscious anxiety, emotional dependence, and idealization (Feeney & Noller, 1990).

Whereas the secure attachment style was associated with an emphasis on love ideals and friendship, the avoidant style displayed a pragmatic approach and anxiety with respect to the self. Results showed that the ambivalent style differed most from the other two styles. It was characterized by romantic, passionate, and caring love, obsessive occupation with the partner, emotional dependence, idealization of the partner, and love addiction (Feeney & Noller, 1990).

Clearly, the attachment style is linked to a general view of rewards and dangers in interpersonal relationships. This is also confirmed by further results reported by Collins and Read (1990). Avoidant persons felt themselves ill at ease with interpersonal closeness and intimacy, while anxious-ambivalent people were afraid of being abandoned and unloved. In contrast to this, persons with a secure attachment style emphasized closeness and expressed few worries about being abandoned or unloved.

Additional results obtained by Hendrick and Hendrick (1989) give rise to the assumption that the secure attachment style and the avoidant attachment style display a certain dichotomy in the trust–distrust dimension. When they were independently measured in single ratings (instead of from a selection of three alternatives), a negative relationship emerged between the two self-classifications of these attachment styles. The results reported by Levy and Davis (1988) point in the same direction. On the other hand, the anxious-ambivalent style seems to have only slightly negative connections to the secure style and none to the avoidant style. The anxious-ambivalent style displayed an affinity to possessive love. This was confirmed by the results of Hazan and Shaver (1987) and Levy and Davis (1988), who ascertained that persons in the anxious group particularly emphasized jealousy and passion. The avoidant style correlated negatively with intimacy, while the secure style correlated positively with intimacy and a caring attitude.

It is also notable that the persons in a secure relationship (more often than insecure persons) ranked their love relationship as important compared to their work and as giving pleasure (Hazan & Shaver, 1990). At the same time, securely attached persons proved happier with their work, especially in respect of job security, co-workers, income, challenge, and advancement. Anxious-ambivalent persons rated their job security and their advancement opportunities as particularly unfavorable. Avoidant people were relatively unhappy about their co-workers.

Kirkpatrick and Davis (1994) also measured relationship styles among heterosexual pairs with the help of Hazan and Shaver's trichotomized item. They addressed the question as to which relationship styles occurred among pairs with pronounced regularity and which rarely. They discovered that in 240 pairs the constellation where both were avoidant or both were anxious-ambivalent in orientation never occurred. Instead, pairs were overrepresented where one partner was avoidant and the other was anxious-ambivalent.

They further examined the stability of the relationship over a period of three years. Is a particular attachment style particularly favorable to the continuance of a relationship? This question was asked of people who were 21 years old or younger at the first time of questioning. When questioned on the depth of attachment and length of the relationship in a control study the results formed the following pattern: women stay in a relationship longer when they are anxious-ambivalent, men when they are avoidant. Women leave a relationship sooner when they are avoidant, men when they are anxious-ambivalent. These results were primarily traced back to the fact that women are mainly responsible for the maintenance or disengagement of a relationship (see below) and that anxious-ambivalent women work particularly hard on their relationships. In contrast, avoidant men tend to avoid conflicts and exaggerated expectations, so that they are unlikely to hinder the maintenance of a relationship, especially if they have an anxious-ambivalent partner (a combination that occurs frequently).

The single-item measurement of attachment styles was extended by the development of questionnaires in which every attachment style was covered by several items (see Collins & Read, 1990). Examples (after Simpson, 1990) include:

- *secure*: I find it relatively easy to get close to others.
- *anxious-ambivalent*: others are often reluctant to get as close as I would like.
- *avoidant*: I'm somewhat uncomfortable being too close to others.

The results from Simpson's study (1990), which was based on 288 persons, will now be given in more detail. The people questioned comprised 144 pairs so that the data collected could be evaluated on the intraindividual level as well as on the pair level. On the intraindividual level the results were as follows: persons who reached a high score on the five-item scale for measuring the secure attachment style expressed more love on Rubin's love scale, also more dependence, attachment, and self-disclosure or trust. Apart from this, they tended more to describe their romantic relationship as happy on the eleven-item scale of partnership satisfaction (after Simpson, 1987).

The avoidant attachment style was measured on a four-item scale. Persons with a high avoidance tendency were less in love, less dependent, less attached, and less willing to self-disclose. Their trust in their partner and their satisfaction tended to be low. On the basis of its correlates the avoidant attachment style appears as a counterpart to the secure attachment style.

The anxious-ambivalent scale consisted of four items. In this case gender differences deserve consideration. As a rule, all anxious-ambivalent persons tend to have little faith in the reliability and trustworthiness of their partner. Apart from this, anxious-ambivalent men characteristically reach little satisfaction in their partnerships, whereas anxious-ambivalent women show less attachment.

Simpson (1990) studied pairs so that in his analysis on the pair level he could draw conclusions from the attachment style correlates of the two partners. Partners of anxious-ambivalent persons express less attachment and dependence. Partners of avoidant persons give a comparatively low rating to the reliability and trustworthiness of their partner. Partners of secure persons express little uncertainty in their relationship.

The following gender differences were found: the satisfaction of men correlated negatively with the anxious-ambivalent attachment style of their partner. On the other hand, the satisfaction of women correlated positively with the secure attachment style of the man and negatively with the avoidant attachment style.

Which emotions do securely and insecurely attached persons experience? Simpson (1990) used 24 adjectives (e.g., elated, surprised, angry, fearful) as a basis of studying four emotional spheres: intensely positive, intensely negative, mildly positive, and mildly negative. The results will be summarized here, as the mild and intense emotional scales display similar correlations with the attachment styles. (An analysis of a German-language frequency of emotion index shows that a positive emotion factor and a negative emotion factor suffice to explain intercorrelations between the emotion adjectives; Grau & Bierhoff, 1994.) A secure attachment style was accompanied by a high frequency of positive emotions and a low frequency of negative emotions. The opposite was the case in anxious-ambivalent and avoidant persons: a higher frequency of negative emotions and less positive emotions. This coincides with the results of Hazan and Shaver (1990), who report a lower level of well-being – that is, loneliness, anxiety, animosity, psychosomatic complaints, and illness – in anxious-ambivalent and avoidant persons than in secure persons.

The frequency of emotion index was used to see how it related to the particular attachment styles of partners. A secure attachment approach was associated with a high frequency of positive emotions. In contrast, anxious-ambivalent and avoidant attachment styles were associated with few positive emotions. This pattern of results applied equally to men and women. On the other hand, connections between a partner's negative emotions and the attachment style were insignificant, particularly in the case of male attachment styles. Attachment styles among women displayed slightly positive connections between negative emotions on behalf of the man and an anxious-ambivalent or avoidant orientation.

The differentiation between one secure and two insecure attachment styles is based on the empirical analysis of data on children observed in separation situations (Ainsworth et al., 1978). This classification may well be inadequate in the case of adults, as the avoidant attachment style can be differentiated further by considering whether avoidance results from lack of interest or from fear. On the basis of these considerations Bartholomew (1990) makes a differentiation between four attachment styles. This classification is based on a 2 × 2 schema produced when self-esteem and the other are categorized as positive or negative. Persons can assess themselves positively, for instance, and distrust others. Or they can assess themselves negatively and be open toward others.

Bartholomew assumes that the cognitive working models in which attachment experiences have crystalized should be differentiated according to models of the self and models of others. In a *secure* attachment style both the model of the self and the model of the other is positive. The person is at ease with intimacy and with autonomy. A positive model of the self and a negative model of the other results in a *dismissing* attachment style. The person avoids intimacy and feels independent. A negative model of the self and a positive model of the other results in a preoccupied attachment style. The person focuses his thought on the relationship and feels uncertain about the durability of the relationship. When both working models are negative a *fearful* attachment style occurs. The person is afraid of intimacy and avoids deeper social relationships. Table 8.1 summarizes Bartholomew's 2 × 2 classification.

Bartholomew suggests an interview procedure for gathering data on the four theoretically derived attachment styles. Empirical results (Bartholomew & Horowitz, 1991) show that, as expected, the four attachment styles are systematically connected with characteristics of the self-image and the image of the other. Items referring to attachment styles were regrouped in a factor-analytical investigation based on the 2 × 2 classification of attachment styles (Bierhoff, Grau & Ludwig, 1993). The two basic dimensions of attachment styles were identified as fear (characterized by jealousy and clinging) and avoidance (characterized by self-sufficiency and little searching for closeness). The secure attachment style was characterized by low fear and avoidance, whereas the preoccupied attachment style was

Table 8.1. *Attachment styles dependent on models of the self and models of the other*

	Model of self	
Model of other	Positive	Negative
Positive	Secure	Preoccupied
Negative	Dismissing	Fearful

Source: Bartholomew (1990).

characterized by high fear and avoidance. The other two styles developed by Bartholomew can also be appropriately classified. The results show that a division into four attachment styles is valid. As the fourfold division was developed from the threefold division (by differentiating the avoidant attachment style), Bartholomew's approach (1990; Bartholomew & Scharfe, 1994) represents a further development of the approach by Ainsworth et al. (1978) and contains no contradiction to the earlier classifications.

Attachment styles versus love styles

If attachment styles create a filter through which adults perceive their heterosexual relationships, then it should be possible to establish some connection between love styles and attachment styles. Rubin (1970) developed a questionnaire that globally covered romantic love and became a model for measuring love styles (see Amelang, 1991). Item examples from his love scale include: "I would do almost anything for ———" and "I would greatly enjoy being confided in by ———." Answers referring to a specific person were obtained from a 9-point scale. Hatfield (1988) points out that love occurs in various forms that can be traced back to two basic variants: passionate love and companionate love. A scale comprising 30 items was developed to measure passionate love. One of these items was: "I would feel deep despair if ——— left me." Hatfield emphasized, as this item illustrates, that passionate love contains both positive and negative emotions.

Companionate love is defined as "The affection we feel for those with whom our lives are deeply entwined" (Hatfield, 1988, p. 191). The main source of companionate love seems to be positive reinforcement as in Byrne's theory of attraction (1971). Negative reinforcement reduces feelings of companionate love. Consequently the development of companionate love or liking is described as being dependent on pleasure and pain.

Lee (1973/1976) goes beyond Hatfield's (1988) two love forms in that he differentiates between six love styles that are measurable by scale (Hendrick & Hendrick, 1986). Love styles, like lifestyles, can be changed, although a tendency to keep a particular style remains. Empirically, the six basic patterns are relatively independent (compare Bierhoff, 1991b):

- *Romantic love (Eros)* refers to immediate attraction to the loved person as expressed in the ideal type of love at first sight. Beauty in appearance and sexual passion play an important role in the development of this love style. Romantic love depends a great deal on satisfaction in the partnership (Bierhoff, 1989, Kraigher, 1991).
- *Game-playing love (Ludus)* represents a variation of passionate affection in which seduction, sexual freedom, and sexual adventure stand in the foreground. Orientation toward longer-term relationships tends to be avoidant and waiting. Game-playing love is connected negatively to satisfaction in the partnership (Bierhoff, 1989, Kraigher, 1991).
- *Best-friends love (Storge)* develops from a previous friendship. The interpersonal orientation is characterized by common interests and mutual trust and tolerance. These characteristics should contribute substantially toward the stability of a relationship, as they greatly facilitate a functioning partnership.
- *Possessive love (Mania)* is an extreme version of romantic love, as it accentuates passionate and seemingly irrational relationship behavior. Idealization and possessiveness are connected to strong feelings that can be positive (achieving fusion with the partner) as well as negative (jealousy because the partner does not seem to give himself in the same way).
- *Pragmatic love (Pragma)* represents a certain contrast to the emotional ebullience of possessive love because rational considerations help determine the choice of partner. The relationship is intended to create desirable living conditions or serve particular ends (e.g., end loneliness, have children).
- *Altruistic love (Agape)* exists where partners are prepared to make sacrifices for each other. Lovers who ascribe to this style of love are prepared to reduce their own aims and desires if this contributes to the well-being of their partner.

Romantic and possessive love can be placed on the same level as passionate love while pragmatic and best-friends love are similar to companionate love (Hatfield, 1988).

The reference system of love developed by Lee (1973/1976) is systematically linked to the attachment styles derived from Bowlby's theory (1969). The first results in this context were reported by Levy and Davis (1988): romantic love was linked positively to the secure attachment style and

Table 8.2. *Love styles, attachment styles, and social interaction*

Love style	Relevant for attachment?	Correlate
Romantic	yes	secure +, avoidant −
Game-playing	yes	secure −, avoidant +
Possessive	yes	anxious-ambivalent +
Pragmatic	no	consequences of interaction
Best-friends	no	coordination of interaction
Altruistic	no	transformation of consequences of interaction

Note: This is a provisional description of love styles based on the results of Levy and Davis (1988) and Hendrick and Hendrick (1989).

negatively to the avoidant attachment style, whereas game-playing love correlated in exactly the opposite way to these attachment styles. Consequently, game-playing love was linked positively to the avoidant attachment style, which confirms expectations considering that the quintessence of game-playing love lies in the avoidance of long-term relationships.

There was also a marked positive connection between possessive love and the anxious-ambivalent attachment style, which resulted from the conceptual overlap between these two styles. This is understandable as they are both based on an "emotional cocktail" combining dependence and anxiety.

In summarizing it can be said that each attachment style can be correlated to certain love styles. Table 8.2 presents an overview supported by the results of Hendrick and Hendrick (1989), which in turn corroborate the findings of Levy and Davis (1988) to a large extent.

A word of caution should, however, be added: the correlations between love styles and attachment styles are relatively low. On the one hand, this could be attributable to the fact that in these studies the attachment style is often recorded by specific items that probably offer little measurement reliability. On the other hand, it should be considered that the effects of the attachment style on the love style are limited: there must be other factors that can affect the formation of love styles, such as role models in the mass media. The given correlations cannot prove any causal connections between attachment styles and love styles. It is possible to surmise from the concepts that the attachment styles developed in early childhood influence the love styles of adults. But until now, no (longitudinal) studies have been carried out to help test causal interdependence in this area.

It is also worth mentioning that few unambiguous connections were found between attachment styles and pragmatic, best-friends, and altruistic love. The theoretical description of these love styles suggests that links between them and attachment styles are limited. This applies particularly to pragmatic love, which includes the criteria of expected usefulness and – more generally – expected consequences and, as such, is to be traced back to social interaction realized in close relationships (see Bierhoff, 1973; Thibaut and Kelley, 1959). This is why this particular love style is associated with the (expected) consequences of the interaction in Table 8.2.

The same also applies to altruistic love. It can be assumed that altruism is closely connected with imitative learning from role models and the positive reinforcement of selfless behavior during childhood (Rushton, 1982). Adhering to altruistic norms is comparable to a transformation of interaction goals, which replaces the maximization of one's own gain with that of the partner (Kelley & Thibaut, 1978).

Finally, best-friends love goes beyond attachment styles insofar as the compatibility of interests and the coordination of actions within the relationship are concerned. Thus, a best-friends relationship can be based on such things as mutual interests or mutual enterprises. Consequently, this love style also indicates general characteristic of social interaction, as described in exchange theory, which are of great importance in coordinating successful relationships (Kelley & Thibaut, 1978). The aim of this class of interaction characteristics lies in successful decision making on behalf of the partners so that they can coordinate their preferences and actions appropriately. In enduring relationships, best-friends love probably represents a foundation for stabilizing and maintaining the relationship.

These considerations lead to a restructuring of love styles, as reflected in Table 8.2. Whereas Lee (1973/1976) classifies according to primary love styles (romantic, game-playing, best-friends) and secondary love styles (possessive, pragmatic, altruistic), it seems sensible – because of the presence or lack of associations with attachment styles – to differentiate between attachment-related love styles (romantic, game-playing, possessive) and attachment-independent love styles (best-friends, pragmatic, altruistic).

Is there a connection between love styles and happiness in a partnership? The romantic love of a male or female partner correlates positively with the personal assessment of satisfaction, whereas game-playing love correlates negatively. Consequently, if a person has a partner who displays high values in romantic love and low values in game-playing love, he or she tends to describe themselves as satisfied with the relationship (Bierhoff, 1991b). Hendrick and Hendrick (1992) have summarized further correlates of love styles. *Eros* is associated with higher levels of self-esteem and more self-disclosure; *Ludus* with less self-disclosure and more sensation seeking (Zuckerman, 1979). *Storge* and *Pragma* display no conspicuous psychological correlates. *Mania* is associated with more communication and relationship turbulence. Finally, *Agape* is associated with more enduring relationships and greater religiosity.

The investment theory of love

References to the significance of exchange theory (Kelley & Thibaut, 1978) for love relationships (see above) signalize a promising new research area that at present is just beginning to develop. The research of Rusbult (1983) does, however, include this perspective. Rusbult differentiates between two fundamental quantities in relationships: satisfaction (SAT) and commitment (COM). Satisfaction is conceptualized as dependent on high rewards (REW), low costs (CST), and high consequences relative to generalized expectations (comparison level; CL). Commitment, which determines the stability of a relationship, is influenced by satisfaction, quality of alternative relationships (ALT), and investments (INV). Investments include extrinsic (e.g., common possessions) and intrinsic contributions (e.g., self-disclosure). If the comparison level is ignored, the following equation in theory holds (Rusbult, 1983):

$$COM = (REW - CST) - ALT + INV.$$

Commitment is a positive function of the reward − cost difference and investment, and a negative function of quality of alternative relationships. Stay/leave behaviors are considered to be a direct function of level of commitment. The investment model predicts relationship disengagement from low commitment. Longitudinal studies over a seven-month and a three-year span, respectively, confirm the importance of commitment for the stability of a relationship (Rusbult, 1983; Kirkpatrick & Davis, 1994). In contrast, the relative importance of costs and comparison level is still unclear (compare Mikula & Stroebe, 1991). As far as alternatives are concerned, it was shown that people who stay in a relationship pass increasingly negative judgments on alternative partners, while dropouts who left a relationship previously think increasingly positively about alternative partners (Johnson & Rusbult, 1989).

In the presentation of love theories emphasis was laid on attachment styles and love styles. But Sternberg's (1986) triangular theory of love should also be mentioned here. This theory differentiates between intimacy, passion, and decision/commitment. Intimacy indicates close communication and self-disclosure. Passion includes sexual desire and satisfaction. Finally, decision/commitment refers in the *short term* to the decision for a particular partner and in the *long term* to the question of shared future planning.

The usefulness of this theory lies, among other things, in the fact that it offers a basis for differentiating eight kinds of love (Sternberg, 1986, 1987).

While consummate love is characterized by all three components, companionate love, for example, represents a type of love in which intimacy and decision/commitment play the major role and passion is of secondary importance. In contrast to this, the condition of infatuated love displays an emphasis on passionate elements.

Certain parallels can be drawn between the love styles defined by Lee and the love types defined by Sternberg (in a similar way to those drawn between the classifications of Hatfield and Lee): for example, romantic love corresponds to infatuated love and best-friends love corresponds to companionate love. Clarification of possible correspondence between different types in these taxonomies will be of particular interest in future research.

The course of relationships

Initiation, maintenance, and disengagement are important aspects in the course of heterosexual love relationships (compare Levinger, 1980). On the basis of initial attraction (phase A) the relationship is built up (phase B); it is then maintained (phase C) and may possibly deteriorate (phase D) until it ends because of separation or death (phase E). As it will not be possible to deal with all the phases in detail here, we will concentrate on two of these phases where changes in the relationship are particularly pronounced: the building phase and the disengagement phase.

Initiation of partnerships

A particular form of pair identity develops within a relationship that does not necessarily derive from the individual characteristics of the two partners (Levinger, 1980). Mutual aspects are related to different spheres (compare Levinger & Snoek, 1972):

- Communication becomes increasingly intimate as self-disclosure intensifies.
- Mutual knowledge increases and a division of labor takes place between the partners.
- Interaction behavior specific to the pair develops.
- Partners assume an active approach to and support of each other instead of a passive observer role.
- Cooperative orientation develops, which gives the achievements of the pair a new, important value.

The selection of a potential partner depends on many idiosyncratic factors as there are few fixed norms for initiating a relationship. This being the situation, we can assume that the behavior of the actors is also influenced by their personality to a certain extent. An important personality characteristic that should be mentioned in this context is self-monitoring. A high level of self-monitoring coincides with an orientation toward external features such as appearance; low self-monitoring coincides with an orientation toward attitudes and convictions ("inner values").

Snyder, Berscheid, and Glick (1985) showed in two studies that high self-monitoring individuals paid great attention to physical attractiveness when choosing a partner while low self-monitoring individuals paid more attention to personality characteristics of their potential partner. In one of the studies a choice was given between an externally attractive Jennifer who apparently had negative personality traits and a far less attractive Kristen who displayed positive personality features. Of the high self-monitoring individuals, 69% preferred the attractive Jennifer, whereas only 19% of the low self-monitoring individuals shared this preference; 81% of these preferred Kristen instead.

Why is this? On the one hand, it is to be assumed that high self-monitoring individuals care particularly about the impression their female partner makes in public. In contrast to this, low self-monitoring individuals tend to consider it more important to find a partner to whom they can express their thoughts and feelings because she appears open to personal communication. Fortunately, partner selection is not always limited by a strict contrast between external appearance and personality. But these studies do show that, depending on personality, different global preferences influence partner selection. It should be mentioned that the influence of self-monitoring in women on relationship initiation has hardly been investigated. But there are some indications that self-monitoring in women also influences the initiation of a relationship. Here it seems likely that not only the external appearance of high self-monitoring men but also the perceived personality of the male counterpart are considered during initiation (Bierhoff & Grau, 1993).

It appears that the development of a relationship is pursued more intensely by the male partner, especially in terms of sexual desires, whereas women tend to display a waiting attitude (Peplau, Rubin & Hill, 1977). Women regularly appear to exercise much more control over the extent of relationship development. This is illustrated by the fact that it is primarily the previous sexual experience of the woman that decides when sexual activity will start in a new relationship (it begins sooner in cases of previous experience than without), whereas the previous sexual experience of the man has little effect in this respect. In particular, anxious-ambivalent women seem to be highly commited to the maintenance of a relationship (Kirkpatrick & Davis, 1994; see above).

In general a distinction can be made between pairs where sexual intimacy precedes emotional intimacy (sexually liberal pairs) and those where emotional intimacy precedes sexual intimacy (sexually traditional pairs). When these two types of pair were compared it was seen that sexually traditional couples displayed greater romantic love than sexually liberal pairs. Sexual satisfaction with the relationship was, however, equally high in both groups and, on the first control measurement two years later, the endurance of the relationship had not been influenced by liberality. The sexual satisfaction of both men and women correlated significantly with romantic love as classified in the love scale of Rubin (1970).

As far as the partners' perception of closeness is concerned, the level of correspondence appeared to be low (Hill, Peplau & Rubin, 1981). On the question of who was more involved in the relationship and who had more to say, there were moderately high intrapair correlations. In addition, men tended to assess the involvement of women higher than the women themselves; they also assessed their own power higher than the women did.

These results indicate interesting gender and gender-role differences in the development of a relationship. Such differences also become evident when the dimensions of love (Lee, 1973/1976) are analyzed with respect to gender and gender role (Bierhofff, 1991a). Men rated their altruistic love higher and their possessive love lower than women did. Apart from this, women tended to be more pragmatic in their approach to love than men. However, the latter result did not prove particularly stable in all of the samples (compare Bierhoff & Klein, 1991, p. 67).

Gender-role orientation is differentiated in the dimensions of instrumentality and expressivity (Spence & Helmreich, 1978). Instrumentality refers to active problem-solving behavior, willingness to take the initiative, and assertiveness. Expressivity refers to such features as social sensitivity, empathy, and interpersonal warmth.

The gender effects were partly mediated by gender-role effects. This is especially true for possessive love, which women expressed more than men. The gender effect vanished after including the instrumentality and expressivity in the prediction of expressive love. Low instrumentality and high expressivity predict high possessive love. In addition, women describe themselves as less instrumental and more expressive than men. Therefore, the gender effect on possessive love might be explained by gender-role effects (Bierhoff, 1991a).

In addition, instrumentality is related to pragmatic love, independent of the gender effects mentioned above. The higher level of pragmatic love in women corroborates results that show women in heterosexual relationships to be more pragmatic than men (Rubin, Peplau & Hill, 1981). The authors ascribe this, at least in part, to the fact that women – more so than men – generally combine their choice of partner with a choice of living standard. Women were less romantically in love during the first phase of a relationship and left sooner than men (Rubin et al., 1981). Whether these results from the 1970s are still valid for the 1990s is another question. Continuity or discontinuity of these orientations and their dependency on cultural influences certainly present an interesting task for future research.

Maintenance and disengagement of relationships

Which factors determine the endurance of a relationship? An important predictor of endurance is the level of closeness in the relationship. Over a period of nine months heterosexual relationships proved more endurable if the relationship was characterized by a high level of relationship closeness (Berscheid, Snyder & Omoto, 1989). Closeness was measured with the help of the relationship closeness inventory (RCI), which embraces three dimensions: frequency of impact, diversity of impact, and strength of impact. The frequency scale refers to the number of hours spent together. Diversity is measured on the basis of 38 activities that people could potentially perform together (e.g., participation in a sporting activity) Strength of impact was assessed by 34 items (e.g., "My partner influences what I watch on TV"). Of the three subscales only the strength-of-impact scale correlated positively with Rubin's love scale. The overall index of relationship closeness, which correlated positively with relationship stability, was constructed on the basis of the three subscales.

Predicting the disengagement of a relationship by measuring variables at a time when the relationship is still intact helps identify significant predictors of separation. Within a space of three months Simpson (1987) questioned over 200 male and female students who were going out with a partner (average age 19.8 years) and divided them into two groups: those who were still together after three months and those who had separated in the meantime. About half of those questioned reported that the original relationship had ended. The following predictors contributed independently to an explanation of relationship disengagement:

- Persons who were more content with the relationship spoke more of the possibility of its continuing than those who were dissatisfed.
- The longer the relationship had lasted at the time of the first measurement, the greater the probability of its continuance.
- The partnership was more likely to be still intact when partners had a sexual relationship at the time of the first measurement than when partners reported no sexual relationship.
- The relationship had better prospects of persisting after three months

when the partners stated at the first measurement that they went out exclusively with each other and not with a third party at the same time.

These results show that when a relationship is characterized by exclusiveness, sexual intimacy, satisfaction, and closeness, it has a greater probability of lasting for more than three months. Correspondingly, it was seen that the RCI was a positive predictor of relationship stability. When the closeness in the relationship appeared to be greater, the probability of its endurance was greater (Simpson, 1987). Finally, there were also indications that self-monitoring was negatively connected to stability, as high self-monitoring individuals had a tendency to separate more quickly than low self-monitoring individuals.

In addition, a later study (Simpson & Gangestad, 1991) showed that an unlimited sexual orientation was related to less romantic love (on Rubin's scale, 1970), attachment, and dependence, and to less involvement in the relationship. An unrestricted sexual orientation is characterized by the willingness to enter a sexual relationship without the presence of a longer-term attachment, greater closeness, or intimacy. In contrast to this, where sexual orientation is restricted, a longer relationship, personal attachment, and self-disclosure are prerequisites of willingness to start a sexual relationship. These results again show that personality traits influence the course of a relationship.

In an earlier passage the question of leaving a relationship was described in connection with Rusbult's investment model (Rusbult, 1983). According to this, the likelihood of leaving a relationship is increased by low commitment. The cause of relationship stability, where high commitment exists, is assumed to be that destructive reactions (such as conflict escalation) are suppressed and constructive solution proposals are intensified (Rusbult, Verette, Whitney, Slovik & Lipkus, 1991).

Partnership conflicts are often connected to dissatisfaction with the relationship, which makes a variety of responses possible (Rusbult, 1987): constructive answers include loyalty and voice; destructive answers include neglect and exit. This exit-voice-loyalty-neglect model, represented in Table 8.3, is derived from Hirschman (1970), who originally described three of the four responses to dissatisfaction.

Active forms of response include exit and voice. *Exit* means avoiding clarification of the conflict and resorting to alternatives instead. *Voice*, on the other hand, aims at negotiating conflicts. Passive forms of reaction include *loyalty*, where conflicts are survived by clinging to the status quo and the hope of improvement. Rusbult expands this classification to include the alternative of neglect among the passive reactions. *Neglect* is associated with indifferent acceptance and ignoring of conflicts (e.g., in the avoidant attachment style; compare Kirkpatrick & Davis, 1994).

Table 8.3. *Exit-voice-loyalty-neglect model*

	Coping strategy	
Level of activity	Destructive	Constructive
High	Exit	Voice
Low	Neglect	Loyalty

Source: Rusbult (1987).

Rusbult (1987) assumes that the exit-voice-loyalty-neglect classification is related to three of the variables from the investment model. For the sake of simplification she assumes that they can be positive or negative: satisfaction (SAT), investment (INV), and quality of alternative (ALT).

Exit is likely when low levels of satisfaction, low investments, and high-quality alternatives are present. Low investments make it easy to leave a relationship when satisfaction is low and good alternatives offer favorable evasive action. Voice is probable when high levels of satisfaction, high investments, and favorable alternatives are present. When high satisfaction and high investments exist, they make negotiations appear profitable, in which case alternatives may offer an effective means of applying pressure. Loyalty is likely in the presence of high satisfaction, high investment, and unfavorable alternatives. Finally, neglect is likely when satisfaction, investments, and the quality of alternatives receive low ratings.

Empirical studies correspond with this model. Low investment and low satisfaction as well as more favorable alternatives relate to the choice of exit as a response to dissatisfaction (see Rusbult, Johnson & Morrow, 1986). Apart from this, it was seen that a rising intensity of the conflict increased all four responses, especially exit and voice.

The following remarks are concerned with the ending of a romantic relationship and are based on the results of a questionnaire answered by people who had already experienced separation (Vaughan, 1986). In general, separation is characterized by long-term preparations on behalf of the person who wants to separate, especially if the relationship has lasted for many years. This preparation often takes place in secret, particularly when a new relationship is developing. This is why the person who wishes to leave often tries to convey the image of an intact relationship during the last phase. Behind this facade, the person who wants to leave drafts out a new social world in which he or she develops a new social identity, independent of the partner. This process of detachment is often unintentional, as the person who disengages from the relationship is searching for some form of self-affirmation. But this incipient dissatisfaction often leads to a deeper rift between the partners, and secrecy tends to worsen the situation.

This development results in the person who wishes to leave becoming increasingly concerned about the weaknesses of the relationship. Whereas at the beginning of a relationship lovers only see positive aspects in their partner, persons who want to separate tend to see only negative aspects in their partner and the relationship. In contrast, people who maintain a relationship emphasize the negative aspects of alternative partners (Johnson & Rusbult, 1989). This redefinition of the partner in negative concepts motivates the dissociating person to intensify his or her efforts to leave. Why should one cling to a relationship that in essence is characterized by mistakes and failure?

Often the whole history of the relationship is rewritten to create consistency with the separation, which means that the relationship is assessed as unsatisfying from the very beginning. The dissociating persons typically ask themselves whether their partner ever loved them. Apart from this, the development of the relationship is no longer traced back to love but to external causes that undermine the perceived love (compare Seligman, Fazio & Zanna, 1980). When dissociating persons have an alternative at hand they tend to develop an extremely critical attitude toward their partner (Vaughan, 1986).

The new negative assessment and emotional rejection create the normative legitimation required to leave the partnership. The result is a cumulative separation that is compensated by the creation of new commitments. But as long as the separation has not been completed the dissociating person feels compelled to participate in the old relationship. These constraints produce anger, which often affects areas of mutual interest, and in particular a disinclination toward sexual relations with the partner – which often continue, however, so as not to cause a premature collapse of intimacy.

This development is associated with a communication problem in that only the person who wishes to dissociate is conscious that a separation is occurring, while the partner unknowingly adheres to the relationship. As Vaughan (1989, p. 68) writes: the parting person may say to his or her partner, "I feel unhappy," and avoids adding, "and I'm seeing someone else." Partners easily become allies in trying to avoid a direct confrontation. Often the partner who wants to separate feels unable to cope with the prospect of talking openly about separation and carries it through more or less without comment to avoid the negative repercussions, especially the helpless reactions of the partner. Indirectness of communication is a widespread characteristic in relationship disengagement (Baxter, 1985).

Separation questions the usual habits of the partners (Vaughan, 1986). The person instigating the separation has a certain advantage in being able to prepare for the reality of separating; but the separator, too, suffers from the change in habits and living conditions, which calls for adaptation. Apart from this the noninstigating partner starts to develop new survival strategies after the separation; he or she forms new relationships and begins redefining him- or herself so that in time weakness is transformed into strength.

Concluding remarks

Initiation and disengagement are particularly striking phases in a close relationship. It should, however, be kept in mind that the maintenance of a relationship often lasts far longer than the initiation and disengagement phases. Nevertheless, far more is known about these two phases, as a result of empirical research, than about the constancy of a relationship. This bias in research is comparable to a similar bias in the mass media. Films and television also tend to concentrate on the development and the ending of a relationship, whereas the course of the relationship over the central phase is generally of less interest.

Although this deficit in research on the maintenance of a relationship is understandable, it should be rectified in the future. Studies on love and partnership (compare Bierhoff, 1991b) as well as on the exchange processes in relationships (compare Mikula, 1992; Rusbult, 1983) can be seen as an important contribution in this respect. One central concept is that the initiation of a relationship is motivated primarily by romantic sentiments of love, while the longer-term maintenance of the relationship is facilitated by the development of a friendly love style. Further research in this area may well contribute to a deeper understanding of the conditions underlying happiness or unhappiness during the course of a relationship.

References

Ainsworth, M. D. S., Blehar, M. S., Waters, S., & Wall, S. (1978). *Patterns of attachment: A psychological study of the strange situation.* Hillsdale, NJ: Erlbaum.

Amelang, M. (1991). Einstellungen zu Liebe und Partnerschaft: Konzepte, Skalen und Korrelate. In M. Amelang, H. J. Ahrens & H. W. Bierhoff (Eds.), *Attraktion und Liebe* (pp. 153–196). Göttingen: Hogrefe.

Bartholomew, K. (1990). Avoidance of intimacy: An attachment perspective. *Journal of Social and Personal Relationships, 7*, 147–178.

Bartholomew, K., & Horowitz, L. M. (1991). Attachment styles in young adults: A test of a four-category model. *Journal of Personality and Social Psychology, 61*, 226–244.

Bartholomew, K., & Scharfe, E. A. (1994). Attachment processes in young couples. Paper presented at the 7th International Conference on Personal Relationships in Groningen.

Baxter, L. A. (1985). Accomplishing relationship disengagement. In S. Duck & D. Perlman (Eds.), *Understanding personal relationships* (pp. 243–265). Beverly Hills, CA: Sage.

Berscheid, E., Snyder, M., & Omoto, A. M. (1989). The relationship closeness inventory: Assessing the closeness of interpersonal relationships. *Journal of Personality and Social Psychology, 57,* 792–807.

Bierhoff, H. W. (1973). Kosten und Belohnung: Eine Theorie sozialen Verhaltens. *Zeitschrift für Sozialpsychologie, 4,* 297–317.

(1989). Liebesstile. *Psychologie Heute, 16*(2), 16–17.

(1991a). Liebe. In M. Amelang, H. J. Ahrens & H. W. Bierhoff (Eds.), *Attraktion und Liebe* (pp. 197–234). Göttingen: Hogrefe.

(1991b). Twenty years of research on love: Theory, results, and prospects for the future. *German Journal of Psychology, 15,* 95–117.

Bierhoff, H. W., & Grau, I. (1993). Die Bedeutung der physischen Attraktivität für interpersonelle Attraktion und Liebe. In M. Hassebrauck & R. Niketta (Eds.), *Physische Attraktivität* (pp. 201–233). Göttingen: Hogrefe.

Bierhoff, H. W., Grau, I., & Ludwig, A. (1993). *Enge Beziehungen.* Unveröffentlichter Bericht für die Deutsche Forschungsgemeinschaft.

Bierhoff, H. W., & Klein, R. (1991). Dimensionen der Liebe: Entwicklung einer deutschsprachigen Skala zur Erfassung von Liebesstilen. *Zeitschrift für Differentielle und Diagnostische Psychologie, 12,* 53–71.

Bowlby, J. (1969). *Attachment.* New York: Basic Books.

(1988). *A secure base: Parent–child attachment and healthy human development.* New York: Basic Books.

Bretherton, I. (1985). Attachment theory: Retrospect and prospect. *Monographs of the Society for Research in Child Development, 50* (2, Serial No. 209), 3–35.

Byrne, D. (1971). *The attraction paradigm.* New York: Academic Press.

Collins, N. L., & Read, S. J. (1990). Adult attachment, working models, and relationship quality in dating couples. *Journal of Personality and Social Psychology, 58,* 644–663.

Eibl-Eibesfeldt, I. (1984). *Die Biologie des menschlichen Verhaltens.* München: Piper.

Feeney, J. A., & Noller, P. (1990). Attachment style as a predictor of adult romantic relationship. *Journal of Personality and Social Psychology, 58,* 281–291.

Grau, I., & Bierhoff, H. W. (1994). Eifersucht als besitzergreifende Liebe (Jealousy as possessive love). Vortrag auf dem 39. Kongreß der Deutschen Gesellschaft für Psychologie in Hamburg.

Grossmann, K. E., & Grossmann, K. (1991). Attachment quality as an organizer of emotional and behavioral responses in a longitudinal perspective. In C. M. Parkes, J. Stevenson-Hinde, & P. Marris (Eds.), *Attachment across the life cycle* (pp. 93–114). London: Routledge.

Hatfield, E. (1988). Passionate and companionate love. In R. J. Sternberg &

M. L. Barnes (Eds.), *The psychology of love* (pp. 191–217). New Haven, CT: Yale University Press.

Hazan, C., & Shaver, P. (1987). Romantic love conceptualized as an attachment process. *Journal of Personality and Social Psychology, 52,* 511–524.

(1990). Love and work: An attachment-theoretical perspective. *Journal of Personality and Social Psychology, 59,* 270–280.

Hendrick, C., & Hendrick, S. (1986). A theory and method of love. *Journal of Personality and Social Psychology, 50,* 392–402.

(1989). Research on love: Does it measure up? *Journal of Personality and Social Psychology, 56,* 784–794.

Hendrick, S. S., & Hendrick, C. (1992). *Romantic love.* Newbury Park, CA: Sage.

Hill, C. T., Peplau, L. A., & Rubin, Z. (1981). Differing perceptions in dating couples: Sex roles vs. alternative explanations. *Psychology of Women Quarterly, 5,* 418–434.

Hirschman, A. O. (1970). *Exit, voice, and loyalty.* Cambridge, MA: Harvard University Press.

Johnson, D. J., & Rusbult, C. E. (1989). Resisting temptation: Devaluation of alternative partners as a means of maintaining commitment in close relationships. *Journal of Personality and Social Psychology, 57,* 967–980.

Kelley, H. H., & Thibaut, J. W. (1978). *Interpersonal relations. A theory of interdependence.* New York: Wiley.

Kirkpatrick, L. A., & Davis, K. E. (1994). Attachment style, gender, and relationship stability: A longitudinal analysis. *Journal of Personality and Social Psychology, 66,* 502–512.

Kraigher, U. (1991). *Similarity and assumed similarity of partners in their attitude toward love and relationship satisfaction.* Unpublished Diploma work, University of Graz.

Lee, J. A. (1973/1976). *The colors of love.* Englewood Cliffs, NJ: Prentice-Hall.

Levinger, G. (1980). Toward the analysis of close relationships. *Journal of Experimental Social Psychology, 16,* 510–544.

Levinger, G., & Snoek, D. J. (1972). *Attraction in relationships: A new look at interpersonal attraction.* Morristown, NJ: General learning Press.

Levy, M. B., & Davis, K. E. (1988). Lovestyles and attachment styles compared: Their relations to each other and to various relationship characteristics. *Journal of Social and Personal Relationships, 5,* 439–471.

Main, M., Kaplan, N., & Cassidy, J. (1985). Security in infancy, childhood, and adulthood: A move to the level of representation. *Monogrographs of the Society for Research in Child Development, 50* (2, Serial No. 209), 66–104.

Mikula, G. (1992). Austausch und Gerechtigkeit in Freundschaft, Partnerschaft und Ehe: Ein Überblick Über den aktuellen Forschungsstand. *Psychologische Rundschau, 43,* 69–82.

Mikula, G., & Stroebe, W. (1991). Theorien und Determinanten der zwischenmenschlichen Anziehung. In M. Amelang, H. J. Ahrens & H. W. Bierhoff (Eds.), *Attraktion und Liebe* (pp. 61–104). Göttingen: Hogrefe.

Peele, S. (1988). Fools for love: The romantic ideal, psychological theory, and addictive love. In R. J. Sternberg & M. L. Barnes (Eds.), *The psychology of love* (pp. 159–187). New Haven, CT: Yale University Press.

Peplau, L. A., Rubin, Z., & Hill, C. T. (1977). Sexual intimacy in dating relationships. *Journal of Social Issues, 33*(2), 86–109.

Reis, H. T., Shaver, P. (1988). Intimacy as an interpersonal process. In S. W. Duck (Ed.), *Handbook of personal relationships* (pp. 367–389). Chichester, England: Wiley.

Rubin, Z. (1970). Measurement of romantic love. *Journal of Personality and Social Psychology, 16,* 265–273.

Rubin, Z., Peplau, L. A., & Hill, C. T. (1981). Loving and leaving: Sex differences in romantic attachments. *Sex Roles, 7,* 821–835.

Rusbult, C. E. (1983). A longitudinal test of the investment model: The development (and deterioration) of satisfaction and commitment in heterosexual involvements. *Journal of Personality and Social Psychology, 45,* 101–117.

(1987). Responses to dissatisfaction in close relationships. In D. Perlman & S. Duck (Eds.), *Intimate relationships* (pp. 209–237). Newbury Park, CA: Sage.

Rusbult, C. E., Johnson, D. J., & Morrow, G. D. (1986). Impact of couple patterns of problem solving on distress and nondistress in dating relationships. *Journal of Personality and Social Psychology, 50,* 744–753.

Rubult, C. E., Verette, J., Whitney, G. A., Slovik, L. F., & Lipkus, I. (1991). Accommodation processes in close relationships: Theory and preliminary empirical evidence. *Journal of Personality and Social Psychology, 60,* 53–78.

Rushton, J. P. (1982). Social learning theory and the development of prosocial behavior. In N. Eisenberg (Ed.), *The development of prosocial behavior* (pp. 77–105). New York: Academic Press.

Seligman, C., Fazio, R. H., & Zanna, M. P. (1980). Effects of salience of extrinsic rewards on liking and loving. *Journal of Personality and Social Psychology, 38,* 453–460.

Shaver, P., Hazan, C., & Bradshaw, D. (1988). Love as attachment: The integration of three behavioral systems. In R. J. Sternberg & M. L. Barnes (Eds.), *The psychology of love* (pp. 68–99). New Haven, CT: Yale University Press.

Simpson, J. A. (1987). The dissolution of romantic relationships: Factors involved in relationship stability and emotional distress. *Journal of Personality and Social Psychology, 53,* 683–692.

(1990). Influence of attachment style on romantic relationships. *Journal of Personality and Social Psychology, 59,* 971–980.

Simpson, J. A., & Gangestad, S. W. (1991). Individual differences in sociosexuality: Evidence for convergent and discriminant validity. *Journal of Personality and Social Psychology, 60,* 870–883.

Snyder, M., Berscheid, E., & Glick, P. (1985). Focusing on the exterior and the interior: Two investigations of the initiation of personal relationships. *Journal of Personality and Social Psychology, 48,* 1427–1439.

Spence, J. T., & Helmreich, R. L. (1978). Masculinity and femininity. Austin: Texas University Press.

Sternberg, R. J., (1986). A triangular theory of love. *Psychological Review, 93,*
    119–135.
    (1987). Liking versus loving: A comparative evaluation of theories. *Psycho-
    logical Bulletin, 102,* 331–345.
Tennov, D. (1979). *Love and limerence: The experience of being in love.* New
    York: Stein & Day.
Thibaut, J. W., & Kelley, H. H. (1959). *The social psychology of groups.* New
    York: Wiley.
Vaughan, D. (1986). *Uncoupling.* Oxford: Oxford University Press.
Zuckerman, M. (1979). *Sensation seeking.* Hillsdale, NJ: Erlbaum.

9

Same-sex couples: Courtship, commitment, context

Virginia Rutter and Pepper Schwartz

The study of same-sex couples and their relationships has grown over the past several decades. While great gaps in our knowledge still exist, the past 15 years have shown substantial interdisciplinary growth of the literature. The literature has proliferated so much that a comprehensive but brief overview is difficult to accomplish. This chapter will confine itself to a few central themes: courtship, maintaining relationships, dissolving relationships, and several problem areas including AIDS, intimate violence, and the political climate in the United States toward same-sex couples. With a few exceptions, our review is limited to research in the United States on gay and lesbian couples.

Nomenclature is especially difficult in these days of interdisciplinary research, since many disciplines have discipline-specific, nonoverlapping terms. Therefore, we will state our working definitions before our substantive discussion. The term "homosexual" describes individuals with a same-sex sexual preference; "same-sex" refers to all homosexual couples; "lesbian" refers to women with a same-sex preference; "gay" refers to men with a same-sex preference; and "bisexual" refers to individuals who are either sequentially or contemporaneously attracted to same-sex and opposite-sex partners. We ask the reader, however, not to reify these labels. These terms are tools to describe behavior. They do not describe strict categories of gays, lesbians, bisexuals, or the wide varieties of identities in between and among the different social-sexual arrangements people move in and out of over the course of a lifetime.

Orienting themes: Gender, gay culture, and history

Three themes organize our analysis of same-sex relationships: gender, gay culture and subcultures, and historical developments and larger contextual influences.

Gender

It is important to remember that lesbian and heterosexual women share early socialization and life experiences. This means that regardless of sexual orientation, all women can be understood in part by their similarities. This analytic approach also provides insight into gay men, who share values, experience, and socialization with heterosexual men. It is a central tenet of our approach that the profoundly gendered way individuals are sorted by society renders greater continuity between lesbian and heterosexual women and between gay and heterosexual men than between gay men and lesbians. In other words, before there is sexual orientation, there is the socially and perhaps biologically constructed sexual identity we refer to as gender. Some argue against our position and believe that gays are more likely to have been "sissies" growing up and lesbians "tomboys," suggesting that gays and lesbians have a unique gender as well as a unique sexual orientation (Hemmer & Kleiber, 1981; Whitam & Mathay, 1991). However, we believe the weight of present research demonstrates that most gays and lesbians do not have an atypical socialization, nor exhibit early and sustained cross-sex behavior (Blumstein & Schwartz, 1983; Eldridge & Gilbert, 1990; Peplau, 1991).

New research suggests that there may be a genetic basis of homosexuality (Bailey, Pillard, Neale & Agyei, 1993; Hamer & Copeland, 1994). This evidence persuasively explains the orientation of at least some proportion of homosexuals. The genetic evidence, however, does not establish a correlation between homosexuality and other behavioral or physical qualities often associated with homosexual orientation, such as effeminacy or being "butch." While there are many different research arenas on the etiology of homosexuality, including brain differentiation and endocrine system differences (LeVay, 1993; Money & Ehrhardt, 1972), behavioral and other studies still find gender, rather than sexuality, central to understanding the values, goals, and practices of lesbian and gay relationships.

Men and women of every sexual preference experience similar socialization into relationship roles and sexual roles. For example, men are not expected to focus on relationships as the center of their lives; women are exhorted to do so. Role models for men stress independence and the provider role, and equate success in work with masculinity and personal success. Although women's socialization is changing, women are more often trained to link their future adult identity to a good marriage, motherhood, and more modest work achievements. Theoretically, then, men interacting with men, and women interacting with women, share approaches, reactions, and role expectations. Contributions the opposite sex might be expected to bring to a heterosexual relationship may be absent in same-sex relationships. Both homosexual partners may expect the other to balance their role behavior at the same time each person claims role prerogatives. For example, if two men slow-dance, both may expect to lead; if two women are cleaning house, both may hope the other will take on mechanical or automotive projects. Lesbians may seek to reject the impositions of gendered norms of behavior and consciously supplement their past socialization by adopting masculine skills or affect. However, this is a case of the exception supporting the rule. That is, whether one accepts or rejects gendered norms, the decision-making process serves to acknowledge the power of gendered norms.

Homosexual culture

While gender norms tend to create similarity between homosexuals and heterosexuals of the same sex, the culture of the gay community modifies these continuities. Evolving and expanding gay norms influence homosexual lifestyles, ideologies, and values. For example, in some lesbian communities appearance norms support a more masculine or androgynous "butch" look. Over time, lesbians who initially looked more traditionally feminine become drawn to the prevailing lesbian community standard. Likewise, in some American gay male neighborhoods and bars, the standard is a hypermasculine look, including "lumberjack" shirts, bluejeans, hiking boots, and cropped hair. New norms are the basis for an alternative culture that supports and expresses the homosexual community's ideology instead of the values of heterosexual courtship.

Of course, gay culture is not a unitary phenomenon. Subcultures exist that shape a variety of behaviors, defining and diversifying homosexual norms. For example, a growing lesbian "sex-positive" subculture is reacting against prevalent lesbian sexual norms that eschew aggression and nonmonogamy. In this sex-positive subculture, women favor recreational, aggressive, and casual sex. Subcultures are defined by rebelling against a well-understood *homosexual* norm, rather than simply against *heterosexual* norms. The anomalous behavior reinforces the gay cultural norms, demonstrating the extent to which the culture has evolved and defined itself.

Historical context

The historical circumstances and larger context in which homosexuals and the gay community exist also exert influence over gay and lesbian relationships. These effects extend beyond proximal community influences and include larger institutional and social forces. Until the 1960s homosexuals were largely "closeted." In the past three decades great openness has evolved, particularly in major metropolitan areas. While a trend of increased tolerance is evident in the increased descriptive attention (as opposed to "scandalizing" attention) same-sex couples obtain in Western popular culture,[1] the circumstances for gays and lesbians vary tremendously by local community. For example, in Seattle, a liberal, medium-sized U.S. city, the mayor and police chief typically march in the gay rights parade. Because of the high income, education, and class level of the residents, these acts of solidarity are supported by the population.[2] In contrast, lesbians in the southeastern United States and other politically and socially conservative parts of the country are subject to vigorous surveillance and social sanctions imposed by less tolerant communities.[3] Even liberal cities with statutes that promote nondiscrimination in housing and employment practices find individual acts of discrimination and even rage against gays and lesbians, as reported by the Anti-Violence Project report on national trends in violence against gays and lesbians (Dunlap, 1995c). These cities usually find it necessary to use all the resources of the law to enforce these statutes.

National movements have organized to increase heterosexuals' tolerance, understanding, and connection to gays and lesbians, who are increasingly likely to be "out." Such movements must square off against countermovements such as those organized by fundamentalist Christian organizations. The course of a couple's life will be altered depending on whether they live in a community or historical period of substantial acceptance and legal protection, or in one where prevailing sentiment is fearful, hostile, and legally tenuous.

Courtship

There is a spare literature on same-sex patterns of courtship. The research has tended to focus on committed relationships, perhaps because the right to be a couple has been uncertain, and the way to be a couple has been unscripted. Recently, however, research has begun to emphasize homosexual courtship. Partly as a consequence of the AIDS epidemic, the process of partnering has become more salient for gay men and health researchers alike. The AIDS epidemic has made casual sex a potentially lethal enterprise for gay men, and to a lesser extent for lesbians and heterosexuals. Thus, social scientists and public health researchers are interested in understanding the mechanisms by which sexual interaction carries as little risk as possible. Establishing and maintaining committed relationships is one mechanism for reducing risk. Researchers have discovered that studying courtship patterns has become at least as complicated as studying sexual interaction. Of course, the issue of reducing risk is also salient to the sex lives of homosexuals. For gay men, HIV status has become part of explicit negotiations about who can have sex with whom and under what conditions. Because so many lesbians (approximately 50%) have had sex sometime in their past with a man, many of them gay or bisexual, these women are also concerned with safer sex (Laumann, Michael & Gagnon, 1994).

Generation is an additional reason for the new focus on creating and maintaining committed same-sex relationships. As the baby boom generation has aged, a substantial proportion of the homosexual population has reached the "settling-down age." Indeed, the trend toward more committed relationships actually preceded the AIDS crisis (Siegle & Glassman, 1989). Thus, while in the 1970s surveys showed approximately 95% of gay men preferring nonmonogamy (McWhirter & Mattison, 1984), surveys done in early 1992 showed over 96% of gay men preferring monogamous relationships (Berger, 1990). As we will discuss later in the chapter, gay men report greater preferences for monogamy, but it is not clear that this ideal always translates into behavior.

The dating marketplace

Heterosexual and homosexual women still link sex and love, and seek to establish some level of intimacy before sexual involvement. Lesbians, like other women, tend to emphasize mental and emotional qualities above physical qualities. They often reject male-derived appearance norms of beauty, and especially reject norms of submissiveness that often govern women in heterosexual courting situations. Many lesbians prefer a "butch" androgynous or boyish look, but a more feminine look, often referred to as "lipstick lesbian," has also recently come into style in some lesbian communities. Although as recently as the 1970s heterosexual-like role playing (butch and femme) was quite common for lesbians and gay men, it has since become less common and is counternormative in gay culture. Nevertheless, role playing persists as one among many tastes for homosexuals (Blumstein & Schwartz, 1983).

Recently there has been an increase in lesbians' use of personal advertisements (Davidson, 1991). Some studies have demonstrated that lesbians tend to emphasize political and sexual identity issues in their search for a partner. For example, women will state "bi's need not apply," indicating a political as well as personal commitment to a homosexual identity. Lesbians' advertisements also emphasize physical characteristics that do not appear in heterosexual women's advertisements, such as indicating a preference for physical strength (Sociology 481 student project, fall 1994). Lesbians persistently emphasize independence and self-sufficiency as valued characteristics in themselves and potential partners. However, lesbians do not usually emphasize job status or high earning (Blumstein & Schwartz, 1983). This may be due to the limited access women generally have to higher-status or higher-earning jobs (Ferree, 1987). It may also be a rejection of the heterosexual norm that women ought to "marry well" by finding a "good provider."

Heterosexual and homosexual men have tended to prioritize attractiveness in potential partners. Gay men, in particular, place a heavy emphasis on looks. The preference is for an extremely attractive face, an athletic body, and 9 well-groomed appearance. There is a common emphasis on specific body parts, especially buttocks, but also penis size and chest. Gay men also seek the accoutrements of manliness, including high-paying or masculine careers (Davidson, 1991).

Meeting places

Gay and lesbian populations in the United States and other Western countries are concentrated in urban areas (Laumann et al., 1994). It is easier to meet other gays and lesbians in cities, especially major cities such as Boston, New York, Seattle, San Francisco, Chicago, and Los Angeles, than in smaller cities or rural areas, where there is likely to be a smaller homosexual community as well as less tolerance for nonheterosexuals (Miller, 1989).

For a homosexual who is "out," the variety of places to meet others like oneself has grown. Gay travel clubs, university alumni groups, and gay and lesbian bars of many types have proliferated. Furthermore, information resources such as *Inn Places*, *The Gay Yellow Pages*, and *International Gay Yellow Pages* list gay and lesbian businesses and meeting places in every city in the world (Huston & Schwartz, 1995). For homosexuals who are not out, or who are only partially out, there is less opportunity to find a relationship. In certain locations, including Providence, Rhode Island; Brooklyn Heights, New York City; Fire Island, New York; Provincetown, Massachusetts; Northampton, Massachusetts; as well as Paris, Berlin, Amsterdam, and Copenhagen, there is a concentration of same-sex courting, meeting, and mating, with a diversity of venues for doing so.

While gays may meet one another in bars and clubs, it is more likely for lesbians and gay men to meet potential partners through other homosexual friends. This is particularly the case for lesbians, attributable in part to women's preference for intimacy and familiarity before sexual involvement, and in part to the way that lesbian social life is strongly organized around friendship networks. When matches are made within friendship circles, the breakup can be socially awkward or disruptive. These are intense social groups, and breakups disturb alliances, loyalties, and social interaction patterns. Notably, heterosexual friends rarely engage in such matchmaking, either because they know very few homosexuals or because they are myopic about gay friends' interests or preferences.

A secondary way for lesbians to meet is through political/feminist organizations and activities. These settings encourage pairs to match on values and ideology, which is an important predictor of lesbian pair satisfaction (Howard, Blumstein & Schwartz, 1992). Lesbians who meet in a political setting are often more activist, independent, and radical than others and are most likely to emphasize the value of autonomy. Thus, paradoxically, while lesbian political settings are an important site for meeting partners, politically minded lesbians are less likely to endorse settling down and monogamy as fundamental relationship values (Andrews, 1990; Vance, 1984).

Finding partners

Even in high-concentration homosexual areas, the dilemma of who makes the first move and how it is done remains. Lesbians are particularly reticent, since they have learned feminine gender norms that discourage initiation and sexual forwardness. Moreover, a lesbian cannot always be sure, even in a homosexual environment, whether a woman she meets is available. Lesbians tend to socialize in couples, and there are strong norms against approaching someone else's girlfriend. Furthermore, unlike the presumption of availability at a gay bar, it is not always clear that all women in a lesbian environment are committed to a homosexual identity and lifestyle.

The recent growth of lesbian "sex clubs" designed for casual sex is a remarkable exception to lesbian sexual norms. In recent years, urban centers such as New York and San Francisco have developed lesbian bathhouses and other venues suitable for casual sexual encounters (Huston & Schwartz, 1995). In contrast, gay men have traditionally had the option of a variety of meeting places, including baths, dance clubs, and "tea rooms," that assume availability and are known as venues for anonymous sexual encounters.

Most meeting places are not organized by any similarity other than sexual orientation. Where the only basis for meeting is sexual preference, couples without shared interests may be paired solely on the basis of physical attractiveness. As a consequence, lesbians and gay men may end up in mismatched couples. A growing number of publications try to bring gays and lesbians with shared interests together, but the problem of haphazard matching continues and tends to generate less stable relationships. In general, homogamous relationships (couples matched by class, education, age and interests) are correlated with higher degrees of satisfaction, and homogamy has positive effects on empathy, communication, and the equitable division of labor (Whyte, 1990). This has implications for homosexual couples as well. For example, Kurdek and Schmitt (1987) found that closeness in age of homosexual partners was positively correlated with satisfaction. Matching on levels of emotional involvement and ability to solve relationship problems is generally a stronger predictor of relationship satisfaction in homosexual couples than matching on demographic variables (Kurdek & Schmitt, 1987). Furthermore, while gays and lesbians are more likely to be in nonhomogamous pairs, there is still quite a high rate of homogamous pairing in all features except age (Howard, Blumstein & Schwartz, n.d.).

What gays and lesbians rarely do is meet openly, as they encounter one another in the day-to-day course of their lives. Not only is homosexuality a nonnormative status, it is also an invisible status. Even liberals, who believe homosexuals should have civil rights, jobs, and fair housing, may be embarrassed by hand-holding, kissing, or just obvious mutual interest between same-sex members of a couple. These acts might be interesting or attractive among courting heterosexuals, but they are disquieting to many heterosexuals when enacted by same-sex couples.

It is particularly difficult for homosexual teenagers to court openly. Very few environments are sufficiently liberal, such that gay teenagers can go to the high school prom or openly date in high school. A few isolated cases of same-sex prom dates have captured media attention in the United States in recent years, more because they are an anomaly than because they are a trend. Gay and lesbian teens' minimal level of dating experience is a considerable impediment to acquiring social skills necessary to navigate intimate relationships. While heterosexuals have the freedom to practice having relationships throughout high school, college, and beyond, homosexuals are curtailed in parallel same-sex relationship experiences.

Committed relationships

Should a couple shift from courtship into commitment, several features are prominent in patterns of communication and conflict negotiation, particularly in problem areas including career, money, housework, sex, and family.

A look at predictors of satisfaction for same-sex couples provides important background to communication patterns. Predictors for lesbian satisfaction and gay satisfaction correspond with gender norms: women seek high emotional intensity while men seek low conflict. Satisfaction for lesbians is correlated with high degrees of emotional intimacy, an equitable balance of power, and high self-esteem (Eldridge & Gilbert, 1990). Where differences are found in mean scores of couple satisfaction, lesbian couples have the higher satisfaction scores of all types of couples (Metz, Rosser & Strapko, 1994). For gay men, satisfaction is correlated with low conflict, high appreciation, stability, and cooperation (Jones & Bates, 1978). Just as with heterosexual couples, same-sex couples' destructive arguing, characterized by criticism, contempt, blame, and stonewalling, is negatively correlated with relationship satisfaction (Kurdek, 1993b). Furthermore, Metz et al. (1994) find heterosexual, lesbian, and gay couples to be fundamentally similar in conflict resolution styles. For heterosexual couples the challenge is to balance the difference between male and female styles in the relationship; for same-sex couples the challenge is to counterbalance the similarities in styles.

Patterns in conversation

Since patterns in satisfaction outcomes for gay and lesbian pairs appear to be influenced by gender, it follows that communication styles are also influenced by gender. In addition, we emphasize that power has a strong, separate influence on communication styles. Communication provides a site for evaluating both styles of communication and issues that arise within communication among different kinds of couples (Steen & Schwartz, in press). A gender approach to conversation hypothesizes that men and women use the act of conversing differently (Tannen, 1990). Along with gendered patterns, the impact of power differentials within same-sex couples emerges when "dominance and support patterns" are identified in couples' conversations. Such dominance tactics as interrupting or steering the conversation reinforce or help to create relationship hierarchy (Kollock, Blumstein, & Schwartz, 1985; Steen & Schwartz, in press). When "power differentials" and gender are used as distinct predictors of conversational control, power differentials, rather than gender, appear to be a better predictor of who maintains conversational control, although gender plays an important role (Kollock et al., 1985). The gender of the participant exerts a similar level of influence on relationship styles of heterosexual and homosexual couples. Furthermore, the participant's power within the relationship dictates patterns of influence and accommodation for heterosexual and homosexual couples.

Research on women's approaches to conversation and problem solving demonstrates that women view conversation as part of intimacy. Women work to keep the conversation going, encourage their interlocutor, fill silences, and ask questions. Women seek consensus because it is emotionally rewarding to them (Gilligan, 1982). They will take time in conversation to find or create common ground. Women, more than men, demonstrate a greater preference for emotional disclosure, both as an opportunity for dominating the issue and for winning the point. Men find the "feminine" supportive style weak; they prefer strong tactics such as interruption and conversational leadership. Women tend to dislike verbal challenges because they believe they violate intimacy and civility; men persistently prefer to spar. "Masculine" tactics facilitate expeditious decision making and reduce the length of the conversation or "debate" (Tannen, 1990).

While researchers have often associated males with conversational power and females with conversational submission, Kollock et al. (1985) find that "gendered" styles of communication are more strongly associated with personal power than with gender. The more powerful speaker will have more control over decisions and the decision-making process, regardless of sex. Powerful tactics, regardless of gender, include the use of minimal responses (such as "hmm" or "uh-huh," thus avoiding the effort of substantive verbal exchange); more frequent interruptions; and not asking for other opinions or input by the use of tag questions (e.g., "This is what I think, what do you think?"), which are commonly used by the less powerful speaker. While for heterosexual couples, the more powerful partner is often the male, this is not always the case. Same-sex couples create an environment without gender differences, so that power differences are more evident.

How do these power- and gender-related styles of communication influence same-sex couples' communication? Lesbian and gay couples both aspire to egalitarian relationships, but their conversational styles reflect different strategies. Lesbians, highly sensitized to power imbalances, seek to minimize conflict and avoid power plays in conversation. Instead, conversation is oriented to a shared goal: creating an emotionally close, fulfilling, disclosing conversation. Indeed, of the four kinds of couples Kollock and colleagues studied (lesbian, gay, married, and cohabiting heterosexual), lesbians had the lowest rate of attempted interruptions, and the fewest conversational challenges. Eschewing conventional power tactics is a path to egalitarianism for lesbians.

Like other men, gay men are more likely to jockey openly for power. Gay men are more likely to acknowledge rank and its privileges and use various strategies to claim it. For example, gay men use minimal responses during conversation more than any other kind of couple (Kollock et al., 1985). While tag questions (e.g., "What do you think?") tend to be used by the less powerful partner among heterosexuals, the more powerful partner uses them among gay men. This means that the man with the obvious advantage is going out of his way to draw his less powerful partner out, and to make him feel his opinion matters and that he has interactive value. Because power and masculinity are prominent issues for gay men, this practice represents an effort to equalize status and curb resentment.

While egalitarianism is the goal, not all same-sex couples achieve it. Conversational problems for lesbians arise from the high levels of emotionality present in woman-to-woman relationships. Such emotionality can generate a high number of relationship issues. This emotional intensity can produce an "implosion" in pursuit of emotional issues. The relationship can collapse under a preponderance of emotional expectations and needs. Interestingly, this potentially claustrophobic environment coexists with what psychologists call an avoidant style (J. M. Gottman, 1994), where the relationship is organized around *not* observing or addressing relationship problems. Because women typically shun conflict, there is a tendency among lesbians to avoid controversial issues, or to have high expectations of partners to intuit or know their feelings without conversation. While emotional expressiveness is high, problem solving may be delayed indefinitely. Problem avoidance may lead to an accumulation of unresolved or seemingly insurmountable relationship problems (Peplau, Cochran, Rook & Padesky, 1978).

The dilemma for gay couples is the inverse of lesbians' high emotionality problem. Gay men, like heterosexual men, engage in a low level of disclosure. When the relationship is troubled, this may become stonewalling, during which no communication occurs. Gay couples may fail to create opportunities to address important relationship issues. Small arguments are avoided, while over time, angry feelings accumulate. By the time a problem is addressed, an explosive argument may erupt, and the enormity of the problem may mean that resolution is much more difficult. Male conversational style may complicate the problem once conflict is identified. Men are more likely to challenge partners without listening to each other. Furthermore, gay men view compromise (Berzon, 1988) as a failure of masculinity, and resolution may be impossible.

Conflicts

The content of same-sex couples' conversations revolves around equality, whether it pertains to career priorities, money, or division of domestic labor. The issues within these categories for gay or lesbian couples, however, have important differences that relate both to gender norms and the different socioeconomic experiences of women versus men.

Career

Male partners tend to be equally career-centered. The dilemma over whose job gets precedence is a difficult, unscripted decision-making enterprise. Most men accept cultural norms that value job achievement, and may even compete with their own partners, as well as with men in general, for prestige and money. Among lesbians, career issues tend to be a lower priority, and therefore somewhat less polarizing. Furthermore, men are not only socialized to value career achievement as a central part of their identity, but they are also more likely than women to have more exciting job opportunities and to be highly rewarded in prestige and money for job performance.

Women are less often socialized to build their whole life and self-concept around career. They are offered fewer tempting, prestigious, or high-paying job opportunities and advances. As the workplace continues to open up to women, this may change. At present, however, a more common work conflict for lesbians involves resentment over relationship time lost to one or the other's professional endeavors. This is particularly the case for couples mismatched in terms of emphasis on career versus relationship. For the smaller proportion of lesbian couples with "competing careers," the conflicts in these couples revolve predictably around independence and equality. These career-oriented women are defying cultural norms by emphasizing career over relationship, and for lesbians as for heterosexual women they often pay a price in their domestic relationships. Where one partner but not the other is highly invested in career, the conflict is commonly cast in terms of class struggle. Indeed, a strong theme in the lesbian literature is that middle-class women have "class prerogatives" that they use unfairly in life and relationships, and which they should relinquish. How this is accomplished is not clear. More radical lesbian literature advocates avoiding class struggles by dropping out of the larger capitalist work structure to become a lesbian "separatist" and live in a world without men and men's economic and social institutions.

Money

The economic provider role has an impact on heterosexual and homosexual relationships. For heterosexuals, men have traditionally functioned in the provider role; the "good provider" engages in work for pay, while the "true woman" engages in domestic work, including household labor as well as the expressive work of maintaining relationships. Although in practice only a small proportion of families have ever had a single good provider, these norms have historically been very powerful (Bernard, 1981; Coontz, 1992). Although these 1950s archetypes are hardly the norm today, married women continue to be economically dependent on their husbands, as a consequence of child bearing, fewer workplace opportunities, and lower pay for similar work. Wives' dependence on husbands tends to influence power dynamics in noneconomic spheres of the relationship. Finally, these patterns are very difficult for heterosexuals to overcome or disrupt (Schwartz, 1994).

Blumstein and Schwartz (1983) found that same-sex couples, because partners' job opportunities tend to be more similar than among heterosexual partners, have fewer financial conflicts than other kinds of couples. However, maintaining relative independence requires fastidious, deliberate money management. Same-sex couples pool financial resources less often than married couples, but those couples who do not pool resources experience higher breakup rates (Blumstein & Schwartz, 1983). Even when great care and equity is emphasized, couples are still vulnerable to tension and conflict over money. Kurdek (1991) finds that negotiating financial matters is central to same-sex couples' stability. Even in couples with high incomes, Berger (1990) found that one-third of same-sex couples mentioned money as a source of conflict.

Both gay and lesbian partners will engage in the provider role, but they each prefer a co-provider situation. Gay men, like other men, do not expect that a provider will take care of them. When one gay partner is the provider, the partner who is being provided for tends to be more dissatisfied with the situation. In contrast, lesbians do not expect to support another person financially, except temporarily. Lesbians are not socialized, as many men are, to take pleasure in a paternalistic provider role. A lesbian who finds herself in the role of provider is likely to be the more dissatisfied partner with the situation. Both gay and lesbian couples are more stable when each partner contributes equally or proportionately.

Money issues are significantly different for men and women. Money heavily influences power relations between gay men. Gay men are more likely to link the couple's economic welfare with relationship satisfaction, and they tend to endorse the belief in the perquisites of the provider role. However, differences in income and attitudes about money can cause long-term tension and conflict. Even if the higher earner in a gay couple does not endorse a power differential that coincides with their economic differences, the lower earner is likely to be sensitive to the difference. Indeed, the research on reasons for breakups demonstrates that the lower earner in gay couples is more likely to be the one who initiates dissolution (Kurdek, 1991).

Lesbians are highly sensitized to the relationship between power and money. Heterosexual norms are seen as problematic in part because of the way in which they perpetuate the dichotomous provider/domestic roles. Conflicts are not typically tied to the issues of the "provider role" and associated privileges, since lesbians rarely enact this kind of role. Nevertheless, the higher earner is more likely to initiate a breakup. A study of lesbian couples together for 10 years or more shows that money was the second-most conflictual issue (Johnson, 1990). In examining the content of lesbians' money conflicts, Clunis and Green (1988) found that the salient issue tends to become whether to live simpler lives, in defiance of patriarchal norms, or spend money more freely, in defiance of the typically limited economic capacity of women. The conservative spenders wish to challenge mainstream materialism. The liberal spenders seek liberation from second-class citizenship and wish to establish the "good life" in the absence of men.

The money issue for lesbians is exacerbated by the constraints of lower incomes and the difficulties of pink- and blue-collar jobs in which workers are less likely to have control personal autonomy. Peplau reports that lower-income, less educated lesbians tend to be more dependent in relationships because of their disadvantaged personal status and resources (Peplau, Padesky & Hamilton, 1982).

Housework

Housework for all couples is a contentious and increasingly politicized issue. The task for gay men is to accomplish necessary traditionally female jobs while avoiding assumptions about feminine or masculine roles. Like heterosexual men, high-earning gay men expect that their provider role should mostly exempt them from household labor. Hiring outside help is an alternative more often used by gay men than lesbians. Gay men have more discretionary income to hire help. Lesbians are less likely to consider hiring a housekeeper, who is typically a working-class woman of color, an act with ideological implications.

The division of labor for lesbian couples is influenced by task knowledge, rather than income or other power-related factors. However, lesbians do less housework overall than other couples: the work simply is not done. Furthermore, lesbians are more likely than gay men to disagree about who engages in traditionally male versus traditionally female domestic tasks (Patterson & Schwartz, 1994). Housework, which is a visible reminder of the domestic inequality in heterosexual households, is extremely stigmatized among lesbians who seek to reject such heterosexual problems.

Couples' isolation and coming-out issues

For same-sex couples, the right to be a couple, to enjoy the privileges and community that couple status affords, influences the course of relationships. Legal institutions influence the rights of same-sex couples, but so do cultural institutions. Thus, issues of coming out, family, and children are unique problem areas for same-sex couples.

Coming out

Gay men and lesbians have strong personal feelings about whether or not sexual identity and couple status should be public or private. Circumstances emerge in which one partner has a status position that he/she needs to protect by maintaining privacy with respect to sexual identity; or in which one partner seeks such a position. Enormous tension and logistical complications arise for couples mismatched on their preferred public identity. Typically the closeted person feels that secrecy is critical to protect a job, parents, children, or custody issues. For the uncloseted person, an openly gay status is a statement of identity, self-respect, political commitment, and a rejection of a previously closeted lifestyle. Research indicates that closeted status is related to negative health consequences, mental stress, and deteriorating relationship satisfaction, and perhaps durability of the relationship (e.g., Turner, Hays, & Coale, 1993).

"Out" lesbians have a particularly strong commitment to their identity, representing a political commitment to being homosexual. Lesbians, more so than gay men, are concerned about a partner's bisexual capacity. Indeed, shifting in and out of heterosexuality is more common among women than among men (Laumann et al., 1994). There is every incentive to do so: women who shift into heterosexuality obtain certain benefits in society (economic advantages, social approval) by being with men. Thus when lesbian personal ads emphasize "bi's need not apply," it is indicative of committed lesbians' aversion to women who switch back and forth between sexual statuses.

Family

The incorporation of parents, in-laws, and children is no simple matter for any couple. For same-sex couples the challenges are multiplied when family relations are already strained, when the couple lacks institutional support, or when the legal system is able to intervene on custodial arrangements.

Berger (1990) found that conflict with family members was the second-most often cited argument in gay couples. However, parents are sometimes supportive of their gay and lesbian children. For example, a national organization, "Parents and Friends of Lesbians and Gays" (P-FLAG), has acquired a growing presence in the United States and abroad, helping family and friends learn how to be supportive of their homosexual loved ones. Nevertheless, few families provide rituals of inclusion that parallel weddings, anniversary parties, or family vacations. Sometimes parents will support their homosexual child, but will minimize the importance of their child's partner, and see him/her as temporary, threatening, or the cause of their child's homosexuality. Some homosexuals may treat family relationships as private, and not attempt to integrate their lovers into their families. Still others may never discuss the issue with their partners or their families.

Individual feelings about identity and couple status are compounded by the obtuseness with which heterosexuals may deal with same-sex couples. In the popular 1994 movie *Four Weddings and a Funeral*, a tight-knit friendship group concerned with dating, mating, and marriage failed to recognize that two of the male members of the group were already "married" to each other. Heterosexuals may simply fail to find ways to honor and recognize same-sex couple relationships, or fail to see the positive impact legitimacy confers on couples.

Legal risks of being out

Depending upon the country, region, or historical period, being out as a couple may invite legal sanctions or punishments. Different historical periods have shown different levels of tolerance of same-sex couples. Populations can even hold simultaneous and contradictory beliefs about homosexuals, which makes it harder for same-sex couples to calibrate how open or closeted they should be. For example, for the past two decades in the United States, a majority of Americans have consistently responded in surveys that they believe homosexuality is wrong; yet during this same period, a majority, or near-majority, of Americans have consistently opposed discrimination against homosexuals (Laumann et al., 1994).

The contradictions and shifts in attitudes toward homosexuality can be traced through court cases. For example, in *Bowers* v. *Hardwick* (1986; see *United States Reports*, Volume 478, p. 186) the U.S. Supreme Court upheld the right of the state of Georgia to enforce an anti-sodomy law in a case that involved a committed, same-sex couple in the privacy of their own home. In the United States in 1995, laws pertaining to sexual orientation and military service were under review. The armed services have historically rejected any tolerance for homosexuality as potentially interfering with necessary discipline and obedience. Gay and lesbian activists, including homosexual members of the armed services, sought the right to serve without threat of discharge. President Clinton enacted a "compromise" policy: in the past, disclosure that a soldier was homosexual was reason for dishonorable discharge; new the regulation supported an individual's freedom to "be" homosexual, but not openly or actively so. A federal district court ruled in March 1995 that the "don't ask, don't tell, don't pursue" policy in the military was an abridgment of the right to free speech. However, this decision may be appealed by the U.S. government as far as the Supreme Court if necessary.

Children

Where laws in different places or in different times may challenge a same-sex couple's right to be together, the issue of children challenges same-sex couples' right to be parents. Having or wanting children raises the contextual factors of fertility technology and family law, and the interpersonal concerns related to the impact of children on same-sex relationships and of same-sex relationships on children. Today, the lesbian literature often discusses issues related to having children (Clunis & Green, 1988). If couples wish to have children, they must choose whether to use artificial insemination or intercourse as a method of conception. Lesbian couples must decide who will be the biological mother, or whether they each wish to become pregnant. They may also debate who should be the primary caretaker, although empirically it is usually the biological parent (Moore & Schwartz, n.d.). The routes to parenthood for gay men are to adopt a child, take in a foster child, or continue to parent a child from a previous, heterosexual union. These men face the challenge of allocating tasks that have been traditionally allocated to women. It is not clear who will do the "feminine" mothering tasks when there are two dads.

Lesbians also often have children from a prior heterosexual alliance. No matter how old the children are, they challenge couple stability. Custody battles occur with regularity, and the outcomes vary widely. When the issue in a court battle is fitness of the mother or propriety of a same-sex union, lesbians often must choose between a lover and a child. Even when the custody case is settled in a lesbian mother's favor, the possibility of the case being reopened remains, especially when the children are younger (Sheppard, 1992).

In cases where there is no custody dispute, children have a complex response to the new partner (as they do in heterosexual stepfamily situations; see Kaiser, Chapter 7 of this volume; Rutter, 1994) that requires great psychological skill to manage. In such cases, children may have difficulty adjusting to new parenting arrangements, and may even disapprove of a mother's choice to be a lesbian, which creates extra problems for the mother. Furthermore, communities may respond negatively to homosexual pairs. Children's response to a parent's homosexual status may be amplified or complicated by a negative response from the child's other parent, from children at school, or from other families or school officials. If both women have children, they may be forced to live in different domiciles (e.g., *Schuster* v. *Schuster*, 1978). Psychological research has shown that children raised by a same-sex couple are no worse or better off than children raised by a heterosexual couple (Gottman, 1990).

Children can influence the balance of power in same-sex couples beyond custodial issues. In married or cohabiting heterosexual couples, the biological mother tends to be in a less powerful position because she is seen as bringing "extra baggage" to the relationship. These women may therefore be less secure and more emotionally vulnerable. Because children tend to be a valued emotional resource to lesbian partners, the nonbiological stepmother is less powerful, less secure, and more emotionally vulnerable. The nonbiological stepmother is likely to have a strong attachment to her stepchildren, which gives the biological mother the power of distributing emotional access to the children (Moore & Schwartz, n.d.). In effect, the children's availability depends on the mother's goodwill. Some couples seek custody rights for the nonbiological stepmother in order to guarantee a relationship, but the courts vary widely on whether such rights are allowed (Leo, 1993). Furthermore, where rights are established, they can always be challenged subsequently, leaving nonbiological lesbian stepmothers in a precarious situation relative to their attachment to their stepchildren.

Sex in committed relationships

Sex requires role innovation for same-sex couples. Since gays and lesbians have been socialized like other men and women into heterosexual sexual norms, homosexuals must create new sexual patterns. They cannot rely on heterosexual sexual scripts. In particular, lesbians must learn to initiate sex; gay men must learn to accept initiation. Similar to heterosexual couples, sexual styles evolved in dating may end up being modified in a long-term relationship.

Initiating sex

The role of initiating sex is largely seen as symbolic in same-sex couples, since there are no gendered norms as there are for heterosexual couples. Egalitarianism is prominent in this domain; the goal is to share the role of initiator between partners. Men view initiating sex as a masculine behavior. Both gay partners will seek to be the desiring partner to confirm their masculinity, and to control the frequency and timing of sexual conduct. The challenge is in learning how to enjoy being desired. Where an imbalance in initiation occurs, one partner will be viewed as usurping the masculine role; ideally partners discover how to share the role. Interestingly, Blumstein and Schwartz (1983) found that when asked who initiates sex more in the relationship *both* partners tended to claim that role, thus highlighting a preference for the initiator role.

Lesbians have trouble with initiation. Initiation tends to be interpreted as a form of sexual aggression associated with insensitive masculine sexual behaviors. Lesbians' sexual task is to engage in careful negotiations for creating completely consensual, mutual sex. The complexity of such negotiation, and lesbians' disdain of sexual leadership as "macho" heterosexual behavior, probably contribute to low sexual frequency among lesbians. Also, since refusal of sex is a legitimate female privilege and is often a method of asserting power among all women, refusal is more likely to happen between lesbian partners. In fact, Blumstein and Schwartz (1983) found that when asked who refuses sex more in the relationship, *both* female partners were likely to claim that role.

Frequency

Sexual frequency for same-sex couples, as for heterosexual couples, can become a problematic issue over time. For many reasons, some of which have already been discussed, lesbians have the lowest sexual frequency of all couples among married, heterosexual cohabiting, gay, and lesbian couples (Blumstein & Schwartz, 1983). While aggressive male sexuality is encouraged regardless of the current emotional closeness in the couple, female sexuality in our culture is shaped into more restricted expression. Lesbians' high emotional standards for intimacy tend to create fewer acceptable circumstances for sexual activity. Furthermore, lesbians may be ambivalent about sex because of bad past experiences. For example, women are more likely than men to be victims of childhood sexual abuse or sexual violence in adulthood. However, the detrimental impact of low sexual frequency among lesbians tends to be modified by higher levels of nonsexual affectionate behavior, such as touching and cuddling. Nevertheless, lesbians in long-term relationships may end up having sex around once a month (Blumstein & Schwartz, 1983).

Rates of oral sex among lesbians vary widely from survey to survey. Some research disconfirms the centrality of oral sex to lesbian sexuality, while other studies support this image. Surveys of rates vary from 39% engaging in oral sex in the early 1980s (Blumstein & Schwartz, 1983) and 53% in the 1990s (Lever, 1994) to higher rates in the recently released National Opinion Research Center's social organization of sexuality survey (Laumann et al., 1994). Laumann and colleagues found self-report rates above 90% for giving and receiving oral sex among women who identify themselves as homosexual or bisexual (as opposed to 67% giving and 73% receiving oral sex among heterosexual women). The rates of oral sex for women who engage in same-gender sex but who do not identify themselves as lesbians is lower. Oral sex is an important issue because of its voluntary nature. While heterosexuals very rarely consider intercourse as optional within a sexual relationship, lesbians must negotiate preferences relative to a menu of sexual options. Problems can arise where preferences differ. Importantly, the frequency of oral sex among lesbians is correlated with relationship satisfaction (Blumstein & Schwartz, 1983).

Although early in the relationship gay men have more frequent sex than other couples, they tend to suffer declines in activity following the first year of romance. The excitement of the new partner quickly fades, and sexual rewards tend to decrease. Sociobiologists have hypothesized that a taste for variety in sexual partners is a general and pervasive male trait (Van Den Berghe, 1979). Such a taste for variety adds to the challenge of remaining monogamous for gay couples. Gay couples may negotiate nonmonogamy, telephone sex, or use of pornography to maintain passion and satisfaction in the relationship. Often, however, couples end up having less sex than either wants, which tends to weaken the relationship (Blumstein & Schwartz, 1983).

Anal sex among gay men has recently become a much less practiced behavior, even with a condom. Not only is anal sex associated with higher risk for transmission of HIV, it is complicated by issues of who is active and who is passive in the act. In a recent survey (Lever, 1994) a third of gay couples reported engaging in anal sex, with partners always taking the same role; a third reported no anal sex at all; and a third said they shared active and passive roles. Laumann et al. (1994), however, report that among men who identify as gay, rates of anal sex (giving and receiving) are between 75% and 81%; rates are around 50% for men who have ever had a same-sex partner. The dilemma of who should give and who should receive is also present with oral sex. Oral sex is more common among gay men than anal sex, with rates around 90%, according to Laumann et al. (1994).

Monogamy

Monogamy has become a life-or-death issue for gay men. As discussed earlier, there has been a reversal in attitudes toward monogamy from the 1970s, when the overwhelming majority of gay men endorsed nonmonogamy, to the 1990s, when the overwhelming majority endorsed monogamy as a relationship ideal. Partners faced with negotiating a consensus related to monogamy actually achieve greater solidarity through establishing shared values. The proliferation of public health campaigns to promote safer sex among homosexuals has contributed to the revision of gay norms related to monogamy. Furthermore, while the tragic incursion of AIDS has decimated the gay community, it has generated a culture of gay solidarity in the face of everyone's mortality and the likelihood of death among one's friends. National-level cultural events in the United States (such as Tony Kushner's touring Broadway play *Angels in America,* which deals with AIDS in the lives of gay men, and the AIDS Quilt, which commemorates AIDS victims in a quilt made of patches memorializing individuals who have died) generate art, community activities, and cultural references for the gay community facing AIDS. *And the Band Played On: Politics, People, and the AIDS Epidemic* (1987), by Randy Shilts, documents the evolution of the AIDS community.

Even though attitudes toward nonmonogamy for gay men have changed tremendously during the AIDS era, behavior lags behind attitudes. For example, in one study, self-described "monogamous" couples report an average of three to five partners (Blasband & Peplau, 1985). Monogamous behavior is influenced by age (younger men are less likely to be monogamous than older men) and by context. Gay men embedded in a gay community are less likely to be monogamous than those outside of a gay community. In a gay community more alternative partners and sexual opportunities are available. Longer-term relationships tend to be associated with lower levels of sexual frequency, and this makes intimacy with others more likely. Furthermore, whether a gay relationship is "open" or closed has very little impact on satisfaction, commitment, expectations for the future, or degrees of liking or loving one's partner (Patterson, 1995).

Lesbians, like heterosexual women, value monogamy. Nevertheless, certain social structures make nonmonogamy more likely. For example, the strong friendship networks in which lesbians tend to be embedded make affairs more likely. Conversely, affairs transform friendship networks into "incestuous" and complex settings. Indeed, an affair between friends, rather than strangers, is more likely to threaten the primary relationship. Long-term lesbian couples cite affairs most often as the cause for considering breaking up (Johnson, 1990). Finally, while lesbians tend to have a preference for monogamy, some subcultures seek to challenge bourgeois images of female sexuality by engaging in noncommitted nonmonogamy.

Breakups and dangerous conflicts

Early research on gays and lesbians was often done by sympathetic and/or gay and lesbian researchers, and it tended to seek normative ratification for this population. Rather than examining sources of conflict, the literature focused on strengths, successes, and normalcy. Conflict and problem-oriented research was downplayed. Books such as *Lesbian Nation: The Feminist Solution* (Johnston, 1973) and *The Homosexual Dialectic* (McCaffrey, 1972) delivered a "gay liberation" message. Other books such as *The Gay World* (Hoffman, 1968) and *Woman Plus Woman: Attitudes Toward Lesbianism* (Klaich, 1974) sought to define and describe homosexuality. Nevertheless, with current, broader, more objective research, same-sex couples appear to experience less conflict than heterosexual couples. Indeed, partners may be unclear as to how much conflict these undersupported relationships can afford or absorb. While we have observed that certain structural disadvantages distress same-sex relationships, it also appears that in some ways living in a hostile world may minimize internal conflict for same-sex couples. Where legally sanctioned marriages have been called a "license to abuse," no such legal sanctioning of conflict is available to same-sex couples. Instead, same-sex couples must create their own rules, based on a common bond rather than on prevailing social norms.

In the late 1980s and 1990s, scholars began to study how the absence of social norms might cause conflict or strain in same-sex relationships. Kurdek (1993b) studied same-sex relationship conflict and its correspondence to instability. He examined stages of vulnerability for same-sex couples, noting that the second and third years are less satisfying than the first year and beyond the third year. Arguments about family, friends, or unequal power are associated with breaking up. As discussed in the section on money, Blumstein and Schwartz (1983) found that lower-earner males and higher-earner females are more likely to initiate breakups. Lesbians may suffer from unrealistic expectations to be empathetic and to prioritize available time for the relationship. Research also indicates that lesbians react with intense levels of jealousy when an affair occurs. This is less true for gay men, who have less rigid definitions of what constitutes intimacy and fidelity, and who are more likely to support norms of nonmonogamy than lesbians or women in general. Same-sex couples also have no guidelines for whose career to protect or advance when conflicts over one partner's job arise. Therefore, they have a higher likelihood of conflict over work and careers.

Gay men often engage in power struggles that revolve around competition. Competition is not uncommon among males regardless of sexual orientation, especially competition related to money and career. In contrast, lesbians more regularly struggle over maintaining personal boundaries, struggling to be intimate and still independent; close, but not fused. These women are faced with finding a delicate balance that maintains hard-earned independence. Indeed, fears of engulfment in the relationship can plague a lesbian couple. In cases where identities revolve too tightly around the relationship, one or both lesbian partners may retreat, rebel, or completely depart from the couple.

Intimate violence

Same-sex couples are not immune from the problem of violent conflict. Early research on gays and lesbians generally ignored this topic (as has much research on heterosexual couples). Furthermore, it is difficult to get accurate rates of violence or to agree upon what constitutes emotional abuse, physical aggression, or systematic battering among more commonly studied heterosexual populations (Koss et al., 1994). Brand and Kidd (1986) found that 25% of lesbians and 27% of heterosexual women report physical abuse in committed relationships; 7% of lesbians report being date-raped by a woman. Waterman, Dawson, and Bologna (1989) studied same-sex sexual coercion and found that about 12% of gay men and 36% of lesbians had experienced some form of sexual coercion. They observed, however, that lesbians were likely to define more acts as coercive.

Interestingly, Renzetti (1992) found that battered lesbians generally had higher levels of income, education, and occupational prestige and had made greater contributions to the relationship than their battering partners. Renzetti hypothesized that violence in these relationships was used to rebalance the distribution of power. Indeed, half of the battered women in the study cited power imbalances as the reason for violence. Sixty-eight percent reported that partner dependency was a source of strain in the relationship. Thus, the more the battered (higher-earning) lesbian sought independence, the more the abuse occurred. In addition, 70% of battered lesbians cited jealousy and accusations of nonmonogamy as a reason for the abuse.

Galvin and Brommel (1991) identify fusion as a source of lesbian violence. They observe that the battering appears to function as a way to intimidate the battered woman into staying in the relationship. This parallels the way a large subgroup of overattached battering heterosexual males use violence against their partners (Jacobson, 1994). Lenore Walker (1986) noted that lesbians tend to fight back more than heterosexual women, citing the lower size differential typical between lesbians than between hetero-sexual partners. Battered lesbians are also more inclined to leave a battering relationship than heterosexuals. In addition, because lesbians are often more evenly matched physically, the outcome of a fight is uncertain, and therefore it is more likely for either woman to be either an initiator or an active resistor than in the case of heterosexual women.

Renzetti (1992) established that 10–20% of gay men experience violence similar to heterosexual wife battering. Waterman et al. (1989) found that men are more likely to reciprocate violence than women. One of the reasons for the higher rates of violence reported by lesbians than by gay men may have to do with beliefs about violence. Lesbians are more likely to be sensitized to the issues of physical aggression, and to define more acts as physically aggressive or coercive. In contrast, gay men are more likely to see physical aggression as a normal part of men's reaction to serious disagreement.

AIDS

AIDS has generated a new source of conflict for same-sex couples that deserves further study. It has changed couples' landscape of opportunities and experiences. In both gay and lesbian communities, tremendous, free-floating grief and anger is pervasive. In gay relationships in particular there is widespread fear of betrayal and death. Indeed, when one gay partner is diagnosed with HIV, this can precipitate a breakup and conflict including bitter recriminations from both partners. For gay men who stay together with AIDS, the level of dependency that evolves can be crushing to the relationship (Gochros, 1992; Paradis, 1991). What is seen as the death sentence of AIDS often brings about increased family contact, which may generate conflict for gay partners (Turner et al., 1993). Families move in, take over caregiving, and may marginalize the gay partner. Alter-natively, the family may merely assume increased emotional or financial salience, which can destabilize the couple's previous existence. Neurological damage associated with AIDS may also generate symptoms such as para-noia or confusion that weaken gay relationships. It is hard to overestimate the extent to which AIDS has changed gay relationships over the past decade.

Summing up: The legal and political status of same-sex couples

Perhaps one of the most significant ways in which same-sex couples differ from heterosexual couples is that committed same-sex couples do not have the option to choose the legal sanction and benefits of marriage. This influences relationship dynamics. Noninclusion in traditional family rituals such as weddings and anniversary parties and nonacceptance by church or professions take a toll on same-sex relationships. These patterns also shape material interests of partners. Among the benefits married couples enjoy and same-sex couples are denied are: spousal benefits, such as social security or other public pensions; income tax benefits; estate tax benefits; health insurance in spouse's group plan; inheritance rights; right to sue for wrongful death of spouse; compensation to families of crime victims; protection against eviction from rent-controlled apartments; visiting rights in hospitals and prisons; power to make medical decisions for partner; and power to make funeral and burial arrangements. Some rights can be acquired by contract, but many cannot, and are only available to couples allowed to marry (Dukeminier & Krier, 1993). Long-term committed same-sex relationships are challenged to survive in the absence of social supports. This condition produces a greater degree of instability for these couples. Some lesbians see the marginal status of same-sex unions as cause for some women to leave same-sex relationships for the greater comfort and legitimacy of heterosexual marriage.

The right to legal marriage has been tested in the United States (e.g., in Hawaii, 1993; see Leo, 1993). Interestingly, historian John Boswell found evidence from medieval documents that same-sex unions were sanctioned by the Roman Catholic Church at various times in its early history (Boswell, 1994). Some U.S. cities, corporations, and other public employers have experimented with same-sex partner benefits, particularly access to health insurance, but this has developed in few places. In 1989, Denmark became the first country in the world to give legal recognition to same-sex couples (Miller, 1992).

Simultaneously, popular discourse in the United States also suggests ambivalence or even hostility toward same-sex couples. Legal advances may occur in one area while they are undermined in another. Whereas March 1995 saw a U.S. Federal Court advancing the rights of homosexuals in the military (as discussed earlier), a May 1995 U.S. Federal Court decision upheld the right of cities and counties to ban legal protections for homosexuals (Dunlap, 1995b). It is clear from the range of public discourse on homosexuality, however, that the status of same-sex couples is far from resolved. Yet this same evidence also demonstrates that the status, experience, and concerns of same-sex couples are not likely to be so widely ignored as they were until recent years.

Nevertheless, some same-sex couples seek to be outside the mainstream, abstaining from the rituals of heterosexual culture. They seek freedom from roles, scripts, and gendered expectations. Like all "outsider" relationships, the outsider stance provides couples with benefits and costs. While same-sex couples may prefer or enjoy an outsider status, this status continues to be the only one available to them. The status of same-sex couples changes over time, in relationship to gender norms, to gay culture, and to cultural sanctions, tolerance, or support for same-sex couples. Same-sex couples will be influenced by the region or country they live in, by class, and by their own particular family relationships. Finally, gay and lesbian couples differ in how they conduct intimate relationships, and in the extent to which politics or public health concerns influence their norms of behavior. Gender is a crucial factor in how these couples differ. The recent direction in Western countries has been to allow gay and lesbian couples some freedom to exist, to love, and to hope for a day when they have the choice to obtain all the protections and rights of heterosexual relationships.

Notes

1. For example, the *New York Times* regularly includes articles that address gay and lesbian lifestyles (e.g., a front-page story on Sunday, April 23, 1995, about the impact on both married partners when one partner recognizes that he/she is homosexual).
2. In fact, an openly lesbian black woman was elected a city council representative in a recent (1995) general election in Seattle.
3. In April 1995, the state of Virginia Supreme Court denied Sharon Bottoms custody of her 3-year-old son, awarding custody instead to the boy's maternal grandmother. The *New York Times* reports that "Noting Ms. Bottoms' relationship with April L. Wade, the court said that 'living daily under conditions stemming from active lesbianism practices in the home may impose a burden upon a child by reason of the social condemnation to such an arrangement.' " The case was brought against Ms. Bottoms by her mother (Dunlap, 1995a).

References

Andrews, C. (1990). *Closeness and satisfaction in lesbian relationships.* Unpublished master's thesis, University of Washington.

Bailey, J. M., Pillard, R. C., Neale, M. C., & Agyei, Y. (1993). Heritable factors influence sexual orientation in women. *Archives of General Psychiatry, 50,* 217–223.

Berger, R. M. (1990). Men together: Understanding the gay couple. *Journal of Homosexuality, 19,* 31–49.

Bernard, J. (1981). The good-provider role: Its rise and fall. *American Psychologist, 36,* 1–12.

Berzon, B. (1988). *Permanent partners: Building gay and lesbian relationships that last.* New York: Dutton.

Blasband, D., & Peplau, L. A. (1985). Sexual exclusivity versus openness in gay male couples. *Archives of Sexual Behavior, 14,* 395–412.

Blumstein, P., & Schwartz, P. (1983). *American couples.* New York: Morrow.

Boswell, J. (1994). *Same sex unions in pre-modern Europe.* New York: Villard.

Bowers v. Hardwick (1986) in *United States Reports* (Vol. 478, pp. 186–220).

Brand, P. A., & Kidd, A. H. (1986). Frequency of physical aggression in heterosexual and female homosexual dyads. *Psychological Reports, 5,* 1307–1313.

Clunis, D. M., & Green, G. D. (1988). *Lesbian couples.* Seattle: Seal Press.

Coontz, S. (1992). *The way we never were: American families and the nostalgia trap.* New York: Basic Books.

Davidson, A. G. (1991). Looking for love in the age of AIDS: The language of gay personals, 1978–1988. *Journal of Sex Research, 28,* 125–137.

Dukeminier, J., & Krier, J. (1993). *Property* (3rd ed.). New York: Little, Brown.

Dunlap, D. W. (1995a, May 1). Support for gay adoptions seems to wane. *New York Times.*

(1995b, May 14). Court upholds anti-homosexual initiative. *New York Times.*

(1995c, March 8). June 1994 produced a record for antigay attacks (N.Y.C. Anti-Violence Project Report). *New York Times.*

Eldridge, N. S., & Gilbert, L. A. (1990). Correlates of relationship satisfaction in lesbian couples. *Psychology of Women Quarterly, 14,* 43–62.

Ferree, M. M. (1987). She works hard for a living: Gender and class on the job. In B. Hess and M. M. Ferree (Eds.), *Analyzing gender: A handbook of social science research* (pp. 322–347). Newbury Park, CA: Sage.

Galvin, K. M., & Brommel, B. J. (1991). *Family interaction: Cohesion and change.* New York: HarperCollins.

Gilligan, C. (1982). *In a different voice.* Cambridge, MA: Harvard University Press.

Gochros, H. L. (1992). The sexuality of gay men with HIV infection. *Social Work, 37,* 105–109.

Gottman, J. M. (1994). *What predicts divorce.* Hillsdale, NJ: L Erlbaum.

Gottman, J. S. (1990). Children of gay and lesbian parents. In Frederick W. Bozett and Marvin B. Sussman (Eds.), *Homosexuality and family relations.* New York: Haworth.

Hamer, D. H., & Copeland, P. (1994). *The science of desire: The search for the gay gene and the biology of behavior.* New York: Simon & Schuster.

Hemmer, J. D., & Kleiber, D. A. (1981). Tomboys & sissies: Androgynous children? *Sex Roles, 7,* 1205–1212.

Hoffman, M. (1968). *The gay world.* New York: Bantam.

Howard, J., Blumstein, P., & Schwartz, P. (1992). *The rights of lesbians and gay men.* Carbondale: Southern Illinois University Press.

(n.d.). *Homogamy in intimate relationships: The advantages of similarity.* Unpublished manuscript.

Huston, M., & Schwartz, P. (1995). The relationships of lesbians and gay men.

In J. T. Wood & S. Duck (Eds.), *Under-studied relationships: Off the beaten track.* Newbury Park, CA: Sage.

Jacobson, N. S. (1994). Contextualism is dead: Long live contextualism. *Family Process, 33,* 97–100.

Johnson, J. (1973). *Lesbian nation: The feminist solution.* New York: Simon & Schuster.

Johnson, S. E. (1990). *Staying power: Long term lesbian couples.* Tallahassee, FL: Naiad.

Jones, R. W., & Bates, J. E. (1978). Satisfaction in male homosexual couples. *Journal of Homosexuality, 3,* 217–224.

Klaich, D. (1974). *Woman plus woman: Attitudes toward lesbianism.* New York: Simon & Schuster.

Kollock, P., Blumstein, P., & Schwartz, P. (1985). Sex and power in interaction: Conversational privileges and duties. *American Sociological Review, 50,* 34–46.

Koss, M. P., Goodman, L. A., Browne, A., Fitzgerald, L. F., Keita, G. P., & Russo, N. F. (1994). *No safe haven: Male violence against women at home, at work, and in the community.* Washington, DC: American Psychological Association.

Kurdek, L. A. (1991). The dissolution of gay and lesbian couples. *Journal of Social and Personal Relationships, 8,* 265–278.

(1993a). The allocation of household labor in gay, lesbian, and heterosexual married couples. *Journal of Social Issues, 49,* 127–139.

(1993b). *The assessment of destructive arguing and personal conflict resolution styles in gay, lesbian, heterosexual nonparent and heterosexual parent couples.* Unpublished manuscript.

Kurdek, L. A., & Schmitt, J. P. (1987). Perceived emotional support from family and friends in members of gay, lesbian, married, and heterosexual cohabiting couples. *Journal of Homosexuality, 14,* 57–68.

Laumann, E. O., Michael, R. T., & Gagnon, J. H. (1994). *The social organization of sexuality: Sex practices in the United States.* Chicago: University of Chicago Press.

Leo, J. (1993). Gay rights, gay marriages. *U.S. News and World Report,* pp. 114–119.

LeVay, S. (1993). *The sexual brain.* Cambridge, MA: MIT Press.

Level, J. (1994, August 23). The 1994 Advocate Survey of Sexuality and Relationships: The men. *Advocate: The National Gay & Lesbian Newsmagazine,* pp. 17–24.

McCaffrey, J. A. (Ed.) (1972). *The homosexual dialectic.* Englewood Cliffs, NJ: Prentice-Hall.

McWhirter, D. P., & Mattison, A. M. (1984). *The male couple: How relationships develop.* Englewood Cliffs, NJ: Prentice-Hall.

Metz, M. E., Rosser, B. R. S., & Strapko, N. (1994). Differences in conflict-resolution styles among heterosexual, gay, and lesbian couples. *Journal of Sex Research, 31,* 293–308.

Miller, N. (1989). *In search of gay America: Women and men in a time of change.* New York: Atlantic Monthly Press.

(1992). *Out in the world: Gay and lesbian life from Buenos Aires to Bangkok.* New York: Random House.

Money, J., & Ehrhart, A. (1972). *Man and woman, boy and girl.* Baltimore: Johns Hopkins University Press.

Moore, M., & Schwartz, P. (n.d.). *The power of motherhood: A contextual evaluation of family resources.* Unpublished manuscript.

Paradis, B. A. (1991). Seeking intimacy and integration: Gay men in the era of AIDS. *Smith College Studies in Social Work, 61,* 260–274.

Patterson, D. G. (1995). *Virtual in-laws: Kinship and relationship quality in gay male couples.* Unpublished master's thesis, University of Washington.

Patterson, D. G., & Schwartz, P. (1994). The social construction of conflict in intimate same-sex couples. In D. D. Cahn (Ed.), *Conflict in personal relationships.* Hillsdale, NJ: Erlbaum.

Peplau, L. A. (1991). Lesbian and gay relationships. In J. C. Gonsiorek and J. D. Weinrich (Eds.), *Homosexuality: Research implications for public policy* (pp. 177–196). Newbury Park, CA: Sage.

Peplau, L. A., Cochran, S., Rook, K., & Padesky, C. (1978). Loving women: Attachment and autonomy in lesbian relationships. *Journal of Social Issues, 34,* 7–27.

Peplau, L. A., Padesky, C., & Hamilton, M. (1982). Satisfaction in lesbian relationships. *Journal of Homosexuality, 8,* 23–35.

Renzetti, C. M. (1992). *Violent betrayal: Partner abuse in lesbian relationships.* Newbury Park, CA: Sage.

Rutter, V. (1994). Lessons from stepfamilies. *Psychology Today, 27,* 30–92.

Schuster v. *Schuster* (1978) in *Washington Reports, Vol. 90, Second Series: Cases Determined in the Supreme Court of Washington,* 626–637.

Schwartz, P. (1994). *Peer marriage.* New York: Free Press.

Sheppard, A. T. (1992). Lesbian mothers II: Long night's journey into day. *Womens Rights Law Reporter, 14,* 185–212.

Shilts, R. (1987). *And the band played on: Politics, people, and the AIDS epidemic.* New York: St. Martin's.

Siegle, K., & Glassman, M. (1989). Individual and aggregate level change in sexual behavior among gay men at risk for AIDS. *Archives of Sexual Behavior, 18,* 335–348.

Steen, S., & Schwartz, P. (in press). Communication, gender and power: Homosexual couples as a case study. In M. A. Fitzpatrick & A. L. Vangelish (Eds.), *Perspectives on family communication* (pp. 310–343). Newbury Park, CA: Sage.

Tannen, D. (1990). *You just don't understand: Women and men in conversation.* New York: Ballantine.

Turner, H. A., Hays, R. B., & Coale, T. J. (1993). The context of AIDS. *Journal of Health and Social Behavior, 34,* 37–53.

Vance, C. S. (1984). *Pleasure and danger: Exploring female sexuality.* Boston: Routledge & Kegan Paul.

Van Den Berghe, P. (1979). *Human family systems.* New York: Elsevier.

Walker, L. (1986). Battered women's shelters and work with battered lesbians.

In K. Lobel (Ed.), *Naming the violence: Speaking out about lesbian battering* (pp. 198–201). Seattle: Seal Press.

Waterman, C. K., Dawson, L. J., & Bologna, M. J. (1989). Sexual coercion in gay male and lesbian relationships: Predictions and implications for support services. *Journal of Sex Research, 26,* 118–124.

Whitam, F. L., & Mathay, R. M. (1991). Childhood cross-gender behavior of homosexual females in Brazil, Peru, the Philippines, and the United States. *Archives of Sexual Behavior, 20,* 151–170.

Whyte, M. K. (1990). *Dating, mating, and marriage.* Hawthorne, NY: Aldine de Gruyter.

PART IV

Private nonkin relationships

10

Adult friendship
Ann Elisabeth Auhagen

The friendship paradox

Friendship is a highly valued asset to almost all people. As an interpersonal phenomenon, it has been in existence for thousands of years. This social relationship was, and is, the object of philosophical analyses, as by Aristotle, Cicero, Epicurus, Hegel, Kant, Lucian, Nietzsche, Plato, Schopenhauer, and Spinoza (see, e.g., Bukowski, Nappi & Hoza, 1987; Pakaluck, 1991). At the same time it represents an important theme of poets and authors: Shakespeare, Goethe, Walt Whitman, Oscar Wilde, and Antoine de Saint-Exupéry have treated it. From ancient Greece to postmodern times the concept of friendship has undergone numerous changes. Depending on the epoch and on people's situation in life during that epoch, friendships were associated with such various terms as blood-brotherhood, family, comradeship, soulmates, emotional and spiritual bonds between friends, friendship with God, young scamp and bachelor unions, vassals, sensible and functional relationships, and heartfelt emotional relationships (Kon, 1979). Friendship knows no limits when it comes to age, gender, and domicile. Therefore friendships seem to have no boundaries. Yet reality is different.

One of the peculiarities of this social relationship is that it makes few explicit demands on those involved. At the same time friendship appears to possess its own particular characteristics. We know which persons are our friends and at the same time we can usually identify those who do not belong to this circle. One precise feature of friendship is that it possesses so few truly clear, unequivocal characteristics. This peculiarity I term the paradox of friendship. This contradiction in itself creates a dilemma for social scientists conducting empirical research on friendship. On the one hand an all-too-narrow theory of friendship and an equally restricted empiricism can, in the long run, result in the systematic exclusion of important areas of the phenomenon. History and ethnology indicate certain limitations to empirical social scientific research into our present culture. Friendship can mean different things depending on the generation, the historical period, and the society. On the other hand, an atheoretical approach based only on description and the collection of data would have few guidelines and would also fail to meet the goals of social scientific research on friendship. The goals are description, analysis, and understanding the phenomenon of friendship as well as gaining practical knowledge of it. This chapter will not offer a simple solution to these questions.

In keeping with the intention of this book, this chapter will present the results of selected, mainly psychological studies of friendship concerned with experiences and behavior in friendships. Sociological, ethnographic, and historical, as well as developmental-psychological (see Krappmann, Chapter 2 of this volume, and von Salisch, Chapter 3 of this volume) aspects of friendship will, for the most part, not be considered here for lack of space (Blieszner & Adams, 1992, provide a more comprehensive survey). To begin with, an explication of friendship will be given, followed by an elaboration of the most important content variables and variants of friendship as represented in current literature. The function of friendship will then be sought, based upon empirical research. In conclusion, perspectives will be offered.

What is friendship?

One of the most important characteristics of friendship is that it makes so few definite demands on those involved. Is it sensible under these circumstances to define it at all? At least two arguments justify the elucidation of friendship. First: it makes sense to establish a common linguistic basis for scientific analysis of the term. Second: operational criteria for friendship are often needed in empirical proceedings.

It is precisely because friendship has so many facets that an explication of it should not be built on content criteria such as respect or trust. With such an approach there is a danger of succumbing to circular reasoning and to designating circumstances as criteria of friendship when in fact they are effects and results of it. These reasons, supported by an extensive study of the literature, have led Auhagen (1991) to formulate an explication of friendship that attempts to define friendship chiefly with theoretical-abstract criteria rather than empirical observations. Here, the aim is to indicate the most important distinguishing characteristics of friendship without exhaustively describing it. A field study in which naive subjects were questioned confirmed that the explication corresponds with the routine understanding of laypersons (Auhagen, 1991). The following definition of friendship does not claim universal validity: it is dependent upon culture or time periods. Moreover, it should be understood as *one* attempt to explicate friendship – other authors select other emphases (Allan, 1989; Duck, 1983/1991; Hays, 1988).

Explication

Friendship is a *dyadic, personal, informal* social relationship. The two people involved are designated as friends. The existence of friendship is based upon *mutuality*. For each of the friends the friendship possesses a *value* of different strength that can comprise different content elements. In addition, friendship is characterized by four further essential criteria: *voluntariness*, in relation to the selection, configuration, and continuance of the relationship; *time perspective*, whereby friendship contains a past and a future aspect; *positive emotion*, an unalterable element being the subjective experience of the positive; and *no overt sexuality*.

Friendship, it must be explicitly said, is seen here as a category of relationship, a specific kind of social togetherness. This relationship category is specified by a certain combination of criteria. Other social relationships may likewise possess some of these attributes.

What is to be understood under the particular aspects of the explication? And what implications could these have for routine experiences in friendships?

Dyadic relationship. To define friendship as a relationship between two people does not deny the existence of friendship circles. A group of friends should be understood as a gathering of people in which there is a friendship, in the above-defined sense, between every possible dyad.

Informal social relationship. No official approval or requirements exist for friendship, in contrast for example to marriages or to some family relationships. In this sense, official responsibilities or regulations do not exist for friendships. If friends feel obligated to one another, it is because of inner motives and inducements or implied social norms or rules.

Personal relationship. Those involved in the relationship view themselves mainly as individual, unique personalities and not as the bearers of formal social roles. In his *person qua person* variable, Wright (1985) suggests that friends mainly relate to these individual aspects in their behavior. One can then ask further: Is there a role for friends, and what does this role look like? It is possible that the expectations of roles of friends are closely related to the concept and the function of friendships (see below). On the other hand, one is a friend, or has a friend, because one appreciates this person or is appreciated by her or him. Based on these considerations, it can be speculated that when the perception of individual esteem in friendships is jeopardized as a result of something, disharmony and conflicts can result.

Mutuality. Friendships cannot be initiated and sustained by one person only. It is possible for one person to show feelings of friendship to others, but a relationship only qualifies as a friendship if both of those involved classify it as such. Consensus over the type of social relationship that two people have may greatly ease the further development of this relationship. In the case of a friendship, the individual arrangement and development remains entirely up to the friends. However, a societally recognized basic understanding of friendship is brought into the relationship by both partners. A certain consensus over implicit rules in friendship must be clear (Argyle & Henderson, 1984; see below).

Value for friends. This rubric includes all emotional, social, and spiritual values related to friendship, for example trust, support, respect, and attachment. The meaning given to such values and behavioral patterns, which may be associated with individual friendships, will usually be implicitly determined by the friends. An example of differences in individual friendships and social support is reported by Auhagen (1994). A cross-sectional study over a two-month period in which pairs of friends described their relationship in written diaries (Auhagen, 1987) produced the following results: with some couples, emotional and instrumental social support arises much more frequently than with others. This indicates that social support in some relationships has greater value than in others.

Voluntariness. Friends are chosen voluntarily – in contrast, for example, to parents or siblings. Contacts and interactions in friendships transpire on a voluntary basis (see also Wright, 1985, "voluntary interdependence"), and those involved are equally free to dissolve the friendship. The criterion of voluntariness in friendships makes special demands on the partners in the relationship. A firm framework of contacts and interactions, as for example in occupational relationships (see Neuberger, Chapter 12 of this volume), does not usually exist. The freedom within the relationship requires those involved to develop a particular awareness of the relationship situation and to make constant efforts to contribute toward activities.

Time perspective. Two people do not immediately become friends on their first meeting. A friendship is developed. How quickly this occurs can vary. Important ways of behaving in the formation phase of a friendship serve to gain information about the potential new friend and his or her reactions (Miell & Duck, 1986; see below). Once a friendship has formed (this does not have to be a conscious process for those involved), it implies the desire and a great probability that the relationship will continue, at least in the near future.

Positive emotion. The subjective experience of the positive as an essential aspect of friendship may differ in individual relationships and from person to person. Conflicts and conflict potential are not excluded by this definition criterion. The criterion of positive emotion has a central meaning in the experience of friendship. Philosophers frequently describe friendship as an ideal or idealistic social relationship. Ideal concepts are in fact expressed when people are asked about their general concept of friendship. In a telephone survey in Germany (Groeneveld, Wißer & Wittstock, 1991), the respondents spontaneously associated friendship with trust, support, conversations, and mutual interests. Only a small number of those questioned believed that criticism was an important element of friendship.

No overt sexuality. Of all of the defining characteristics of friendship introduced here, this one is the most controversial. This is true not only because a number of research projects do not exclude sexuality from friendship (e.g., Reisman, 1981), but also because sexual partnerships very often possess a number of characteristics that can also be identified as elements of friendship, such as trust or support. Apart from this, in everyday life there appear to be individual relationships that defy classification as either friendships or sexual partnerships.

No overt sexuality, in the narrow sense of the phrase, is defined here as: no sexual intercourse or similar sexual practices (Auhagen & Friedrich, 1994). Sexuality is a critical area, especially in cross-sex friendships. Even if no partnership or romantic relationship exists between a man and a women, sexual attraction is certainly possible. Initial evidence confirming sexual attraction in cross-sex friendships already exists (Matthews, 1986; Monsour, 1992). With the help of a survey of cross-sex pairs of friends in Germany, Auhagen and Friedrich (1994) found, among other things, that in approximately half of all cases friends find their opposite-sex friends sexually attractive. This is based mainly on reciprocity and is also frequently interpreted as a validation of one's own attractiveness as a woman or man.

Which continuing considerations involve the criteria of friendship? If the aspects of the definition mark out important areas of the relationship, one can speculate that these aspects can also be meaningful and possibly even critical areas in the everyday life of friendships. However, it is not necessary for people to consciously experience these aspects or be able to identify them. If, one can further suppose, the criteria of friendship are jeopardized in the practice of the relationship, conflicts can develop because the existence of the relationship as a friendship may well be questioned. If, for example, subliminal sexual attraction in a cross-sex friendship transforms into overt sexual practices, those involved must decide with the onset of this change how the relationship should be shaped in the future. This could result in a crisis in the friendship or in a transformation of the friendship into a partnership.

Variables and variations: Toward a description of friendship

Over the last 10 years research on friendship laid particular emphasis on its description. Description, as a first step toward understanding relationships, is meaningful (see Hinde, Chapter 1 of this volume); nevertheless, the abundance of variables and variations of friendships in the relevant literature is confusing. Without any generally binding theoretical statements this will remain the case. It is, however, possible to develop a pragmatic classification of important friendship variables based on existing literature. Here, the following pattern often appears: researchers order friendships or persons who report on friendships according to graduated characteristics and then test the degree to which these characteristics correlate with the degree of expression of other variables. The rationale behind such mainly quasi-experimental research designs is the idea that criteria can be forecast through predictors. However, when reference is made in the following to independent and dependent variables, this does not imply a straightforward causal connection. (For this reason the terms are placed in quotation marks.) On the contrary, manifold interdependencies may well exist between the "independent" and "dependent" variables used in surveys (Hinde, Chapter 1 of this volume).

The "independent variables" may be characterized in terms of qualities or traits of the person and characteristics of friendships. Personal qualities that have often interested researchers are gender and age. But variables and qualities such as family status or the nature of motives in relation to the friendship (McAdams, 1985), among other variables, can also be mentioned here. Characteristics of friendship relationships addressed by research include the length and the closeness of the friendship as well as the developmental phases of friendship, such as the beginning, maintenance, and end (Blieszner & Adams, 1992). The "dependent variables" are often measured in terms of costs, benefits, resources of the friendship, frequency, content and quality of the interaction, content of conversations, intimacy, self-disclosure, emotional and instrumental social support, and conflicts (Aries & Johnson, 1983; Auhagen, 1987, 1990, 1994; Baxter, Wilmot, Simmons & Swartz, 1993; Floyd, 1994; Hays, 1984, 1985; Milardo, 1982; Monsour, Betty & Kurzweil, 1993; Planalp, 1993; Planalp & Benson, 1992).

Of course this is not an exhaustive list of variables. It should also be noted that the same variables are used by some researchers as "independent" variables while others use them as "dependent" variables. In addition, not every work fits into this general pattern. Simple enumeration may also give the impression of a complete absence of theory, but this would do injustice to the state of research. Even though at present there is no generally accepted concept of friendship, the terms summarized here under "dependent" variables are derived from diverse models or theories from the field of research on interpersonal relationships. The concepts of costs and benefits are derived from the pool of exchange theories (see below). Intimacy and self-disclosure, as a further example, have their theoretical basis in social penetration theory (Altman & Taylor, 1973). A pioneering attempt to place the abundance of variables and variations in an integrative framework was undertaken by Adams and Blieszner (1994; Blieszner & Adams, 1992). Their approach elaborated on the relationship between individual characteristics, for example age, sex, and friendship patterns. It was the authors' intention to combine psychological and sociological approaches to friendship patterns as well as to utilize the corresponding literature. They assume structural and process components as two fundamental qualities of friendship.

In the following pages a closer look will be taken at four aspects of friendship that the author considers particularly central to the relevant literature. They are friendship and gender, friendship and age, friendship as a process, and the function of friendship.

Friendship and gender

No other question has preoccupied friendship research so long and so persistently as the connection between friendship and gender. This interest has a tradition dating back to ancient Greece, though, admittedly, there friendship was considered an exclusively male domain (Kon, 1979). Current empirical research reveals another picture clearly summed up by Wright (1982): women are more involved in face-to-face friendships, men are more involved in side-by-side friendships. Differences between female and male friendships can be found in a number of variables: preferred topics of conversation in female friendships are the friends themselves, close social relationships, feelings, and problems, in contrast to male friendships in which the emphasis is on shared activities (Aries & Johnson, 1983; Johnson & Aries, 1983). Interactions within female friendships are described as being more intimate than interactions in male friendships (Wheeler, Reis & Nezleck, 1983). Social support plays a greater role in friendships among women than in those among men (Auhagen, 1991; Auhagen & Schwarzer, 1994; Winstead & Derlega, 1984). Many studies indicate that women approach their same-sex friendships more intimately and holistically, but also in more richly faceted ways than men (Auhagen, 1991; Wright, 1982; for a review of differences between the sexes, see Winstead, 1986). However, women appear to have greater problems with conflict in friendships than men (Wright, 1982).

Frequently replicated gender differences (Winstead, 1986) lead to the conclusion that in the daily practice of friendships, traditional, and in our society widespread, gender roles are effective. For women these provide a more affective, expressive behavioral basis and for men a more instrumental and assignment-oriented behavioral basis. However, there are also other opinions. Utilizing two sets of data obtained from different procedures (diaries and questionnaires) Duck and Wright (1993) concluded that both men and women in same-sex relationships show socioemotional behavior. Women, however, appear to express this behavioral aspect in a more direct and overt manner. A differential approach to the often replicated gender differences in friendships is also supported by studies that have discovered that gender differences in friendship can be modified by other variables. Wright (1982) proposes that the closer friendships are and the longer they exist, the more gender differences tend to disappear. The same author (Wright, 1988) cautions against an all too global interpretation of gender differences – even on methodological grounds. Despite significant differences in statistical comparisons of groups, there is a certain lack of overall magnitude of effect. Moreover, frequently too little allowance is made for the variability within the groups being studied. Lastly, Wright argues that gender, as a personality variable, can often be potentially confused with variables that, per se, are correlated with gender – for example, sex role orientation.

On the question of family status as a further moderator of gender differences, Tschann (1988) points out that when single, both women and men disclose themselves more to their friends on less intimate topics than when they are married. More promising approaches in the attempt to shed further light on the debate over gender differences are provided by two other studies. According to Sapadin (1988), both sexes have similar expectations concerning the ideal concept of friendship. Their actual experiences in same- and cross-sex friendships, however, are different – corresponding to the above-sketched direction. The same values, namely self-disclosure and enjoyment, equally satisfy both women and men in friendships. Nevertheless, there are gender differences in these variables and they are revealed more strongly in women (Jones, 1991). Overall, a fairly consistent picture emerges from empirically based gender differences in friendships, but interpretations of the results display less clarity. The application of meta-analyses and solid theoretical approaches could lead to further clarification. The discussion on gender differences in same-sex friendships will certainly continue.

More recently a new focus has developed in research into gender and friendship: the long-neglected area of cross-sex friendships. The first analyses of this relationship include the perception of intimacy, respect, and sexual aspects (Auhagen & Friedrich, 1994; Bell, 1981; Gaines, 1994; Monsour, 1992; Monsour et al., 1993; O'Meara, 1989).

Friendship and age

As a variable in friendship, age is similar to gender: it is not necessarily the genuine source of variations in different types of experiences and behavior in friendships. Rather, it is generally understood that at different stages in life, people in our society are subjected to different demands, which, according to the usually implicit hypotheses of research on friendship, also affect the practice of friendship.

Research on friendship has resulted in the convention of dividing the life cycle into four general phases: childhood, adolescence, adulthood, and old age. Friendship in childhood and adolescence is influenced by the different developmental stages of young people (LaGaipa, 1977; Selman, 1984; Schneider, 1994; see also Krappmann, Chapter 2 of this volume; and von Salisch, Chapter 3 of this volume). The tendency here is that with increasing age adolescent friendships become more intimate. Uncommon but interesting are studies that investigate intergenerational aspects. Doyle, Markiewicz, and Hardy (1994) were thus able to predict childhood behavior in friendships based on the quality of the mother's closest friendship. According to Argyle and Henderson (1985), friendships in adulthood lose significance while family relationships grow. Relationships with neighbors and colleagues are important during this phase. In a review of relevant literature, Dickens and Perlman (1981) arrive at the following synopsis: in advanced age the frequency of friendship contacts and the degree of intimacy often decrease in relationships. However, a study by Dickson-Markman (1986) shows that clearer differentiations should be made because when the length of time invested in a friendship is taken into consideration, hardly any differences in the degree of self-disclosure can be observed. Further results on adulthood in relation to friendship variables, structure, and processes are provided by Blieszner and Adams (1992). Increased interest in the psychology of gerontology has resulted in a number of studies of friendships in old age (overview in Adams & Blieszner, 1989). Main areas of interest differ little from those already known – for instance, social support (Crohan & Antonucci, 1989), exchange and equity (Roberto, 1989), friendship groups and friendship networks (Litwak, 1989), and conflicts and stress (Rook, 1989).

In general, virtually the same applies to friendship and age as to friendship and gender: with the exception of childhood and early adolescence, which entail such fundamental changes for people that they have a genuine impact on social relationships, there is little empirical support for the assumption that friendships are experienced any differently at various stages of adulthood. For example, satisfaction with a friendship, even in advanced age, depends on the perceived balance in the relationship (Roberto & Scott, 1986). The age variable itself appears to have less effect on the practice of friendship than the psychological and accompanying sociological circumstances during various life phases.

Friendship as a process

Friendship is a process between two people. In accordance with Barker (1978), Auhagen defined this process on the molecular level of concrete behavioral patterns as "the totality of the interactions of the streams of experience and behavior of two friends" (Auhagen, 1991, p. 22). The analysis of sequences and contingencies of certain behavioral patterns between friends that is deductable from this approach has thus far hardly been pursued (for an exploratory study of sequences of types of contact between friends, see Auhagen, 1991). In contrast to this, the appropriate literature usually divides the course of friendship into three main phases: (1) emergence and development, (2) maintenance, and (3) dissolution and the end of friendship (for summaries of relevant theories and works, see Blieszner, 1989; Blieszner & Adams, 1992; Hays, 1988). The phases should be understood more in the sense of a rough working model rather than as established theoretical elements of friendship.

The greatest attention by far has focused on the emergence and development of friendships. It should, however, be noted that in the main the suggested theories and models are not specifically tailored to the development of friendships as they usually apply to social relationships in general. They include approaches that attempt to explain the development and maintenance of interpersonal relationships on the basis of classical (e.g., Lott & Lott, 1974) and operant conditioning (in particular for friendships, see Wright, 1984): under certain circumstances interactions with people are experienced as rewarding or reinforcing and therefore striven for and/or pursued. These theories also emphasize that people in social relationships strive for maximum benefits and minimum costs. Both exchange theory and equity theory are characterized as classics among the explanatory approaches to interpersonal relationships (e.g., Homans, 1961; Rusbult, 1980; Walster, Walster & Berscheid, 1978). They also share the idea of the exchange of values or goods that Foa and Foa introduced as resources (1980; see also Hinde, Chapter 1 of this volume).

Various models postulate increasing intimacy and self-disclosure as content variables in the developmental process of friendship (Social Penetration theory, Altman & Taylor, 1973; Levels of Pair Relatedness, Levinger & Snoek, 1972; Levinger's ABCDE-Model, Levinger, 1980). If and how a friendship relationship intensifies is reflected in the experience and behavior of the partners. According to Miell and Duck (1986), people have different cognitive strategies depending on whether they are establishing a friendship, communicating with a close friend, or wanting to relax a close friendship. People believe that when establishing the relationship many questions are posed and self-disclosure is reciprocated; the other person is carefully observed and one responds to him or her. The opposite occurs when a relationship is dissolving. When friendships are in the developmental phase the intimacy of contacts increases (Hays, 1984, 1985). At the beginning of a relationship the frequency of interactions determines the quality of the friendship. When a friendship is further developed, the degree of intimacy is the determining factor (Hays, 1984, 1985). As trust increases so do costs such as stronger emotional commitment or additional responsibilities (Hays, 1985).

Little is known about the individual mechanisms that hold friendships together in everyday life. Pioneering work has been carried out by Wright (e.g., 1969, 1978, 1984), both in the theoretical and the empirical sense. Wright's model, or rather theory of friendship, combines self-concept research and learning theory. Every person strives to assure that her or his "self," as an important personality reference point, is doing well and that she or he has a positive self-image. Friendships are formed because they help to achieve the goals and desires people have with respect to their self-image. According to Wright, friendship itself is characterized by *voluntary interdependence* and an emphasis on the individual aspects of those involved (*person qua person*), in contrast to the role-oriented aspects of the friend as a person. The more strongly these criteria are developed, the closer the friendship is, according to Wright (1978). Impairments of friendships, such as conflicts or aggravations, are defined by Wright as *maintenance difficulties*. The goal of the "self" is promoted in friendships as a result of rewarding interactions. According to Wright, different values are important here. They include *ego support value*: one friend conveys to the other that she or he is a competent person, with whom it is meaningful to spend time together; *self-affirmation value*: the behavior of the partner reflects and strengthens what are felt to be positive aspects of one's self; *stimulation value*: the friend brings new ideas, increases knowledge; *security value*: the degree to which the friend is felt to be nonthreatening; *utility value*: the friend is prepared to provide concrete resources. In order to test his friendship model, Wright created a questionnaire that he called the Acquaintance Description Form (Wright, 1985).

Wright's friendship theory predicts that friendships end with decreased interdependence and diminished reward in the relationship (Wright, 1978). However, the exact causes and consequences during the dissolution of a relationship still need clarification. Few studies exist concerning the end of friendships. Until now researchers were concerned mainly with the dissolution of relationships in general (Duck, 1982) and the termination of romantic relationships or partnerships (Baxter, 1985; see also Bierhoff, Chapter 8 of this volume). In view of the formal differences in content between partnerships and friendships, it can hardly be assumed that the ends of both types of relationship are announced or manifested in the same manner. In the case of friendships no explicit, formal criteria for the end of the friendship exist. Within the boundaries of societal norms, implicit criteria to determine whether a friendship is still a friendship may vary from case to case, depending on the individuals' concepts of friendship, which by no means have to concur. Furthermore, it is also possible to imagine dyad-specific friendship concepts (see below). Rose (1984) identified four types of patterns in the ending of friendships: spacial separation; new friends replacing old; increasing dislike of the friend; disruption of the friendship as a result of marriage or a partner relationship. The last reason for the dissolution of friendships was more frequently identified among women. According to Rose's findings, male friendships dissolve more frequently as a result of spatial separation.

Mutual appreciation and mutual support as functions of friendship

In addition to all other social relationships friendship clearly offers people something of great value. Determining the functions of friendship is not a simple task. Almost all the functions fulfilled by friendship could also be attributed to other interpersonal relationships. Not only do friends help one another; so too, for example, do relatives, neighbors, and colleagues. The pure enumeration of various functions of friendship hardly differentiates it from other social relationships. Litwak (1985, 1989) offers a sociological explanation for the importance of friendships in modern societies: friendships demarcate and supplement other societal primary groups such as married couples and families. In contrast to formal organizations in society, such primary groups are characterized by internalized, noninstrumental commitment, a common lifestyle, and constant face-to-face contact. Technical knowledge and detailed division of labor play no role in primary groups. Their main concern lies in supporting people in nontechnical life tasks that harbor uncertainties. To be able to live within our society people have to be socially mobile in various ways, for example in relation to the practiced career, the workplace, or the intimate sphere. The primary group of friends often shares a similar lifestyle and extreme flexibility in beginning and ending social ties and is thus particularly well-equipped for interpersonal tasks that can be solved more easily as a result of similar social status and similar values. However, according to Litwak, three different types of friendship are necessary for overcoming the enormous multiplicity of life's responsibilities and problems at various times: long-term, medium-term, and short-term friendships.

Other authors place a more psychological emphasis on the function of friendships. These include Kon (1991): friendship has instrumental-utilitarian and emotional-expressive functions. Duck (1983/1991): friends give us a feeling of belonging, emotional integration and stability, and the opportunity to discover ourselves and to help others; they provide us with spiritual and physical support and show us that we are valuable as people. Hays (1988, p. 395): "Friendship is intended to facilitate social-emotional goals." Wiseman (1986): the functions of friendship are enjoyment and the maintenance of the friendship as such. In this case implicit agreements apparently prevail between people. Argyle and Henderson (1984, p. 234) postulate rules of friendship for which they designate special functions. They include the *exchange function*: sharing news of successes with the other; showing emotional support; volunteering help in times of need; striving to make the other happy while in each other's company; repaying debts and favors; the *intimacy function*: trusting and confiding in the other; the *third party function*: standing up for the other person in their absence; being tolerant of other friends; not criticizing the other in public; keeping confidences; not being jealous or critical of the other's relationships; the *coordination function*: not nagging; and respecting privacy.

Which preliminary conclusions can be drawn from these considerations of the functions of friendship? Friends are people chosen by us ideally to achieve a maximum sense of well-being. By the same token we will also act in a way that enhances their feeling of well-being. Therefore, the ideal picture that has been sketched by philosophers and writers over thousands of years seems to have a certain amount of justification (Kon, 1979). In practice, friendship shows that our friends, and we ourselves in the role of friends, are unable to satisfy these needs under all circumstances (on conflict in friendships, see Auhagen, 1994; Perlman, 1990). Wiseman (1986) even suggests that friendship contains its own dialectic, which makes the bond between friends particularly delicate and fragile: freedom and intimacy. The voluntary aspect of friendship contrasts with expectations directed toward the friend, which include being pleasant and displaying desirable behavior. Friends should always remain that way and should honor their unwritten contract in which mutual affection and support are anchored.

Conclusion and perspectives

Friendship is a social relationship different from most other interpersonal relationships because it does not demand any concrete instrumental responsibilities or societal requirements from those involved. As a result of its basic voluntariness and open character, friendship provides people with a rich store of experiences. In short, the function of friendship is the mutual building and sustenance of a good form of togetherness.

However, without any form of personal understanding or agreement, interpersonal relationships are hardly possible. The absence of explicit norms and obligations in friendships places demands on friends that are different, though not necessarily simpler, than those in other types of relationship. In order for friendships to work, friends have to develop a perception of the relationship and of the partner within the relationship. Furthermore there has to be open communication and an exchange of information, as well as an internal commitment to the relationship that is made known to the partner. The combination of unusual freedom in structuring a friendship on the one hand, and human requirements and expectations of the friendship on the other, makes this relationship similar to walking on a knife's edge. The sense of balance is affected by the finest, almost imperceptible disturbances. Even when other, superficial problems are blamed for the breakup of a friendship, the cause can almost always be traced back to an infringement of the mutually agreed relationship structures developed by the friends. Friendships do not end *eo ipso* as a result of physical separation. More often the cases is a lack of commitment of those involved. Among other things, an unsatisfactory exchange of intimacy and information can make contact with the friend less rewarding, which, according to learning theory, can lead to a further decrease in commitment.

The description of important areas of emphasis in current empirical studies has made their merits and limitations visible. We are able to describe friendship quite well with different global variables, but we possess few theoretical foundations to help understand friendship as a whole and as a process. Apart from this, the validity of the results cited in the studies is limited: data were often obtained from samples hardly representative of the general population. Most were collected from university students in English-speaking countries. Many results are based upon retrospective self-report studies, predominantly questionnaires and interviews used in cross-sectional studies. These techniques tend to assess somewhat general concepts of friendship between people, but they do not tell us much about actual experiences and behavior of people in day-to-day friendship. From attitude research it is known that fictive or retrospective responses concerning behavior often do not correspond with what actually happened. In addition, global concepts of friendship mirror the expectations and norms that people in a society generally associate with this social relationship. Yet every friendship is in itself unique. Therefore it can be assumed that people also develop and carry within them relationship-specific scripts that they apply appropriately to different friendships. What these dyad-specific friendship concepts and behavioral patterns look like and what effect they have on the friendships still remains unanswered.

For the empirical-psychological analysis and the understanding of friendship, we need more theoretical concepts tailored specifically to friendship rather than to interpersonal relationship in general. Such theories or theoretical elements should attempt to integrate the different levels from which friendship can be scientifically examined. These are, for example, general concepts of people concerning friendship, concrete behavior in friendship, and societal expectations of friendship. Naturally, interdisciplinary problems are also involved, for example clarification of the relationship between social structures and psychological variables (see Blieszner & Adams, 1992). The theoretical approach used in this chapter offers a number of indicators for the analysis of friendship. The criteria of friendship denote fundamental characteristics of the relationship; the functions of friendship provide information about its tasks. These two keystones of friendship could form the basis for considering theoretical concepts of friendship. The general question, then, is: What effects do the criteria and functions of friendship have on the experience and behavior of people in friendships? Examples of a more precise line of questioning would be: What types of conflicts occur in friendship when the criteria of friendship are put to the test, and how are these conflicts solved? Under what circumstances is the function of help particularly addressed? The third, related keystone of theoretical considerations on friendship is the level of concrete experiences and behaviors. Here, the various concepts of learning theory, for instance, could be used to explain and predict manifest behavioral sequences. However, to fully understand the phenomenon of friendship we need theoretical concepts that reflect the real nature of friendship: a whole characterized at the same time by its great diversity.

References

Adams, R., & Blieszner, R. (Eds.) (1989). *Older adult friendship*. Newbury Park, CA: Sage.
   (1994). An integrative conceptual framework for friendship research. *Journal of Social and Personal Relationships*, 11, 163–184.
Allan, G. (1989). *Friendship: Developing a sociological perspective*. Brighton, England: Harvester Wheatsheaf.
Altman, I., & Taylor, D. A. (1973). *Social penetration: The development of interpersonal relationships*. New York: Holt, Rinehart & Winston.
Argyle, M., & Henderson, M. (1984). The rules of friendship. *Journal of Social and Personal Relationships*, 1, 211–237.
   (1985). *The anatomy of relationships*. London: Heinemann.
Aries, E. J., & Johnson, F. L. (1983). Close friendship in adulthood: Conversational context between same-sex friends. *Sex Roles*, 9, 1183–1196.
Auhagen, A. E. (1987). A new approach for the study of personal relationships: The double diary method. *German Journal of Psychology*, 11, 3–7.
   (1990). Friendship and sibling dyads in everyday life: A study with the new method of double diary. Paper presented at the Fifth Conference on Personal Relationships, July 1990, Oxford, England.
   (1991). *Freundschaft im Alltag. Eine Untersuchung mit dem Doppeltagebuch*. Bern: Hans Huber.
   (1994). Similarity and dissimilarity in friendship pairs: Support, conflict, and sexual attraction. Paper presented at the Seventh International Conference on Personal Relationships, July 1994, Groningen, Netherlands.
Auhagen, A. E., & Friedrich, D. (1994). Subliminal sexual attraction in cross-sex friendships. Paper presented at the Thirteenth World Congress of Sociology, July 1994, Bielefeld, Germany.
Auhagen, A. E., & Schwarzer, R. (1994). Ein neues Leben mit neuen Freunden. Zum Prozeß der sozialen Integration bei Übersiedlern aus der DDR. *Zeitschrift für Entwicklungspsychologie und Pädagogische Psychologie*, 26, 166–184.
Barker, R. G. (1978). The stream of individual behavior. In R. G. Barker & associates (Eds.), *Habitats, environments, and human behavior*. San Francisco: Jossey-Bass.
Baxter, L. A. (1985). Accomplishing relationship disengagement. In S. Duck & D. Perlman (Eds.), *Understanding personal relationships*. London: Sage.
Baxter, L. A., Wilmot, W. W., Simmons, C. A., & Swartz, A. (1993). Ways of doing conflict: A folk taxonomy of conflict events in personal relationships. In P. J. Kalbfleisch (Ed.), *Interpersonal communication: Evolving interpersonal relationships*. Hillsdale, NJ: Erlbaum.
Bell, R. R. (1981). Friendship of women and men. *Psychology of Women Quarterly*, 5, 402–417.
Blieszner, R. (1989). Developmental processes of friendship. In R. Adams & R. Blieszner (Eds.), *Older adult friendship*. Newbury Park, CA: Sage.

Blieszner, R., & Adams, R. G. (1992). *Adult friendship.* Newbury Park, CA: Sage.

Bukowski, W. M., Nappi, B. J., & Hoza, B. (1987). A test of Aristotle's model of friendship for young adults' same-sex and opposite-sex relationships. *Journal of Social Psychology, 127,* 595–603.

Crohan, S., & Antonucci, T. C. (1989). Friends as a source of social support in old age. In R. Adams & R. Blieszner (Eds.), *Older adult friendship.* Newbury Park, CA: Sage.

Dickens, W. J., & Perlman, P. (1981). Friendship over the life-cycle. In S. Duck & R. Gilmour (Eds.), *Personal relationships,* Vol. 2: *Developing personal relationships* (pp. 91–122). London: Academic Press.

Dickson-Markman, F. (1986). Self-disclosure with friends across the life cycles. *Journal of Social and Personal Relationships, 3,* 259–264.

Doyle, A. B., Markiewicz, D., & Hardy, C. (1994). Mother's and children's friendships: Intergenerational aspects. *Journal of Social and Personal Relationships 11,* 363–377.

Duck, S. (Ed.) (1982). *Personal relationships,* Vol. 4: *Dissolving personal relationships.* London: Academic Press.

(1983/1991). *Friends for life.* Brighton, England: Harvester Wheatsheaf.

Duck, S., & Wright, P. H. (1993). Reexaminating gender differences in same-gender friendships: A close look at two kinds of data. *Sex Roles, 28,* 709–727.

Floyd, K. W. (1994). Gender and intimacy among same-sex friends and same-sex siblings. Paper presented at the Seventh Conference on Personal Relationships, July 1994, Groningen, Netherlands.

Foa, E. B., & Foa, U. G. (1980). Resource theory: Interpersonal behavior in exchange. In K. J. Gergen, M. S. Greenberg & R. H. Willis (Eds.), *Social exchange: Advances in theory and research.* New York: Plenum.

Gaines, S. O. (1994). Exchange of respect-denying behaviors among male–female friendships. *Journal of Social and Personal Relationships, 11,* 5–24.

Groeneveld, T., Wißer, B., & Wittstock, R. (1991). *Freundschaft im Erwachsenenalter* (Unveröffentlichte Magisterarbeit). Hagen: Fernuniversität.

Hays, R. B. (1984). The development and maintenance of friendship. *Journal of Social and Personal Relationships, 1,* 75–98.

(1985). A longitudinal study of friendship development. *Journal of Personality and Social Psychology, 48,* 909–924.

(1988). Friendship. In S. Duck (Ed.), *Handbook of personal relationships* (pp. 391–408). Chichester, England: Wiley.

Hinde, R. A. (1979). *Towards understanding relationships.* London: Academic Press.

Homans, G. (1961). *Social behavior.* New York: Harcourt.

Johnson, F. L., & Aries, E. J. (1983). Conversational patterns among same-sex pairs of late adolescent close friends. *Journal of Genetic Psychology, 142,* 225–238.

Jones, D. C. (1991). Friendship satisfaction and gender: An examination of sex differences in contributors to friendship satisfaction. *Journal of Social and Personal Relationships, 8,* 167–185.

Kon, I. S. (1979). *Freundschaft.* Reinbeck bei Hamburg: Rowohlt Taschenbuch Verlag GmbH.

LaGaipa, J. J. (1977). Testing a multidimensional approach to friendship. In S. Duck (Ed.), *Theory and practice in interpersonal attraction* (pp. 249–270). New York: Academic Press.

Levinger, G. (1980). Toward the analysis of close relationships. *Journal of Experimental Social Psychology, 16,* 510–544.

Levinger, G., & Snoek, J. D. (1972). *Attraction in relationships: A new look at interpersonal attraction.* Morristown, NJ: General Learning Press.

Litwak, E. (1985). *Helping the elderly: The complementary roles of informal networks and formal systems.* New York: Guilford.

(1989). Forms of friendships among older people in an industrial society. In R. Adams & R. Blieszner (Eds.), *Older adult friendship.* Newbury Park, CA: Sage.

Lott, A. J., & Lott, B. E. (1974). The role of reward in the formulation of positive interpersonal attitudes. In T. L. Huston (Ed.), *Foundations of interpersonal attraction* (pp. 171–189). New York: Academic Press.

Matthews, S. H. (1986). *Friendship through the life course.* Beverly Hills, CA: Sage.

McAdams, D. P. (1985). Motivation and friendship. In S. Duck & D. Perlman, (Eds.), *Understanding Personal Relationships: An interdisciplinary approach* (pp. 85–106). London: Sage.

Miell, D., & Duck, S. (1986). Strategies in developing friendships. In V. J. Derlega & B. A. Winstead (Eds.), *Friendship and social interaction* (pp. 129–143). Heidelberg: Springer.

Milardo, R. M. (1982). Friendships networks in developing relationships. *Social Psychology Quarterly, 45,* 162–172.

Monsour, M. (1992). Meanings of intimacy in cross- and same-sex friendships. *Journal of Social and Personal Relationships. 9,* 277–295.

Monsour, M. Betty, S., & Kurzweil, N. (1993). Levels of perspectives and the perception of intimacy in cross-sex friendships: A balance theory explanation of shared perceptual reality. *Journal of Social and Personal Relationships, 10,* 529–550.

O'Meara, J. D. (1989). Cross-sex friendship: Four basic challenges of an ignored relationship. *Sex Roles, 21,* 525–541.

Pakaluck, M. (1991). *Other selves: Philosophers on friendship.* Indianapolis: Hackett.

Perlman, D. (1990). You bug me: Some preliminary data and reflections on hassles in close relationships. Paper presented at the Fifth Conference on Personal Relationships, July 1990, Oxford, England.

Planalp, S. (1993). Friends' and acquaintances' conversations II: Coded differences. *Journal of Social and Personal Relationships, 10,* 339–354.

Planalp, S., & Benson, A. (1992). Friends' and acquaintances' conversations I: Perceived differences. *Journal of Social and Personal Relationships, 9,* 483–506.

Reisman, J. M. (1981). Adult friendships. In S. Duck & R. Gilmour (Eds.), *Personal Relationships* (Vol. 2, pp. 205–230). London: Academic Press.

Roberto, K. (1989). Exchange and equity in friendships. In R. Adams & R. Blieszner (Eds.), *Older adult friendship.* Newbury Park, CA: Sage.

Roberto, K. A., & Scott, J. P. (1986). Friendships of older men and women: Exchange patterns and satisfaction. *Psychology and Aging, 1*(2), 103–109.

Rook, K. S. (1989). Strains in older adults' friendships. In R. Adams & R. Blieszner (Eds.), *Older adult friendship.* Newbury Park, CA: Sage.

Rose, S. M. (1984). How friendships end: Patterns among young adults. *Journal of Social and Personal Relationships, 1,* 267–277.

Rusbult, C. E. (1980). Satisfaction and commitment in friendships. *Representative Research in Social Psychology, 11,* 96–105.

Sapadin, L. A. (1988). Friendship and gender: Perspectives of professional men and women. *Journal of Social and Personal Relationships, 5,* 387–403.

Schneider, B. H. (Ed.) (1994). Special Issue: Children's friendships. *Journal of Social and Personal Relationships, 11.*

Selman, R. (1984). *Die Entwicklung des sozialen Verstehens.* Frankfurt: Suhrkamp.

Tschann, J. M. (1988). Self-disclosure in adult friendship: Gender and marital status differences. *Journal of Social and Personal Relationships, 5,* 65–81.

Walster, E., Walster, D. W., & Berscheid, E. (1978). *Equity: Theory & research.* Boston: Allyn & Bacon.

Wheeler, L., Reis, H., & Nezlek, J. (1983). Loneliness, social interaction, and sex roles. *Journal of Personality and Social Psychology, 45,* 943–954.

Winstead, B. (1986). Sex differences in same-sex friendships. In V. Derlega & B. Winstead (Eds.), *Friendship and social interaction* (pp. 81–99). Heidelberg: Springer.

Winstead, B., & Derlega, V. (1984). The therapeutic value of same-sex friendships. Paper presented at the annual meeting of the Southeastern Psychological Association Convention, New Orleans.

Wiseman, J. P. (1986). Friendship: Bonds and binds in a voluntary relationship. *Journal of Social and Personal Relationships, 3,* 191–211.

Wright, P. H. (1969). A model and a technique for studies of friendship. *Journal of Experimental Social Psychology, 5,* 295–309.

(1978). Toward a theory of friendship based on a conception of self. *Human Communication Research, 4,* 196–207.

(1982). Men's friendships, women's friendships and the alleged inferiority of the latter. *Sex Roles, 8,* 1–20.

(1984). Self-referent motivation and the intrinsic quality of friendship. *Journal of Social and Personal Relationships, 1,* 115–130.

(1985). The Acquaintance Description Form. In S. Duck & D. Perlman (Eds.), *Understanding personal relationships: An interdisciplinary approach.* London: Sage.

(1988). Interpreting research on gender differences in friendship: A case for moderation and a plea for caution. *Journal of Social and Personal Relationships, 5,* 367–373.

11

Neighbors and acquaintances
Christian Melbeck

Introduction

Current studies on relationships in neighborhoods and between acquaintances often assume that these two types of relationship are very similar. Is a neighbor an acquaintance who lives in the vicinity? Are there other aspects, apart from spatial proximity, that indicate differences between neighborhood and acquaintance relationships?

Most authors agree that changes in interpersonal relationships took place at the beginning of the century as a result of industrialization and urbanization. In preindustrial times, neighborhood relationships represented a specific type of relationship that later formed the strongly idealized basis of numerous studies on neighborhoods. The following points were characteristic of this type of study:

(1) The neighborhood formed a network providing community support and emergency services and was of fundamental importance to the individual (illness, fire fighting, pump brigades for water supply, etc.). It formed an institutionalized structure with defined limits and precise rules and duties for its members.
(2) Neighborhood relationships were close, primary relationships that strongly resembled those with relatives.

In his now-classic essay, Wirth (1938) considered changes in social structure depending on the level of industrialization, population size and density, and duration of settlement, which he viewed as the foundations of urban lifestyle. According to Wirth, the quality of interactions changes as the population increases in size. Increasing population density leads to stronger formalization, symbolized by the clock and traffic signs as a basis of order in urban society (1938, p. 15f). Growing heterogeneity leads to a higher level of industrialization as individuals can only participate in social, political, and economic life by joining intermediary organizations. The separation of home and work, and the possibility of setting one's own priorities in leisure activities, lead to contacts with persons who may belong to very different social groups. Contacts with various groups affect only certain aspects of the personality. According to Wirth (p. 12), they are compelled to be "impersonal, superficial, transitory, and segmental," and he terms them as "secondary contacts." In contrast, "primary contacts" are those with relatives and neighbors, which, Wirth maintains, disappear with urban lifestyle.

Wirth views acquaintances as typical secondary contacts of urban dwellers. "Our acquaintances tend to stand in a relationship of utility to us in the sense that the role which each one plays in our life is overwhelmingly regarded as a means for the achievement of our own ends" (Wirth, 1938, p. 12). Wirth regards the shift from primary to secondary contacts as decidedly negative, as – simplified – contacts with a great variety of personality types lead to status insecurity that can finally result in anomie.

Wirth's contemporaries often judge acquaintances differently. In their view, this type of relationship encourages individuality and the development of a separate personality. Extreme positions related to Wirth's, which maintained that urban inhabitants no longer had any primary contacts, were quickly contradicted and have not been corroborated by later research.

The analytical differentiation made by Tönnies (1963; German original 1887) between community (primary relations) and society (secondary relations) is more helpful here, as it is not conceived as a dichotomy. According to Tönnies, the different social formations (e.g., family, groups of friends, neighbors) include both types of relationship, but he maintained that the development of society leads to a decline in the community element and a corresponding increase in the societal element.

The term "community" includes both aspects: the personal community built up by interpersonal ties and the administrative community as a common locality. The idea that a personal community can exist independent of a local community became popular during the 1970s. Wellman (1979), in particular, should be mentioned in this context. He differentiates among three theoretical approaches, which he terms generally as "community lost," "community saved," and "community liberated" (1979, p. 1204–1208; Wellman & Leighton, 1983). The approach that proposes the loss of community contacts (at least in urban neighborhoods) is associated with Wirth's position. In contrast to this, the second approach maintains that primary contacts also exist in urban neighborhoods. Gans (1962, 1982), in particular, represents this viewpoint. The final approach, which assumes independence of spatial limitations, is from Wellman. It includes the possibility of maintaining primary contacts over great distances as a result of modern transport and communication channels.

Wellman's "community liberated" approach requires a completely different method of sampling design, in contrast to those of the "community lost" and "community saved" approaches. Instead of first defining a space in which the social relationships of people living within it are examined, the reverse is necessary. First of all the relationships between people have to be defined. Only then can the question of the spatial distance between the persons be asked.

Wellman's approach has a higher theoretical content but poses difficulties concerning empirical substantiation, as standard procedures of empirical social research cannot be applied to test it. Two prerequisites have to be satisfied in an empirical analysis of these questions: first, relational data are required; second, a number of methodical instruments are needed to analyze such data. In relational data the basis unit of analysis is the relationship between a pair of actors as opposed to a characteristic of an individual actor. In this case the analysis procedure for assessing relational data should not be restricted to the individual pair but should also be able to encompass all other relationships connected with this pair. Network analysis, based on graph theory and matrix algebra, is the most suitable methodical procedure for this purpose.

Methodological basis: Network analysis

In network analysis a differentiation is made between the overall network and the personal (ego-centered) network (Pappi, 1987). Whereas the overall network contains the relationships of all the actors to all other actors from the perspective of a single actor, the personal network contains only the relationships of a fixed actor (*ego*) to the people associated with him or her (*alteri*). In the ideal case, the personal network is augmented by the relationships that the ego perceives among the alteri. In principle an overall network is conceivable that combines a number of personal networks, providing that all ego and alteri belong to the same social system.

The prerequisite for gaining data on overall networks is a meaningful system definition. In comparison to personal networks, overall networks provide a much higher information content and far more analysis possibilities, but analysis will not be particularly productive if the system definition is inadequate. In personal networks, system definition involves the question of defining relationship content.

Both in overall networks and in personal networks a differentiation is made between partial and total networks. Partial networks contain only relationships of a particular type (e.g., political discussions, aid, etc.), while the overall network comprises the totality of all relationship types. Empirical research based on questionnaires enables the collection of data only on partial networks, but approximations of the overall network can be achieved by linking a number of partial networks. Additional evaluation of data can often only be achieved with partial networks. The potential volume of data is considerable, as shown by Boissevain's (1974) study of the networks of two Maltese, one of whom had contacts with 1,751 persons, the other with 639 persons. This illustrates how essential it is to make more exact data specifications.

The alteri in ego-centered questionnaires can only be selected in connection with certain contents. Various investigations have concerned themselves with which contents, or bundles of contents, are particularly appropriate here. The following name generators were of particular significance:

(1) Question on the three best friends (Laumann, 1973).
(2) Question about the persons with whom ego had discussed important matters over the past six months (Burt, 1984).
(3) Combination of various contents. In Fischer (1982) people were asked who looked after their apartment when they were away; who they talked with about work, shared hobbies and leisure activities, and personal matters; who they had undertaken activities with in the past three months (e.g., going out, invitations, etc.); whose opinion they consider important, and whom they would borrow money from.

The original theoretical considerations lead to the central question of how many different contents are included in relationships to alteri. When my sole connection with a person consists of discussing the current football results, then the relationship is uniplex. If, however, I also participate in some sport with this person, go out for meals with him or her, or borrow money, then the relationship is multiplex. The degree of multiplexity can, however, vary.

The partial networks resulting from the above-mentioned questions are not necessarily uniplex too. For instance, a variety of more detailed studies on friendship networks show that friendships have a number of contents. In this connection a study by Burt (1983) is of particular interest as it provides an empirical examination of the overlap of various contents.

The introductory theoretical considerations on relationships between neighbors and between acquaintances referred not only to the individual dyadic relationships of a person, but also to the structure of the personal network. Analysis here requires a shift from the dyadic to the triadic level

(Pappi & Melbeck, 1988). Primary, strong relationships are present when the relationships are multiplex and transitive, whereas secondary, weak relationships are uniplex and intransitive. Here, transitivity refers to the relationships between the alteri. When ego has a relationship with A and B, then the triad comprising ego, A, and B is transitive if A and B also have a relationship. If the latter is not the case, then the triad is intransitive.

Neighborhoods: Selected empirical findings

Relationships that are not defined as kinships, friendships, or contacts at work are often classified as "remaining relationships" in empirical studies. Of all the various forms of relationships between acquaintances, only neighborhood contacts have received any special attention.

Interest in neighborhood relationships has a long tradition in the sociology of the community. A wealth of information on neighborhoods is provided by socioecological studies that commenced at the beginning of the century with the works of the Chicago School (e.g., see Park, Burgess & Mckenzie, 1925). General questions on the significance of neighborhood usually lead to the conclusion that a "good" neighborhood is important to those interviewed. But when questioned more exactly about personal contacts with neighbors, the resulting picture shows little actual involvement. Most people know a few neighbors by name and greet them when they meet, but they have very few close contacts with them. An impression of the extent of contacts is provided by Table 11.1, which Wellman prepared in the first East York study. It will be referred to in more detail in the remainder of this section.

The table illustrates that a large number of the subjects have at least weak relationships (names known, conversations) with a few neighbors. The majority of subjects had more intense relationships (visits, help in times of need) with only a few of their neighbors. In this case only a few of the subjects noted six or more neighbors. On the one hand, it can be maintained that the number of relationships with neighbors decreases as relationship intensity increases; on the other hand, over 80% of the respondents have at least one neighbor on whom they can rely in an emergency. Other studies (see Friedrichs, p. 246f) gathered data not only on the actual contacts but also on the degree of need for more, and more intense, contacts. It was seen that a certain distance to neighbors was usually desired and maintained in most cases.

The results show that the normative concept of considering an integrated neighborhood important is present, but that individuals do not necessarily aim to realize this. If one departs from the ideal image of a comprehensive, highly integrated neighborhood – which some authors suggest never coin-

Table 11.1. *Extent and intensity of contacts between neighbors*

| | Number of ties between neighbors | | | | | |
	None	1–2	3–5	6–10	11+	Total
Names of neighbors known	55 (7.0%)	131 (16.6%)	186 (23.5%)	212 (26.8%)	206 (26.1%)	790 (100.0%)
Neighbors talked to	45 (5.7%)	173 (21.8%)	268 (33.8%)	198 (24.9%)	110 (13.9%)	794 (100.0%)
Neighbors' homes visited	187 (23.6%)	272 (34.3%)	247 (31.1%)	66 (8.3%)	21 (3.6%)	793 (100.0%)
Neighbors to be called on in emergencies	144 (18.2%)	408 (51.6%)	194 (24.5%)	30 (3.8%)	15 (1.9%)	791 (100.0%)

Source: Wellman (1976, p. 18), slightly modified.

cided with reality – and considers the separate dyadic relationships, it becomes clear that most people have slightly more intense relationships only with a few selected neighbors.

The type and extent of these selective relationships depend on certain characteristics of the neighborhood, the respondents, and the households in which they live. Various studies show that the following variables affect contacts between neighbors: type of architecture (high-rise versus detached houses), neighborhood socioeconomic status, and (at least in the United States) the ethnic status of the inhabitants, as well as individual character- istics such as length of habitation in the area, presence of (small) children in the household, and employment outside the home. Campbell and Lee (1992) adopt a general approach. They maintain that variables such as gender, age, family status, and socioeconomic status influence general social integration in society, and that neighborhood relationships depend on the level of social integration. Their empirical investigations discovered an exception to this in that people with a low socioeconomic status tend to have more frequent and longer-lasting relationships with neighbors than might be expected from the social integration theory.

The figures given in various studies are not easy to compare because the definitions of neighborhood, its composition, and data-collecting methods vary too much. However, the general tendency in recent studies is that the absolute number of reported contacts with neighbors show a decrease that could be attributed to a general increase in mobility, but that the above- mentioned variables still have similar effects on the number and intensity of contacts. In addition, there are a number of other variables, such as gender and owning versus renting one's home, which lead to different results. These stem partly from high correlations with other variables.

Campbell's (1990) reanalysis of a 1939 study showed that the above-mentioned characteristics had similar effects in the past to those found in more recent studies. Apart from this, Campbell's results also confirm the above-mentioned supposition that the concept of a highly integrated neighborhood in earlier times is not necessarily realistic.

In contrast to the overall network researched in the Bloomington study, Wellman's East York study collected data on personal networks from the ego perspective. East York has a population of about 100,000 and is the smallest of six districts in Toronto. The majority of inhabitants live in small self-owned homes or in high-rise apartments. Hardly any homes have more than two adult members. East York has the reputation of being the district with the highest sense of social cohesion.

The first study was based on a random sample of 845 adult East Yorkers. Wellman conducted the study together with the psychiatrist Donald B. Coates (Coates, Moyer & Wellman, 1969; Coates, Moyer, Kendall & Howatt, 1976), who was primarily interested in the significance of networks on psychological well-being. The questionnaire contained questions on the number of particular neighborhood contacts on the one hand (see Table 11.1) and questions about personal networks on the other. In a first step the respondents were asked to name a maximum of six persons they felt closest to outside their home. Data were collected on these alteri concerning the characteristics of gender, age, and socioeconomic status; on the dyads concerning strength of the relationship, frequency of contacts, type of contact (e.g., telephone, visit), and the origin of the relationship (e.g., mother, neighbor); and on the triads concerning closeness among the alteri. Although Wellman's analyses were designed primarily to answer the more general community question, they still contain important information about relationships between neighbors.

Almost all East Yorkers had a close relationship to at least one person, but the majority report five or more. Out of 3,930 dyadic relationships reported by the 845 respondents, about half involved relatives. When the strengths of the relationships are compared, those with relatives dominate even further. When relatives and nonrelated persons were named as close partners, these two groups rarely showed any links.

Persons generally classify a relationship with a spatially close kin not as a neighborhood relationship. The decision whether a spatially close person should be termed a friend or a neighbor presented a problem in some cases. Table 11.2 reflects the subjective categorization of a relationship by the respondents as well as the "objective" criterion of geographical distance. The classification of a relationship is cross-tabulated with the distance from

Table 11.2. *Close relationships reported by a sampling of East Yorkers, by residence and identity of the partner*

Residence	Relationship							
	Child	Parent	Sibling	Other Relative	Friend	Neighbor	Co-worker	Total
Same neighborhood	9 (4.0%)	23 (6.8%)	25 (4.2%)	54 (6.9%)	194 (13.1%)	182 (74.3%)	18 (8.3%)	505 (13.0%)
Elsewhere in East York	23 (10.1%)	35 (10.3%)	63 (10.6%)	85 (10.9%)	211 (14.3%)	38 (15.5%)	28 (13.0%)	483 (12.5%)
City of Toronto	26 (11.5%)	94 (27.6%)	130 (22.0%)	176 (22.6%)	441 (29.9%)	10 (4.1%)	83 (38.4%)	960 (24.8%)
Elsewhere in Metro Toronto	108 (47.6%)	50 (14.7%)	147 (24.8%)	227 (29.1%)	359 (24.3%)	10 (4.1%)	71 (32.9%)	972 (25.1%)
Outside Metro Toronto	61 (26.9%)	138 (40.6%)	227 (38.3%)	237 (30.4%)	271 (18.4%)	5 (2.0%)	16 (7.4%)	955 (24.6%)
N	227	340	592	779	1,476	245	216	3,875
% of total	5.9%	8.8%	15.3%	20.1%	38.1%	6.3%	5.6%	100.0%

Source: Wellman (1979, p. 1212).

the domicile. Looking first at the marginals, it can be seen that 75% of contacts were situated in the same town but only 13% were in the same neighborhood. The individual entries in the table read in the following way: in 9 out of 227 close relationships with children (4%), the children live in the same neighborhood. The proportion of "real" neighborhood relationships was only 4.7% of the total number of dyadic relationships when former neighbors who had moved away and with whom contacts still existed are excluded. According to Wellman, only very few of the respondents nominated more than one neighbor as a close contact person. Accordingly, only 20% of the 845 persons questioned named a neighbor as a close partner.

This result seems to contradict Table 11.1, where 80% of the same respondents stated they had at least one neighbor to whom they could turn in an emergency. But this simply leads to the conclusion that no particularly close relationship was maintained with those neighbors on whom one could rely in an emergency.

Wellman and his coresearchers carried out a second study in 1977–1978 on a subsample of the original study subjects. Here, a more general name generator was used to gain data on a much larger section of the overall network. The subsample comprised 33 interviewees who were first asked about persons with whom they were in touch at present. The results of this interview can be found in Wellman, Carrington, and Hall (1988). Although the interviews each lasted between 10 and 15 hours, it was still not possible to define clearly the type of aid received from the alteri. As a result it was followed up by a written questionnaire. However, the small number of subjects and the method of selection limit the possibility of generalizing the results. Nevertheless, it is possible to estimate the effect of the extension of the network by including less intimate relationships.

In the case of neighborhood contacts, two extreme groups could be juxtaposed. On the one hand there were the networks of four housewives who cooperated closely with neighbors in childminding and also exchanged goods, services, information, and emotional support with them. At the other extreme were the networks of 10 employed women who had no contacts with the neighbors except for exchanging greetings. Six of them stated that they consciously avoided contacts with the neighbors in order to protect their private sphere and remain independent. The remaining four persons were men who had no contacts with the neighbors but stated that their wives did.

Results on which kinds of support could be given by neighbors as opposed to persons in other relationships are summarized in Table 11.3.

The study by Wellman and Wortley was published in 1990 and was based on a subsample of 29 of the 845 respondents of the first study. In contrast to Table 11.2, it includes not only the strong relationships but also

Table 11.3. *Forms of aid provided by various relationship types (in percentages)*

	Emotional aid	Small services	Large services	Financial aid	Companionship
Parent/child:					
Significant	7	5	13	15	2
Strong	8	7	11	15	6
Sibling:					
Significant	8	7	8	7	7
Strong	16	15	20	1	12
Extended kin:					
Significant	5	5	0	2	2
Strong	2	2	2	2	2
Neighbor:					
Significant	8	10	11	2	8
Strong	13	14	16	13	15
Friend:					
Significant	4	5	4	6	4
Strong	20	21	15	9	25
Organizational tie:					
Significant	5	5	0	9	10
Strong	4	4	0	6	7
Total	100	100	100	100	100
All significant ties	37	37	36	41	33
All strong ties	63	63	64	59	67

Source: Wellman and Wortley (1990, p. 567).

less intimate relationships (labeled "significant" in Table 11.3). Of the 344 dyadic relationships reported, approximately 40% were close relationships (similar to Table 11.2) and 60% were additional, weaker relationships. Data were collected on 18 special forms. In a factor analysis, Wellman and Wortley discovered five dimensions of aid: emotional, small services, large services, financial aid, and companionship. The individual dyadic relationships could contain one, several, or all five dimensions. Table 11.3 shows each of the five aid dimensions and the percentages attributed to the various relationship types. For example, 8% of emotional aid came from neighbors with whom only weak dyadic relationships existed and 13% from neighbors with strong relationships. In sum 21% of emotional aid came from neighbors. The last two lines of the table show the support given by weak and strong relationships. Here it is clear that support from strong ties covered far more dimensions than weak ones because, although only 40%

of the relationships were strong, they provided almost two-thirds of each single type of support.

There were specialists for certain forms of support. For example, financial aid often passed between parents and children, whereas companionship usually occurred between friends. As far as relationships with neighbors are concerned, it is striking that strong relationships with neighbors covered all five aid dimensions. Although aid from neighbors never ranked first, it always came second or third. Weaker relationships with neighbors were rarely a source of financial aid, but they still covered the remainder of the spectrum fairly well. It is interesting that the weak relationships with neighbors were similar to weak relationships with parents, children, and siblings as far as emotional aid, small services, and large services were concerned. Divergences appeared only in the case of financial aid, which was rendered by parents to children, and companionship, which was not shared by parents and children.

The type of aid among relatives is subject to normative regulations (in the case of close relatives there are additional legal regulations). It is quite possible that even in relationships between neighbors there are still surviving normative concepts according to which neighbors should help one another in times of need. It is "the right thing to do" to help the old lady from next door to carry her heavy shopping bag even though one may not like her very much. One is more likely to help a person only connected by local proximity than a comparable stranger who does not live in the neighborhood.

Apart from the small number of people questioned in these studies by Wellman, the examination of a district with very particular characteristics further limits the possibility of generalizing the results. In a study by Fischer (1982), data were also collected on personal networks from the ego perspective. The name generator already mentioned in the section on network analysis was used to collect data on the networks of specific relationship contents. These can be analyzed either individually or in aggregated forms. One great advantage of this study is that different types of community were taken into consideration. Interview subjects were taken from a sample of 50 Californian communities ranging from small towns with less than 10,000 inhabitants (villages were excluded) to inner-city districts of San Francisco and Oakland.

Fischer works on the assumption that the size and density of a community do not directly influence the type of relationships between inhabitants, but do so only indirectly, as they are associated with greater social homogeneity. In his "subcultural theory of urbanism," Fischer (1975) assumes that various minorities and highly specialized individuals prefer larger cities because the chances of meeting similar people are greater there, and the critical mass necessary to form groups is also more likely to be present. As the population of a town increases, so too does the number of groups with different lifestyles. The group members, or rather the people who feel attached to a certain lifestyle, are not usually neighbors with close local proximity. They tend to be distributed over a certain town or city district and meet at particular "insider" places. To quote Keller (1968, p. 61), one could speak of a change from "neighboring of place to neighboring of taste." If, by definition, neighborhood is supposed to be associated with local proximity, then Fischer's theory postulates that increasing urbanity relationships with neighbors tend to be replaced by relationships with friends or acquaintances.

Fischer's data also show that most respondents had contacts with their neighbors but that in most cases these were fairly weak. Only half of those questioned said they had ever borrowed something from neighbors, and a third of those classified as neighbors were only named once as somebody who had kept an eye on the apartment while the respondent was away. In Fischer's study, data concerning the type and extent of neighborhood contacts were also determined by characteristics such as homogeneity and heterogeneity in sociostructural composition, number of children, employment outside the home, housewife, pensioner, population increase or decrease, stagnation of the district, and home ownership or rental. On the question of the effects of the community size, the problem arises that all these variables correlate with it.

Fischer's central explanation for the varying number of contacts focuses on opportunity structure. When people are less mobile they depend more on contacts with neighbors. An increase in choice outside the neighborhood tends to decrease the probability of selecting a neighbor for contacts.

A further point seldom treated in the literature should also be mentioned here. Relationships between people are not always positive; in many cases conflicts of varying magnitude arise. If and when conflicts are investigated, they are usually examined in close social relationships. As a rule it is assumed that a relationship must first exist before it can be disturbed. When the relationship is weak there is little cause for conflict. If conflicts do arise, then contact with a person in a weak relationship can be reduced, if necessary by avoiding him or her. Conflict potential is greater in strong relationships and there is less opportunity to withdraw. At first it appears that conflicts between neighbors do not fit into this picture very well. Although relationships with neighbors are often only weak or nonexistent, there is still a multitude of conflicts within neighborhoods.

Bergmann (1992) provides a variety of very lucid examples. He cites an extremely large annual number of court cases in which neighbors file suits against each other. Considering the indirect involvement of family members associated with the plaintiffs and defendants, the extent of potentially negative experiences with neighborhoods soon becomes clear. Linneweber

(1990) confirms this in his telephone survey of personal negative experiences with neighbors. Only 18% of those interviewed reported wholly positive experiences, while 60% reported negative personal experiences. On closer scrutiny such results show that relationships between neighbors are weak social relationships but strong spatial relationships. Even if someone does not know neighbors personally, he or she can still be annoyed, as by their noise or garbage, and come into conflict with them by complaining to a third party (a janitor, the police).

The above-mentioned changes that have taken place in social relationships since the beginning of the century have led to a situation in which the strength of spatial and of social relationships no longer have to coincide. Socially strong kin relationships can be maintained over great distances and relationships with neighbors can be socially weak.

On the theory of acquaintances

Until now, this chapter has primarily considered the effects of structural phenomena in living areas on the probability of relationship existence. The probability of a relationship in the case of housewives with young children in a residential area with detached houses is greater than in the case of people in full employment outside the home. This does not mean that all housewives in a certain area have relationships with all the other housewives. It simply means that in the case of a housewife the probability of her network containing someone from the neighborhood is greater than that among other groups of people. This cannot explain the concrete selection of a contact partner. In this case individual approaches are needed that consider the characteristics of each person concerned. Fischer (1982, p. 251ff) has evaluated a number of individual characteristics such as education, age, gender, and income. Education proved to be the central individual characteristic in explaining network characteristics, but the other variables listed also played a certain role.

Individualistic approaches on attractiveness cannot contribute much toward characterizing the relationship between neighbors as a specific relationship type. On the other hand, the present result – that different opportunity structures in certain living areas and population groups influence the nature and extent of the relationship – is a bit too general. The link is missing between the structure of a living area and its population on the one hand, and the establishment and development of relationships among the inhabitants on the other. This link is provided by Feld's (1981; see also Wegener 1987) suggested focus theory of social relationships.

According to this theory, the opportunity structure is created by a number of foci. Foci are crystallization points for social relationships that can consist of a great variety of contents. "A 'focus' is any social, psychological, or physical entity around which joint activities of individuals are organized" (Feld, 1981, p. 1025). Family, club, workplace, playground, neighborhood are just as much foci as religion, philosophy of life, or a person's clothing. While referring to Homans (1951, 1961), Feld departs from the basic assumption that two persons who have a common focus are more likely to undertake activities together than two persons to whom this does not apply.

The particular strength of this approach lies in the exact specification of focus properties and their effects. First of all, foci differ in the level of constraint exercised on the relationships of those involved (focus restrictiveness). For instance, two members of a family are under greater pressure to interact than two residents in the same neighborhood. Apart from its content, the focus size, which is determined by the number of persons associated with it, also influences the level of constraint to interact. Large foci principally exercise less constraint than small ones, although there are exceptions. According to Feld, "A focus is 'constraining' to the extent that it leads each pair of individuals to devote time and energy to participating in joint activities associated with that focus" (Feld, 1981, p. 1025).

Similar to the concept of multiplexity in the above-mentioned network approach, people can be associated with one another through one or more foci. Foci can be categorized according to the level of compatibility depending on the similarity of activities and interactions (focus compatibility). This means, for instance, that neighborhood, club, and family foci are more compatible than the workplace and a parent–child group.

Weak relationships with neighbors can be explained by the fact that the neighborhood focus itself is not particularly restrictive. The strong relationships observed between neighbors in certain neighborhoods or in certain subgroups are not caused directly by the neighborhood focus itself but result from foci that are compatible with it and also share a similar spacial relationship. Foci of particular relevance to the neighborhood as a whole tend to increase the community spirit of the residents. Here, neighborhood organizations, local initiatives, street festivals, and the like play an important role. Publications that consider the influence of such foci tend to concentrate on their influence on the development of community spirit and the associated increase of neighborhood contacts. Examples include Lee, Oropesa, Metch, and Guest (1984); Chavis and Wandersman (1990); Oxley, Haggard, Werner, and Altman (1986); and Werner (1987). Foci that lead to strongly associated subgroups in a neighborhood include especially those centered on children. People who have children generally spend a great deal of time in places that other parents also visit. A similarity in certain attitudes can be concluded and interpreted as a common psychological focus from the frequency the same parents meet at different foci.

262   *Christian Melbeck*

Although in most cases a common focus already exists, the initiation of a social relationship between two people does not necessarily depend on the presence of a common focus. However, usually a common focus is sought or newly developed in order to maintain the relationship.

The probable strength of a relationship between ego and alter can be derived from the propositions of focus theory. The lower the number of connecting foci and the less restrictive and compatible they are, the weaker the relationship is between ego and alter. The theory also allows statements on the presence of connections between the alteri. The more restrictive a focus is, the greater the likelihood that connections exist between the associated alteri. A simple example can be seen in the kinship focus: two persons who are related to ego will probably also be related to one another. The probability of a connection between the alteri increases when the foci connecting them and ego are compatible.

Focus theory sees the cause of transitivity in the number and type of underlying foci. Transitivity can emerge later with the development of a new focus. According to this theory, not all relationships have a tendency to transitivity. Certain weak relationships in which a person invests little time, energy, and emotion, or those with incompatible foci, may well be intransitive.

Such intransitive relationships are typical for many acquaintances. Respondents generally categorize persons as acquaintances with whom they are connected by only a few special foci. If the relationship is to be strengthened, additional foci will be sought or developed that are compatible with the exisiting ones. The relationship is thus strengthened and the categorization of the relationship between the two persons involved shifts in the direction of friendship. In contrast to balance theory approaches based on Heider (1958), focus theory maintains that intransitive relationships can also be long-term and stable (see Hummel & Sodeur, 1987).

Acquaintances can be more than an intermediary stage in a process of relationship development. Many relationships between neighbors are of long duration but do not develop into close relationships. Such relationships do not necessarily depend on spatial proximity, although proximity can prevent the complete dissolution of a weakening relationship. Acquaintances can also be maintained over long distances, and they can remain stable over long periods despite their low strength. In his often-quoted articles, Granovetter (1973, 1982) has indicated the significance of these weak ties for the integration of the individual within society. Members of the primary groups of kin and friends are often connected through strong, transitive relationships. In order to gain access to other groups people need local bridging relationships that are intransitive and weak.

Access to the information of other groups is greatly facilitated when a person is connected to others who in turn have links with other groups.

With the exception of kin relationships, members of primary groups are often homogeneous in status, but persons of higher status have information that could lead to personal advancement. This kind of constellation can lead to the paradox described by Granovetter, whereby weaker relationships are sometimes more productive than strong ones. Granovetter's data include details on who informed a person about a particular job opportunity. In the United States at least, personal contacts are very important in job hunting. In approximately three-quarters of cases where work was found through personal contacts, weak relationships were involved (Wegener, 1987, p. 285).

In his essay on strangers (Simmel, 1968, p. 509ff), written in 1908, Simmel provided a very vivid description of the particular role that acquaintances have always played and their typical characteristics. What is described as a relationship with an acquaintance in this chapter is described by Simmel as a relationship with a stranger, a person who belongs on the one hand, but who is an outsider on the other. Simmel's historical example of a stranger is the traveler or merchant who is mobile and comes into contact with many people, but who has no permanent ties with individuals through kinship, profession, or local relationships. The stranger is thus exempt from group pressure. He or she is not bound to particular role within the group and can remain "objective." As an outsider, the stranger can be told personal confidentialities that one keeps secret from close members of one's own group. On the other hand, the stranger can report on other countries and people and their customs and habits, which can stimulate otherwise unknown desires as well as changes in value hierarchies. To this extent the stranger always represents a danger to one's own group.

Nowadays a great variety of media and institutional counseling services provide information. But where very specialized information is needed at a particular time, acquaintances are still more appropriate, because personal information often has higher credibility than information received through the media.

Acquaintances are not only important for relaying information but also for leisure activities that require a partner. These can be selected according to the particular requirements of the activity without considering whether this person fits into the primary group on the basis of additional criteria.

Finally, it can be said that acquaintances display not only general characteristics, but that their more specialized forms can also possess additional properties. In this chapter it was only possible to consider the characteristics of one specialized type: neighborhood relationships. Until now there have been virtually no similar studies on the other particular forms of acquaintances.

References

Bergmann, T. (1992). *Giftzwerge. Wenn der Nachbar zum Feind wird.* München: Beck.

Boissevain, J. (1974). *Friends of friends: Networks, manipulators and coalitions.* Oxford: Blackwell.

Burt, R. S. (1983). Distinguishing relational content. In M. J. Minor et al. (Eds.), *Applied network analysis: A methodological introduction* (pp. 35–74). Beverly Hills, CA: Sage.

—— (1984). *Network items should be included in the General Social Survey.* New York: Department of Sociology and Center for the Social Sciences reprint series.

Campbell, K. E. (1990). Networks past: A 1939 Bloomington neighborhood. *Social Forces, 69,* 139–155.

Campbell, K. E., & Lee, B. A. (1992). Sources of personal neighbor networks: Social integration, need, or time? *Social Forces, 70,* 1077–1100.

Chavis, D. M., & Wandersman, A. (1990). Sense of community in the urban environment: A catalyst for participation and community development. *American Journal of Community Psychology, 18,* 55–81.

Coates, D. B., Moyer, S., Kendall, L., & Howatt, M. G. (1976). Life-event changes and mental health. In I. G. Sarason & C. D. Spielberger (Eds.), *Stress and Anxiety* (Vol. 3, pp. 225–249). New York: Halsted Press.

Coates, D. B., Moyer, S., & Wellman, B. (1969). The Yorklea study of urban mental health: Symptoms, problems and life events. *Canadian Journal of Public Health, 60,* 471–481.

Feld, S. L. (1981). The Focused organization of social ties. *American Journal of Sociology, 86,* 1015–1035.

Fischer, C. S. (1975). Toward a subcultural theory of urbanism. *American Journal of Sociology, 80,* 1319–1341.

—— (1982). *To dwell among friends: Personal networks in town and city.* Chicago: University of Chicago Press.

Friedrichs, J. (1977). *Stadtanalyse. Soziale und räumliche Organisation der Gesellschaft.* Reinbek bei Hamburg: rororo studium.

Gans, H. J. (1962). Urbanism and suburbanism as a way of life: A re-evaluation of definitions. In A. M. Rose (Ed.), *Human behavior and social process* (pp. 625–648). Boston: Houghton Mifflin.

—— (1982). *The urban villagers: Group and class in the life of Italian-Americans* (rev. ed.). New York: Free Press.

Granovetter, M. S. (1973). The strength of weak ties. *American Journal of Sociology, 78,* 1360–1380.

—— (1982). The strength of weak ties: A network theory revisited. In P. V. Marsden & N. Lin (Eds.), *Social structure and network analysis* (pp. 201–233). Beverly Hills, CA: Sage.

Heider, F. (1958). *The psychology of interpersonal relations.* New York: Wiley.

Homans, G. C. (1951). *The human group.* London: Routledge, Paul & Kegan.

(1961). *Social behaviour: Its elementary forms*. New York: Harcourt, Brace & World.

Hummell, H. J., & Sodeur, W. (1987). Triaden- und Triplettzensus als Mittel der Strukturbeschreibung. In F. U. Pappi (Ed.), *Methoden der Netzwerkanalyse* (pp. 129–161). München: Oldenbourg Verlag.

Keller, S. (1968). *The urban neighborhood*. New York: Random House.

Laumann, E. O. (1973). *Bonds of pluralism: The form and substance of urban social networks*. New York: Wiley Interscience.

Lee, B. A., Oropesa, R. S., Metch, B. J., & Guest, A. M. (1984). Testing the decline-of-community thesis: Neighborhood organizations in Seattle, 1929 and 1979. *American Journal of Sociology, 89,* 1161–1188.

Linneweber, V. (1990). Konflikte in nachbarlichen Beziehungen als Gegenstand sozial- und umweltpsychologischer Forschung. *Magazin Forschung der Universität des Saarlandes, 1,* 15–20.

Oxley, D., Haggard, L. M., Werner, C. M., & Altman, I. (1986). Transactional qualities of neighborhood social networks. A case study of "Christmas Street." *Environment and Behavior, 18,* 640–677.

Pappi, F. U. (1987). Die Netzwerkanalyse aus soziologischer Perspektive. In F. U. Pappi (Ed.), Methoden der Netzwerkanalyse (pp. 11–37). München: Oldenbourg Verlag.

Pappi, F. U., & Melbeck, C. (1988). Die sozialen Beziehungen städtischer Bevölkerungen. In J. Friedrichs (Ed.), *Soziologische Stadtforschung, Sonderheft 29 der Kölner Zeitschrift für Soziologie und Sozialpsychologie* (pp. 223–250). Opladen: Westdeutscher Verlag.

Park, R. E., Burgess, E. W., & McKenzie, R. D. (1925). *The city*. Chicago: University of Chicago Press.

Simmel, G. (1968). *Soziologie*. Berlin: Duncker & Humblot.

Tönnies, F. (1963). *Community and society* [original title: *Gemeinschaft und Gesellschaft*]. Translated and edited by Charles P. Loomis. New York: Harper Row.

Wegener, B. (1987). Vom Nutzen entfernter Bekannter. *Kölner Zeitschrift für Soziologie und Sozialpsychologie, 39,* 278–301.

Wellman, B. (1976). Urban Connections. Research Paper No. 84. Centre for Urban and Community Studies, University of Toronto.

(1979). The community question: The intimate networks of East Yorkers. *American Journal of Sociology, 84,* 1201–1231.

Wellman, B., Carrington, P. J., & Hall, A. (1988). Networks as personal communities. In B. Wellman & S. D. Berkowitz (Eds.), *Social structures: A network approach* (pp. 130–184). Cambridge: Cambridge University Press.

Wellman, B., & Leighton, B. (1983). Networks, neighborhoods, and communities: Approaches to the study of the community perspectives of the American community. In R. L. Warren & L. Lyon (Eds.), *New perspectives on the American community* (pp. 246–262). Homewood, IL: Dorsey Press.

Wellman, B., & Wortley, S. (1990). Different strokes from different folks:

Community ties and social support. *American Journal of Sociology, 96,* 558–588.

Werner, C. M. (1987). A transactional approach to neighborhood social relationships. In S. Oskamp & S. Spacapan (Eds.), *Interpersonal processes* (pp. 25–57). Newbury Park, CA: Sage.

Wirth, L. (1938, July). Urbanism as a way of life. *American Journal of Sociology, 44,* 1–24.

PART V

Relationships at work

12

Relationships between colleagues
Oswald Neuberger

Human relations in organizations?

In the following chapter the term "colleagues" has two meanings:

(1) those people who occupy different hierarchical levels in a work organization but share the same rank, although they may have nothing to do with one another in both senses of the phrase (all workers; all foremen/ women; all those in higher managerial positions). Together these different bodies of colleagues form the (work) collective or personnel.
(2) those people of similar rank who work together in a clearly perceptible work unit and who share direct interpersonal relationships.

Both of these perspectives will be used here to elucidate characteristic features of "relationships between colleagues."

Being a colleague, female or male, is a social classification. It does not denote an individual accomplishment on the part of a specific person; it is a prescribed role that is accepted and either formed individually or negotiated. Classifications are "prescribed" in two ways: on the one hand they are prefabricated *descriptions* (prefabricated both in terms of time and form, i.e., generalized and stereotyped); on the other hand they are *prescriptions* that function as valid premises for actions and decisions in a particular context. Classification gains its regulating power from this dual definition as a norm, which unites the usual with the demanded. It shapes expectations and mutual expectations: thus, if a woman sees herself in a classified relationship to another person – for instance another female colleague – she will expect the other to have specific legitimate expectations of her.

Classifications are stimulating in that they create order and orientation and yet – more important for organizational purposes – they can still be shaped and contain elements of surprise. Knowing that someone is a female colleague explains quite a lot but by no means everything, so that statements in this respect always need indicators that provide closer definitions – for instance, the colleague in question has been with the organization for many years, she is motivated, under pressure, self-centered, burned out, or in sales or production. The decisive difference that separates the relationship between colleagues from other interpersonal relationships lies in the organization of the social context in which the relationship develops. When referring to colleagues the reference to organizations becomes inevitable.

From the very beginning empirical research in the social sciences has addressed the question of social relationships within organizations: the so-called Hawthorne Studies were conducted between 1927 and 1932 and one of their most quoted results was that human relations within an enterprise – as a combination of formal and informal organization – are of fundamental importance. The ideology behind this discovery (or rather invention) originates from the *spiritus rector* of the program: Elton Mayo saw his "rabble hypothesis" confirmed in the big American companies of the time. According to this hypothesis the workforce was composed of uprooted, greatly differing individuals who had been torn from their traditional family and community ties and tended toward "anomic" behavior. In order to counteract the disintegration of society, the companies would have to act as the seedbeds of a new order. Superiors were to ensure by means of "Human Relations" (a respectful, understanding, and friendly approach to subordinates) that the isolated individuals in the various working groups grow into a kind of substitute family. In this way it would be possible to counteract such widespread phenomena as boredom with work, restriction of output, and aggression toward objects and people. The useful side effect would be that collective interest group formation (particularly unions) would become superfluous. Human Relations between superiors and colleagues, modeled on the image of the "works family" or the small group, concentrate solely on interpersonal aspects and neglect the apersonal aspects of organizational structures and rules. As a result they fail to consider the founding conditions of relationships within the work context.

Human Relations is based on an emphatic understanding of "humaneness" that stresses such relationship attributes as openness, trust, mutual respect, authenticity, solidarity, warmth, supportiveness, sensitivity, directness, empathy, and emotionality. To demonstrate the ideological nature of the argument for this type of "humane relationships" among the workforce of an organization it is necessary to establish that, on the whole, "humane behavior" is often neither authentic nor realizable, not because the people involved are incapable of such behavior but because the conditions of organization are opposed to it.

These basic conditions will therefore be described in the following passages. It must first be noted that the framework for all interactions, interrelations, and inter-experiences of colleagues is set by the fundamental formal definition of "worker" or "personnel." When conflicts or solidarity arise between the people so formed, this is not (only) because of particular personality attributes but (also) because of structural prerequisites. An *organizational-psychological* perspective proceeds beyond the "interpersonal" toward the "apersonal" (i.e., organizational) and is thus embedded in a superior order that is not created within the relationships themselves but is preexistent and superpotent. This calls for preliminary clarification of the specifics of a (work) organization, since we are not concerned here with "applied social psychology," which concentrates on face-to-face relationships between "people in general," but rather with relationships between colleagues – and these are "people within organizations." Work organizations are to be understood as efficiency-oriented social systems (e.g., firms, public authorities, universities, the military) that are so large that it is no longer possible to coordinate cooperation within them by means of directly communicated verbal agreements, thus making the introduction of structural control mechanisms necessary.

We now need to name the major characteristics that, as objective conditions, create the foundations for differences between colleague relationships and other types of relationship (parenthood, partnership, friendship, etc.). It

mind that this list is additive, as some of the
y to other types of relationship.

pes of relationship, interpersonal relationships in
following characteristics:

larger social context. All relationships – including
e seen within the framework of manifold connec-
ationship partners whereby boundary-spanning
d the limits of the group, the department, the
hment.

ated. This is often accompanied by the cultivation,
of emotions in the pursuit of efficiency.

nination; that is, people are compelled to accept
ctions.

evaluation (permitting oneself to be assessed or
s of such assessments may be made available to
ng processes.

ation through *pay*. This is the most important

generalized symbolic code that regulates relationships to and within work organizations.

- Encounters and relationships are *unavoidable*: it is impossible to simply "keep out of the way" of certain people even if they have not selected each other. Precautionary measures become necessary to keep undesired emotions and actions under control.
- They simultaneously demand *personal identity and role conformity*. As a result border demarcation and marking and exceeding limits become both important and precarious.
- Size, complexity, and dynamics create a *partial lack of transparency* in processes and relationships.
- There is a *scarcity of and competition for resources* (personnel, finance, tools, information, time, etc.). Acting economically means consuming values to create values. The pooling of resources becomes necessary and competition for their control develops.

"Organizing" takes place under these framing conditions; the most important methods will be sketched in the following sections. They show what turns "normal people" – to use a somewhat exaggerated term – into colleagues. Of course there are interpersonal relationships in organized establishments that resemble those in neighborhoods, leisure associations, families and their extensions, and so forth, and of course there are friendships, intimate relationships, and power constellations in enterprises and public authorities. The singularity of "colleague relationships" is based solely on the specific design of the context in which they are embedded. This will now be elucidated.

Characteristics of organized interpersonal relationships

Structure – that is, the continuous and binding order of relationships – is recognized as the central characteristic of organization. The main focus of organizational psychology is often described as "the experience and behavior of individuals within organizations." This defines organization as something external that intervenes in actions and experiences in a limiting and determining way. However, as already indicated, organization should in fact be seen as the determinant of the form of *relationships* within and between objects and subjects (for more detail see Neuberger, 1991). It is *their* structuring that concerns us here. People's decisions and actions are made possible, constrained, or channeled by this structuring while at the same time (re)producing the structure (Giddens, 1988). This type of dual conception of structure avoids the categorization of the acting individuals as perpetrators or as victims; they are simultaneously both – though of course with different weightings – because, through their actions, they (co)produce the structure they are reacting to.

The general characteristic of formal determination (structure) can be broken down into separate components that illustrate the dual aspect of every organization: on the one hand their is rationalization (i.e., the unremitting and consistent direction of all processes toward defined goals), and on the other there is domination. In describing the characteristics below I am neither attempting to provide a comprehensive list nor endeavoring to derive them from any particular theoretical system. I am presenting those structuring measures that have received most attention in literature on organizational theory (e.g., Kieser & Kubicek, 1983).

Hierarchy

"Relationships between colleagues" can hardly be investigated without a concept of hierarchy. When talking about colleagues we also have to talk about superiors. Not because they too are, or have, colleagues in the general sense, but because relationships between fellow employees are formed by the existence of hierarchy. When two or more people work together, the third element in the constellation is hierarchy (disregarding, for the moment, power, rank, or status differentials). As the hierarchy-free relationship is solely a regulative idea – even in so-called "alternative enterprises" that themselves exist within the traditions and environment of hierarchy – we necessarily start from the facts of subordination, surveillance, and external determination (which can be responsible for competition, aggression, solidarity, secrecy, etc.). Hierarchy also has to be juxtaposed to the vision of self-control or self-organization because these are only possible or permitted locally and noncentrally (!).

Experience in group-dynamic sensitivity training shows just how far hierarchy has become second nature to members of organizations. The usual initial situation generates a great deal of irritation: the trainer starts the seminar and simply remains silent. Frustrated expectations of guidance, structuring, and supervision are discharged in aggression, withdrawal and annoyance, and so forth (Gebert, 1972). Hierarchy creates order and power order implies repression. Alternatively conceivable relationships are suppressed; the individuals are not free to decide what, how, and with whom they want to work; rather, this is prescribed and is kept under surveillance. However, repression manifests itself not only in the personal intervention of superiors: "structural power" is often more effective in that it is invisibly installed in rules, programs, objective technological restrictions, and so forth.

Formalization and standardization

Formalization is often viewed as the keystone of organizations; references are even made to a generic concept of formal organization. "Formalized" means set in (written) form, documented, pre-scribed. (As already mentioned, this last term in particular indicates that the formal is not only generalized and codified but is also binding!) Things have to be put in writing because individual people are no longer free to converse when they like and because negotiations have to be held simultaneously in different places in the absence of all-channel communication. The framework or corridor of interactions and interrelationships is more rigidly fixed in organizational relationships than in spontaneous relationships – not that the latter have ever been excluded; on the contrary, reference is more often made to the simultaneous existence of "formal" *and* "informal" relationships, which occur in mixed forms and are mutually conditioned (see Gaska & Frey, Chapter 13 of this volume).

The much-lamented "legal regulation" of relationships is an extreme expression of formalized relationships. The special feature of this conditioning becomes clear when it is projected onto other relationships: if friends or lovers were to claim "rights," their relationship would be disrupted or destroyed. Legal formalization – as indicated by exchange theory – signifies loaned authority in a coalition with a powerful third party (e.g., the state power monopoly). In this respect formalization is a technique and strategy of control in social relationships, a form of supervised guidance. The specific quality of bureaucratically controlled guidance can be seen more distinctly when contrasted with so-called clan control: locally valid, informal, and traditional influence techniques are used in intimate social relationships such as a family or a group of relatives. To some extent the organizational culture movement aims at familiarizing relationships in a firm and propagates appropriate myths for control purposes ("We're all in the same boat"; "We're one big family"; "We've got team spirit").

Abstractification

This characteristic is inextricably bound up with formalization and is occasionally used synonymously. I am presenting it separately to highlight a special aspect of *general regulation*, as this generalization (typification) has a number of important consequences for relationships among colleagues. When Max Weber (1921/1972) emphasized that decisions are taken in (bureaucratic, rational-legal) organizations "irrespective of a person's standing" and "*sine ira et studio*," he was referring to the essentially determining factor of multiple deconcretization in formal organizations. Examples of such generalizations of particular relevance to relationships among colleagues are:

- *De-emotionalization.* Indifference, substitutability, neutralization of contacts and relationships that "officially" conform with factual and organizational conditions.
- *Desensualization and decorporalization.* People become objects(!) of reference – for example, holders of a position, providers of services, items of cost accounting.
- *Decontextualization and desituation.* Rules and directives are valid "generally," "in principle," "fundamentally."Decontextualization is particularly manifest in temporal and spacial generalizations; rules are valid "always and everywhere."
- *Desolidarization. Divide et impera* (this strategy for the "division of labour" will be considered in depth later).
- *Distancing.* This is a general characterization that, in a sense, includes those already mentioned. It denotes the progressive introduction of specific media into organizations. This signifies two things. First, immediacy in social relationships is lost due to the introduction of technical, verbal, or factual media. A work routine "mediated" (i.e., enforced) by PC software is, for example, different from one specified by a superior or a procedure recommended by a colleague. Second, people themselves become means (things, objects) that are available, plannable, replaceable, rationalizable, and so forth. In this respect people are removed from organizations and replaced by objects or reduced to objects. *Things* are at the disposal of others; they can be moved to and installed in rooms, their "timing" can be monitored, they can be kept under constant surveillance – this is not as simple with *people.* Employees have been successfully "disciplined" (Foucault, 1977) when they have adopted external determination as their own will and in so doing reduce themselves to objects. Under such conditions it is bound to appear out of place when colleagues clearly love one another (see below). As an "object" the individual is permanently threatened with replacement by others (objectivized) or by technology or by organization. In contrast to this, human beings are irreplaceable on principle: if one's girlfriend or lover leaves one, is he or she replaced by a substituted "similar one"?

Colleagues decide and act under these generalized conditions not simply on the basis of common sense and personal preference. They are subject to factual, temporal, and social typifications. This gives "the organization" the opportunity of formulating its demands in a nameless and faceless fashion: they are valid for everyone and cannot be modified to the idiosyncratic needs of the individual. Tolerance of possible deviations then becomes a tacit concession that – since it is made evident that the deviant is really in the wrong – obliges him or her to respond with gratitude and reciprocal services.

The above conditions offer an explanation for a particular differentiation often quoted in literature on small groups and leadership – the differentiation between socioemotional relationships as opposed to task-oriented relationships. This differentiation is also identifiable in (seemingly) nonformalized contexts and is considered a social psychological universal. Bales and Slater (1969) interpreted the role divergencies they observed in small group discussions (between the "efficient" and the "popular") as a consequence of exaggerated task orientation: someone who unilaterally pursues a task and frustrates socioemotional needs upon which someone else stands in as a "specialist" to satisfy them. The dominance of achievement, time pressure, the dictates of efficiency, depersonalization, and so forth, means that social, emotional, physical, and sensual needs are permanently at a deficit. There are no formal(!) provisions for relief, which remains an additional personal activity and in the strict sense even qualifies as a violation of the above-mentioned official demands.

To what extent the situation is simplified by drawing a line between task orientation and socioemotional orientation becomes clear when we consider the many different kinds of experiences, actions, and relationships subsumed under this pair of concepts (Haubl & Spitznagel, 1983). In addition it is assumed – as in the symlog extension of the approach (Bales, Cohen & Williamson, 1979) – that these orientations or qualities can be "objectively" ascertained. Laing, Phillipson, and Lee (1971) pleaded in favor of considering not just the *different* perspectives of ego and alter but also their respective meta- and meta-metaperspectives. This immediately spotlighted complexity of the diagnosis should act as a warning against oversimplified objectivization. At the same time it pinpoints the often overlooked fact that it is impossible to operate on complete or objective information in the field of social relationships and actions. Uncertainty, ambiguity, the necessity for interpretation, contradictoriness, and instability are basic characteristics of social relationships. They are basic to the foundation of trust and the risk of disillusionment.

Division of labor

Dividing up the "overall task" of an organization into partial tasks (positions) is not simply restricted to the objective process of dividing up work; it also entails social division and the splitting of relationships. Specialization carried out under the primacy of controllability and rationalization hinders natural and spontaneous collaboration. Application of the differentiation program results in the necessity to create specialized(!) positions, programs, and processes for purposes of coordination, coorientation, cooperation, and communication, which in addition – following the line of objectivist-rational logic – have to be formalized and generalized.

Cooperation does not just mean pooling individual resources; it also means being dependent on and being able to rely on each other. Linked to this is the temptation to bring asymmetry into this relationship, that is, to introduce external dependency and reduce one's own so that questions of power and control are latent or embodied in all organized social relationships. Openness, trust, vulnerability, sympathy, and the like are attitudes that can be placed under suspicion of instrumentalization and in turn can trigger unexpected "perverse" counterreactions that then export the objective division of labor into the social sphere: duplicity, concealment, mistrust, assurance seeking, precaution, and so forth, result, and they then have to be reduced by the introduction of confidence-building measures through integration (cooperative leadership, teamwork; etc.; Neuberger, 1994). Enforced division of labor also means demarcation of competences and responsibilities that again – whether desired or not – produces job and departmental egoism, rivalry, competition, micropolitics, and similar phenomena (Küpper & Ortmann, 1988). Finally, as the organizational culture approach proves, when "technical" solutions are no longer effective in complex systems, the remedy is sought in the "mental programing" of basic attitudes, mentalities, and values, and the problem is defined as the dialectic of individual (individually rewarded) performance and (in the final instance) overall success, a problem that has to be solved by *persons* (Neuberger & Kompa, 1987). A further form of overcoming excessive differentiation can be found in those personal connections between colleagues known ironically as "relationships" (or "vitamin C"), in which formally prescribed channels of communication and influence are short-circuited.

When looked at soberly it is clear that "all-channel" networking renders the person (or position) incapable of effective action. This can be attributed to the contradictory combination of information, action, and relationship: whoever seeks more assuring information no longer acts, and whoever permits themselves to be dominated by relationships when acting restricts his or her horizon. It is for this reason that organization theory has introduced the concept of "loose coupling" as a form of relationship between organizational actors (be they persons or groups); this reflects the necessity for a certain degree of boundary defenses or buffer zones in relationships to avoid the possibility of people becoming overwhelmed by information or action impulses where high levels of networking are involved (Weick,

1976). The resulting compulsory selectivity of perception and actions also causes blind spots, misunderstandings, coordination difficulties, and the pursuit of particularist interests.

But this also shows that maxims invoked by so-called cooperative leadership, the free and open exchange of information and mutual, object-focused decision making, are unrealistic propositions from the point of view of organizational theory: the filtering or concentration of information and asymmetrical decisions are unavoidable when operating under conditions of scarcity of time and resources.

Social psychological cooperation games (based on the prisoners' dilemma; Bierhoff, 1991) work with fixed payoffs (nonaugmentable by negotiations, etc.) on conditions already known in principle. In organizational reality both aspects are questionable or rare. To counteract the dangers that paralyze action or are at least difficult to master, and to reduce complexity and contingency, decision-making rules are introduced to permit algorithmic solution possibilities (e.g., payment systems, work evaluation schemes). During the process it becomes evident that the *concrete* composition of a relationship network can strongly influence the assessments and evaluations.

In recognizing the fact that boundaries, demarcation, differentiation, and specialization are inevitable, it becomes obvious that organizations go to great lengths to symbolize oneness and unity (e.g., by means of "corporate identity" programs; personality cults; speech regulation; ceremonial occasions such as anniversaries, outings, achievement celebrations, shop-floor meetings; socialization methods; etc). This creates a framework of official events for unofficial encounters within which interpersonal relationships can be developed. At the same time an increase in subgroup cohesion leads to clique development, breakaway tendencies, special interests, exclusive relationships, and the like, which then come under pressure for legitimation, but which are also an essential item on the agenda when it comes to bridging regulation gaps and contradictions!

The time dimension

This structural quantity is important when analyzing relationships between colleagues for several reasons:

- These relationships take (consume) time to develop and they always have a (pre)history and a tradition. A momentary picture in time may provide a description but it explains nothing. Investigations of inter organizational socialization by and with colleagues (summarized in Rehn, 1990) consistently point out that it is a time-consuming process for newcomers to get to know, and act on, the wealth of tacit and informal rules that exist besides the few official rules – and that they will hardly be able to cope unless colleagues provide the necessary introduction.

• The development and form of relationships between colleagues are under *time pressure* because, on the one hand, achievement processes are tailored to each other (synchronized), making timing and scheduling necessary and, on the other hand, the pace of capital turnover is of paramount importance in a capitalist economy (time is money). Characteristics of style, patience, a relaxed approach, and allowing time for growth are particularly suspect in a culture where time is considered a scarce resource and where doing has priority over letting things happen.

• Relationships between colleagues are programed for duration: the same people continually meet in typified situations. This implies that short-term opportunism at the expense of others is risky because "payback" is likely. An attitude of not wanting to hurt one another can, however, produce a veneer of friendliness and cooperation that leaves painful clarifications unsaid. The danger here is that the dynamics of social relationships, which are normally in constant flow, become artificially frozen and the status quo becomes rigid. Experiences in communication trainings that practice open, constructive feedback show just how difficult it is to question ingrained, foregone conclusions or at least to raise them for discussion.

Instrumentalization and the facades of rationality and efficiency

Relationships are instrumentalized and functionalized in organizations. They are not an end in themselves but a means supposed to fulfill tasks and produce products, services, and achievements. Personnel are employed individually to fulfill tasks and not to help them on the road to self-fulfillment, nor to provide enriching social relationships. Because inevitable but undesired relationships form with potentially destructive tendencies, they have to be controlled and utilized. This presupposes that there is point of reference outside the relationship (generally, "success"), that its achievement or nonachievement can be confirmed, and that it functions as a parameter of selection and order.

In business administration it is basic knowledge that goals in organizations are multidimensional, equivocal, unstable, and antagonistic, that various "parties of interest" (or coalitions) compete on the definition and interpretation of goals, and that they have very different concepts of measuring and attributing achievement.

The dominant coalition is operationally defined when it succeeds in pushing through and legitimating *its* goal specifications. This gives them the chance to place the other participants under pressure for justification and to demand consequent decisions and actions with reference to the goal in question. But it is because, for reasons already mentioned, this is neither unequivocally nor uncontroversially possible that legitimization patterns and rationality facades play such a major role in organizations. Relationships between colleagues are also subject to the pressure for justification and have to appear functional for declared purposes, so that the construction and procurement of legitimization become separate, strenuous achievements in themselves. Confirmation of this can be gained by a simple glance at the argumentation necessary to acquire personnel, equipment, gradings, premiums, promotions, project finance and annual budgets, and so forth.

If and when colleagues not only share organizational but also personal interests, their formation of relationships is characterized not only by solidarity but also by attempts to conceal special strategies and goals. As already noted, work organizations are directed in particular toward gainful employment, not toward unspecified "action." This means that – under our societal-historical conditions – work is distinguished from interaction (communicative action) and from self-determined, goal-oriented production by the characteristic of *valorization*. This aspect introduces the demand of the anonymous third party into the scenario (the "market"), which regulates the exchange value of the achievement in question. The value of an achievement or a relationship to one personally is not decisive, but its value to the market is. Here again we recognize the compulsion to objectify the valorization of relationships, which in turn forces other, differently motivated relationships to be formed rationally or efficiently, or at least for them to be *presented* in this light.

The listed conditions of "organization" are to be understood normatively, not empirically. They are the postulates to which organizational work feels itself committed and that are particularly upheld because they are so often infringed in practice. We can even formulate the general thesis: in each "healthy" organization every system-designed imperative of action will have an antagonist to keep it in check. Hypertrophic pathological developments are hindered when formalization is counteracted by informalization, hierarchy by egalitarian relationships, and abstraction by concretization. In this respect organizations are an ingenious system of "checks and balances" (Neuberger, 1994). The formal(!) renunciation of an organization's maxims would result in the collapse of spontaneous cooperation (and this represents by far the greatest proportion within the framework). Modern conceptions of organization theory (system-oriented, political, symbolic, and symbolic-interactionist approaches; see the summary in Türk, 1989) offer models of organizational processes. Although these models consider the actor perspective, interpretative accounts, contingency, and the almost uncontrollable complexity, as well as power and interest spheres, they still place great emphasis on the importance of apersonal structures (that is, patterns of orientation, legitimization, and domination).

When colleagues relate to one another with envy, jealousy, malevolence, rivalry, recognition, counseling, helpfulness, friendliness; when they treat each other insincerely, disconcertedly, proudly, calculatingly; or when they terrorize or harass each other, tell tales, support, inform, then this confusing simultaneity of the incompatible seems to defy any system of ordering. Escape routes into individual, situative, or historical explanation attempts seem to be the only alternative.

In this situation the previously sketched basic conditions can serve as a reference system to help understand the empirically ascertainable heterogeneity of relationships between colleagues without attributing contradictoriness to personal characteristics or motives, nor to emergent interpersonal phenomena or apersonal structurally generated phenomena. Interpersonal relationships between colleagues do not lead a separate abstract existence that can be examined on its own; they are embedded in organizational structures. This is a basic characteristic that makes them relationships between colleagues in contrast to other types of relationship presented in this book. In the following an example will be used to demonstrate this contrast and show what changes (or changed evaluations) take place in a particular class of social relationships existing or developing in the context of organizations – that is, among colleagues. Examples abound: social support, mutual problem solving, conflict resolution, team development, collective achievement regulation ("goldbricking"), solidarity to protect against organizational measures, plus many more, equally useful examples treated in organizational psychology handbooks (Gebert & von Rosenstiel, 1988; Greif, Holling & Nicholson, 1989; von Rosenstiel, 1987; Roth, 1989; Weinert, 1987).

I have selected the example of gender relationships. People are employed for the object of working and are themselves supposed to be, or become, objects. Among other things this stands in contrast to their inalienable genderness. It offers a highly appropriate illustration of the special features of *organizational* social relationships because gender always manifests itself – despite efforts to deny, suppress, or officially censor it out of existence. There are no "pure" interpersonal relationships, they are always "contaminated" by apersonal form specifications. Conversely, the "contamination" of the organization's formal-rational "purity" through sexuality is an undeniable fact that clearly demonstrates the precarious nature of apersonal structuring.

Sexual relationships between colleagues

Colleagues have "relationships" – not relationships in the general meaning of the term, but rather the subgroup of erotic or sexual relationships between colleagues. This particular case seems well suited to demonstrate the influence of organization on social relationships because the existence of affairs, liaisons, amours, intimate relationships, encroachments, harassments, represents a violation of or deviation from formalized patterns of order in all the named structural characteristics. If there are "romances" between employees and superiors – these represent quite a large proportion of relationship compositions reported in empirical studies (Dillard & Miller, 1988, p. 454) – then intimate relationships will neutralize characteristic steering mechanisms of the hierarchy; also, close erotic relationships between equal-ranked employees represent a restriction to hierarchical steering procedures, because they are a form of (usually clandestine) "coalition formation." Similarly, if division of labor is seen as an instrument of *divide et impera*, it will be undermined by social relationships if they become too close. As "relationships" are often turbulent and not "programed for duration," they introduce elements of incalculability and unplannability. They also violate the primacy of rationality and efficiency because they give expressly non-work-related activities priority. But the most important fact is that sexual relationships between colleagues diametrically oppose organizational typifications of formalization and abstraction: they are not directed toward respecting or realizing codified and documented regulations (secrecy, inadvertence, and nonstandardization of the relationship illustrate this), nor do they fulfill the concept of generalization, according to which demands have to apply on principle and context-free ("irrespective of a person's standing") and the work scenario in organizations is supposed to be desensualized, decorporalized, de-emotionalized, and so forth.

The irritation caused by the discussion of "sexuality in organizations" (or even: *The Sexuality of the Organization*, Hearn, Sheppard, Tancred-Sheriff & Burrell, 1989) is partly due to the fact that work organizations have been systematically desexualized as part of a long historical process that corresponds with the process of civilization (Burrell, 1984): the pleasure principle had to give way to the reality principle. Organizations are collective instruments and institutions of self-control, external control, and world control, their agents and expression. A program that prescribes and enforces drive control is permanently disturbed by evidence that affect, fantasy, and the articulation of needs of a nonutilizable nature can neither be excommunicated nor eliminated, but in fact flourish quite abundantly off stage. Irrationality, spontaneity, and emotionality are the natural enemies of plan, number, and calculation, while at the same time justifying their existence and giving cause for continuously renewed efforts to improve control.

There is a quasi–incest taboo within organizations; this also explains why they often like to picture themselves as a "family" on which people are subordinate to the head and sexual partners are to be sought externally during leisure time. The "no relationship illusion" prevails in organizations (Dillard & Miller, 1988, p. 460). The previous extreme division between work and the private sphere is gradually dissolving (in the sense of a colonization of life by the system world: Habermas, 1981) and the so-called value changes taking place in the form of hedonism and enjoyment is the reverse aspect of disciplining. The suppressed reemerges, also within work contexts that were previously characterized by the ascetic "spirit of capitalism."

Sexual relationships within organizations are usually researched from either of two angles, as "sexual harassment" or as "sexual attraction." Both rely on conditions outside the individuals involved: men and women work together without handing in their sexuality to security at the entrance: in spite of all efforts to exclude sexuality people still are not reduced to the sexless "work people" desired. The organization specifically selects employees on the basis of similar characteristics (Josefowitz refers to "cloning" that produces "homosociality"; 1982, p. 93). Proximity and contact belong to conditions of attraction. Anderson and Hunsaker (1985) found that 94% of partners in office affairs worked in the same building and that 64% worked in the same or adjacent rooms. The development not only of solidarity and collegiality but also of affection, erotic attraction, and sexual behavior is hardly surprising when men and women work together daily, develop and realize projects together, suffer common failures, survive stress phases and celebrate successes, help, comfort, and encourage one another, travel together to external branches, subsidiaries, or congresses, stay overnight in new places, do overtime or nightwork together, or work together in rooms secluded from public view.

Sexual behavior – particularly in feminist literature as a result of outrageous collective disregard – has received a heavy stress as "sexual harassment," something that is as widespread as it is minimized. Gutek and Dunwoody (1987, p. 254) summarized various studies on the percentage of employed women who felt themselves "sexually harassed" and reported levels between 20% and almost 100%. This enormous span resulted partly from the fact that there were variations in the number of years examined ("the last 2 years," "in the past 5 years," "during your whole working life"); that questions were asked about self-experienced or observed harassment; that the interviewees were previously sensitized to varying degrees by advance knowledge of the interests and aims of the researchers; and that the definitions of "sexual harassment" also varied (wolf-whistling, compliments on the figure, dirty jokes, offensive posters, "accidental" and intentional touching of various parts of the body up to and including rape; see lists in Gutek, 1985; Hemphill & Pfeiffer, 1986; Plogstedt & Bode, 1984; Tangri, Burt & Johnson, 1982; Terpstra & Baker, 1989). At least it is clear that this is by no means a marginal phenomenon but that unwelcome sexual approaches – suffered in the great majority by women – and an intimidating, humiliating, insulting atmosphere at work (slang, jokes, pornographic posters, gestures, discrimination) are sad everyday reality in what is ostensibly a purely objective, efficiency-oriented working world.

Sexuality is not restricted to genital satisfaction. I can also be motivated by the lust for power and possession (particularly in the claims of superiors and men who extort sexuality from dependent – subjected – women or expect it as a foregone conclusion). It is also motivated by the need to belong and the search for recognition. It can be a means of "sensation seeking" to enliven drab work routines (adventure, suspense, risk) and a playful, pleasurable pastime, a transfer-determined reenactment of earlier relationship constellations, a means of testing personal attractiveness and confirmation of self-esteem, and so forth. This complex mixture of motives is relevant to organizations because it can complement existing satisfaction possibilities and compensate forced denials.

It is, however, important not to restrict our vision to unwelcome sexual approaches because sexual relationships that are both welcome and pleasurable also play an important role. Dillard and Millar (1988, p. 453) ascertained in a weighted comparison of five studies containing relevant data that 71% of those questioned had observed at least one romance and 31% had been personally involved. "Naturally," that is, due to the intimate and tabooed nature of the relationships and in contrast to "sexual harassment," data in this area are not particularly comprehensive; in her overview of 19 publications, Mainiero (1988) found only two systematic questionnaires (Anderson & Hunsaker, 1985; Quinn, 1977). Quinn questioned waiting air passengers and, in a later study, Dillard (1987) called randomly selected phone numbers.

In "office romances" Quinn focused on three of the above-mentioned complex bundles of motives for sexual relationships (see also the expansion by Dillard & Miller, 1988): romances are sought for "ego motives" (adventure, pleasure, confirmation), "love" (authentic, sincere affection), and "job motives" (buying a favor, e.g., in the form of promotion, pay raises, better working conditions, and job security). Assuming that both partners in a romance have independent, varying motives, six relationship patterns emerge. Quinn found that three "pure" forms occurred particularly frequently: sincere love (the partners developed a deep, lasting partnership), the affair (both were looking for a brief, passionate adventure outside an existing relationship), and the utilitarian relationship (where both calculate the advantages of the enterprise). Dillard and Segrin's (1987) preference for quantitative approaches resulted in the following figures after they questioned 128 "observers": 36% of office romances were classified as passionate love (ego and love motives), 23% as partnership (authentic) love, 19% as extra-partnership relationships (pure ego motives), 14% as female-dominated utilitarian relationships, and 8% as male-dominated utilitarian relationships.

Finally, we take a look at why sexual relationships between colleagues are so problematic in and for organizations and why they cause such ambivalent reactions, that is, why they are followed informally with great interest and ignored formally for as long as possible. The reasons for this can be found in the typical structuring dimensions of organizations:

- "Relationships" are exclusive because of their intimacy: the partners separate themselves off, exclude others, and try – in vain – to hide their relationship: "Despite the fact that everyone knows, and everyone knows that everyone knows, the participants continue to behave as if the relationship is secret, and members of the organization act as if they know nothing about it" (Quinn, 1977, p. 37). Intimacy and exclusiveness make surveillance and control more difficult. Normally private enclaves in organizations are only tolerated if they can be instrumentalized. In romances this in particular seems questionable because partners are "distracted from work" and those who know become involved in endless gossip.
- Individual people take the liberty to disregard the expected typification and fulfill their own needs. Even though the form of the relationship is by no means idiosyncratic but instead follows cultural and conventional patterns, the illusion of privacy, exceptionality, and novelty exists along with the pleasure of momentarily escaping the "iron cage of compliance" (Max Weber). In particular there are no proven and accepted norms, standards, and scripts on how confidants, colleagues, and superiors should react to such situations and this can lead to uncertainty or overreactions.
- Because privileged relationships develop between members of organizations, there is a dange of reversals, blurring, or blockading or power: in an often-quoted example, a subordinate woman is involved in an intimate relationship with her superior so that the original dependency structure is reversed, she receives privileges, influences decisions to her advantage, and obstructs objectively better alternatives. This case illustrates how important organizational myths can be shattered (rationality, fairness, achievement principle, equal opportunity, etc.).
- Intimate, exclusive, and privileged relationships result in rumors, jealousy, and rivalry among observers and those excluded – if only through projection of their own denied wishes, which lead to envy of the "happier

person." Here too, violation of the norms of formalization, abstraction, and instrumentalization plays a central role.

- An intimate relationship absorbs energy, time, and imagination for sexuality (and secrecy), so that they are no longer available for task-fulfillment roles – an act of deception against the organization, which, on account of the payment relationship, deems itself entitled to have the whole person at its disposal during working time.
- The renunciation of fantasy, vitality, emotionality, satisfaction – otherwise an accepted inevitability within the work experience as a normal abstractification – appears particularly painful and unnecessary to the worker presented with an intensely experienced alternative. In such situations organizational normality is experienced as abnormal, which can encourage further de-alienation attempts, thus jeopardizing "control."
- If "the organization" decides to part company with one or both of the partners (in most cases women are threatened with dismissal: Gutek, 1989) because of social irritation, it can mean the loss of valuable employees.
- Tabooing and secrecy can lead to extortion, denunciation, sabotage, threats, and the like, so that the meta-aim of (management-organized) comprehensive control is also undermined.
- Seen from the positive side, sexual relationships between colleagues can radiate happiness, pleasure, activity, and fulfillment, which in turn can increase dedication and sociability. In many cases – especially where "true" love is involved and less in utilitarian liaisons – "observers" react with approval, encouragement, and understanding. But even if the relationship is kept secret, the partners might, as a reaction to an implied deterioration in work results, increase their efforts to avoid confirming existing suspicions.

The desire to exclude or domesticate something as both harmless and powerful as sexuality within organizations proves just how presumptuous the claim is to organize all spheres of life. The example of sexual relationships between colleagues seems especially suited to demonstrate with greater clarity the extent of organizational formation. Sanctions against them can be added to the list of unreasonable restrictions that prescribe everything in minute detail and to which people have become accustomed in work organizations (e.g., restrictions on clothing, speech, manners, self-presentation, territorial behavior).

References

Anderson, C. A., & Hunsaker, P. L. (1985). Why there's romancing at the office and why it's everybody's problem. *Personnel, 62,* 57–63.

Bales, R. F., Cohen S. P., & Williamson, S. A. (1979). *Symlog, a system for the multiple level observation of groups.* New York: Free Press.

Bales, R. F., & Slater, P. E. (1969). Role differentiation in small decision making groups. In C. Gibb (Ed.), *Leadership* (pp. 255–276). Harmondsworth, England: Penguin.

Bierhoff, H. W. (1991). Soziale Motivation kooperativen Verhaltens. In R. Wunderer (Ed.), *Kooperation. Gestaltungsprinzipien und Steuerung der Zusammenarbeit zwischen Organisationseinheiten* (pp. 21–38). Stuttgart: Poeschel.

Burrell, A. (1984). Sex and organizational analysis. *Organization Studies, 5,* 97–118.

Dillard, J. P. (1987). Close relationships at work: Perceptions of the motives and performance of relational participants. *Journal of Social and Personal Relationships, 4,* 179–193.

Dillard, J. P., & Miller, K. I. (1988). Intimate relationships in task environments. In S. Duck (Ed.), *Handbook of personal relationships. Theory, research and interventions* (pp. 449–465). Chichester, England: Wiley.

Dillard, J. P., & Segrin, C. (1987). *Intimate relationships in organizations: Relational types, illicitness, and power.* Paper presented at the annual meeting of the International Communication Association, Montreal, in Dillard & Miller (1988).

Foucault, M. (1977). *Überwachen und Strafen. Die Geburt des Gefängnisses.* Frankfurt: Suhrkamp.

Gebert, D. (1972). *Gruppendynamik in der betrieblichen Führungsschulung.* Berlin: Duncker & Humblot.

Gebert, D., & von Rosenstiel, L. (1988). *Organisationspsychologie. Person und Organisation.* Stuttgart: Kohlhammer.

Giddens, A. (1988). *Die Konstitution der Gesellschaft. Grundzüge einer Theorie der Strukturierung.* Frankfurt: Campus.

Greif, S., Holling, H., & Nicholson, N. (Eds.) (1989). *Arbeits und Organisationspsychologie. Internationales Handbuch in Schlüsselbegriffen.* München: Psychologie Verlags Union.

Gutek, B. A. (1985). *Sex and the workplace: Impact of sexual behavior and harassment on women, men and organizations.* San Francisco: Jossey Bass.

(1989). Sexuality in the workplace: Key issues in social research and organizational practice. In J. Hearn, D. L. Sheppard, P. Tancred-Sheriff & G. Burrell (Eds.), *The sexuality of organization* (pp. 56–70). London: Sage.

Gutek, B. A., & Dunwoody, V. (1987). Understanding sex in the workplace. In A. H. Stromberg, L. Larwood & B. Gutek (Eds.), *Women and work: An annual review* (Vol. 2, pp. 249–269). Newbury Park, CA: Sage.

Habermas, J. (1981). *Theorie des kommunikativen Handelns,* Band 1 u. 2. Frankfurt/M.: Suhrkamp.

Haubl, R., & Spitznagel, A. (1983). Diagnostik sozialer Beziehungen. In K.-J. Groffmann & L. Michel (Eds.), *Verhaltensdiagnostik* (pp. 702–858). Göttingen: Hogrefe.

Hearn, J., Sheppard, D., Tancred-Sheriff, P., & Burrell, G. (Eds.) (1989). *The sexuality of the organization.* London: Sage.

Hemphill, M. R., & Pfeiffer, A. L. (1986). Sexual spillover in the workplace: Testing the appropriateness of male–female interaction. *Women's Studies in Communication, 9,* 52–66.

Josefowitz, N. (1982). Sexual relationships at work: Attraction, transference, coercion or strategy. *Personnel Administrator, 27,* 91–96.

Kieser, A., & Kubicek, H. (1983). *Organisation.* Berlin: de Gruyter.

Küpper, W., & Ortmann, G. (Eds.) (1988). *Mikropolitik. Rationalität, Macht und Spiele in Organisationen.* Opladen: Westdeutscher Verlag.

Laing, R. D., Phillipson, H., & Lee, A. R. (1971). *Interpersonelle Wahrnehmung.* Frankfurt/M.: Suhrkamp.

Mainiero, L. A. (1986). A review and analysis of power dynamics in organizational romances. *Academy of Management Review, 11,* 750–762.

Neuberger, O. (1991). Organisationspsychologie. Eine Disziplin auf der Suche nach ihrem Gegenstand, *Augsburger Beiträge zu Organisationspsychologie und Personalwesen, 12,* 1–47.

(1994). *Führen und geführt werden.* Stuttgart: Enke.

Neuberger, O., & Kompa, A. (1987). *Wir, die Firma. Der Kult um die Unternehmenskultur.* Weinheim: Beltz.

Plogstedt, S., & Bode, K. (1984). *Übergriffe. Sexuelle Belästigung in Büros und Betrieben. Eine Dokumentation der Grünen Frauen im Bundestag.* Reinbek: Rowohlt.

Quinn, R. E. (1977). Coping with Cupid: The formations, impact, and management of romantic relationships in organizations. *Administrative Science Quarterly, 22,* 30–45.

Rehn, M.-L. (1990). *Die Eingliederung neuer Mitarbeiter. Eine Längsschnittstudie zur Anpassung an Normen und Werte der Arbeitsgruppe.* München und Mering: Rainer Hampp Verlag.

Rosenstiel, L. von (1987). *Grundlagen der Organisationspsychologie. Basiswissen und Anwendungshinweise.* Stuttgart: Poeschel.

Roth. E. (Ed.) (1989). *Organisationspsychologie.* Göttingen: Hogrefe.

Tangri, S. S., Burt, M. R., & Johnson, L. B. (1982). Sexual harassment at work: Three explanatory models. *Journal of Social Issues, 38,* 33–54.

Terpstra, D. E., & Baker, D. D. (1989). The identification and classification of reactions to sexual harassment. *Journal of Organizational Behavior, 10,* 1–14.

Türk, K. (1989). *Neuere Entwicklungen in der Organisationsforschung.* Stuttgart: Enke.

Weber, M. (1972). *Wirtschaft und Gesellschaft. Grundriß der verstehenden Soziologie.* Tübingen: Mohr.

Weich, K. (1976). Educational organizations as loosely coupled systems. *Administrative Science Quarterly, 21,* 1–19.

Weinert, A. (1987). *Lehrbuch der Organisationspsychologie.* München: Urban & Schwarzenberg.

13

Occupation-determined role relationships
Anne Gaska and Dieter Frey

Introduction

Interpersonal relationships can develop in different ways. There are relationships within families and with relatives, those centered on leisure and sport activities, contacts that come about by chance and those that develop at work or through the occupation, that is, work-determined relationships. By this we mean interactions between colleagues in an organization or institution, interactions between business partners, and interactions that are work-determined in only a "unilateral" way (such as salesperson–customer or doctor–patient). This chapter focuses on work-determined role relationships. After a discussion of the role concept and levels of formality or informality in a relationship, the following aspects will be addressed: what significance does the occupational role have in society, for the concept of self, for personal experience, and for the social interactions of a person? What conflicts develop when particular work roles are taken on? Are roles and role relationships inflexible? Do they restrict our interactions? Is there also evidence of attitude and value change in role relationships? Finally, we illustrate the theoretical aspects by considering the doctor–patient relationship.

Concept definitions

The role concept

Sociological role definitions emphasize the aspect of expectations that are associated with a social position; the person occupying the position is acting a role. A role is defined as the sum of normative expectations that other people have of someone occupying a position (compare Joas, 1980; Wiswede, 1977). Increased precision and unambiguity of such behavioral rules and expectations make it more difficult for the role bearer to exercise the role in keeping with his or her own personality and individuality. The role itself strongly influences both with whom we (have to) interact and how we (have to) interact. Norms also regulate our chance encounters in everyday life. The difference between these and work-conditioned norms is that the latter are set down in laws and rules, and these legitimize expectations in a special way (Krappmann, 1971). We are in a way the prisoners of formal role relationships (above all occupational roles) in which our behavior is more or less specifically defined by regulations. Whoever wishes to fulfill an occupational role in an adequate way must act within certain limits.

Someone who takes on the role of a minister, for instance, is automatically restricted with respect to time and whom he or she will be able to meet. The minister, who might prefer to sleep longer on a Sunday, has to preach and be concerned with believers (and nonbelievers) in the community with an equal level of commitment. But within these limits every minister has a certain amount of leeway to set personal accents, such as concentrating on confirmees or children or elderly people in the community. Thus the occupational role influences the behavior and the personality of a person on the one hand, while on the other there is a certain amount of scope for personal accents and formation of the role. Every role leaves an "essential remainder which escapes calculation and control" (Dahrendorf, 1958). (Occupational) roles should by no means be understood simply as restrictions on our personality. They facilitate communal life by making behavior more predictable.

Differences between formal and informal relationships

In the final instance people meet in formal (e.g., work-determined) relationships and in informal relationships (e.g., in the family) as bearers of particular roles, and each role represents just one particular part of the human being as a whole. Role relationships can be described according to levels of formality or informality. This does not mean that every family relationship is automatically informal, nor that every work-dependent relationship is automatically formal, but that every type of human relationship can fall on either side of the continuum. Similarly, the relationship's modality is by no means fixed but can vary along this continuum. Take the example of the doctor–patient relationship. Is the relationship between a doctor and a patient still formal if they often play tennis together? Is a romantic relationship still informal if the couple only interacts within certain specified role structures? The different relationship patterns (formal versus informal) can be characterized in the following way as ideal types (Weber, 1922):

(1) *Particularist versus holistic perspective*: in a formal relationship a person tends to be seen in a particularist way; in an informal relationship the view is more holistic. Here, particularist perception means that one gets to know just one specific aspect of another person and sees him or her acting in one role only (e.g., as a business partner). But if one lives with another person in a close relationship, then one gets to know him or her from many angles and in many roles (e.g., partner role, father role, mother role) that unite to form an overall image.

(2) *Structuredness and rationality versus unstructuredness and emotionality*: formal relationships are characterized by structure, that is, not only are the aims and purposes clearly prescribed but so are the means and norms with which they are to be attained. Informal relationships contrast with this in that they are usually unstructured, less aim- and purpose-oriented and have greater socioemotional and affective components. A decisive factor is that there is a high degree of similarity and sympathy between the interacting partners (Byrne, 1971; see also below).

(3) *Behavior specification versus behavior freedom*: a further characteristic of formal relationships is that the contents are prescribed by an external source as well as by a particular objective, and that the respective participants have to abide by these within the relationship. They may, for example, have to work on a shared task, conduct sales negotiations, or reach a diagnosis. This means not only that the participants are often obliged to ignore their individuality to a great extent but also that they cannot arbitrarily end the relationship. Informal relationships offer interacting partners a much greater range of behavioral alternatives. To a large extent they are free to determine the content of their interactions by themselves.

(4) *Depersonalization versus individuality*: we can conclude from the above characteristics that a formal relationship depends far less on specific persons than an informal relationship. Whereas the individuality of the partners is of particular importance in a friendship (see Auhagen, Chapter 10 of this volume), interacting partners in a formal relationship are relatively easily exchanged and substituted: a business discussion, for instance, can also be held with a substitute if one's expected partner is absent. In contrast to friendships or partner relationships, formal relationships are characterized by the avoidance of intimacy (Argyle, Henderson & Furnham, 1985).

This differentiation has been made to clarify ways of interacting, especially in work-determined role relationships. We would again like to stress that such characterization illustrates the two poles of a continuum and that less strict criteria may well be present or develop during the relationship, depending on the attitudes of the interacting partners. To a certain extent interacting partners can reach mutual understandings on their interpretation of norms and actively define their social relationships ("role making"; on the role concept in interaction research, see Joas, 1980). Problems in interactions often occur when one of the two interacting partners operates on different premises concerning levels of informality or formality so that the mode of encounter is not clearly defined. In this case the interacting partners are unsure whether they should react according to formal or informal structures. If just one of the partners behaves in an unpredictably inconsistent way, it can lead to a great deal of ambivalence and role ambiguity.[1]

The significance of the occupational role in interpersonal relationships

The central significance of the occupational role

Work and the occupation are of central importance to people in our Western society. To a greater or lesser degree they also tend to structure the remaining areas of activity (Klages, 1983; Seifert, 1992). Rapid technological and economic development would probably not have been possible without our work ethos. Apart from satisfying existential needs, work is a basic element in the search for social identity; it furthers experience of one's own competence and strongly influences a person's self-esteem (e.g., Frese, 1982). People gain social recognition through their achievements. Satisfaction with the occupational role is closely connected to an intrinsic motivational orientation that simultaneously acts as a buffer against stress and increases efficiency (Keaveney & Nelson, 1993). In turn, satisfaction and identification with the occupational role as well as commitment are important for a person's well-being. But contrary to expectations, Greenberger and O'Neil (1993) discovered in their study that a high level of commitment did not automatically lead to a greater sense of well-being. The authors' explanation for this is that a high level of commitment is often accompanied by a high level of work intensity. The resulting pressure could have negative effects on the person's health. An interesting result was that the health of a man highly committed to his work depended greatly on the level of support he received from his wife.

The occupational role and leisure-time activities

The occupational role forms a person in many dimensions, but here we will concentrate especially on research into its effects on leisure activities and the family. According to Bamberg (1989) there are three different approaches to explaining the behavior of working people inside and outside the work context: compensation, generalization, and independence. The *compensation hypothesis* (compare Staines, 1980) says that people try to compensate deficits or negative experiences at work during their leisure time. The *spillover hypothesis* assumes that people try to adapt their leisure-time behavior to that of their role at work and that their leisure time displays similar attitudes and competences to those found in their occupational role (compare Staines, 1980). In this case leisure-time activities are seen as a continuation of work – for example, when informal contacts and social activities take place with colleagues during leisure time (compare Meissner, 1971; Salaman, 1974; and the sections below). The *independence hypothesis* postulates that work and leisure time are two independent spheres. Bamberg (1989), however, points out that until now no empirical studies have been made to test the various models by going beyond simple studies of correlations between leisure-time behavior and professional behavior. In addition, more attention should be paid to the fact that the direction of effects between the two spheres is not solely one-way; two-way effects are certainly present.

Some empirical studies showed quite clearly that the professional role has an effect on actions in other areas: a limited scope of activity among workers results in passive leisure activities (Karasek, 1981; Ulich & Ulich, 1977). Complex, freely structurable activities in the occupational role are linked to less authoritarian behavior and greater personal responsibility (Kohn & Schooler, 1982). People who enjoy a high level of cooperation opportunities, autonomy, and personal responsibility at work display these abilities and motivations outside their profession. On the other hand, people who are restricted by their occupational role will probably be unlikely or unwilling to assume much control and autonomy outside it (Frese, 1982). In Volpert's view (1975), this is explained by the fact that action competence deteriorates within the context of a rigidly structured occupational role, leading to "cognitive atrophy." People in such occupational roles lose their motivation and ability to act because of lack of competence and fatalism.

That the occupational role strongly influences personal experience and interaction opportunities outside work has been established by the fact that certain negative conditions in the occupational sphere give rise to psychological ailments and disturbances that also manifest themselves outside the work situation (see Frese, 1982, 1985). In particular, the combination of limited action opportunity and stress at work has negative effects on psychological health and interaction with other people. People who are chronically overtaxed in the occupational role with find that sooner or later this affects their other roles. For example, they may have a lower level of stress tolerance and be more impatient and intolerant in the family context.

This does not necessarily mean that such negative characteristics at work automatically lead to less job satisfaction. Research on work satisfaction shows that the personality of the individual also plays an important part in the perception of work characteristics such as opportunities for cooperation and autonomy. In their longitudinal study, Staw and Ross (1985) examined whether work satisfaction could also be a consistent disposition inherent in a person. Their results showed a stable attitude, that is, a significant level of consistency, in work satisfaction or dissatisfaction in a variety of work situations. This indicates that it is not only the occupation but also the person that is responsible for the level of job satisfaction. This does not invalidate the results on the effects of work on leisure, family, and well-being, but it does illustrate that work does not always have the same value in a person's life, that not everyone has the same expectations for a job, and that the meaning and purpose of work can vary from person to person (see, e.g., Friedmann & Havighurst, 1962; Hulin, 1971).

Loss of the occupational role

The significance of the occupational role for the self-image and for social interactions becomes especially clear when the consequences of role loss are analyzed. When identification with the occupational role is very strong and important to self-esteem, the loss of such a role will lead to significant identity crises. Role loss occurs not only through unemployment but also through retirement. Both represent a major change in the life of an individual.

Cobb and Kasl (1977) showed that even the fear of unemployment has a negative influence on psychological health. It is the greatest stressor next to role conflicts, role ambiguities, mobbing, and adaptation processes. Numerous studies have shown that in the long run unemployment leads to difficulties in time structuring, social contacts, and physical and psychological well-being (Layton, 1986; overview in Aschenbach & Frey, 1985, and in Hartley & Mohr, 1989). For example, Mohr and Frese (1978) were able to show that unemployment not only increases depression and anxiety but also social isolation within a few weeks: contacts and activities with former colleagues and with informal interaction partners are reduced or completely broken, as are activities in clubs or communities (compare also Brinkmann, 1986). The loss of work is accompanied by the loss of a great number of social interaction relationships that were based on the work role and built up outside the workplace. However, the negative effects of unemployment are less pronounced when people take on a new role such as voluntary activities in clubs or political or social organizations (compare Frese, 1985; Warr, 1984).

Available studies on the self-esteem of unemployed people are non-uniform, but they consistently indicate a loss of self-esteem: the classic study by Jahoda, Lazarsfeld, and Ziesel (1933) established feelings of guilt and disappointment over unemployment; Jahoda (1982) found a loss of trust and fluctuations in emotional equilibrium. Loss of work entailed a loss of ties to an organization, the loss of "compulsory" activity, and loss of financial security and social status. The central status of the work role in our society results in stigmatization (compare Goffman, 1967) of the unemployed (people without a role) and to a feeling of no longer "belonging" (Brinkmann, 1986). Unemployment not only affects the person in question but also his or her family (Walper, 1988), because unemployment means a role change and a redistribution of responsibilities within the family. Studies also document a negative association between the unemployment of fathers and their children's school performance, psychological well-being, and attractiveness as interaction partners (Aschenbach & Frey, 1985).

Retirement usually means that the people in question have to restructure their time and spatial organization. In contrast to unemployment, retirement is foreseeable and expected and the decision to retire is generally made by the person in question. Parnes and Somers (1994) found in male subjects that the probability of carrying on working depends strongly on their commitment to work, distaste for retirement, level of education, and whether their wife also worked. The age of retirement in women was related to the question of child care: women who work while bringing up their children retire earlier (Henretta, O'Rand & Chan, 1993). Because retirement is foreseeable it is also viewed as a typical developmental task in the process of aging (e.g., Havighurst, 1963). Even so, it still possesses a great deal of conflict potential because of role and activity loss and the break in old relationship structures.

To many people retirement means a reduction in self-esteem and a feeling of reduced personal control, a phenomenon often referred to as retirement shock or retirement bankruptcy (compare Frey, Gaska, Möhle & Weidemann, 1991). A great number of communication needs satisfied during work now remain unmet. As occupational contacts – which are often cultivated in leisure time (see below) – are forced into the background, the retired person often becomes socially isolated. This is particularly the case if the retired person was highly committed to his or her occupation. Thus the loss of the occupational role has extreme consequences not only for a person's self-concept but also for a person's social contacts.

The close connection between psychological, physical, and social components and employment is demonstrated clearly by people who take up employment again. As in the case of unemployed people who find new work and display improvements in their physical and psychological well-being (Layton, 1986), pensioners who take up employment again display better social adjustment than those who remain unoccupied (Jayashree & Rao, 1991).

Does the occupation determine interaction partners?

From the perspective of occupation determined role relationships, we can differentiate between three different areas of interaction in employed people: (*a*) exclusively occupational interactions (e.g., salesperson–customer), (*b*) informal occupational contacts (e.g., personal contacts between colleagues outside work), and (*c*) exclusively informal interactions that in the final instance, are also influenced by work.

Exclusively occupational interactions. Occupational work is rarely isolated; it requires cooperation with others. A great number of our relationships with other people take place within the framework of our occupation. These are mainly formal, work-oriented exchange relationships such as a sales conversation, a conference, or interactions with colleagues, superiors, and subordinates. Cooperation with others creates a field of social contacts, which means that personal communication needs can also be satisfied by occupational communication. The occupational role determines whether, with whom, and to what extent we interact. Considered in the light of the above-named characteristics, such occupation-determined interactions tend to be more particularist, structured, and depersonalized, and they have prescribed contents (see also Neuberger, Chapter 12 of this volume). This type of interaction gives us insights into only a small part of the personality of the role bearer, yet we often see this as the most important or essential part and draw conclusions about the whole personality from it. The more we base our social interactions exclusively on occupation-determined interactions, the greater the danger of developing a restricted view of reality. This increases the risk of seeing the world solely from the perspective of one's own institution.

Informal occupation-determined role relationships. According to Argyle (1988) the workplace is one of the commonest places, apart from the neighborhood and (sports) clubs, for making social contacts. The fact that spatial proximity and frequency of interactions lead to the selection of friends was shown by Festinger, Schachter, and Back (1950) in their studies of hostels. But a further condition for developing closer contacts is a similarity of attitudes, opinions, and values between the interaction partners (Berscheid, 1985; Lea & Duck, 1982).

Personal contacts can develop within initially formal, occupation-determined relationship patterns. These can lead to shared activities and friendships outside the work context. Informal relationships develop mainly during coffee breaks, during (business) meals, or on other occasions. At this stage gossip, humor, and game playing are of major significance in the interaction (Argyle, 1988; Homans, 1950). The occupational situation forms the point of departure for the relationship. It creates an opportunity not simply to see the interaction partners (at least when regular occupation-determined contacts are involved) in their position as role bearer (business-woman, doctor), but also to appreciate and respect them in their personality. The more similar attributes, similar values, and common interests can be attributed to the other, the greater the sympathy will be between the interaction partners. As a result, interaction frequency increases and with it the readiness to maintain contacts and extend them to the informal sphere (see also the attitude-attraction hypothesis of Byrne, 1971, and the exchange theory of Homans, 1961; Blau, 1964; Thibaut & Kelley, 1959; and the above-mentioned studies by Lea & Duck, 1982, and Berscheid, 1985). An increasingly holistic type of perception develops within this gradually informalized relationship; the individuality of the persons involved plays a greater role and behavioral freedom increases (unless a person is speculating in other directions, such as increasing informal contacts with a superior to improve one's career prospects). If an occupation-determined relationship is characterized by tension and competitive thinking and the interaction "costs a great deal of energy," then the probability of informal contacts is limited (they will even be actively avoided). In addition, already existing informal contacts may well be overtaxed by occupational commitment (e.g., by the sudden occurrence of a competitive situation). Ending this type of relationship then proves difficult because the relationship itself usually has to be maintained on account of external circumstances – the occupational role. The relationship can weaken or even turn to enmity, but the frequency of occupation-determined contacts is largely beyond the control of the persons involved (Argyle & Henderson, 1985).

If our social interactions outside the occupational sphere are restricted to persons we know from our occupation-determined role relationships, then the danger of developing a distorted view of the world increases.

Informal interactions that are codetermined by the occupation. In the final instance the occupation also determines with whom we interact outside the occupation-determined role structure. Depending on the occupation, technical and time structures promote or hinder the development of relationships with other people to varying degrees. This can be illustrated by the example of shift work: shift work (particularly night work) presents a fundamental problem in that it desynchronizes the rhythmic human processes. Numerous studies demonstrate the negative effects of shift work in various areas, such as alertness, quality and length of sleep, general health, and social and family life (compare Parkes, 1994; Rosa, 1993; Smith & Folkard, 1993a; Spelten, Barton & Folkard, 1993). Naturally, disturbances in the sphere of social contacts influence not only intraorganizational relationships but also relationships with family and friends, and the opportunity to participate in social activities (cultural and sporting events, political parties) as well (compare Nachreiner, Baer, Diekmann & Ernst, 1984; Nachreiner, Streich & Wettberg, 1985). In their study, Smith and Folkard (1993b) also documented the negative effects of shift work on partnerships. Partners were unhappy about the shift work of their spouse and felt that their life was being interrupted by it.

Different occupations further different social skills for developing interpersonal relationships. For example, working in a clothing store calls for the ability to approach and talk to customers as part of the occupational role; such people are more likely to be able to remove conflict barriers in the private sphere. The structural process and content of work also promotes or restricts contacts between colleagues during working hours (noisy machinery, for instance, hinders almost all interaction). Thus, social-communicative skills and abilities that have been learned and developed in connection with an occupational role can be transferred to outside spheres.[2]

Members of the same occupation tend to come into contact outside the work context. Many occupation display a form of solidarity that manifests itself in a veritable "we feeling" or "in-group mentality" in the sense of social identity (Mummendey, 1985; Tajfel, 1982). Social stratification also plays an essential role in interactions: as a result, mixing of academic and nonacademic occupational groups in the informal sphere rarely takes place (for instance, informal contacts between doctors in a hospital are more common than those between doctors and nursing staff). Because of their significance in our society, respective occupational roles also have a very strong influence on how attractive someone is as an interaction partner outside his or her occupational role. In this case the specific level of occupational prestige determines who belongs to the informal circle of interaction.

The significance of role conflicts in occupational interpersonal relationships

The complexities of the occupational role have already been illustrated in the above sections and it is only logical to conclude that conflicts are likely to occur among the many roles we happen to bear. According to Gross, Mason and McEachern (1958), role conflicts can be seen as contradictory (incompatible) role expectations in which the role bearer in question is usually aware of this incompatibility, that is, it does not simply exist in the opinion of external observers. *Interrole conflicts* exist when role expectations of a particular person are difficult to fulfill or are incompatible (e.g., a woman as mother, partner, and teacher). *Intrarole conflicts* exist when divergent expectations are directed toward the single role of a person. These inconsistent expectations may be expressed by one person (e.g., a husband expects his wife to cook and to go to the theater with him at virtually the same time), or they may be expressed by different persons (e.g., the expectations of parents and the head teacher toward the teacher) (compare also Griese, 1989). Such role conflicts can often lead to interpersonal conflicts or even intergroup conflicts.

Interrole conflicts: The conflict between occupational role and family role

One and the same person is the bearer not just of one, but of many different roles (multiple roles). Anna Jonas is not only a teacher; at the same time she is a mother, wife, chairwoman of the local branch of an ecological party, treasurer at the local branch of a national motor club, and a member of the church choir. In theory these roles could well be highly compatible. But there may also be cases where they conflict; for instance, time clashes could occur or conflicts between the interests of the ecological party and the motor club. As a result this interrole conflict leads not only to an intrapsychic conflict but also to conflicts in interactions as the expectations of the interaction partners cannot be fulfilled. The interrole conflict escalates to an interpersonal conflict. It should be noted, however, that such interrole conflicts do not develop in direct dependence on the person, Anna Jonas, but because of the roles she has adopted. Admittedly, actors and observers often confuse intrapsychic and interpersonal conflicts with interrole conflicts.

The classic role conflict is the conflict between family and occupation. This has been the object of many empirical studies. The negative effects of this role conflict are consistent throughout: the greater the conflict between occupational role and family role, the worse the family climate is perceived to be by both men and women (Wiersma & Van den Berg, 1991). Frone, Russell, and Cooper (1993) even found a positive correlation between the level of role conflict and abusive alcohol consumption. Interrole conflicts are of great significance particularly in women and/or mothers who often have multiple roles (as in the case of Anna Jonas). In his summary of relevant literature, Piechowski (1992) found that these roles consistently lead to discontent and stress, which are significant predictors for depression and other psychological symptoms. Ranking (1993) found that 62% of mothers who also worked in employment experienced high levels of stress. The major stress indicators they named were "lack of time," "child-related problems," and "maternal guilt." In a longitudinal study of married working women with at least one child between 1 and 6 years of age, it was seen that stress generated by the occupational role (operationalized by perceived lack of authority and influence in the occupation, sexual discrimination, pressure of work, etc.) coincided with increased depressive symptoms (Reifman, Biernat & Lang, 1991). However, the alternative of having no occupational role besides the maternal role did not appear to be the right solution: a study carried out by Hock and DeMeis (1990) showed that women who wanted to have an occupational role but had to stay at home displayed much stronger symptoms of depression than women who chose to stay at home or those employed outside the home.

How the conflict between career and family is solved depends largely on self-esteem and satisfaction with life. High self-esteem and life satisfaction best predict the resolution of this conflict. People who say "my family comes first" have the least conflicts because this means they have made a clear decision in favor of the family (compare Kinnier, Katz & Berry, 1991). Admittedly, it is mostly women who give the family priority; men give it less emphasis (Bielby & Bielby, 1989).

Intrarole conflicts

There are many influences on an occupational role, and any one of them can spark off a conflict. The causes can lie in the objective circumstances or in certain subjective elements, such as personality traits (e.g., Szewczyk, 1968). Many other role bearers are associated with the role of a teacher: parents, colleagues, students, the school principal. Each of these parties has specific expectations of the teacher's role, which, in extreme cases, may be diametrically opposed (Griese, 1989). Doing things right for the children does not mean satisfying colleagues, the school principal, or, least of all, the parents. Siegall (1992) was able to show that the level of stress perceived in an intrarole conflict – defined here as inconsistent expectations of one person directed toward the role of another – depends on the power of the person or persons generating the conflict (where power was operationalized as control over valued resources and outcomes). This means that the expectations of the principal will cause more stress for the teacher than those of the students.

The example of the teacher can easily be transferred to any other occupation and shows that in most people intrapsychic conflicts often develop because irreconcilable expectations are being directed toward their position. These intrapsychic conflicts can weigh extremely heavily on social relationships with other role bearers. But the reasons for the conflicts should not be sought in the person, but rather in the incompatibility of roles. However, both interrole and intrarole conflicts also have a definite positive function in informal as well as formal conflicts: on the one hand they are a "cleansing agent" for clearing up difficulties, on the other hand they prevent informal and formal relationships from becoming encrusted and leading to more involved problems than if they had been articulated in time. Last but not least, overcoming a conflict is often the motor of change (Dahrendorf, 1958).

The doctor–patient relationship: An example of an occupation-determined role relationship

Characteristic features of doctor–patient interaction

Structure of the interaction. People with ailments become "patients" (formal role) when they place themselves in the hands of the professional medical system. Doctor and patient meet out of absolute necessity (e.g., because of pain) and their meeting pursues a particular goal (recovery). The interaction partners meet in a prescribed way in which the conversation is structured and directed toward a particular purpose: the doctor asks questions in the occupational role of medical expert in order to acquire information from the patient, on which he or she can then base a diagnosis and propose a therapy.

Prescribed behavior and a particularist view. Two further features of the formal relationship are present: on the one hand, content and behavior of the interaction are clearly prescribed to the extent that the topic is the patient's complaint, to which the doctor reacts with appropriate actions (questions, physical examinations). On the other hand, a particularist view of the interaction partners results from this topic and behavior restriction. The patient sees the doctor in his or her role as an expert and helper in medical questions, and the doctor sees the patient in his or her role as a sick person seeking help. Although the doctor may try to gain a comprehensive view of the patient as a personality in order to reach an adequate diagnosis, he or she is unlikely to be interested in the patient's political affiliations, brand of car, or home furnishings. Especially within the hospital context, doctors display an overtly particularist view of the patient: the doctor has an "objective scientific" approach and assumes responsibility for the afflicted organ; the nursing personnel assume the "motherly" role in that they are responsible for the care and psychological support of the patient.

Yet results from compliance research have shown that interaction and communication between doctor and patient are in fact the keystone of medical treatment. The doctor has to be a good listener and create the ideal empathic context in order to encourage the patient to describe his or her problem (compare Wiemann & Giles, 1988). The quality of the relationship often determines to what extent the patient can be motivated to cooperate constructively; otherwise, a "relationship dilemma" can result, possibly with serious consequences (Siegrist, 1982). Negative attitudes toward the doctor's instructions (noncompliance) often have their origins in heartlessly conducted five-minute consultations. American studies showed a great imbalance in the communication between the doctor and patient: the doctor does most of the talking and determines the agenda, the change of topic, and the termination of the encounter; the doctor interrupts the patient more (except when the doctor is female); and the doctor keeps asking further questions before the patient has answered the last one (compare Fisher & Todd, 1983; West, 1994).

This has led to demands for a more patient-centered approach. Results from various studies (overview in Haisch, 1991) unanimously confirm the favorable effects of a patient-centered approach by doctors, especially concerning the quality of symptom presentation and symptom processing. The doctor has to feel the way between rationality and emotional support when relating to a patient, because too much empathy in the patient-centered approach can cause the patient to overestimate the seriousness of the symptoms (Haisch & Zeitler, 1991). Calming the patient also has its dangers. It is a form of emotional attention that entails withholding information on important characteristics of the illness and this can make the patient anxious and insecure (Wimmer, 1991). When information is being suppressed, we can assume an asymmetrical relationship between doctor and patient with strong dominance on the part of the doctor (Siegrist, 1982).

The patient as an individual? When applying the fourth of the given characteristics of formal relationships, namely depersonalization versus individuality, the asymmetry we have just referred to also manifests itself in a similar way because the doctor–patient relationship is a "unilateral," occupation-determined relationship. From the point of view of the doctor, it is of a more objective nature; he or she expects the patient to pay for the help provided and to abide by given instructions. To the doctor, the individual patient is almost a number, an index card with a particular clinical picture (especially in everyday hospital life). From the point of view of the patient, the doctor is a human being from whom he or she hopes for help. The patient might see the doctor as a kind, competent, and helpful person in whom he or she has complete trust. Such an attitude can be regarded as perfectly functional, as it gives the patient the illusion that he or she is not simply case X confronting a role bearer but a human being. Here, it again becomes clear that the doctor is interested in a maximum of objective distance when absorbing the information, whereas the patient is preoccupied with personal concern and the subjective perception of symptoms. But it is questionable whether we can really refer to a depersonalization of the patient, as this depends largely on the doctor's attitude to his or her professional role. A doctor who consciously decides to become a general practitioner often accompanies patients throughout their lifetime. In this case deeper, more personal attachment may well develop (Haisch, 1991). Such relationships become more informal in the above-mentioned sense; personal contact develops on the basis of occupation-determined encounters. In the clinical context a change in doctors is an everyday occurrence, so that this type of transformation of the doctor–patient relationship is much more difficult.

Occupation-determined relationships and conflicts in the doctor's role

As already shown, the occupational role determines and forms the part of reality we perceive and, at the same time, a large proportion of our interpersonal interactions in both the formal and the informal spheres. Of course, the doctor meets only a certain kind of people in everyday professional life: ill, help-seeking, and sometimes hypochondriac people. Were the doctor to restrict his or her interpersonal relationships to these interactions, he or she would develop a human image characterized solely by illness, helplessness, and depression. Because of the profession, a doctor experiences only a very small selection of interactions. On the other hand, these interactions may be very rewarding in terms of self-esteem: the patient often shows deference, respect, and gratitude, and usually the patient's health improves after a visit to the doctor, which results in a successful experience (for both). The medical profession enjoys a high level of prestige in our society because of these helping, and often life-saving, activities.

The doctor's role inevitably involves conflicts: the daily routine of a doctor (and the nursing staff) includes the overcoming of personal feelings such as antipathy, anxiety, and revulsion. Conflicts can arise between the role concept and personal experience, particularly in the case of seriously ill patients. Many doctors use diverting conversation to spare themselves from dealing with the patient's situation in depth (Siegrist, 1982). On the account of their role they should give the patient sufficient information and support, but personal anxiety often prevents them from doing so, especially when the patient's imminent death is involved (von Uexküll, 1990). This is the topic studied by Martin and Julian (1987): they investigated doctors who were treating chronically or terminally ill patients. According to them, doctors come under increasing pressure from advancing technology, increased patient assertiveness, higher professional expectations, and more demanding bureaucratic evaluations. This is accompanied by a declining doctor–patient relationship. The importance of a psychotherapeutic component in the doctor–patient relationship, particularly in the case of chronically ill patients, is emphasized in this context by Priel, Rabinowitz, and Pels (1991).

How rigid are roles?

We would like to continue with the example of the doctor–patient relationship in this section and use it to illustrate some theoretical points.

Role inconsistency leads to social irritation

When answering the questions of how far individual leeway is restricted by clearly defined prescriptions on behavior and content and how far expectations form a framework within which role conformity is required, it is useful to note the reaction of the interacting partners when nonconformity occurs. Research shows that the favorable effects of social attachment and constant counseling by a doctor are limited to doctor–patient contact within the prescribed framework (Haisch & Zeitler, 1991). Contacts that go beyond this bear the risk of seeming implausible and can lead to irritation in the patient. To a certain extent the patient has a distorted view of such contacts in that he or she tends to view the doctor purely in the professional role and this often obscures perception of the doctor as a person acting privately (Haisch, 1991). If a doctor were to tell a patient that he or she was no longer interested in diagnosing illnesses or prescribing therapies, the patient would be very irritated, doubt the competence of the doctor, and probably never go back again. Why do such irritations occur? A patient has precise expectations of how a doctor should behave toward patients, that is, with interest in the patient's illness and without conversations about lack of professional motivation. Conversely, the doctor also has specific expectations of the patient: the doctor would certainly be surprised if the patient were to say he was not ill at all, he just wanted to talk about the weather, to ask the doctor if she liked his new necktie and if he could borrow yesterday's paper. Why would the doctor be irritated? Doctors work on the assumption that people who come to them need help because they are suffering from a complaint and this is the main focus of the interaction. This clearly illustrates that our behavior toward others is not coincidental but that it is distinctly structured by the definition of the role we ascribe to ourselves and others.

Occupation-determined role relationships are thus prescribed with respect to form and content, and nonconformity on behalf of one of the participants leads to irritation. This is because every relationship is governed by unwritten rules that guide our interactions (Argyle, 1988; Argyle, Furnham & Graham, 1981). These rules are informal and are based on social consensus. Even if both partners act contrary to the rules of an occupation-determined role relationship, as in love affairs between doctor and patient or teacher and student, society reacts with irritation and disapproval. Such relationships are often initially condemned and negatively sanctioned before they succeed in achieving social acceptance.

Changes in attitudes and values in occupation-determined role relationships

Over the past decades changes can be observed in personal values and in societal aims within Western industrialized nations (Inglehart, 1977, 1985; Klages, 1983). These have led to significant changes in private lifestyles as well as in the work sphere, and this in turn has affected role descriptions.

Considerable attitude changes have also been observed in the health care system. They are reflected in efforts to extend psychological knowledge to the area of medicine. On the basis of this, ecological and social psychological aspects of the health system, such as doctor–patient relationships, psychological effects of intensive care on patients and medical personnel, as well as organizational psychological aspects of hospital life, were also increasingly addressed (Lütjen & Frey, 1987, 1992). Empirical studies confirm the relevance of psychological factors in the convalescence of accident patients (Frey & Rogner, 1987; Frey, Rogner, Schuler, Korte & Havemann, 1985). For the first time connections were assumed to exist between the satisfaction of the patient with the doctor's treatment and the patient's recovery. Supposed effects of the clinical or hospital atmosphere on the psychic and somatic condition of the patient (the call for the "humanization of hospitals," Prochazka & Schmalzriedt, 1981) increased efforts to integrate psychosomatics into general hospitals as well (compare Forster, 1981; Schmeling-Kludas, Niemann, Jäger & Welder, 1991). Efforts to create a qualitative improvement in the doctor–patient, relationship are also visible in discussions in the area of psychosomatics; studies have focused on the effects of patient-centered approaches to treatment, including the social support of the patient by the doctor (see Balint, 1989; Haisch, 1991; von Uexküll, 1989). Despite the observed attitude changes, the everyday view of many doctors and patients is still predominantly characterized by traditionally somatic concepts of illness (Overbeck, 1984); it will surely take some time before a new understanding of the role is routinely accepted in clinics and private practices. This clearly shows that roles can be redefined and changed but that continuing stereotypes and lethargy tend to slow down the process. The described trend toward humaneness, toward the humanization of the profession and professional interaction, signifies a shift in characteristic features along the continuum from the formal to the informal pole (e.g., a holistic view of the other). Admittedly, this process of change will only be possible up to a certain point (with good reason) and it does not affect all characteristics to the same degree (e.g., the prescribed content of an occupation-determined interaction would be less affected).

Concluding remarks

The fundamental question, whether the personality forms the role or the role the personality, cannot be solved here. It is clear that human beings do not preside over an unlimited behavioral repertoire that can be applied in every role and that is also in keeping with personal ideas. Nevertheless, people are definitely able to shape roles through their individuality and personality. This is particularly clear in politics; for example, the role of head of government depends heavily on the individual in office. People interpret events and make decisions within the framework of their role but according to their own personality. Personalities can change situations by their different approaches to shaping a particular role.

People with a high level of integrity, the courage of their own convictions, and self-confidence are perfectly capable of overcoming certain highly restricting rules and redefining a role; in extreme cases they can even fundamentally change it. Efforts to redefine a role can, however, take a negative course, as when dictators redefine the role of head of state. The success of role bearers also depends on their ability to solve problems, irrespective of conformity. The self-identity that a person introduces into a role relationship should "not be seen as a barrier to successful role behavior but as its prerequisite" (Krappmann, 1971).

It is important that we never stop questioning norms, despite their internalization, and we should always be prepared to change them if necessary. We should not accept specific role definitions, especially when they collide with our ethical and moral principles. In this case courage should be shown by rejecting role conformity even if it could result in tough negative sanctions and enormous role pressure. People who act with total role conformity are completely adapted, "simple" citizens, but at the same time they can be dangerous, especially when they just go along with the rest and support a criminal regime, as during the German Third Reich – in fact it is they who make it possible in the first place! Such extreme role conformity – that is, adaptation to the *Zeitgeist* combined with the fulfillment of expectations and demands in the occupational role – very often earns privileges and promotes careers. Demonstrating resistance and nonconformity and more or less departing from the role is without a doubt more difficult and demands courage. But when high moral and ethical values are to be established, this type of behavior is often essential. Most people, unfortunately, tend to fulfill their (occupational) roles too doggedly. More personal courage and individuality, in occupation-determined role relationships as well, would benefit our society not only with variety instead of monotony, but also with innovation and creativity.

Notes

1. The different roles become blurred, especially for the role bearer, but the respective accompanying or opposing roles have quite specific expectations in the particular situation and of the particular role. If, for instance, the child of a teacher meets its mother acting as supervisor during break, the mother-teacher may be able to change roles briefly (the role contours become blurred) but the child will experience difficulty in changing its own roles.
2. The reverse is also conceivable, i.e., a person's social skills could determine his or her choice of occupation. This would mean, for example, that socially and communicatively skilled people would go into sales while highly introverted people might withdraw into quiet laboratory work. "Trait and factor" approaches to vocational suitability do in fact make it possible to identify certain personality characteristics that enhance a person's prospects for a particular occupation with its specific demands; they also show that certain types of personality tend to choose particular professions (Crites, 1981; see also Fletcher & Williams, 1985; Williams, 1989).

References

Argyle, M. (1988). Social relationships. In W. Stroebe, M. Hewstone, J.-P. Codol & G. M. Stephenson (Eds.), *Introduction to social psychology: A European perspective* (pp. 222–245). Oxford: Blackwell.

Argyle, M., Furnham, A., & Graham, J. A. (1981). *Social situations.* Cambridge University Press.

Argyle, M., & Henderson, M. (1985). *The anatomy of relationships.* London: Heinemann. Harmondsworth: Penguin.

Argyle, M., Henderson, M., & Furnham, A. (1985). The rules of social relationships. *British Journal of Social Psychology, 24,* 125–139.

Aschenbach, G., & Frey, D. (1985). Arbeitslosigkeit. In D. Frey & S. Greif (Eds.), *Sozialpsychologie. Ein Handbuch in Schlüsselbegriffen,* 2. erw. Aufl. (pp. 529–542). München: Psychologie Verlags Union.

Balint, M. (1989). Der Arzt, sein Patient und die Krankheit. Wiederabgedruckt in C. Nedelmann & H. Ferstl (Eds.), *Die Methode der Balint-Gruppe.* Stuttgart: Klett-Cotta.

Bamberg, E. (1989). Freizeit und Familie. In S. Greif, H. Holling & N. Nicholson (Eds.), *Arbeits- und Organisationspsychologie. Internationales Handbuch in Schlüsselbegriffen* (pp. 227–234). München: Psychologie Verlags Union.

Berscheid, E. (1985). Interpersonal interaction. In G. Lindzey & E. Aronson (Eds.), *Handbook of social psychology* (3rd ed.). New York: Random House.

Bielby, W. T., & Bielby, D. D. (1989). Family ties: Balancing commitments to work and family in dual earner households. *American Sociological Review, 54*(5), 776–789.

Blau, P. M. (1964). *Exchange and power in social life.* New York: Wiley.

Brinkmann, C. (1986). Finanzielle und psychosoziale Folgen der Arbeitslosigkeit. *Materialien der Arbeitsmarkt- und Berufsforschung, 8,* 1–8.

Byrne, D. (1971). *The attraction paradigm.* New York: Academic Press.

Cobb, J. B., & Kasl, S. V. (1977). *Termination: The consequences of job loss.* Washington, DC: U.S. Department of Health, Education, and Welfare. NIOSH Research Report, 76-1261.

Crites, J. O. (1981). *Career counseling; Models, methods and materials.* New York: McGraw-Hill.

Dahrendorf, R. (1958). *Homo sociologicus.* Opladen: Westdeutscher Verlag.

Festinger, L., Schachter, S., & Back, K. W. (1950). *Social pressures in informal groups.* New York: Harper.

Fisher, S., & Todd, A. D. (Eds.) (1983). *The social organization of doctor-patient communication.* Washington: Center for Applied Linguistics.

Fletcher, C., & Williams, R. (1985). *Performance appraisal and career development.* London: Hutchinson.

Forster, T. (1981). Psychologische contra medizinische Behandlung? Modell einer Integration gleichberechtigter Ansätze. In M. Hockel & F. J. Feldhege (Eds.), *Handbuch der Angewandten Psychologie, Bd. 2, Behandlung und Gesundheit* (pp. 135–149). Verlag Moderne Industrie.

Frese, M. (1982). Occupational socialization and psychological development: An underemphasized research perspective in industrial psychology. *Journal of Occupational Psychology, 55,* 209–224.

(1985). Arbeit. In T. Herrmann & E. Lantermann (Eds.),

Persönlichkeitspsychologie. Ein Handbuch in Schlüsselbegriffen (pp. 139–149). München: Urban & Schwarzenberg.

Frey, D., Gaska, A., Möhle, C., & Weidemann, J. (1991). Age is just a matter of mind: Zur (Sozial-)Psychologie des Alterns. In J. Haisch & H. P. Zeitler (Eds.), *Gesundheitspsychologie* (pp. 87–108). Heidelberg: Roland Asanger.

Frey, D., & Rogner, O. (1987). The relevance of psychological factors in the convalescence of accident patients. In G. R. Semin & B. Krahé (Eds.), *Issues in contemporary German social psychology.* London: Sage.

Frey, D., Rogner, O., Schuler, M., Korte, C., & Havemann, D. (1985). Psychological determinants in the convalescence of accident patients. *Basic and Applied Social Psychology, 6,* 317–328.

Friedmann, E. A., & Havighurst, R. J. (1962). Work and retirement. In S. Nosow & W. H. Form (Eds.), *Man, work and society* (pp. 98–120). New York: Basic Books.

Frone, M. R., Russell, M., & Cooper, M. L. (1993). Relationship of work–family conflict, gender, and alcohol expectancies to alcohol use/abuse. *Journal of Organizational Behavior, 14*(6), 545–558.

Goffman, E. (1967). *Stigma. Über Techniken der Bewältigung beschädigter Identität.* Frankfurt: Suhrkamp.

Greenberger, E., & O'Neil, R. (1993). Spouse, parent, worker: Role commitments and role-related experiences in the construction of adults' well-being. *Developmental Psychology, 29*(2), 181–197.

Griese, H. (1989). Rolle. In G. Endruweit & G. Trommsdorff (Eds.), *Wörterbuch der Soziologie, Bd. 2* (pp. 547–553). Stuttgart: Ferdinand Enke.

Gross, N., Mason, W. S., & McEachern, A. W. (1958). *Explorations in role analysis.* New York: Wiley.

Haisch, J. (1991). Soziale Unterstützung durch den (Haus-)Arzt – Positive Effekte auf die Gesundheit von Patient und Patientenfamilie. In J. Haisch & H. P. Zeitler (Eds.), *Gesundheitspsychologie* (pp. 173–183). Heidelberg: Roland Asanger.

Haisch, J., & Zeitler, H. P. (Eds.) (1991). *Gesundheitspsychologie.* Heidelberg: Roland Asanger.

Hartley, J., & Mohr, G. (1989). Arbeitsplatzverlust und Erwerbslosigkeit. In S. Greif, H. Holling & N. Nicholson (Eds.), *Arbeits- und Organisationspsychologie. Internationales Handbuch in Schlüsselbegriffen* (pp. 118–126). München: Psychologie Verlags Union.

Havighurst, R. J. (1963). Successful aging. In C. Tibbitts & W. Donahue (Eds.), *Processing of aging* (pp. 299–320). New York: Williams.

Henretta, J. C., O'Rand, A. M., & Chan, C.-G. (1993). Joint role investments and synchronization of retirement: A sequential approach to couples' retirement timing. *Social Forces, 71*(4), 981–1000.

Hock, E., & DeMeis, D. K. (1990). Depression in mothers of infants: The role of maternal employment. *Development Psychology, 26*(2), 285–291.

Homans, G. C. (1950). *The human group.* London: Routledge & Kegan Paul.
(1961). Social behavior as exchange. *American Journal of Sociology, 63,* 597–606.

310 *Anne Gaska and Dieter Frey*

Hulin, C. L. (1971). Individual differences and job enrichment: The case against general treatments. In J. R. Maher (Ed.), *New perspectives in job enrichment*. New York: Van Nostrand.

Inglehart, R. (1977). *The silent revolution*. Princeton: Princeton University Press.

(1985). New perspectives on value change. Response to Lafferty and Knutse, Savage, and Böltken and Jagodzinski. *Comperative Political Studies, 4*, 485–532.

Jahoda, M. (1982). *Employment and unemployment*. Cambridge University Press.

Jahoda, M., Lazarsfeld, P. F., & Zeisel, H. (1933). *Die Arbeitslosen von Marienthal*. Frankfurt: Suhrkamp.

Jayashree, V., & Rao, T. R. (1991). Effects of work status on adjustment and the life satisfaction of the elderly. *Indian Journal of Clinical Psychology, 18*(2), 41–44.

Joas, H. (1980). Rollen- und Interaktionstheorien in der Sozialisationsforschung. In K. Hurrelmann & D. Ulich (Eds.), *Handbuch der Sozialisationsforschung* (pp. 147–160). Weinheim: Beltz.

Karasek, R. A. (1981). Job socialization and job strain: The implications of two related psychosocial mechanism for job design. In B. Gardell & G. Johansson (Eds.), *Working life*. New York: Wiley.

Keaveney, S. M., & Nelson, J. E. (1993). Coping with organzational role stress: Intrinsic motivational orientation, perceived role benefits, and psychological withdrawal. *Journal of the Academy of Marketing Science, 21*(2), 113–124.

Kinnier, R. T., Katz, E., C., & Berry, M. A. (1991). Successful resolutions to the career-versus-family conflict. *Journal of Counseling and Development, 69*(5), 439–444.

Klages, H. (1983). Wertewandel und Gesellschaftskrise in der sozialstaatlichen Demokratie. In J. Matthes (Ed.), *Krise der Arbeitsgesellschaft* (pp. 341–352). Frankfurt: Campus.

Kohn, M. L., & Schooler, C. (1982). Job conditions and personality. A longitudinal assessment of reciprocal effects. *American Journal of Sociology, 87*, 1257–1286.

Krappmann, L. (1971). *Soziologische Dimensionen der Identität*, Stuttgart: Ernst Klett Verlag.

Layton, C. (1986). Employment, unemployment, and response to the General Health Questionnaire. *Psychological Reports, 58*(3), 807–810.

Lea, M., & Duck, S. (1982). A model for the role of similarity of values in friendship development. *British Journal of Social Psychology, 21*, 301–310.

Lütjen, R., & Frey, D. (1987). Gesundheit und Krankheit/Gesundheitspsychologie. In D. Frey & S. Greif (Eds.), *Sozialpsychologie. Ein Handbuch in Schlüsselbegriffen* (pp. 567–579). 2. Aufl. München: Psychologie Verlags Union.

(1992). Gesundheit und Medizin. In D. Frey, C. Graf Hoyos & D. Stahlberg

(Eds.), *Angewandte Psychologie* (pp. 405–426). Weinheim: Psychologie Verlags Union.

Martin, C. A., & Julian, R. A. (1987). Causes of stress and burnout in physicians caring for the chronically and terminally ill. Special issue: Stress and burnout among providers caring for the terminally ill and their families. *Hospice Journal, 3*(2–3), 121–146.

Meissner, M. (1971). The long arm of the job. A study of work and leisure. *Industrial Relations, 10,* 239–260.

Mohr, G., & Frese, M. (1978). Arbeitslosigkeit und Depression unter besonderer Berücksichtigung einer empirischen Untersuchung zur Langzeitarbeitslosigkeit älterer Arbeiter. In A. Wacker (Ed.), *Vom Schock zum Fatalismus?* (pp. 179–193). Frankfurt: Campus.

Mummendey, A. (1985). Verhalten zwischen Gruppen: Die Theorie der sozialen Identität. In D. Frey & M. Irle (Eds.), *Theorien der Sozialpsychologie, Bd. 2, Gruppen- und Lerntheorien* (pp. 185–216). Bern: Huber.

Nachreiner, F., Baer, K., Diekmann, A., & Ernst, G. (1984). Some new approaches in the analysis of the interference of shift work with social life. In A. A. Wedderburn & P. Smith (Eds.), *Psychological approaches to night and shift work.* Edinburgh: Heriot-Watt University.

Nachreiner, F., Streich, W., & Wettberg, W. (1985). Schicht- und Nachtarbeit. In Bundesanstalt für Arbeitsschutz (Eds.), *Handbuch zur Humanisierung der Arbeit, Bd. 2* (pp. 905–928). Wilhelmshaven: Wirtschaftsverlag Nordwest.

Overbeck, G. (1984). *Krankheit als Anpassung.* Frankfurt: Suhrkamp.

Parkes, K. R. (1994). Sleep patterns, shiftwork, and individual differences: A comparison of onshore and offshore control-room operators. *Ergonomics, 37*(5), 827–844.

Parnes, H.-S., & Somers, D.-G. (1994). Shunning retirement: Work experience of men in their seventies and early eighties. *Journal of Gerontology, 49*(3), 117–124.

Piechowski, L.-D. (1992). Mental health and women's multiple roles. *Families in Society, 73*(3), 131–139.

Priel, B., Rabinowitz, B., & Pels, R. J. (1991). A semiotic perspective on chronic pain: Implications for the interaction between patient and physician. *British Journal of Medical Psychology, 64*(1), 65–71.

Prochazka, R., & Schmalzriedt, L. (1981). Psychologie im Allgemein-Krankenhaus. In M. Hockel & F. J. Feldhege (Eds.), *Handbuch der Angewandten Psychologie, Bd. 2, Behandlung und Gesundheit.* Verlag Moderne Industrie.

Ranking, E. D. (1993). Stresses and rewards experienced by employed mothers. *Health Care for Women International, 14*(6), 527–537.

Reifman, A., Biernat, M., & Lang, E. L. (1991). Stress, social support, and health in married professional women with small children. *Psychology of Women Quarterly, 15*(3), 431–445.

Rosa, R. R. (1993). Napping at home and alertness on the job in rotation shift workers. *Sleep, 16*(8), 727–735.

Salaman, G. (1974). *Community and occupation: An exploration of work–leisure relationships.* Cambridge University Press.

Scheller, R. (1976). *Psychologie der Berufswahl und der beruflichen Entwicklung.* Stuttgart: Kohlhammer.

Schmeling-Kludas, C., Niemann, B. M., Jäger, K., & Wedler, H. (1991). Das Konzept der integrierten internistisch psychosomatischen Patienten-Versorgung – Erfahrungen und Ergebnisse bei der Umsetzung im Allgemeinen Krankenhaus. *Psychotherapie, Psychosomatik, Medizinische Psychologie, 41,* 247–294.

Seifert, K. H. (1992). Berufswahl und Laufbahnentwicklung. In D. Frey, C. Graf Hoyos & D. Stahlberg (Eds.), *Angewandte Psychologie* (pp. 187–204). Weinheim: Psychologie Verlags Union.

Siegall, M. (1992). Some effects of role conflict source on the experience of role conflict. *Journal of Applied Social Psychology, 22*(8), 628–637.

Siegrist, J. (1982). Asymmetrie der Arzt-Patient-Beziehung im Krankenhaus. In D. Beckmann, S. Davies-Osterkamp & J. W. Scheer (Eds.), *Medizinische Psychologie – Forschung für Klinik und Praxis* (pp. 375–401). Berlin: Springer.

Smith, L., & Folkard, S. (1993a). The impact of shiftwork. *Work and Stress, 7*(4), 341–350.

(1993b). The perceptions and feelings of shiftworkers' partners. Special issue: Night and shiftwork. *Ergonomics, 36*(1–3), 299–305.

Spelten, E., Barton, J., & Folkard, S. (1993). Have we underestimated shiftworkers' problems? Evidence from a "reminiscence" study. Special issue: Night and shiftwork. *Ergonomics, 36*(1–3), 307–312.

Staines, G. L. (1980). Spillover versus compensation: A review on the literature on the relationship between work and nonwork. *Human Relations, 33*(2), 111–129.

Staw, B. M., & Ross, J. (1985). Stability in the midst of change. A dispositional approach to job attitudes. *Journal of Applied Psychology, 70,* 469–480.

Szewczyk, H. M. (1968). Konflikte im Beruf. Berlin: Deutscher Verlag der Wissenschaften.

Tajfel, H. (1982). Social psychology of intergroup relations. *Annual Review of Psychology, 33,* 1–39.

Thibaut, J. W., & Kelley, H. H. (1959). *The social psychology of groups.* New York: Wiley.

Uexküll, T. von (1989). Patientenkarrieren. In C. Nedelmann & H. Ferstl (Eds.), *Die Methode der Balint-Gruppe.* Stuttgart: Klett-Cotta.

(1990). *Psychosomatische Medizin.* 4. Auflage. München: Urban & Schwarzenberg.

Ulich, E., & Ulich, H. (1977). Über einige Zusammenhänge zwischen Arbeitsgestaltung und Freizeitverhalten. In T. Leuenberger & K. H. Ruffmann (Eds.), *Bürokratie* (pp. 209–227). Bern: Lang.

Volpert W. (1975). Die Lohnarbeitswissenschaft und die Psychologie der Arbeitstätigkeit. In P. Groskurth & W. Volpert (Eds.), *Lohnarbeitspsychologie.* Frankfurt: Fischer.

Walper, S. (1988). *Familiäre Konsequenzen ökonomischer Deprivation.* München: Psychologie Verlags Union.

Warr, P. (1984). Job loss, unemployment and psychological well-being. In V. Allen & E. von D. Vliert (Eds.), *Role transition* (pp. 121–136). New York: Plenum.

Weber, M. (1922). *Wirtschaft und Gesellschaft.* Tübingen: Mohr.

West, C. (1994). *Routine complications.* Bloomington: Indiana University Press.

Wiemann, J. M., & Giles, H. (1988). Interpersonal communication. In W. Stroebe, M. Hewstone, J.-P. Codol & G. M. Stephenson (Eds.), *Introduction to social psychology: A European perspective* (pp. 199–221). Oxford: Blackwell.

Wiersma, U. J., & Van den Berg, P. (1991). Work–home role conflict, family climate, and domestic responsibilities among men and women in dual-earner families. *Journal of Applied Psychology, 21*(15), 1207–1217.

Williams, R. (1989). Berufsentwicklung, Laufbahn und Beratung. In S. Greif, H. Holling & N. Nicholson (Eds.), *Arbeits- und Organisationspsychologie. Internationales Handbuch in Schlüsselbegriffen* (pp. 193–199). München: Psychologie Verlags Union.

Wimmer, H. (1991). Krankheitsbearbeitung durch den Patienten. *Wiener Medizinische Wochenschrift, 141,* 90–95.

Wiswede, G. (1977). *Rollentheorie.* Stuttgart: Kohlhammer.

Epilogue

Selected remarks on relationship research
Gerold Mikula

This final chapter will sketch out a few of the thoughts and considerations prompted by a reading of the contributions in this volume. The book's intention was to cover the whole spectrum of relationships experienced by people in everyday life, and the following remarks refer to questions and problems arising from this spectrum. The questions are not new, nor are any solutions offered to the problems addressed here. But it appears useful for an appropriate assessment of existing results and the future tasks of relationship research to address these questions and problems not just once but time and again.

The complete catalogue of interpersonal relationships?

In view of the broad spectrum of interpersonal relationships treated in this volume, it is tempting to consider whether some important types of relationship have been neglected. Apart from the fact that some readers may be surprised to discover that marital relationships have not received an independent chapter, it appears that most relevant interpersonal relationships, at least those in our cultural and historical context, have been addressed: parent–child relationships, peer and sibling relationships during childhood, relationships between adult siblings, child–parent relationships in adulthood, different types of relationships in families and among relatives, friendships, heterosexual and homosexual relationships, relationships with acquaintances and neighbors, and occupation-determined relationships between colleagues, and role relationships. This extensive list could conceivably be lengthened to include thematically oriented relationships that develop when people share the same interests or aims (see also Krappmann, Chapter 2 of this volume), but this type of relationship can also be seen as a subgroup of the heterogeneous and less clearly definable category of acquaintance relationships (see also Melbeck, Chapter 11 of this volume).

Quite apart from this playful search for "forgotten" relationships, the reader might also ask whether it is at all possible to develop a complete list of interpersonal relationships and how this should be done. Perhaps the most common (unscientific) method of compiling such a list would be to recall all (or as many as possible) of the people one knows and to identify the relationships to and between them by drawing on everyday terminology of role and relationship concepts. Apart from the fact that, at their best, lists compiled in this manner can claim a certain validity only for a particular cultural and historical framework, the resulting number of types of relationship is highly arbitrary and depends heavily on the level of differentiation in distinctions made. This automatically leads to the question of how many and which of the relationships distinguishable in principle should be considered. Take, for example, the great variety of relationships between family members and relatives. How valuable is it to consider relationships such as those with sisters- or brothers-in-law, or to cousins, as independent types of relationship? How useful is it to differentiate further in relationships such as the parent–child relationship and to take a closer look at mother–daughter, mother–son, father–daughter, or father–son relationships? Decision on the meaningfulness of such differentiations cannot be made in a general form. In the final instance it depends on whether there is reason to assume that the relationships, which can be differentiated in principle, also differ in a psychologically relevant way, or more generally speaking, in a way that is of interest for the particular researcher. It is, however, impossible, even within a given cultural and historical framework, to produce a comprehensive catalogue of interpersonal relationships that is universally acceptable and relevant to relationship research.

Comparisons between different types of relationship

This book is conceived in a way that invites comparisons between different types of relationship. Such comparisons can be made on numerous levels and with a variety of purposes. For example, the specific formal and structural characteristics of relationships can be examined and compared. But from a psychological point of view comparisons only become interesting and revealing when they consider the implications of different relationship characteristics for the formation of a relationship or for other interpersonal and intrapersonal processes (e.g., dependence, loyalty, commitment, trust, conflict potential). Systematic relationship comparisons can also give indications of certain regularities that are specifically associated with particular types of relationship and so help prevent inappropriate generalizations.

But at present, systematic comparisons of different types of interpersonal relationship are inhibited for several reasons. The first reason is that, although the terminology coincides, central variables and concepts are used and defined quite differently by various authors (compare Mikula, 1984, 1992). Despite the fact that efforts have increased in recent times to gain more conceptual clarity (as several of the contributions to this book show), the consistent use of concepts required for systematic comparisons and the integration of results remain things of the future.

Systematic comparisons are further obstructed by the fact that research into particular types of relationship is localized in particular disciplines. While simplifying somewhat, we can make the following distinctions: social psychologists tend to concentrate their interest on affection-based relationships, such as friendships and partnerships; developmental psychologists prefer parent–child relationships and child–child relationships; clinical psychologists and communications researchers are mainly concerned with marital and family relationships; and sociologists focus on relationships in the family and between neighbors. The responsibility of different scientific disciplines for individual types of relationships tends to hamper comparisons because the respective disciplines pose different questions and employ different research methods. One consequence of this is that the knowledge available about different types of interpersonal relationships refers to different things. This stimulates two ideas. On the one hand, research programs could be started in which particular kinds of relationship are analyzed simultaneously by several different disciplines in keeping with their usual questions and methods. On the other hand – and probably of more importance – specific comparative studies could be carried out to analyze and compare particular relationship phenomena (e.g., dealing with conflicts and differences of opinion) in different types of relationships (e.g., sibling relationships, friendships, parent–child relationships). This could give some indication of the significance of particular relationship characteristics (e.g., status and power differences) for the occurrence, development, and form of the particular phenomenon; it could also lead to the recognition of possible specifics of relationship types. Studies of this kind hardly exist at the moment.

Wanted: an accepted descriptive terminology

The above discussion of comparisons of different types of relationship brings another problem to light that is of central importance to the development and progress of relationship research. There is still no generally accepted catalogue of characteristics or variables for the description of relationships. As Berscheid and Peplau (1983, p. 11) correctly stress, the problem does not lie in the lack of a descriptive language but in the fact that there are too many different varieties of such language. The categories of descriptive dimensions suggested in this book by Robert Hinde (Chapter 1; see also Hinde, 1979) can be seen as a valuable preliminary contribution to a general catalogue of characteristics, yet both his suggestions and those developed by Kelley et al. (1983) have been used far too little by relationship researchers. As a result, the relevant research literature describes and defines the individual relationship types with different "languages" and with respect to different aspects and features. This not only makes comparisons difficult, it also hinders the establishment of relationship research as an interdisciplinary and yet coherent scientific discipline. It is to be hoped, lest the project be abandoned prematurely, that relationship researchers prove more successful in their development of a common language conducive to their own relationship than the builders of the Tower of Babel.

On the arbitrary nature of taxonomies

Apart from creating simple lists, it is always tempting to develop, or at least call for, classifications or taxonomies of interpersonal relationships. The types of relationships treated in this book could, for example, be classified according to factors determining their development: family relationships (parent–child relationships, sibling relationships, relationships in the extended family), affection-based relationships (heterosexual and homosexual love relationships, friendships), and ecologically determined relationships (neighbor relationships and acquaintance relationships, relationships between colleagues, and occupation-determined role relationships). Quite apart from this type of classification, an almost infinite number of other classification alternatives is conceivable. Relationships could equally well be ordered according to formal characteristics, such as the age or gender of the persons and their respective constellations, according to the phase in the life cycle of those concerned, according to their (primary) aim and function, levels of voluntariness, or status and power relations, to name but a few. The existence of so many different and yet equally plausible possibilities of order illustrates the arbitrary nature of classifications and taxonomies when they are developed independent of a theory or a clearly defined purpose. Consequently it is advisable to treat demands for a generally binding taxonomy of interpersonal relationships with a certain amount of reserve.

Reciprocal influences and relations among relationships

The great variety of interpersonal relationships treated in this book also invites interest in the question of how different types of relationship are interwoven and what influence they have on each other. This fact, which is self-evident for system theory, is considered by a number of contributions to this book. It is also increasingly addressed by developmental psychologists (Dunn, 1988; and the special issue on "Family–peer Relationships" of the *Journal of Social and Personal Relationships*, edited by Ladd, 1991). But in other disciplines, such as social psychology, the question has been virtually ignored. There are two topics of interest in this connection: proof of the presence of such influences and the identification of processes that mediate such influences. Whereas until now the main focus of studies was on the significance of attachment experiences in early childhood and the influence of various characteristics of the parent–child relationship on the quality of relationships in later life, in future more attention should be directed toward investigating the influence of other relationship characteristics and other types of relationship as well as toward the reciprocal influence of multiple relationships in which people are involved simultaneously.

Reciprocal information and stimulation between different areas of research

Theme-oriented books that compile a variety of contributions from different (sub)disciplines of scientific research offer opportunities to analyze to what extent reciprocal information, influence, and stimulation can be observed between the different disciplines. Judging by bibliographies, it appears that reciprocal information between (sub)disciplines interested in interpersonal relationships has increased since the beginning of the 1980s (Mikula, 1988). However, more immediate reciprocal stimulation between areas of research still seems to be the exception rather than the rule. One of the themes that has been taken up by representatives of various disciplines illustrating a certain level of integration of insights among different disciplines is the concept of attachment, or more generally, the significance of relationship experiences during early childhood for interpersonal relationships in later phases of life.

Apart from such exceptions, questions posed and methods used by the different disciplines interested in interpersonal relationships certainly differ greatly; the impression conveyed by this book is representative in this respect. Therefore it is more appropriate to view relationship research as a plurality of research interests and forms rather than as a unitary research corpus. Considering the diversity and complexity of this area of research, the great variety of research approaches is both necessary and welcome. Whether this will result in a differentiation between various relationship sciences or whether we move toward a more unified science of interpersonal relationships, as long propagated by many authors (Duck & Perlamn, 1985), will depend on whether and to what extent insights gained from various areas of existing disciplines can be integrated. These closing remarks indicate some of the important prerequisites for such integration.

References

Berscheid, E., & Peplau, L. A. (1983). The emerging science of relationships. In H. H. Kelley, E. Berscheid, A. Christensen, J. H. Harvey, T. L. Huston, G. Levinger, E. McClintock, L. A. Peplau & D. R. Peterson (Eds.), *Close relationships* (pp. 1–19). New York: Freeman.

Duck, S. W., & Perlman, D. (1985). The thousand islands of personal relationships: A prescriptive analysis for future explorations. In S. W. Duck & D. Perlman (Eds.), *Understanding personal relationships; An interdisciplinary approach* (pp. 1–15). London: Sage.

Dunn, J. (1988). Relations among relationships. In S. W. Duck (Ed.), *Handbook of personal relationships* (pp. 193–209). Chichester, England: Wiley.

Hinde, R. A. (1979). *Towards understanding relationships*. London: Academic Press.

Kelley, H. H., Berscheid, E., Christensen, A., Harvey, J. H., Huston, T. L., Levinger, G., McClintock, E., Peplau, L. A. & Peterson, D. R. (Eds.) (1983). *Close Relationships*. New York: Freeman.

Ladd, G. W. (Ed.) (1991). Family–peer relationships [Special issue]. *Journal of Social and Personal Relationships, 8*(3).

Mikula, G. (1984). Personal relationships: Remarks on the current state of research. *European Journal of Social Psychology, 14*, 339–352.

  (1988). *Von zwischenmenschlicher Attraktion zu zwischenmenschlichen Beziehungen: Die Entwicklung eines Forschungsgebietes*. Berichte aus dem Institut für Psychologie der Karl-Franzens-Universität Graz.

  (1992). Austausch und Gerechtigkeit in Freundschaft, Partnerschaft und Ehe: Ein Überblick über den aktuellen Forschungsstand, *Psychologische Rundschau, 43*.

Author Index

Milardo, R.M., 235, *246*
Milgram, J.I., 121, 123, 127, 129, 131, 133, 135, *139*
Milhoj, P., 106, *118*, 133, *139*, 143, *169*
Millar, F.E., 9, 24, *34*
Miller, D.T., 21, *32*
Miller, K.I., 282, 283, 284, *287*
Miller, N., 202, 221, *224*
Miller, N.B., 85, *102*
Mills, R.S.L., 20, *33*
Minkler, M., 134, *138*
Minnett, A., 65, *75*
Minuchin, P., 9, *34*
Minuchin, S., 9, *34*, 151, 156, *167*
Mitterauer, M., 106, *117*
Moane, G., 130, *138*
Möhle, C., 295, *309*
Mohr, G., 294, *309, 311*
Money, J., 198, *225*
Monsour, M., 233, 235, 237, *246*
Montemayor, R., 90, *102*
Montgomery, B.M., 15, 23, *34*
Moore, M., 213, 214, *225*
Morrow, G.D., 190, *195*
Mosatche, H.S., 121, 123, 131, 135, *138*
Moss, M.S., 134, *138*
Moss, S.Z., 134, *138*
Mount, N.S., 85, *104*
Moyer, S., 254, *264*
Mueller, E., 39, *57*
Mueller, E.C., 41, *58*
Mühlfeld, C., 142, *167*
Müller, B., 155, 158, 160, 161, *167*
Mummendey, A., 298, *311*
Munn, P., 62, 67, *74*
Murstein, B.I., 23, *34*
Myers, D.R., 120, 123, *139*

Nachreiner, F., 298, *311*
Napp-Peters, A., 159, *167*
Nappi, B.J., 229, *245*
Nauck, B., 143, 144, 150, *167*
Nave-Herz, R., 142, 143, *167*
Neale, M.C., 198, *222*
Neidhardt, F., 109, *117*, 142, *167*

Nelson, B., 20, 21, *30*
Nelson, J.E., 292, *310*
Nettles, M., 96, *99*
Neuberger, O., 272, 277, 280, *288*
Neugarten, B.L., 114, *117*
Nezlek, J., 236, *247*
Nias, D.K.B., 19, *34*
Nicholson, N., 281, *287*
Niederberger, J.M., 156, *167*
Niemann, B.M., 306, *312*
Nienstedt, M., 156, *168*
Noam, G., 90, *100, 103*
Noam, G.G., 93, *100*
Noberini, M.R., 121, 123, 131, 132, 135, *137, 138*
Noller, P., 16, *34*, 176, *193*
Norpoth, A., 146, 148, 153, 156, *165*
Notarius, C., 16, *32*

O'Bryant, S.L., 125, *139*
O'Connor, P., 28, *34*
Oliver, J.E., 148, *168*
Olson, D.H., 83, 94, *102*, 156, *168*
Olson, D.H.L., 23, *30*
O'Meara, J.D., 237, *246*
Omoto, A.M., 188, *193*
O'Neil, R., 292, *309*
Opie, I., 59, *75*
Opie, P., 59, *75*
O'Rand, A.M., 295, *309*
Oropesa, R.S., 261, *265*
Ortmann, G., 277, *288*
Osgood, C.E., 13, *34*
O'Shea, G., 147, *164*
Osofsky, H.J., 84, *102*
Osofsky, J.D., 84, *102*
Oswald, H., 46, 48, *57*, 61, 62, 65, 68, 70, *75*, 110, *117*
Overbeck, G., 306, *311*
Oxley, D., 261, *265*

Padesky, C., 207, 210, *225*
Paikoff, R.L., 89, *102*
Pakaluck, M., 229, *246*
Palkovitz, R., 84, *102*
Pannor, R., 159, 160, *169*

Subject Index